Lecture Notes in Computer Science 9506

Commenced Publication in 1973
Founding and Former Series Editors:
Gerhard Goos, Juris Hartmanis, and Jan van Leeuwen

Editorial Board

More information about this series at http://www.springer.com/series/7408

Zhiming Liu · Zili Zhang (Eds.)

Engineering Trustworthy Software Systems

First International School, SETSS 2014
Chongqing, China, September 8–13, 2014
Tutorial Lectures

Springer

Editors
Zhiming Liu
Southwest University
Chongqing
China

Zili Zhang
Southwest University
Chongqing
China

ISSN 0302-9743   ISSN 1611-3349   (electronic)
Lecture Notes in Computer Science
ISBN 978-3-319-29627-2   ISBN 978-3-319-29628-9   (eBook)
DOI 10.1007/978-3-319-29628-9

Library of Congress Control Number: 2016931300

LNCS Sublibrary: SL2 – Programming and Software Engineering

Printed on acid-free paper

This Springer imprint is published by SpringerNature
The registered company is Springer International Publishing AG Switzerland

Preface

This volume contains the lecture notes of the courses given at the School on Engineering Trustworthy Software Systems (SETSS), held during September 8–13, 2014, at Southwest University in Chongqing, China. The school was aimed at postgraduate students, researchers, academics, and industrial engineers who are interested in the theory and practice of methods and tools for the design and programming of trustworthy software systems.

It is widely known that software engineering aims to develop and study theoretical foundations and practical disciplines for software design and production, ones that are as effective as as those already established in traditional branches of engineering. Yet although formal theories of programming, techniques, and tools do exist, already developed with their underpinnings, they are in fact not widely practised by software engineering practitioners; and so the impact of formal methods on commonly used software systems is still far from convincing. Indeed, it is not widely understood where and how the practices of software engineering are informed, and by what theories. Here we quote the question that Carroll Morgan raised in his first lecture at the school:

Trustworthy <u>Systems</u>: *Would you trust...*

A mechanical engineer
who did not understand torque?
$$\frac{\mathrm{d}(r \times \omega)}{\mathrm{d}t} = r \times \frac{\mathrm{d}\omega}{\mathrm{d}t} + \frac{\mathrm{d}r}{\mathrm{d}t} \times \omega$$

An electrical engineer
who did not understand impedance?
$$e^{j\omega t} = \cos(\omega t) + j\sin(\omega t)$$

A civil engineer
who did not understand trigonometry?
$$\sin(\theta + \phi) = \sin\theta\cos\phi + \cos\theta\sin\phi$$

$\vdots$

A *software engineer*
who did not understand assertions?
$$\{post[x\backslash E]\}\ x := E\ \{post\}$$

Carroll Morgan, SETSS 2014
Chongqing, China, 8 September 2014

Carroll continued to discuss in the class how a traditional engineer learns the above fundamental theories "in the first/second year of undergraduate university studies, or even in high school," but that the situation for a software engineer is quite different.

The courses of SETSS 2014 aimed to improve the understanding of the relation between theory and practice in software engineering, in order to contribute to narrowing the gap between them. This volume contains the lecture notes of the five courses and materials of one seminar. The common themes of the courses include the design and use of theories, techniques, and tools for software specification and modeling, analysis, and verification. The courses cover sequential programming, component and object software, hybrid systems, and cyber-physical systems with challenges of termination, security, safety, fault-tolerance, and real-time requirements. The techniques include model checking, correctness by construction through refinement and model transformations, as well as synthesis and computer algebra.

Lecturers and Editors

JONATHAN P. BOWEN was Professor of Computer Science in the Faculty of Computing, Engineering, and the Built Environment and Deputy Head of the Centre for Software Engineering of Birmingham City University (UK) between 2013 and 2015. He has been Emeritus Professor of Computing at London South Bank University since 2007. During 2008–2009, Bowen worked on a major air traffic control project at Altran Praxis (now Altran UK), applying the formal Z notation to a real industrial application. Bowen originally studied engineering science at Oxford University. He has been working in the field of computer science since the late 1970s, mainly in academia but also in industry. His previous academic affiliations include Imperial College (London), the Oxford University Computing Laboratory, and the University of Reading, as well as a number of visiting positions internationally, most recently at the Israel Institute for Advanced Studies during 2015–2016. Bowen is Life Fellow of the British Computer Society and the Royal Society of Arts. His professional interests include formal methods, software engineering, and museum informatics.

ZHIMING LIU just joined Southwest University (Chongqing, China) as a professor, leading the development of the Centre for Software Research and Innovation (SIRC). Before that, he was Professor of Software Engineering and Head of the Centre for Software Engineering at Birmingham City University (UK, 2013–2015) as well as Senior Research Fellow of the United Nations University – International Institute for Software Technology (Macao, 2002-1013). His is known for his work on the transformational approach to real-time and fault-tolerant system specification and verification, and the rCOS formal-model-driven-software engineering method.

ANNABELLE McIVER is a professor in the Department of Computing at Macquarie University in Sydney, where she is also Director of Research. She was trained as a mathematician at Cambridge and Oxford universities and in her research she uses mathematics to analyze security flaws in computer systems.

She is a member of the Programming Methodology Technical Working Group of the International Federation of Information Processing.

CARROLL MORGAN is a professor at the University of New South Wales and Data61 (formerly NICTA). He is known for his work, with his colleagues, on formal methods generally: originally Z, then refinement calculus, then probabilistic weakest-preconditions, and most recently "The Shadow" model for abstraction and refinement of non-interference security properties. These last two together are combined in his current work on quantitative information flow.

He also has a keen interest on how formal methods can be taught to beginner programmers… before it is too late.

BERND-HOLGER SCHLINGLOFF is a professor for software technology at the Humboldt University of Berlin, with a research focus on specification, verification, and testing theory of embedded systems. At the same time, he is a chief scientist at the Fraunhofer Institute of Open Communication Systems FOKUS in Berlin. His research interests are in the quality assurance of cyber-physical systems, in particular, in the automated generation and execution of software tests with formal specifications. Prof. Schlingloff is an internationally acknowledged expert in this field and has published more than 20 scientific articles and book chapters on this subject within the last five years. He coordinates several European and national projects in these areas, and uses the results in industrial projects within the domains of railway, traffic, automation, and medicine.

NAIJUN ZHAN is a distinguished professor of the Chinese Academy of Sciences, Deputy Director of the State Key Laboratory of Computer Science at the Institute of Software of the Academy, and a professor of the University of the Chinese Academy of Sciences. He is known for his work on formal design of real-time systems, and, in particular, his work on formal verification of hybrid systems.

ZILI ZHANG is Professor and Dean of the Faculty of Computer and Information Sciences at Southwest University. He is also a senior lecturer in the School of Information Technology at Deakin University. He has over 130 refereed publications in journal and conferences, one monograph, and six textbooks. He has been awarded about 30 grants from both China and Australia. His research interests include bio-inspired artificial intelligence, agent-based computing, big data analysis, and agent–data mining interaction and integration. He is a member of the Chinese Computer Federation (CCF) Big Data Task Force, the chief expert of the Chongqing Agricultural and Rural Digitalization Program, and a member of the Expert Committee for the Chongqing Cloud Computing Program.

Lecture Courses

Course 1: (In-)Formal Methods: The Lost Art — A Users' Manual by Carroll Morgan. The course draws from an experimental course in "(In-)Formal Methods," taught for three years at the University of New South Wales to fourth-year undergraduate computer science students. An adapted version was then taught (disguised as "Software Engineering") to second-year undergraduate students. The purpose is to "lower the barrier" for the use of those techniques, to show how astonishingly useful they are even without using propositional calculus, or predicate calculus — even if you figure out your invariants using pictures or by waving your hands in the air. Thus even students who have heard of Hoare triples might benefit from this course if they have not actually used them. The material is supported by the use of the program-correctness prover Dafny: students will see how to design correctness arguments, develop programs guided by those arguments, and then finally submit the arguments and the programs together for automated checking. This volume is divided into two parts, Part I on the generalities and Part II on the specifics.

Course 2: Program Refinement, Perfect Secrecy, and Information Flow by Annabelle McIver. This course is about a method for security by construction, which extends traditional "programming by stepwise refinement" as described in Course 1. This "comparative approach" features in stepwise refinement: describe a system as simply as possible so that it has exactly the required properties, and then apply sound refinement rules to obtain an implementation comprising specific algorithms and data structures. The stepwise refinement method has been extended to include "information flow" properties as well as functional properties, thus supporting proofs about secrecy within the program refinement method. In this course, the security-by-refinement approach is reviewed and it is illustrated how it can be used to give an elementary treatment of some well-known security principles.

Course 3: The Z Notation – Whence the Cause and Whither the Course? by Jonathan P. Bowen.

This is a course on the Z notation for the formal specification of computer-based systems that has been in existence since the early 1980s. Since then, an international Z community has emerged, academic and industrial courses have been developed, an ISO standard has been adopted, and Z has been used on a number of significant software development projects, especially where safety and security have been important. This chapter traces the history of the Z notation and presents issues in teaching Z, with examples. A specific example of an industrial course is presented. Although subsequent notations have been developed, with better tool support, Z is still an excellent choice for general-purpose specification and is especially useful in directing software testing to ensure good coverage.

Course 4: Model-Driven Design of Object Component Systems by Zhiming Liu. This course identifies a set of UML notations and textual descriptions for representing different abstractions of software artifacts produced in different development stages. These abstractions, their relations and manipulations all have formal definitions in the rCOS formal method of component and object systems. The purpose is to show how model-driven development seamlessly integrates the theories that have been well developed in the last half century, including abstract data types, Hoare logic, process calculi, I/O automata as well as their underlined techniques and tools for software specification, refinement, and verification. A major theme is to show that models of component-based architectures and interface contracts are essential for designing and maintaining large-scale evolving systems, including cyber-physical systems (CPS), Internet of Things (IoT), and Smart Cities, which have multi-dimensional complexities. The lecture notes in this volume are divided into three consecutive parts:

- Part I describes the background motivation and organization. It especially gives a historic account of software engineering, which is usually missing in textbooks and lecture notes, and discusses basic concepts and principles of model-driven software design.
- Part II is devoted to use-case-driven object-oriented requirements gathering, modeling and analysis, and the UML models used for representing requirement artifacts.
- Part III covers component-based architecture design, and object-oriented design architectural components based on their contracts of interfaces.

Course 5: Cyber-Physical Systems Engineering by Holger Schlingloff. Cyber-physical systems, that is, connected devices that support technical processes and human users, have become ubiquitous in our environment. Examples range from connected AV home entertainment and smart home automation systems, via intelligent cars, UAVs, and autonomous robots, to fully automated factories. However, the complexity of these systems is steadily growing, making it increasingly harder to design them correctly.

Building complex embedded and cyber-physical systems requires a holistic view. Systems engineering must provide means to continuously consider both the design process and the final product:

- The development processes must provide a seamless transition between different stages and views.
- The constructed system must offer a smooth interaction with its physical environment and its human users.

Thus, for cyber-physical systems engineering, modeling techniques and methods have been developed that support such an integral design paradigm.

In this course the fundamentals of cyber-physical systems engineering are presented: identification and quantification of system goals; requirements elicitation and management; modeling and simulation in different views; and validation to ensure that the system meets its original design goals. A special focus is on the model-based design process. All techniques are demonstrated with appropriate examples and engineering tools.

Course 6: Combining Formal and Informal Methods in the Design of Spacecrafts by Naijun Zhan. This course presents a combination of formal and informal methods for the design of spacecrafts. In the described approach, the designer can either build an executable model of a spacecraft using the industrial standard environment Simulink/ Stateflow, or construct a formal model using Hybrid CSP, which is an extension of CSP for modeling hybrid systems. Hybrid CSP processes are specified and reasoned about by hybrid Hoare logic, which is an extension of Hoare logic to hybrid systems. The connection between informal and formal methods is realized via an automatic translator from Simulink/Stateflow diagrams to Hybrid CSP and an inverse translator from Hybrid CSP to Simulink. The course shows the following advantages of combining formal and informal methods in the design of spacecrafts:

- It allows formal verification to be used as a complement of simulation that, by itself, would be incomplete for system correctness.
- It allows the design of a hybrid system to be formally specified in Hybrid CSP and simulated and/or tested economically using the Matlab platform.

The method is demonstrated by analysis and verification of a real-world industry example, that is, the guidance control program of a lunar lander.

Acknowledgments. We would like to thank the lecturers and their co-authors for their professional commitment and hard work, the strong support of Southwest University, and the enthusiastic work of the local organizing team led by Dr. Li Tao, without which the school would not have been possible. We are grateful for the support of Alfred Hofmann and Anna Kramer of Springer's *Lecture Notes in Computer Science* team in the publication of this volume.

January 2016   Zhiming Liu
                                                                     Zili Zhang

Contents

(In-)Formal Methods: The Lost Art

A Users' Manual

Carroll Morgan[1,2]([✉])

[1] School of Computer Science and Engineering,
University of New South Wales, Sydney, Australia
[2] Data 61 (formerly NICTA), Sydney, Australia
carroll.morgan@unsw.edu.au

Abstract. This article describes an experimental course in "(In-)Formal Methods", taught for three years at the University of New South Wales to fourth-year undergraduate Computer-Science students (http://www.cse.unsw.edu.au/~cs6721/). An adapted version was then taught (disguised as "Software Engineering") to second year undergraduate students (http://webapps.cse.unsw.edu.au/webcms2/course/index.php?cid=2332).

Fourth-year CS students at UNSW are typically very-good-to-excellent programmers. Second-year students are on their way to the same standard: but many of them have not yet realised how hard it will be actually to get there.

Either way, whether good or on the way to good, few of these students have *even heard* of static reasoning, assertions, invariants, variants, let alone have learned how to use them... None of the simple, yet profoundly important intellectual programming tools first identified and brought to prominence (more than 40 years ago) has become part of their programming toolkit.

Why did this happen? How can it be changed?

What will happen if we do change it?

Below we address some of those questions, using as examples actual material from the two related courses mentioned above; they were given in the years 2010–4. As an appendix, we present feedback from some of the students who took one course or the other.

At the same time, some suggestions are made about whether, when and how courses like this one could possibly be taught elsewhere.

1 Part I - Generalities

1.1 Background, Genesis and Aims

Here is an excerpt from *βeta*, the fortnightly magazine of UNSW's Computer Science and Engineering student society. It appeared the year after the first *Informal Methods* course:[1]

---

[1] In 2011: http://beta.csesoc.unsw.edu.au/2011/05/getting-max-right/.

© Springer International Publishing Switzerland 2016
Z. Liu and Z. Zhang (Eds.): SETSS 2014, LNCS 9506, pp. 1–79, 2016.
DOI: 10.1007/978-3-319-29628-9_1

Practical applications of formal methods
for Computer Scientists

Last year one of my lecturers posed a very simple question to a class containing about fifteen 3rd and 4th year students: "Write a function that, given an array A containing n integers, computes (and returns) the maximum value contained in the array". Essentially, write the "max" function. Naturally, I thought at the time that this was obvious and simple. I proceeded to write...

⋮   (actual code omitted; but it had some problems...)   ⋮

By using this simple example, the lecturer made a beautiful point: formal methods can be practical!

You can use formal methods in two ways. You can study formal methods from a theoretical perspective. You can rigorously and thoroughly apply formal methods to algorithms or systems in an isolated, academic exercise. Nice results can be obtained from this, such as the work done on [mechanically proved correctness of critical software]. This process, however, is too long and time-consuming for most developers working in industry.

Alternately, you can learn the techniques of formal methods and apply them in practical ways. This means you don't have to prove every statement and every property to the nth degree. Instead, by using simple reasoning during the coding process [...] you can help reduce the number of bugs introduced into a system. Additionally, it will make finding bugs easier by being able to eliminate from consideration parts of the codebase that you can quickly show are correct.

If you ever get an opportunity to learn the techniques of formal methods from a practical perspective, take it. The techniques will change how you write code, making you a more efficient and accurate developer.

What is remarkable about this (unsolicited) article is not so much its content, but that it was written at all. One is surprised that the author was surprised...

Of course formal methods can be practical. In fact they are basic, and essential to any kind of good programming style. As the writer points out, it's a question of degree: it does not have to be "to the nth".

We knew that already... *didn't we?*

1.2   Who is This "We"? And Where Did Formal Methods Go?

Who We Are... and Who "They" Are. Imagine this situation, black-and-white simple in its significance: the "we" above is having a casual conversation with a fourth-year computer-science student who – it is already established – is a very good programmer, respected for that by both peers and teachers. We're discussing a small loop.

"Ah, I see. So what's the loop invariant?" I ask.

"What *is* a loop invariant?" is the reply.

"We" are talking to a "they"; and that we-they conversation, and others like it, is where the motivation for an "Informal Methods" course came from. It was not that these students couldn't understand invariants etc. It was that they had never been given the chance.

We have to turn "them", those students, into "us".

Where Formal Methods Went. Formal Methods did not start in one place, with one person or one project. But in the early 1970's there were a few significant publications, from a small number of (already, or soon to be) prominent authors, that set the stage for a decade of progress in reasoning carefully about how programs should be constructed and how their correctness could be assured. Amongst Computer Science academics generally the names, at least, of those authors are well known: not a few of them are Turing Award winners. But outside of Formal Methods itself, which is a relatively small part of Computer Science as a whole, few academics can say what those famous authors are actually famous for. And even fewer can say what some of them are still doing, right now, as this article is being written.

Why aren't those authors' works now the backbone of elementary programming, not a part of every student's intellectual toolkit? Part of the reason is that although the ideas are simple, learning them is hard. Students' brains have to be ready, or at least "readied" by careful conditioning: the ideas cannot be pushed in by teachers. They have to be *pulled* in by the students themselves. Teachers operate best when answering questions that students have been tricked into asking. Even so, many excellent teachers simply are not interested in those ideas: they have their own goals to pursue, and not enough time even for that.

Another problem with Formal Methods is evangelism: there was, and continues to be, an urge to say to others "You have to do this; you must follow these rules... otherwise you are not really programming. You are just hacking, playing around." Formal Methods, like so many other movements, generated a spirit of epiphany, of "having seen the light" that encouraged its followers too much to try to spread the message to others, and too eagerly. And often that brought with it proposals for radical curriculum re-design that would "fix everything" by finally doing things right. Another "finally", again. And again.

In general those efforts, so enthusiastically undertaken, never made it out of the departmental-subcommittee meeting room — except to be gently mocked in the corridors, by our colleagues' shaking their heads with shrugged shoulders, wondering how we could be so naïve. And now, years later, those efforts are mostly gone altogether, forgotten.

So that is where Formal Methods went, and why it has not become a standard part of every first-year Computer-Science course. And "we" are the small group of Computer Scientists who are old enough to have had no way of avoiding Formal-Methods courses during those "decades of enthusiasm" Or we might be younger people who are intellectually (genetically) pre-disposed to seek, and achieve that kind of rigour: after all, in every generation there are always some.

But now we leave the matter of "us", and turn to the question of "they".

1.3   Operating by Stealth: Catching "Them" Early

In my own view, the ideal place for an informal-methods course is the second half of first year. A typical <u>first-half</u> of first year, i.e. the first computing course, is summarised

> Here's a programming language: learn its syntax. And here are some neat problems you never thought you could do; and here are some ideas about how you can program them on your very own.
> *Experience* for yourself the epic late-night struggle with   (1)
> the subtle bugs you have introduced into your own code; *savour* the feeling of triumph when (you believe that) your program finally works;*gloat*over the incredible intricacy of what you have created.

This is true exhilaration, especially for 18-year-olds, who are finally free to do whatever they want (in so many ways), in this case with "grown-up" tools to which earlier they had no access: most first-years have been exposed to computers' effects for all of their conscious lives, and there is nothing like the thrill of discovering how all these mysterious and magical devices actually work and that, actually, you can do it yourself.

Become a Tenth-Level Cybermancer! Your younger siblings, non-CS friends and even parents will now have to cope with cryptic error messages and bizarre functionality that you have created.

Once we accept (or remember ☺) the above emotions, we realise that the key thing about formal-methods teaching is that for most students there is *no point* in our trying to introduce it until after the phase (1) above has happened and has been fully digested: if we try, we will just be swept out of the way.

A typical <u>second-half</u> first-year course is elementary data-structures; and indeed second-half first-year is a good place for it. But informal methods is more deserving of that place, and it is far more urgent. Survivors of the first half-year will now understand something they didn't have any inkling of before:

> Programming is easy, but programming *correctly* is very hard.

This moment is crucial, and must be seized.

They have not yet *mistakenly* learned that making a mess of your initial design, and then gradually cleaning it up, is normal, just what "real programmers" do — and that lost nights and weekends, sprinting with pizza and Coke, are simply how you play the game. And it is not yet too late to stop them from *ever* learning that mistaken view. This is the moment we must teach them that programming should not be heroic; rather it should be *smart*.

We want programmers like Odysseus, not Achilles.[2]

---

[2] See this equivalently as whether you'd like to have Sean Bean or Brad Pitt on your programming team.

So the "stealth" aspect of informal methods, in second-half first year, is that it should be called something like

- Programming 102, or
- Taking control of the programming process, or
- Practical approaches to writing programs that Really Work, or
- Getting your weekends back.[3]

Having just experienced the pain (and pleasure) of over-exuberant coding, and its consequences, they are now – just for this small moment of their lives – in a small mental window where their teen-aged energy can be channelled into forming the good habits that will help them for the rest of their professional careers. In short, they are vulnerable, at our mercy — and we should shamelessly take advantage of it.

By second year, it could be too late.

1.4   Making Contact

After six months' exposure to university-level programming, many first-year students are on a trajectory to a place that you don't want them to go: they think that their journey in Computer Science is going to be a series of more elaborate languages with steadily increasing functionality, a growing collection of "tricks of the trade" and more skill in dealing with the unavoidable quirks of the software tools we have. And it will be all that. But it should be more: how do we catch that energy, and deflect these would-be tradesmen onto a path towards proper engineering instead?

In my view, our first move has to be making contact: you must first "match their orbit", and then gradually push them in the right direction. It's like saving the Earth from an asteroid — first you land on it, and then a slow and steady rocket burn at right-angles does the job. The alternative, a once-off impulse from a huge space-trampoline, simply won't work: the asteroid will just punch through and continue in its original direction.

In Sect. 2, below, some suggestions are made for doing this, the gradual push. For second-years,[4] it's to develop in the first lectures a reasonably intricate (for them) program, on the blackboard in real-time, in the way they are by then used to: guesswork, hand-waving and even flowcharts. You indulge in all the bad habits they are by now developing for themselves, and in so doing establish your programming "street cred" — for now, you are one of them.[5]

---

[3] Only this last suggestion is meant as a joke: for undergraduates, that phrase is more likely to mean "breaking up with your boy/girlfriend".

[4] I say "second years" here because that is what I have actually been able to try. As should be clear from above, in my opinion this is better done in first year.

[5] Your aim in the end is, of course, that they should become one of you.

But this is where, secretly, you are matching their orbit. (For fourth years, paradoxically, you should use an even simpler program; but the principle is the same.[6])

In both cases, once you have caught their attention, have "landed on the asteroid", by going through with them, sharing together, all the stages mentioned in Sect. 1.3 above – the epic struggle, the subtle bug, the savour of triumph, the gloat over intricacy – you "start the burn" at right angles, and gradually push them in the direction of seeing how they could have done it better.

Your aim is to train them to gloat over simplicity.

2   The Very First Lecture: *Touchdown*

2.1   Begin by Establishing a Baseline

Much of this section applies to any course, on any subject, and experienced lecturers will have their own strategies already. Still, as suggested just above, it's especially important in this course to make a strong connection with the students and to maintain it: you are going to try to change the way they think; and there will be other courses and academics who, with no ill will, nevertheless will be working in the opposite direction, suggesting that this material is unimportant and is consuming resources that could be better used elsewhere. With that said...

First lectures usually begin with administrative details, and that is unavoidable. But it's not wasted, even though most people will forget all that you said. It's useful because:

- Although no-one will remember what you said, to protect yourself later you will have to have said it: "Assignments are compulsory", "Checking the website is your responsibility", "Copying is not allowed".
- It will give the students a chance to get used to your accent and mannerisms. To reach them, you first have to let them see who you are.

---

[6] A simpler program is better for more advanced students because they have developed, by then, an impatience with complexity introduced by anyone other than themselves. (First-years are still indiscriminatingly curious.) Furthermore, older students have begun to realise that their lecturers actually might have something to teach them. Remember Mark Twain:

When I was a boy of fourteen, my father was so ignorant I could hardly stand to have the old man around. But when I got to be twenty-one, I was astonished at how much the old man had learned in seven years.

And finally, older students have learned to suspect that if something looks really obvious than there's probably a catch: so warned, they'll stay awake. The "find the maximum" program used for fourth years was the topic of the quote in Sect. 1.1. For the second-years, I used part of an assignment they had been given in the first-year introduction-to-programming course.

- You can say really important things like "No laptops, phones, newspapers, distracting conversations, reading of Game of Thrones are allowed in the lectures." *Really, not at all.* (If you don't say this at the beginning, you can't say it later because, then, it will look like you are picking on the person who is doing that thing. Only at the very beginning is it impersonal.) This one is really important, because part of getting students to want to understand what you are presenting is showing them that you are interested in them personally. If you don't care about students who are not paying attention, you will be perceived as not caring either about those who are.
- You can warn them not to be late for the lectures. (Do it now, not later, for the same reasons as just above.) Being on-time is important, because if they are not interested enough to be punctual they won't be interested enough to be responsive in the lecture itself, and so will form a kind of "dark matter" that will weigh-down your attempts to build a collaborative atmosphere.

But do not spend too much time on this initial stage: remember that most of it won't sink in and that, actually, that doesn't matter. Your aim with all the above is simply to get their attention.

Once all that is done, continue *immediately* with a programming exercise — because by now they are beginning to get bored. Wake them up!

The details of the exercise I use are the subject of Sect. 4.1. The exercise is not used for making people feel stupid; rather it's used instead for showing people, later, how much smarter they have become.

The exercise is handed out, very informally, on one single sheet of paper, handwritten (if you like); and then it's collected 10 min later. It's not marked at that point, and no comment is made about when it will be returned: just collect them up; store them in your bag; say nothing (except perhaps "thank you").

Like the introductory remarks, this exercise will probably be forgotten; and that's exactly what you want. When it returns, many weeks later, you want them to be (pleasantly) surprised.

2.2 Follow-Up by Cultivating a Dialogue with the Class: And Carry Out an Exercise in Triage

Delivering a course like this one can be seen as an exercise in triage, and the point of the initial dialogue is to carry this out. A (notional) third of the students, the very smart or very well-informed ones, will get value from the course no matter how badly you teach it, and you should be grateful that they are there. Amongst other things, they provide a useful validation function — for if they don't complain about what you say, you can be reasonably sure that any problems you might have are to do with presentation and not with correctness. And they can be used as "dialogue guinea-pigs" (see below). In fact these students *will* listen to and attempt to understand your introduction. But it wouldn't matter if they didn't, since they have already decided to do the course, and for the right reasons.

Another third of the students might be there because they think the course is easy, and that they can get credit while doing a minimal amount of work. They are not a problem in themselves; but neither should they consume too much of your effort and resources. They will not listen to your introduction, and it will make no difference to them, or to you, that they do not. If you're lucky, they will get bored and leave the course fairly early (so that they don't have to pay fees for it).

It's the last third, the "middle layer", who are the students you are aiming for. It's their behaviour you want to change, and it's them you want to excite. They will listen to your introduction, but not so much because they will use it to help them in planning or preparation; instead they will be trying to figure out what kind of person you are, and whether the course is likely to be fun. You must convince them that it will be.

So your constraints are mainly focussed on the top- and the middle groups: for the first, tell the truth (because they will know if you do not); for the second, simply be enthusiastic about what you say and let them see your genuine pleasure that they have come to take part in your course. The introduction could therefore go something like the following:

> *(In-)Formal Methods* are practical structuring and design techniques that encourage programming techniques easy to understand and to maintain. They are a particular kind of good programming practice, "particular" because they are not just rules of thumb. We actually know the theory behind them, and why they work. In spite of that, few people use them. But – by the end of this course – *you* will use them, and you will see that they work.
>
> Unusually, we do not take the traditional route of teaching the theory first, and only then trying to turn it into the practice of everyday programming methods. Instead, we teach the methods first, try them on examples; finally, once their effectiveness is demonstrated, we look behind the scenes to see where they come from.
>
> Thus the aim of this course is to expose its students – you – to the large conceptual resource of essentially *logical and mathematical* material underlying the construction of correct, usable and reliable software. Much of this has been "lost" in the sense that it is taught either as hardcore theory (quite unpopular) or – worse – is not taught at all. So there will be these main threads:
>
> 1. How to think about (correctness of) programs.
> 2. Case studies of how others have done this.
> 3. How to write your programs in a correctness-oriented way from the very start.
> 4. Case studies of how we can do that.
> 5. Why do these techniques work, and where would further study of them lead.

For (1) the main theme will be the use of so-called *static* rather than operational reasoning, that is thinking about what is true at various points in a program rather than on what the program "does" as its control moves from one point to another. This is harder than it sounds, and it takes lots of practice: explaining "static reasoning" will be a major component of the course.

The principal static-reasoning tools, for conventional programs, are *assertions*, *invariants* and *variants*. If you have never heard of those, then you are in the right place. Usually they are presented with an emphasis on formal logic, and precise step-by-step calculational reasoning. Here however we will be using them informally, writing our invariants etc. in English, or even in pictures, and seeing how that affects the way we program and the confidence we have in the result.

For (2), the programs we study will be chosen to help us put the ideas of (1) into practice, as they do need *lots* of practice. Usually the general idea of what the program needs to do will be obvious, but making sure that it works in all cases will seem (at first) to be an almost impossible goal. One's initial approach is, all too often, simply to try harder to examine every single case; and "success" might then be equated with exhaustion of the programmer rather than exhaustion of the cases.

Our alternative approach (3) to "impossible" programs will be to try harder to find the right way to think about the problem they are solving — often the obvious way is not the best way. But getting past the obvious can be painful, and tiring, though it is rewarding in the end: a crucial advantage of succeeding in *this* way is that the outcome – the correctness argument – is concrete, durable and can be communicated to others (e.g. to yourself in six months' time). Further, the program is much more likely to be correct.

Doing things this way is fun, and extremely satisfying: with (4) we will experience that for ourselves. It's much more satisfying that simply throwing programs together, hoping you have thought of every situation in which they might be deployed, and then dealing with the fallout when it turns out you didn't think of them all.

Finally, in (5), we recognise that the above (intellectual) tools all have mathematical theories that underlie them. In a full course (rather than just this article), we would study those theories — but not for their own sake. Rather we would look into the theories "with a light touch" to see the way in which they influence the practical methods they support. Those theories include *program semantics*, *structured domains*, *testing* and *compositionality*, and finally *refinement*.

2.3 Making Contact with the Top Layer: The "Dialogue Guinea Pigs"

In this first lecture, you should begin figuring out who the smart, confident people are. You will use them as a resource to help the other students learn to take the risk of answering the questions you will ask throughout the course. Although the goal is to make the students feel that they can dare to answer a question even if they are not sure, in the beginning you have to show that this is not punished by embarrassment or ridicule.

So: find the smart people; but still, when you ask your first question, ask the whole room and not only them. Pause (since probably no-one will answer), and then pick a smart person, as if at random, who will probably give an answer that will be enough to work with even if it's not exactly right. Make having given an answer a positive experience, and others will be keen to join in.

As the weeks pass, you will increase your pool of smart targets; and you will establish that answering the questions is not threatening. Furthermore, having established a question-and-answer style allows you to fine-tune the pace of a lecture as you go: a conversation is always easier to manage than a prepared speech.

2.4   Making Contact with the Middle Layer: The Importance of "street Cred"

By now, the students have sat through your introduction, and they have probably completely forgotten that they did a small test at the beginning of the lecture (Sect. 2.1).[7] Do not remind them.

Instead, grab the middle layer of your audience by actually writing a program collaboratively, i.e. with their help on the board, right before their eyes — that is, after all, what the course is supposed to be about. Writing programs. But choose the program from material they know, ideally a program they have encountered before, and do it in a way they expect. Your aim here is not to dazzle them with new things which, you assure them, they will eventually master. Rather you are simply trying to *make contact*, and to reassure them that you really understand programming in exactly the way they do, and that you "can hack it" just as they can. Roll up your sleeves as you approach the board; literally, roll them up. This is the Street Cred.

A second aim of this first exercise is to establish a pattern of joint work, between you and them and among them. You aim to form a group spirit, where they will help each other; this is especially important later, when the students who understand the new ideas will enjoy helping the ones who have not yet "got it". Again there is something peculiar about this course: the message sounds so simple that people, initially, will think they understand when in fact they do not understand it at all. A camaraderie operating *outside* the lecture room is the best approach to this. It is terribly important.

In the second-year version of this course, I chose a programming assignment from those very students' first-year course and abstracted a small portion, a slightly intricate loop, and obfuscated it a bit so that they wouldn't recognise it except perhaps subliminally. (It's described in Sect. 5 below.) I then did the

---

[7] Have you forgotten too, as you read this? That's precisely the idea.

program with them, on the board, in exactly the same style I thought a second-year student might do it.[8] It was careful, operational and hand-waving... but the program worked,[9] and the class experienced a sense of satisfaction collectively when, after a hard but enjoyable struggle, we had "got it out".

I then had an insight (simulated), suggested a simplification, and did the same program again, the whole thing all over, but this time using a flowchart. Really, an actual flowchart in a course on "formal methods". The resulting program, the second version, was simpler in its data structures (the first version used an auxiliary array) but more complicated in its control structure: exactly the kind of gratuitous complexity a second-year student enjoys. When we finished that version, as well, we had begun to bond.

This program, and its two versions, are described in Sect. 5 below. What the students did not know at that stage was that the very same program would be the subject of their first assignment, where they would develop a program that was smaller, faster and easier to maintain than either of the two versions we had just done in class (and were, temporarily, so proud of). Having developed the earlier versions with them, all together, was an important emotional piece of this: the assignment shows them how to improve *our* earlier work, not theirs alone. It's described in Appendix B below.

3   Follow-Up Lectures, "Mentoring", and the Goal

A difference between the fourth-year version of the course and the second-year version was that "mentoring" was arranged for the latter. Neither course was formally examined: assessment was on the basis of assignments, and a subjective "participation" component of 10 %.

Mentoring (explained below) was used for second-years because of the unusual nature of this material and, in particular, its informal presentation. As mentioned just above (the "second aim") the risk is that "young students" can convince themselves that they understand ideas and methods when, really, they do not. The point of the mentoring is to make sure every single student is encouraged to attempt to solve problems while an expert is there who can give immediate feedback and guidance. In that way, a student who does not yet understand the material will, first, find that out early and, second, will be able to take immediate action.

The 40+ students in the second-year course in 2014 were divided into groups of 8 students, and met once weekly for 30 min with one of three mentors who (already) understood the material thoroughly. (Two of the mentors were Ph.D. students; and all three were veterans of the fourth-year version of the course.) The student-to-mentor allocations were fixed, and attendance at the mentoring sessions was compulsory (and enforceable by adjusting the participation mark).

---

[8] In fact I tested this beforehand on a small sample of such students, to find out whether they agreed that my hand-waving and picture-drawing could be regarded as a typical approach.

[9] Almost: see the "small problem" identified in Fig. 3.

The mentors were instructed (and did) ask questions of every student in every session, making sure no-one could avoid speaking-up and "having a go". In addition, the three mentors and I met for about 30 min each week so that I could get a bottom-up view of whether the message was getting through. The mentors kept a week-by-week log with, mostly, just a single A, B or C for each student: excellent, satisfactory or "needs watching". (If you ask the mentors to write too much, instead they won't write anything: this way, the more conscientious mentors will often put a comment next to some of the C results without your having to ask them to.)

With all that said, it is of course not established that the mentoring was effective or necessary: the course has not been run for second-years without it, and so there is no "control" group. And the course has no exam. So how do we know whether it was successful?

Success is measured of course against a goal; and the goal of this course is not the same as the goal for a more theoretical course on rigorous program-derivation. For the latter, it would be appropriate to an examination-style assessment testing the ability (for example) to calculate weakest preconditions, to carry out propositional- and even predicate-logic proofs, to find/calculate programs that are correct by construction wrt. a given specification etc.

In fact the two goals for this course are as follows: the first targets the "upper layer" identified in Sect. 2.2 above. Those students will do very well in this course, and it will probably be extremely easy for them. Indeed, it will probably not teach them anything they could not have taught themselves. Are they therefore getting a free ride?

No, they are not: the point is that although they *could* have taught themselves this material, they probably *would not have done so* — simply because without this course they'd have been unaware that this material existed. As educators we strive to maintain standards, because the society that pays for us relies on that. In this case, the good students, the longer view is that it's precisely these students who will take a real "formal" Formal Methods course later in their curriculum, and then will become the true experts that our increasing dependence on computers mandates we produce. Without this course, they might not have done so.

The second goal concerns the "middle layer". These students would never have taken a real Formal Methods course and, even after having taken this course, they probably still won't. But, as the comments in Appendix F show, their style and outlook for programming have been significantly changed for the better — at least temporarily. They will respect and encourage precision and care in program construction, for themselves and – just as importantly – for others; and if they ever become software-project managers or similar, they will be likely to appreciate and encourage the selective use of "real" formal methods in the projects they control.

These people will understand this material's worth, and its benefits; and they will therefore be able to decide how much their company or client can afford to pay for it — they will be deciding how many top-layer experts to hire and, because they actually know what they are buying, they will be able to make an informed hard-cash case for doing so. Given the current penetration of rigour in Software Engineering generally, that is the only kind of case that will work. *References to Section* 4.1 *and beyond can be found in Part II; appendices are at the end of Part II.*

4   Part II – Specifics

4.1   Binary Search: The Baseline Exercise in Lecture 1

We now look at some of the actual material used for supporting this informal approach to Formal Methods. We begin with the "baseline" exercise mentioned in Sect. 2.1.

Binary Search is a famous small program for showing people that they are not as good at coding as they think. But that is not what we use it for here. Instead, it's used to establish a starting point against which the students later will be able to measure their progress objectively.

The exercise is deliberately made to look informal, "unofficial", so that very little importance will be attached to it, and it's done (almost) as the very first thing, to give people the greatest chance of forgetting that it happened at all. Thus it's a single sheet, with instructions on the front and boxes to fill-in on the back, almost like a questionnaire or survey. The actual version used was handwritten,[10] further increasing its casual appearance. Furthermore, doing it that way makes the point that the emphasis is on *concepts* and precision in thought, not on LaTeX- or other word-processed "neatness" of presentation. (For this article, however, I have typeset it to avoid problems with my handwriting: in class, they can just ask what any particular scrawl is supposed to be.)

A typical answer is in Fig. 1, on the reverse side of the handwritten version. (The front side, including the instructions, appears in Appendix A.) The typewriter-font text and ovals were added in marking. The hand-written comments and arrows were there in the handed-out version, in order to give very explicit help about what was expected and what the possible answers were. The light-grey text in the boxes of Fig. 1 are the student's answers.

The (typewriter-font) comments in the marking are important, even if it's only a few: if the program is wrong, for your credibility as a teacher you must identify at least one place it clearly *is* wrong. That way the student won't blame you; and it also makes the point that you actually bothered to read the work.[11]

---

[10] The handwritten version was done with a tablet app, and then converted to PDF. It's important that it be done that way so that – even handwritten – it can easily be corrected and improved as it's used and re-used in subsequent years.

[11] Annotating a PDF on a tablet is a remarkably efficient way of doing all this. Not only can you come back and alter your remarks later, but you can do the marking on the bus or train, a few each day, in time you wouldn't otherwise be using. And it's important to spread-out the marking as much as possible, so that your comments are fresh each time: as much as possible your comments should seem personal.

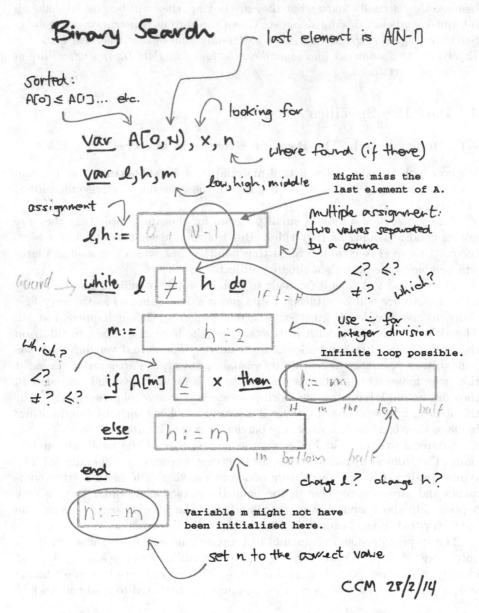

The exercise itself is at App. A: this figure is the answer. The (orange) notes in courier are the marker's comments; all other material, including (red) handwriting with arrows, was present in the handout beforehand.

The student's answers are within the grey boxes.

Fig. 1. Typical marked answer to the Binary-Search exercise of Sect. 4.1(Color figure online).

You don't have to find *all* errors, however, since this test is not marked numerically for credit. The aim is merely to find *enough* errors so that the students will be pleased, later, when they realise that the techniques they have learned would have allowed them to write this program, first time, with no errors at all.

5   The Longest Good Subsegment

This problem forms the basis for the first assignment, whose role in the overall course was described in Sect. 2.4 above: in summary, the problem is solved using "traditional" methods, in class – in fact, it is done twice. Once that has been endured, this assignment does it a third time, but using instead the techniques that the course advocates. The hoped-for outcome is that they will achieve a better result, by themselves but using these methods, than they did with the lecturer's help without these methods.

5.1   Problem Statement

Assume we are given an array A[0,N) of N integers A[0], A[1],..., A[N-1] and a Boolean function Bad(n) that examines the three consecutive elements A[n], A[n+1], A[n+2] for some (unspecified) property of "badness". We write A[n,n+3) for such a subsegment, using inclusive-exclusive style.

Just what badness actually is depends of course on the definition of Bad; but for concreteness we give here a few examples of what Bad might define. If subsegment A[n,n+3) turned out to be $[a, b, c]$ then that subsegment might defined to be "bad" if a, b, c were

- All equal: $a = b = c$.
- In a run, up or down: $a+1 = b \wedge b+1 = c$ or $a-1 = b \wedge b-1 = c$.
- Able to make a triangle: $a+b+c \geq 2(a \max b \max c)$.[12]
- The negation of any of the above.

Note that however Bad is defined, using Bad(n) is a programming error, subscript out of range, if $n < 0$ or $n+3 > N$.

Now a subsegment of A is any consecutive run A[i,j) of elements, that is A[i],A[i+1],...,A[j-1] with $0 \leq i \leq j < N$. We say that such a subsegment of A is *Good* just when it has no bad subsegments inside it. A Good subsegment of A can potentially have any length up to the length N of A itself, depending on A; and any subsegment of length two or less is Good, since no Bad subsegment can fit inside it. (Bad subsegments of A have length exactly 3; and since they can overlap, it's clear that A can contain anywhere from 0 up to N−2 of them.)

The specification is of our program is given in Fig. 2.

---

[12] The operator (max) is "maximum".

We are to write a program that, given `A[0,N)`, sets variable `l` to the length of the longest Good subsegment of `A[0,N)`. More precisely, the program is to

> Set `l` so that for some n[a]
> - `A[n,n+1)` fits into `A`, that is $0 \leq n \wedge n+1 \leq N$; and
> - There is no bad subsegment `A[b,b+3)` such that both
>
> $$n \leq b \wedge b+3 \leq n+1 \qquad \text{— } A[b,b+3) \text{ fits into } A[n,n+1)$$
> $$\text{and } \text{Bad}(b) . \qquad \text{— } A[b,b+3) \text{ is bad}$$

---

[a] The "l" at left is the letter ℓ, not the digit one. The latter is 1.
We write actual program variables in `Courier` (i.e. typewriter) font. Mathematical variables like n are in *mathsfont*, to avoid giving the impression that there has to be some variable `n` in the program. (There *might* be an `n` that stores the value n; but there does not have to be.)

Fig. 2. Specification of the first programming assignment

5.2   First Idea

An Operational Approach. A typical second-year student's first thoughts about this problem might be along these lines. First go through all of `A` and store its "bad positions" b in an auxiliary array `B`. Then find the largest difference *maxDiff* between any two adjacent elements b of `B`. Then – after some careful thought – set `l` to be *maxDiff*+2... or something close to it.[13]

Notice the operational phrasing "go through...", and the slightly fuzzy "something close to it" (one more than that? one less? exactly that?) A typical student would code up the program at this point, using the guess above, and see whether the answer looked right. It's only an assignment statement, after all, and if it contains a one-off error well, it can be "tweaked", based on trial runs, without affecting the structure of the rest of the program. This is how second-years think. (And they are not alone.)

We developed such a program (given below), interactively at the board, without hinting even for a moment that there might be a better way: indeed the whole

---

[13] The "careful thought" here, which most students will enjoy, is to figure out what the longest Good subsegment can be that includes neither of the bad subsegments $A[b_0, b_0 + 3)$ and $A[b_1, b_1+3)$, where $b_0 < b_1$ are the two adjacent bad positions with $maxDiff = b_1 - b_0$.

It must start at-or-after b_0+1, in order to leave out $A[b_0, b_0 + 3)$, and it must end at-or-before $b_1+2 - 1$ to leave out $A[b_1, b_1+3)$. So its greatest possible length is $(b_1+2-1) - (b_0+1) + 1$, that is b_1-b_0+1. Since the largest such b_1-b_0 is $maxDiff$ itself, the correct value for length `l` is $maxDiff+1$ for the largest $maxDiff$ — and not $maxDiff+2$ as suggested above. This "guessing wrong" and then "calculating right" can be simulated in your presentation, and increases the students' sense of participating in the process.

point of sneaky exercise is to get away with having the students agree that this is a reasonable solution, one indeed that they might have come up with themselves.

"Interactive", by the way, is important. The ideas of "static reasoning", invariants, assertions and so on are so simple when finally you understand, but so hard to grasp for the first time. (That's why the mentoring described in Sect. 3 is important: the students who are not yet assimilating the approach must be helped to *realise for themselves* that they are not.) Building a "let's all work together" atmosphere encourages the students to help each other; and so another contribution of this program-construction exercise carried out collectively is to build that collegiality in the context of something they understand: operational reasoning about a program. They *understand* operational reasoning.

Our aim is to change the reasoning style while maintaining the collegiality.

The Program Developed at the Board. The program we came up with is given in Fig. 3.[14] It uses an auxiliary array but, in doing so, does achieve a conceptual clarity: first find all the bad segments; then use that to find the (length of) the longest Good segment.

5.3   Second Idea

Use a "Conceptual" Extra Array. The more experienced programmers in the group will realise that, although having the auxiliary array B is useful for separating the problem into sub-problems, logically speaking it is also "wasteful" of space: a more efficient program can be developed by using a *conceptual* B's whose "currently interesting" element is maintained as you go along. After all, that's the only part of B you need.

This idea of a "conceptual" B is very much a step in the right direction. (It's related to auxiliary variables, and to data-refinement.) This is an insight that can be "simulated" during the presentation of this problem.

A second more advanced technique that the better students might consider is to use "sentinels", in order not to have to consider special cases.

But the resulting control structure turns out to be a bit complicated; and so, in order to see what's going on, we use a flowchart. The flowchart in Fig. 4 is the one we developed at the board, all together interactively in class. Again, this was very familiar territory (at least for the better students).

The code shown in Fig. 5 is the result.

5.4   Static Reasoning and Flowcharts

Ironically, the flowchart Fig. 4 gives us the opportunity to introduce static reasoning just as Floyd did in 1967:[15] one annotates the arcs of a flowchart. Experience seems to show that, initially, students grasp this more easily than the idea of something's being true "at this point in the program text".

---

[14] The syntax is based on **Dafny**, for which see Sect. 6. **Dafny** does not however have `loop`, `for`, `repeat` or `exit` constructions.

[15] R.W. Floyd. Assigning Meanings to Programs. *Proc Symp Appl Math.*, pp. 19–32. 1967.

```
// Find length of longest subsegment of A[0,N)
// that itself contains no "bad" subsegments.
// (Array A is referred to from within Bad.)

m:= 0
for b:= 0 to N-3 { // Don't go too far!
    if (Bad(b)) { B[m],m:= b,m+1 }
}
// Now B[0,m) contains the starting indices of all bad subsegments.

l= 0
for i:= 0 to m-1 { // For each bad-subsequence index...
    if (i==0) { l= l max (b[i]+2) } // compare first with start...
    else { l:= l max (B[i+1]-B[i]+1) } // else compare with previous.
}
l:= l max (N-B[m-1]-1) // Compare end with the last one.
```

This program is not supposed to be especially well written (it isn't), but neither is it supposed to be really badly done (it isn't *that* bad, for a second-year). It's supposed to be *credible*, something the students might have done themselves.

The special end-cases (the i==0 case) and the +1's and –1's lying around: these should be familiar instances of the sort of irritating details that the students, by now, are beginning to accept as "just a part of programming".
We want them to learn *not* to accept them.

A "small problem" though is that this program will fail (indexing error in its last statement) if there are no "bad" subsegments at all. How many students would miss this? And why is the first case b[i]+2 rather than b[i]+1?

Of those that understand those points, how many would revel in discussing these "deep subtleties" with their friends, over a beer? Is that part of the fun of programming? Should it be?

Fig. 3. First approach to the "bad segment" problem

An example of that applied to this problem is given in Figs. 6 and 7: no matter that the assertions there are complicated, even ugly. The point is that the assertions are *possible at all*, a new idea for the students, and crucially that their validity is entirely local: each "action box" in the flowchart can be checked relative to its adjacent assertions alone. There is no need to consider the whole program at once; no need to guess what it might do "later"; no need to remember what it did "earlier".

That's a very hard lesson to learn; experience with these courses suggests that it is not appreciated by course's end, not even by the very good students. It is only "planted", and grows later.

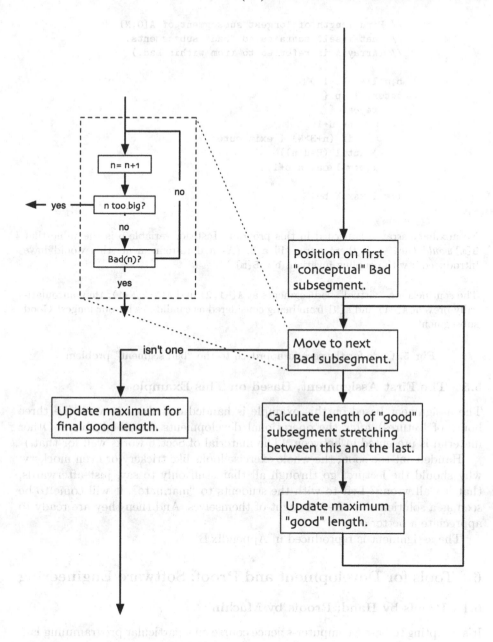

Like the first approach, this one also has a problem if **A** contains no **Bad** subsegments.

Fig. 4. Flowchart for the second approach to the "bad segment" problem

```
// Find length of longest subsegment of A[0,N)
// that itself contains no "bad" subsegments.
// (Array A is referred to from within Bad.)

b,n,l:= -1,-1,0
outer: loop {
    repeat {
        n= n+1
        if (n+3>N) { exit outer }
    } until (Bad(n))
    l,b:= l max n-b+1,n
}
l:= l max N-b-1
```

No auxiliary array B is needed in this program. Instead, variable b is the value that B[m] *would have* — if there were still a B. (As a data-refinement, this would have introduced b with coupling invariant $b = B[m]$.)

The sentinels are "virtual" bad segments at A[-1,2) and A[N-2,N+1): they automatically prevent A[-1] and A[N] from being considered as candidates for our longest Good subsegment.

Fig. 5. Code for the second approach to the "bad segment" problem

5.5   The First Assignment, Based on This Example

The assignment based on this example is handed out about a week (i.e three hours of lectures) *after* the operational developments described above. Other material is presented in between. (The material of Sect. 6 works well for that.)

Handed out too soon, the whole exercise looks like trickery or even mockery: why should the lecturer go through all that stuff only to say, just afterwards, that it's all wrong? Left to with the students to "marinate", it will come to be seen as a solution that they thought of themselves. And then they are ready to appreciate a better one.

The assignment is reproduced in Appendix B.

6   Tools for Development and Proof: Software Engineering

6.1   Proofs by Hand; Proofs by Machine

It's tempting to base a computer-science course on a particular programming language, a particular *IDE*, a particular program-verifier. If the lecturer is already familiar with the tools, then the lectures and exercises can very easily be generated from the specifics of those tools; and indeed "not much energy required" lectures can easily be given by passing-on information that you already know to people who just happen not to know it yet (but don't realise they could teach themselves). The lecturer can simply sit in a chair in front of the class, legs crossed, and read aloud from the textbook.

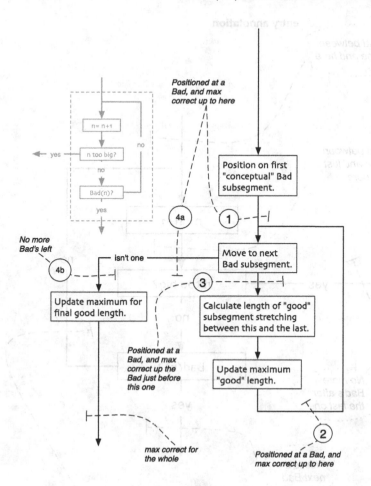

Fig. 6. Annotated flowchart for "bad segment" problem: outer code

To understand a flowchart, we can annotate the arcs that connect one action to the next. The annotation states a fact that must be true whenever program execution reaches that arc, *no matter how execution got there*. This is called "static" reasoning. To understand static reasoning like this, you can check the action boxes of the flowchart one-by-one: there is no need to understand them all at once. Just make sure for each box that if the fact annotating an entry arc holds, and the action takes place, then any fact annotating an exit arc holds too.

For example, the box "Move to next Bad segment" has two entry arcs (1 and 2) and two exit arcs (3 and 4). The facts on the input arcs (1,2) are the same, "Positioned at a Bad, and max correct up to here". We therefore can *assume* it is true whenever this box is reached.

The box has two exits (3,4); one of them is labelled by two facts (4a,4b). All those facts hold *given* that the entry facts held, the box's action was taken *and* that control left the box along the path labelled by the fact.

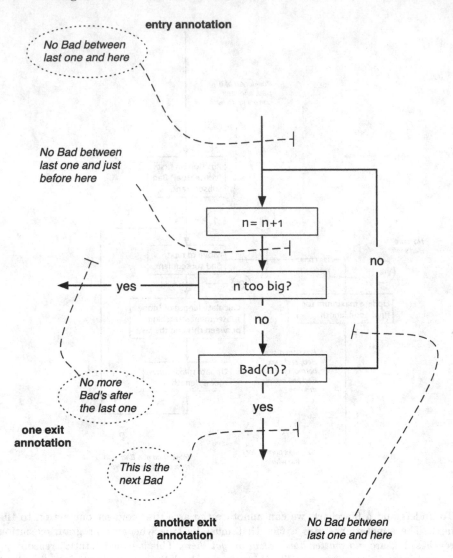

entry annotation

No Bad between last one and here

No Bad between last one and just before here

n= n+1

n too big?

yes

no

Bad(n)?

yes

no

No more Bad's after the last one

one exit annotation

another exit annotation

This is the next Bad

No Bad between last one and here

These are the annotations for the "inner" portion of the "bad segment" program. If we understand this part, we can the understand its role in a larger program (e.g. Fig. 6) simply by concentrating on the annotations of its entry and exits.

Fig. 7. Annotated flowchart for "bad segment" problem: inner code

There are, however, some disadvantages too. The first two of them apply to any tool presentation in class; and the third is more specific to formal methods. They are:

- Even if it's easy to describe programming-language syntax to the class, there is no guarantee that they will be listening or, if they are, that they will remember what you have said. In the end, they'll have to look it up anyway. And then what were the lectures for?
- From the fact that the lecturer seems to think the particular sequence of buttons to push in an *IDE* is important, the students will conclude that the sequence indeed is important. But is it really?
- Since an automated prover can check your reasoning and find any mistakes, one could conclude that it's not necessary to try to avoid making mistakes in the first place. In that case, why don't we get machines to write the programs, instead of merely check them?

In spite of all those caveats, there is an overwhelming advantage to using tools: without them, no serious (software) project of any size can be rigorously completed. It is simply not possible to master that complexity, either alone or in teams. How do we navigate between these two opposites?

What's important is how a tool is *presented*: it's just a tool. If you're lecturing about building circuit boards, you don't spend hours describing which end of a soldering iron to hold: students will figure that out pretty quickly for themselves. And in the end, a robot will do the soldering anyway. What's crucial is that they know what solder is for, and what therefore the robot is doing. The details of a *particular* robot are uninteresting and unimportant.

In this course, the (experimental) principle was adopted that things should not be done using *with* computer-based tools until those same things, perhaps in smaller instances, have been done by hand *without them*.[16]

In the case of static reasoning over programs, then, do we explain what an invariant is informally, conceptually, and how you intuit your way into finding

---

[16] The *reductio ad absurdum* arguments, e.g. that students must translate their programs manually into assembler before being allowed to use a compiler, are escaped by recognising the role of abstraction.

A compiler provides a layer of abstraction that its user can pretend is reality. The programmer can believe, and reason as if, assignment statements really do assign (instead of loading into a register and then storing somewhere else), as if while loops really do "loop while" instead of comparing, setting condition bits and then (conditionally) branching back, whatever that latter might mean to a second-year. And such abstractions are usually good enough for a first course: more hostile, demanding applications can break them; but by that stage, students are ready to go to lower levels.

On the other hand, a typical *IDE* doesn't abstract from anything: it's a cookbook, not a chemical analysis of edible compounds and their reactions with each other. To make and run a program, you type its text into the left-hand window and keep pressing a button on the right, and fiddling with your text, until all the red highlights go away. Press another button at that point, and some outputs might appear somewhere else. It's hard to explain what is going on without knowing the primitives over which these actions operate: source files, compilers, libraries, linkers, archives, object-files, debuggers. And indeed some teachers think that they are doing their students a favour by hiding those details from them. If, on the other hand, the primitives are explained and used first, on small examples, the *IDE* can be explained as a convenience rather than as an incantation.

one? Or do we explain an invariant as something which when typed into a particular tool will allow it to say "loop verified". (Or do we pretend that the invariant follows inescapably, inevitably by careful manipulation of the symbols in the predicate-calculus formulation of your loop's postcondition?)

In this course the motto for finding invariants is "beg, borrow or steal". It makes absolutely no difference where an invariant comes from; but it makes all the difference that you insist on having it, and then what you do with it from that point on.

6.2   Proofs by Hand

The very first example in the list below is used early in the course, informally:

"If you know that x equals 1 now, and the statement $x := x+1$ is executed, what can you say about the value of x afterwards?"[17]

It's easy, and indeed it looks too easy. With the further exercises in that list, we build our way from easy cases to hard ones, looking for the painful point where the problem is still small enough that you think you should be able to work it out in your head but, whenever you try you keep getting the wrong answer. By doing that, we are creating an irritation, a curiosity and, actually, a need.

That need should be satisfied by the "Hoare assignment rule", but instead of presenting it as an axiom of a beautiful programming logic (while remembering that the very idea of have a *programming* logic is beautiful in itself), it is simply presented as an algorism[18] for assertions and programs. Presenting it as a definition is premature: remember that the students have not yet realised that there even is a thing that needs defining.[19]

Thus what these exercises are designed to do is to take the students from simple assertional reasoning, where operational thinking works, to more complicated examples where they still understand what they are trying to do but find the details have become difficult to control. At that point, they are ready to be given a method — but still, crucially, a method to be used by hand.

---

[17] Just after introducing flowcharts is a good moment. (Recall Sect. 5.3.).

[18] *Algorisms* are the techniques for calculating with notations denoting numbers, viz. they are algorithms for arithmetic.

[19] Although the compelling rigour of logic, meta-language and object language, is what guided the creators of formal methods and is what makes sure that, in the end, it all comes together into a coherent whole, for most programmers it's best not to present it that way initially.

Try explaining to a second year that "actually" there are at least four kinds of implication in Formal Logic: the ordinary "if/then" of natural language, the horizontal line in a sequent, the single turnstile, the implication arrow... and then, underneath it all, the double turnstile (which makes five).

Those things have to be *asked for* when a person reaches the point of being too confused to proceed without them. Only then will you be thanked for giving the answer.

precondition program	postcondition

$\{x=1\}\ x:= x+1;$ $\{???\}$

$\{x=2\}\ x:= x/2;$ $\{???\}$

$\{x=3\}\ x:= x/2;$ $\{???\}$

$\{???\}\ x:= x/2;$ $\{x=1\}$

$\{x=A \wedge y=B\}\ x:= y;$ $\{???\}$

$\{x=A \wedge y=B\}\ x:= y; y:= x;$ $\{???\}$

$\{x=A \wedge y=B\}\ x:= x+y; y:= x-y;$ $\{???\}$

$\{x=A \wedge y=B\}\ x:= x+y;$

$\qquad\qquad y:= x-y;$

$\qquad\qquad x:= x-y;$ $\{???\}$

$\{x=A \wedge y=B\}\ t:= x;$

$\qquad\qquad x:= y;$

$\qquad\qquad y:= t;$ $\{???\}$

$\{\ \ x=A$

$\wedge\ y=B$

$\wedge\ z=C\}\ ???; ???; ???; ???;$ $\{\ \ x=B$

$\qquad\qquad\qquad\qquad\qquad\qquad\qquad \wedge\ y=C$

$\qquad\qquad\qquad\qquad\qquad\qquad\qquad \wedge\ z=A\ \}$

$\{???\}\ y:= x*x - 2*x + 1;$ $\{y=0\}$

$\{???\}\ y:= x*x - 3*x + 2;$ $\{y=0\}$

$\{x=A\}\ \text{if}\ (x<0)\ \{x:= -x;\}$ $\{???\}$

$\{x=A \wedge y=B\}\ \text{if}\ (x<y)\ \{x,y:= y,x;\}$ $\{???\}$

$\{x=A \wedge y=B\}\ \text{if}\ (x\leq y)\ \{x,y:= y,x;\}$ $\{???\}$

$s:= x;$ $\{???\}$

$s:= s+y;$ $\{???\}$

$s:= s+z;$ $\{???\}$

$\{???\}$

$p:= x;$ $\{???\}$

$p:= p*y;$ $\{???\}$

$p:= p*z;$ $\{???\}$

$\{???\}$

$s:= 0;$ $\{???\}$

$s:= s+x;$ $\{???\}$

$s:= s+y;$ $\{???\}$

$s:= s+z;$ $\{???\}$

$\{???\}$

<u>precondition</u> <u>program</u>   <u>postcondition</u>

$p := 1;$ $\{???\}$
$p := p*x;$ $\{???\}$
$p := p*y;$ $\{???\}$
$p := p*z;$ $\{???\}$
$\{???\}$

$m := x;$ $\{m = x\}$
if $(m{<}y)$ $\{m := y;\}$ $\{m = x \max y\}$
if $(m{<}z)$ $\{m := z;\}$ $\{???\}$
$\{???\}$

$\{\texttt{minInt} \le x\}$
$m := \texttt{minInt};$ $\{m = \texttt{minInt} \wedge \texttt{minInt} \le x\}$
if $(m{<}x)$ $\{m := x;\}$ $\{???\}$
if $(m{<}y)$ $\{m := y;\}$ $\{???\}$
if $(m{<}z)$ $\{m := z;\}$ $\{???\}$
$\{???\}$

$m := -\infty;$ $\{???\}$
if $(m{<}x)$ $\{m := x;\}$ $\{???\}$
if $(m{<}y)$ $\{m := y;\}$ $\{???\}$
if $(m{<}z)$ $\{m := z;\}$ $\{???\}$
$\{???\}$

$m := +\infty;$ $\{???\}$
if $(m{>}x)$ $\{m := x;\}$ $\{???\}$
if $(m{>}y)$ $\{m := y;\}$ $\{???\}$
if $(m{>}z)$ $\{m := z;\}$ $\{???\}$
$\{???\}$

$m, n := -\infty, 0;$ $\{m = \max A[0, 0)\}$
while $(n{\neq}|A|)$ invariant $\{m = \max A[0, n)\}$
$\{\quad m := m \max A[n];$ $\{m = \max A[0, n{+}1)\}$
$\qquad n := n{+}1;$ $\{???\}$
$\}$
$\{??? \wedge n{=}|A|\}$ $\{m = \max A\}$

$s, n := 0, 0;$ $\{???\}$
while $(n{\neq}|A|)$ invariant $\{s = \sum A[0, n)\}$
$\{\ s, n := s{+}A[n], n{+}1;\ \}$
$\{???\}$

$p, n := 1, 0;$
while $(n{\neq}|A|)$ invariant $???$
$\{\ p, n := p*A[n], n{+}1;\ \}$
$\{???\}$

$\{|A| \ge 1\}\ m, n := A[0], 1;$ $\{???\}$
while $(n{\neq}|A|)$ invariant $\{m = \max A[0, n)\}$
$\{\ m, n := m \max A[n], n{+}1;\ \}$
$\{m = \max A\}$

6.3   Proofs by Machine

By the time the examples above have been worked through, using by-hand calculation based on the substitution definition of an assignment's action on a postcondition, a second boundary has been reached. Even with that assignment rule, it's become too easy to make simple mistakes in the calculations — not because they are difficult to understand, but because they have become larger and are more encumbered with the trivial complexities common in programs generally. And, indeed, the amazing effectiveness and the novelty of the rule has, by then, worn off as well. Having grown used to calculation rather than guesswork, the students are ready for the transition to a tool that does those calculations for them. Crucially, however, they know what those calculations are and thus what the tool is doing (although not, perhaps, how it does it).

It's the same two transitions that move, first, from counting on your fingers to using positional notation on paper and then, second, from paper to a pocket calculator. For us, the pocket calculator is a program verifier. Having done this in stages, though, we understand that the calculator/verifier is just doing what we did on paper, but faster and more reliably. And what we were doing on paper was just, in turn, what we were doing with our fingers/operationally, but with a method to control detail.

In Appendix C we give the same exercises as above, Figs. 12, 13, 14, 15, 16, and 17, written in the language of the program-verification tool Dafny: it will be our pocket-calculator for program correctness. Naturally the exercises should however be done by hand, in class, before the "pocket calculator" is used. Or even before it's revealed that there is one.

6.4   Dafny

From the Dafny website:[20]

> Dafny is a programming language with a program verifier. As you type in your program, the verifier constantly looks over your shoulders and flags any errors.

One presentation of Dafny is embedded in a web-page, where you can simply type-in a program and press a button to check its correctness with respect to assertions you have included about what you want it to do.[21] In Fig. 8, the first part of the assertion exercises from p. 25 above has been (correctly) completed using the template of Fig. 12 (in Appendix C), and that has been pasted into the Dafny online-verification web-page.

In Fig. 9, the same has been done but with a deliberate error introduced; and it shows that Dafny found the error. When explaining this to the students, *it cannot be stressed too much* what a remarkable facility this is. They will be used to syntax errors (annoying, but trivial); and they will be used to run-time errors (fascinating, unfortunately, but also time-consuming). What they

---

[20] http://dafny.codeplex.com.
[21] http://rise4fun.com/dafny.

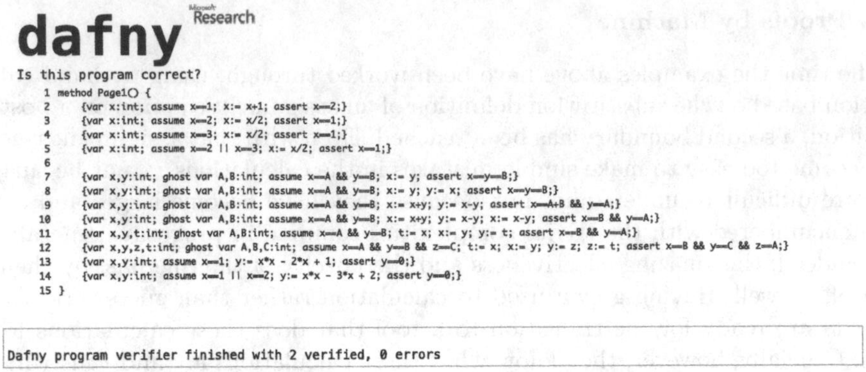

dafny Research

```
Is this program correct?
 1  method Page1() {
 2      {var x:int; assume x==1; x:= x+1; assert x==2;}
 3      {var x:int; assume x==2; x:= x/2; assert x==1;}
 4      {var x:int; assume x==3; x:= x/2; assert x==1;}
 5      {var x:int; assume x==2 || x==3; x:= x/2; assert x==1;}
 6
 7      {var x,y:int; ghost var A,B:int; assume x==A && y==B; x:= y; assert x==y==B;}
 8      {var x,y:int; ghost var A,B:int; assume x==A && y==B; x:= y; y:= x; assert x==y==B;}
 9      {var x,y:int; ghost var A,B:int; assume x==A && y==B; x:= x+y; y:= x-y; assert x==A+B && y==A;}
10      {var x,y:int; ghost var A,B:int; assume x==A && y==B; x:= x+y; y:= x-y; x:= x-y; assert x==B && y==A;}
11      {var x,y,t:int; ghost var A,B:int; assume x==A && y==B; t:= x; x:= y; y:= t; assert x==B && y==A;}
12      {var x,y,z,t:int; ghost var A,B,C:int; assume x==A && y==B && z==C; t:= x; x:= y; y:= z; z:= t; assert x==B && y==C && z==A;}
13      {var x,y:int; assume x==1; y:= x*x - 2*x + 1; assert y==0;}
14      {var x,y:int; assume x==1 || x==2; y:= x*x - 3*x + 2; assert y==0;}
15  }
```

```
Dafny program verifier finished with 2 verified, 0 errors
```

The first part of the exercises from 26 has been completed, and put into **Dafny**-format based on Fig. 12. **Dafny** reports "verified".

Fig. 8. The **Dafny** on-line verifier applied to Fig. 12 completed correctly.

will never have seen before is a computer-generated warning that means "Your program compiles correctly but, even if it does not actually crash at runtime, there are circumstances in which it will give the wrong answer." It is – or should be – one of those moments we all remember from our undergraduate days that we were truly amazed, that mentally we "went up a level".[22]

7   Return to Binary Search

In Sect. 2.1 the one-page handwritten *Can you write Binary Search?* question-naire was described, given almost at the beginning of the very first lecture and then (we hope) forgotten. What happens when we return to it? What material should have been covered in the meantime?

7.1   Why Return to Binary Search at All?

Our aim is to convince students that the techniques we are presenting are worth their while. Most people, at least when they are young, are curious: curiosity can almost be defined as the urge to find out things irrespective of their expected utility. But university students have begun to lose that, at varying rates of course; but the effect that teachers must confront is that many students will learn things

---

[22] As a teacher, however, be prepared for the later moment when they realise that Dafny can sometimes fail to prove correctness even when the program is correct. Of course it shares that problem with all verifiers: but the pedagogical issue is "How far can you get before reality bites?".

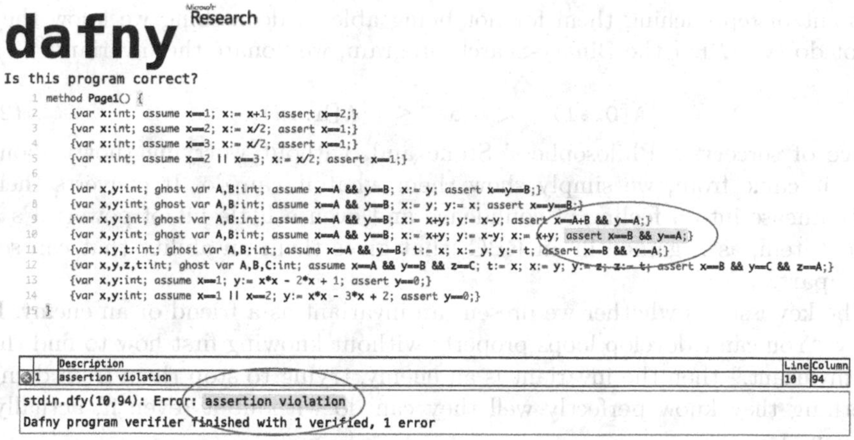

```
dafny    Research

Is this program correct?
 1 method Page1() {
 2   {var x:int; assume x==1; x:= x+1; assert x==2;}
 3   {var x:int; assume x==2; x:= x/2; assert x==1;}
 4   {var x:int; assume x==3; x:= x/2; assert x==1;}
 5   {var x:int; assume x==2 || x==3; x:= x/2; assert x==1;}
 6
 7   {var x,y:int; ghost var A,B:int; assume x==A && y==B; x:= y; assert x==y==B;}
 8   {var x,y:int; ghost var A,B:int; assume x==A && y==B; x:= y; y:= x; assert x==y==B;}
 9   {var x,y:int; ghost var A,B:int; assume x==A && y==B; x:= x+y; y:= x-y; assert x==A+B && y==A;}
10   {var x,y:int; ghost var A,B:int; assume x==A && y==B; x:= x+y; y:= x-y; x:= x+y; assert x==B && y==A;}
11   {var x,y,t:int; ghost var A,B:int; assume x==A && y==B; t:= x; x:= y; y:= t; assert x==B && y==A;}
12   {var x,y,z,t:int; ghost var A,B,C:int; assume x==A && y==B && z==C; t:= x; x:= y; y:= z; z:= t; assert x==B && y==C && z==A;}
13   {var x,y:int; assume x==1; y:= x*x - 2*x + 1; assert y==0;}
14   {var x,y:int; assume x==1 || x==2; y:= x*x - 3*x + 2; assert y==0;}
15 }
```

	Description	Line	Column
1	assertion violation	10	94

```
stdin.dfy(10,94): Error: assertion violation
Dafny program verifier finished with 1 verified, 1 error
```

The first part of the exercises from P. XX has been completed, and put into **Dafny**-format based on Fig. 12 but with a deliberate mistake introduced. **Dafny** reports an error: it's not a syntax error; and it's not a run-time error, since indeed the program hasn't been run yet. It's an error-report of the kind the students probably will *never have seen before.*

Fig. 9. The **Dafny** on-line verifier applied to Fig. 12 with a deliberate error.

(from the teachers) only if they believe it will somehow repay the effort. So we have to convince them of that.

Once they are reminded of the Binary-Search exercise in Lecture One, they will probably also recall that they felt uncomfortable, a bit at a loss. That is exactly what we want, because we want them to feel comfortable now, a few weeks later, to notice that difference, and then to attribute their happiness to what they have learned between then and now.

7.2 The Invariant: Begging, Borrowing, Stealing? or Maybe Donating?

In Sect. 6.1 we suggested that, for students at this level, it does not matter where an invariant comes from. In simplest terms, that is because techniques of invariant *synthesis* can't effectively be taught unless the students are already convinced that they want an invariant at all; and that will take more than a few weeks, or even a few terms. We begin here.

For the moment, we will simple give invariants to the students, without pretending that they should be able to figure them out for themselves. What is the point of reproaching them for not being able to do a thing we know they cannot do (yet)? For the Binary-Search program, we donate the invariant[23]

$$A[0..1] \quad < \quad a \quad \leq \quad A[h..N), \tag{2}$$

a piece of sorcery, a Philosophers' Stone and, without worrying (now) about where it came from, we simply show them what it can do. It converts their earlier unease into a feeling of confidence and even a little bit of power: it's a magical item, as if gained in an RPG, that gives them an ability that can set them apart.

The key issue is whether we present an invariant as a friend or an enemy. If we say "You can't develop loops properly without knowing first how to find the loop invariant." then the invariant is an enemy, trying to stop them from doing something they know perfectly well they can do without it (even if, actually, they can't).

The invariant is a friend if you say "Remember that program, Binary Search, that seemed so hard to get right? If only you'd had one of these, like (2) above, then it would have been easy." And then you go on to show how easy indeed it now is *for them*. (Showing that it is easy for you would be missing the point: more about that immediately below.) Once they understand that, then they will be motivated to learn how to find "one of these", by themselves, for other programs that they encounter later.

There will be an exhilarating moment, for you, when finally one of the students asks "How do you figure out invariants in the first place?" The spark of pleasure you will get is that they *want to know*. That's completely different from your having to convince them that they need to know.

---

[23] The comparison operators here operate over all elements of the structure. It's a neat bit of notation, but at some point it must be mentioned that it is not transitive (when the intermediate structure is empty). Given that most of the students in the class won't have heard of transitivity, now is probably not the time. Remember that the idea of operators' having (algebraic) "properties" itself is a higher level of awareness than most will have at this stage.

Save this, thus, until at some later stage in the class the topic of algebraic reasoning comes up naturally. It will: how do you initialise a loop whose invariant is that some variable holds the product "so far"? What's the product of an empty sequence? Why is there a "right" answer? (It's so that product is a homomorphism.) At that moment, you can suddenly remember this operator, and discuss its abstract properties too. Having a store of deferred "Did you notice?" items, like this one, is useful for time-management during your interactive-style lectures. If you look like you're going to run out of material, pull one of them out and connect it to earlier material. Spend a happy ten minutes discussing with them how to think about it properly.

Have also a few really intriguing "puzzles" that you can look at with the upper-layer students; from about one-third of the way through the course, the others will be happy to listen and they won't be bored. A good one for "What's the sum/product of...?" is "What's the determinant of an empty matrix?" Only the upper layer will know what matrices and determinants are: but they will be pleased that you recognise their extra knowledge and expertise.

7.3 Collaboration and Local Reasoning; Cardboard and Masking Tape

Now the aim is to use (2) to solve the problem posed in Sect. 2.1. Recall that the class has been divided into groups, for mentoring (Sect. 3).

Write the mentoring-group names on small pieces of paper, and bring them to class together with a small cup.[24] Pick one of the slips from the cup, thus picking a mentoring-group "randomly". (In fact, you should rig this to make sure you get a strong group. The theatre here is not in order to seem clever — rather it's to avoid any sense among the students that you might be picking on individuals. Standing in front of the class is a challenge, for them, and you defuse that by making them feel relaxed by the process and maybe even amused by way you carry it out.)

The First Group: Writing the Loop Skeleton. Call the selected group to the front, and explain to them that they will write the loop initialisation, guard and finalisation. Write on the board at the left and explain that "we" (you and they) are going to fill in the ???'s.[25]

The (something), you explain as you glance at the cup, will be another group's problem. (Nervous laughter from the audience.)

```
l,h:= ?L?,?H?
{ A[0..1) < a <= A[h..N) }
while ?G? do
{ A[0..1) < a <= A[h..N) }
    (something)
end
{ A[0..1) < a <= A[h..N) and not ?G?}
{ A[0..1) < a <= A[1..N)}
n:= ?E?
{ A[0..n) < a <= A[n..N) }
```

Now you have to lead them through the steps of filling-in the missing pieces. You will have to say most of it; and it will be hard because, at first, either they will not speak at all, or they will give incorrect answers. The point of having them at the front, even if they say little, is that afterwards what they will remember is that they contributed collectively to finding the solution (just by standing there) even if actually they contributed nothing concrete. The alternative, of pointing to the group still sitting in the audience, does not work nearly so well.

A good piece to start with is ?L?,?H?, because it's the simplest but also a little bit unexpected. What, you ask them, will establish $A[0..1) < a \leq A[h..N)$ trivially? Drag out of them (you will probably have to) that $A[0..1) < a \leq A[h..N)$

---

[24] An Australian styrofoam "stubby holder" gets a good reaction, especially a brightly coloured one whose beer-brand logo will be recognised even from the back of the classroom.

[25] The use of ?L? etc. just below is to be able to refer to them in this text. On the board, simply ??? is fine, since you can point to the one you mean.

is trivially true when $1 = 0$ and $h = N$, because both array segments are empty. *Watch them struggle* to interpret what this might mean for the coming loop; *discourage them* from doing so; *assure them* that it is unnecessary.

Work similarly on ?G? — what is the simplest test you could pick so that $A[0..1) < a \le A[h..N) \land \neg?G?$ implies $A[0..1) < a \le A[1..N)$. Again, it's "obviously" $1 \ne h$, since $\neg(1 \ne h)$ is of course $1 = h$, just what's needed for that implication. Again you will have to drag; again they won't really believe that you can program this way.

Finish off with ?E?, and then ask them to sit down.

The Second Group: Sketching the Loop Body. Now take a piece of cardboard big enough to cover the work just done, and tape it over the board so that the work is no longer visible. Pick a second group's name from the cup, and invite them to come to the front. Write in the middle of the board

```
{ A[0..1) < a <= A[h..N) and l!=h}
m := ?M?
{ l <= m < h }
if ?C?
    then { l <= m < h and A[m]<a }  (something for then)
    else { l <= m < h and A[m]>=a } (something for else)
(something)
{ A[0..1) < a <= A[h..N) and h-l has strictly decreased }
```

and go through the same process with this group. Of course the $A[m] < a$ after the **then** gives the text ?C? away; but they will hesitate because they think it can't be that simple. You are teaching them, by doing this, that it *is* that simple.

Cover-up the results when it's done.

The Third Group: Finishing Off. For the third group, write

```
{ A[0..1) < a <= A[h..N) and l <= m < h and A[m]<a }
?T?
{ A[0..1) < a <= A[h..N) and h-l has strictly decreased }
```

and

```
{ A[0..1) < a <= A[h..N) and l <= m < h and A[m]>a }
?E?
{ A[0..1) < a <= A[h..N) and h-l has strictly decreased }
```

and split the group in two. Get one half to do ?T? and the other half to do ?E?.

You might have to explain why it is allowed for the $A[0..1) < a <= A[h..N)$ suddenly to reappear. Explain (remember this is *in*formal methods) that it carries through from the beginning of the loop body and you really should have written it for the previous group — but you left it out to reduce clutter: there was no assignment to any of its variables.

Once it's done, just ask them to sit. No need to cover this up.

The Fourth Group: Finishing Up. Now remind the class what has been done: three independent groups, working effectively in separate parts of the program, from the outside-in (not from first-line to last-line), and "no idea" whether the three bits will fit together, however correct they might be with respect to their individual assertions.

Then invite a fourth group to come up and remove the cardboard, and to write a single program combining the pieces already there. Tell them that they don't have to write the assertions, except for two: the invariant, just at the beginning of the loop body, and the overall postcondition, at the end of the whole program.[26]

Be sure they write it neatly, so that the whole class can read the program (they believe) they collectively have just written. Then hand back their earlier answers, from the first lecture long ago, without commenting on them:

Really, no comment: say nothing. Nothing at all.[27]

Just wait until you see that people are looking up, starting to pack their things away, ready to go. The minute or two (in my experience) before that is usually so quiet you can almost hear the neurones firing. Make it last, let it run: you won't get many moments like it.

Then simply end the lecture at that point: no announcements or reminders. Just "See you next week."

8 Using Dafny to do Top-Down Development

Getting the most out of Binary Search, in Appendix D we hammer home the idea of program development "from the outside in" rather than from first statement to last. This approach, though known instinctively by many, was brought especially to prominence by Niklaus Wirth in the early 1970's.[28]

Surprising to me personally, though taught this principle as an undergraduate, was that use of Dafny on a program of any complexity actually forces you to do this "stepwise refinement": it is not an option. In effect, Dafny makes a necessity out of a virtue. And here is why.

Novices with Dafny (as I still am) at first expect to be able to write the complete code of a small program (i.e. Binary Search in this case) and then to "do the right thing" by including the assertions and invariants that they have

---

[26] Depending on the grip you feel you have on their attention at this point, you could ask them whether they found it odd to be developing a program without a specification of what it should do. But do not force this: if they look confused enough already, do not add to it.

[27] Saying nothing (aside from, obviously, "Here are your answers from Lecture 1") is important: it's right now, for a few minutes only, that they will be most receptive and will draw conclusions of their own. You cannot draw *their* conclusions for them.

Any distraction (e.g. your voice) will dilute the effect. Silence!.

[28] N. Wirth. Program development via stepwise refinement. *Communications ACM* 14,4, pp. 221–7. 1971.

worked out for themselves, perhaps on paper. Then – one push of the magical button – Dafny will tell you whether those assertions verify. That's the theory.

In practice, Dafny can sometimes give a third answer, and that in two forms. One is "Can't verify." (paraphrased) which means literally that: Dafny has not found your assertions to be wrong; but neither can it prove them to be right. The second form is the "whirring fan" where your laptop simply never returns from the proof effort; eventually you must interrupt the verification yourself.[29]

Once you have experienced this often enough, you realise that a step-by-step approach is much better, where you check at each stage that Dafny can verify what you have done so far. And – crucially – the "so far" has to be from the outside-in if you are not to run the risk ultimately of finding e.g. that your very last assertion won't verify, forcing you to start all over from the very beginning.

Appendix D shows this step-by-step approach with Binary Search. Although it looks like an awful lot of text for such a simple program, in fact each stage is made from the previous one by a cut-and-paste copy followed by alteration of a very small part. It's much more efficient than it looks.

And, most important of all: it works.

9   Fast Forward: Meeting the Real World

9.1   Motivation and Principles

Finally, we must leave (in this presentation) the Binary Search: we "fast forward" from there to the very end of the course.

The material above describes a prefix of the course, perhaps the first third. The middle of the course (not described here) charts a course through examples and techniques that aim to end with a real-world example, briefly treated in this section. The precise trajectory taken through that middle part depends on the characteristics – strengths and weaknesses – of the students in that particular year; and being able to adapt in that way requires a store of ready-made topics that can be selected or not, on the fly. That store will naturally build up as the course is repeated year by year.

But however we pass through the middle, we want to end with the feeling "This stuff really works. It's practical. And it makes a difference." The topic chosen to finish off the course, and its associated assignment, is deliberately designed to be one that, as a side effect, dispels the mystery around some part of the undergraduate computing experience.[30]

---

[29] The Dafny documentation explains why this is a risk with "SMT solvers", which is the kind of prover (Z3) that Dafny uses.

[30] For me, as an undergraduate, the computing courses that had the most impact, both at the time and lasting even until now, were the "de-mystifiers" — the course on compiler construction, that showed how that impossible task could be routinely done if only you looked at it the right way (and read the literature); the course on operating systems, that followed a single character from the moment you typed it in until its arrival in your program's char-buffer; and the course we would have had, had it been 10 years later, of how to program a full-screen editor.

In this case the mystery was "What *really* happens when you type in a command to a terminal window?" As we all know (but some students do not), a program is run. But how does that program access the resources it needs? And how do you use the methods here in order to make sure it does that correctly?

9.2 Programming the cp Command

We chose the copy command "cp", which must read and write files from... somewhere. To do that, it uses system calls, and it must use them correctly.

The assignment begins with an abstract model of the system calls open, creat, read and write that – crucially – are based on *real* operating system calls, complete with the nondeterminism of how much is read or written (not necessarily as much as you asked for), and the operating-style convention for end-of-file that is indicated by reading zero characters.[31]

Only this faithful modelling of what really is "out there" will give the students the conviction that they can and should apply these methods to what they will find when they really get "out there" themselves.

The assignment text is given in full in Appendix E, and is commented upon there. About one third of the students got high marks for this, more than expected. They used all these techniques that were new to them in February, but which after June they will never forget:

- Abstraction of interfaces.
- Refinement of code through increasing levels of detail.
- Invariants and static reasoning.
- Automated assistance with verifying program correctness.
- Programs that work first time, even under the most bizarre scenarios.

Imagine what Software Engineering would be like today if all students experienced those exciting accomplishments in their very first year.

Can we make it that way tomorrow?

10 Conclusions. . . and Prospects?

It would be tempting to conclude from the remarks in Appendix F that this course has been an outstanding success. But we can't. Whether the students enjoy a course, and whether they *think* they benefitted is quite different from whether a course actually achieved its objectives.[32] And, so far, we have no real,

---

[31] Calling it "creat", rather than sanitising it to something sensible, is an important part of this experience. The students should be able to find that *exact* command using "man 2 creat", and they should see that the behaviour described in the manual page matches their abstraction.

[32] Indeed it's often the unpopular lecturers and courses that turn out in the end to have been of the most value. Remember your time at school, what you thought then and what you realised twenty years later.

objective evidence that these are better programmers than they were before or, more significantly, than they would have been without (In-)Formal Methods.[33]

I think it's fair, though, to say this course has at least not been a failure. Why is that important? It's because so many Formal Methods courses *have* failed. That is a critical problem: the skills the students never get a chance to learn, because of those failures, are precisely the skills they need. And they need them at an early stage, to bring about a significant improvement in both their own accomplishments *and* the expectations that they have of others both now and later, of their future colleagues and employers. It's ridiculous, actually scandalous that they do not have these elementary techniques at their disposal.

As for prospects: it depends on whether this approach is *portable* and *durable*. It has already been taught by two other lecturers, who report positively. But true progress will come with an integration so inextricably into the matrix of conventional curricula that it cannot be undone when its patron moves on. Rather than being the icing on the cake, which can always be scraped off, Informal Methods must be the rising agent distributed throughout.

Invariants, assertions and static reasoning should be as self-evidently part of the introductory Computer Science curriculum as are types, variables, control structures and I/O in the students' very first programming language.

Can you help to bring that about?

Acknowledgements. The ideas in this course description distill what I have learned from many years of teaching students and of interaction with my fellow lecturers, both in Australia and, earlier, at Oxford in the UK. Some of those ideas I thought of myself; but most I have copied from colleagues whose style I admire. The key is, of course, in having consistent principles of what to copy and what to leave aside. In spite of the difficulty Formal (or Informal) Methods has had in gaining traction against more conventional courses, I have personally never felt that I lacked the support of my fellow academics in trying this material out. In earlier teaching of rigour in programming, I took a very strict approach; here (obviously) it is not strict at all. I have been encouraged by others in both cases, and I appreciate it. It is not clear yet how to combine the informal and the formal: there is still more experimenting to do. Thanks therefore to all my students, friends, colleagues and even skeptics who have allowed this exploration the space to breathe, and who have given me fair and constructive criticism that has helped to make it better. Finally, I would like to thank Zhiming Liu, Jonathan Bowen and Zili Zhang for organising the *Summer School on Engineering Trustworthy Software Systems* at which lectures based on this "users manual" were given, and for the opportunity to publish it here. I am also grateful also for the institutional support of the University of New South Wales and of NICTA, both during the running of these courses and during the preparation of this article.

---

[33] This is a problem with any form of teaching, of course. But it's especially an issue with Formal Methods because those who haven't "got it" don't want it and, furthermore, don't realise that actually they need it. On the other hand, those who have got it are so amazed at their new perspective that they tend to run ahead of the evidence and so discredit the whole enterprise. Formal-Methods proselytisers must play by the same rules as anyone else if they are not to be branded as zealots — which is the usual prelude to being ignored.

A   Binary-Search Class Test

A.1   Teacher's Notes

1. Hand the exercise out as a _single double-sided A4 sheet_ with the instructions on the front and the template on the back. The fact it's just a single sheet reinforces the feeling of informality that we want to achieve: this exercise should not be a big deal.
2. Use an audible, but gentle alarm to give them 10 min to complete it. (I used a countdown timer on a smart phone that played _2001: A Space Odyssey_'s theme _Thus Sprach Zarathustra_. It begins softly, and so doesn't startle anyone; and in the end it gets a laugh.) Use an alarm sitting on the table, rather than e.g. checking a clock or wrist-watch yourself, because that removes you from the "enforcement zone" — you become the good cop. It's the automated alarm that's the bad cop.
   (This is the same strategy used by some libraries that put their photocopiers on a timer that switches them off automatically at ten minutes before closing. Can't blame the nasty librarian, in that case.)
3. Just collect the answers, and then move on immediately. You want the students as quickly as possible to forget that they have done this test, because they'll regard Binary Search as trivial, as "old stuff" (in spite of the fact their answer is almost certainly wrong), and if you dwell on it they will start to wonder whether they have enrolled in a course that's beneath them.
4. Look at the answers only later, e.g. when you get home: you will probably be amazed. Out of a class of 42 beginning second-year Computer-Science students I found just one answer that was correct. A second one was nearly correct; and the remaining 40 (= 95 %) were quite wrong. Figure 1 in Sect. 4.1 above shows a typical example.
5. Scan them all to PDF's and mark them (at your leisure — you won't need them for a while) by annotating them. (See example marking also in Fig. 1.)
6. Remember that the point of this exercise isn't humiliation, of course. What you will do is choose your moment, somewhere further down the course, where their coding is clearly better than it was on the first day.
   At that stage you return the marked PDF's of Binary Search, and you let them see for themselves how much they have improved.

A.2   The Test Itself

The next two pages are the test itself. The second page is a typeset version of Fig. 1 before it was answered. Probably the handwritten version is more effective, since it reinforces the informality.

(In-)Formal Methods
In-class exercise

Binary Search

Student Name: ┌─────────────────────────────┐
              │   │
              │   │
              └─────────────────────────────┘

Your program is to read from three variables A,N, and a:

- A sorted array A of integers, of size N, indexed from 0 (inclusive) up to N (exclusive). Thus the array elements are

$$A[0] \ \leq \ A[1] \ \leq \ \cdots \ \leq \ A[N-1].$$

- An integer a to be sought in the array.

The program is to assign to a single variable n the least value such that $A[n] = a$, if there an a in A at all. Otherwise n should be the least value such that $A[n] > a$; and if no value in A is greater than a, then n should be set to N.

   You can use other, temporary variables.

Write your binary-search program by filling in the seven boxes on the back of this sheet.

Do not change anything else.

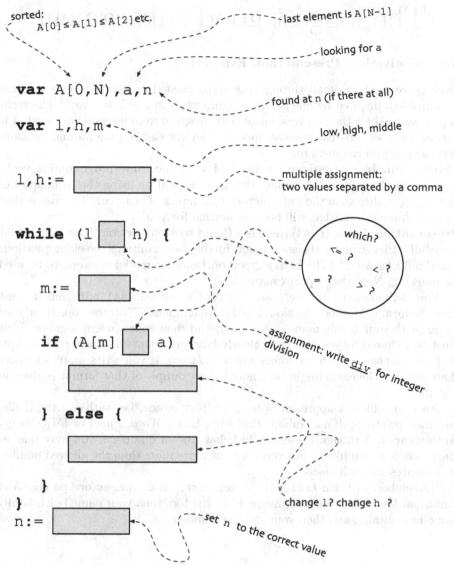

The original version of this was handwritten. (See Fig. 1.)

B   Assignment 1: Good Subsegments

The assignment follows, adapted for this article. Footnotes in italics have been added in this text; footnotes in normal font were in the original.

The longest good subsegment

B.1   Motivation, Presentation, Evaluation

In class we went in detail through the steps needed to program-up a solution to a problem inspired by one of the assignments you had last year:[34] The techniques we used for the two versions of that program were intended to be what is normal for a second-year student: indeed, they (or similar) are normal for more experienced programmers too.

Motivation. In this assignment we deal with the same programming problem, i.e. we do it for a third time. But now we will be using the techniques of <u>this course</u> rather than the introductory techniques of last year. The aim is that *these* techniques are what will become normal for you.

Presentation. Below (p. 43) there is a (hand-written) section "The Assignment — detail " that explains the assignment further, and contains the eight questions you should answer.[35] (The blurry green portions are model answers, to be used for marking. Note their approximate size!)

Your submission must be a single PDF file named **Ass1.pdf**, and it must have "Informal Methods Session 1 2014 Assignment 1" at the top, then your name (with your family name in capitals), and then your student number. That must be followed by your answers, clearly labelled Answer 1, Answer 2 etc. *Note that the number-of-sentence limits are mandatory.* If you write more sentences than allowed, the extra might be ignored. An example of that format is given in Fig. 10.

An easy, efficient approach is to use a text editor, i.e. with an ASCII file, and then print-to-pdf and submit that PDF. Using *Word*, *Pages* or LaTeX is <u>*not*</u> <u>*recommended*</u>. Although the example below fits on one page, you may take as many pages as you like — but you may not write more than the allowed number of sentences for each answer.

Remember: PDF file **Ass1.pdf** — not .txt, .doc, .pages or .ps etc. And "Informal Methods 2014 Assignment 1" at the top, then your name (with family name in capitals), and then your student number.

---

[34] *For these students, that was first-year introductory programming in C.*

[35] *The hand-writing of assignments is deliberate. (In the course as given, most of the material was hand-written; much of this article has been typeset from those hand-written notes just for this publication.)*

First, hand-writing is a much faster way of getting material ready when it mixed text, program code, marginal notes, arrows etc. . . .

Second, and more important, is that it sends the message that clever, glossy, beautiful typesetting is not the aim of the course: we are interested in clever, glossy, beautiful ways of thinking. Hand-written notes and on-the-board lectures reinforces that.

```
Informal Methods Session 1 2014
Assignment 1
Jack SPRAT
#1234567
```

Answer 1: All work and no play makes Jack a dull boy.

Answer 2: All work and no play makes Jack a dull boy. All work and
no play makes Jack a dull boy. All work and no play makes Jack a
dull boy.

Answer 3: All work and no play makes Jack a dull boy. All work and
no play makes Jack a dull boy.

Answer 4: All work and no play makes Jack a dull boy. All work and
no play makes Jack a dull boy.

Answer 5: All work and no play makes Jack a dull boy.

Answer 6: All work and no play makes Jack a dull boy. All work and
no play makes Jack a dull boy. All work and no play makes Jack a
dull boy.

Answer 7: All work and no play makes Jack a dull boy.

Answer 8: All work and no play makes Jack a dull boy. All work and
no play makes Jack a dull boy.

All work and no play makes Jack a dull boy. All work and no play
makes Jack a dull boy.

```
    All work and
    no play makes
        Jack a dull boy
        All work
        and no play makes Jack a
    dull boy
```

Fig. 10. Sample answer format

Evaluation. The markers will be trying to make sure that you understand the
material that the questions are covering. That's a two-part process: first figuring
out, from what you've written, what you are actually thinking; and second,
figuring out whether you are thinking the right thing. *Make the first part easy
for the markers by writing clear and concise answers.*

You will get marks only for the second part (evidence that you are thinking the right thing); but you cannot get marks there unless the markers successfully interpret the first part. So neatness is important.

Your marked answers will be emailed to you as annotated PDF's. The general marking conventions will be as follows:[36]

- Phrases the marker wants to emphasise as *good* will be highlighted in green. Green means "You got it."
- Phrases the marker wants to emphasise as not understood, or dubious, will be highlighted in yellow. Yellow means "Are you sure?" There might be a short query nearby.
- Phrases the marker wants to emphasise as *bad* (e.g. completely wrong) will be highlighted in red. Usually those will have a short explanation nearby.[37]
- Next to each question in blue will be a fraction: that's the number of marks gained (numerator) over the number of marks available (denominator) for that question.
- At the top of the assignment will be an overall mark as a blue fraction in a box, obtained by summing the individual numerators and denominators for each question. The numerator is your mark, and the denominator is the total mark for the whole assignment. (That total mark will be scaled to a percentage, later, depending on the proportion of marks this assignment represents in the whole course.)
  The "numerator/denominator" scheme makes it easy to check for marking errors: check the numerator-sum to make sure the marks given were added correctly; check the denominator-sum to make sure every question was marked and its mark included in the total.
- Any annotation numbers that are *not* fractions are merely marker's notes, and should be ignored.

---

[36] An example is given in Fig. 11.

[37] Often the red highlight and the short explanation will be enough for you to see what is wrong. But not always. This scheme is chosen to make things efficient *for the marker*, to reduce fatigue and so allow more real thought while marking.

Thus the marker's principles in choosing the explanation will be to keep it short, and to act as a reminder *to the marker* what the problem really was. That way the marker can check your work more thoroughly (less fatigue), but will also be able to remember what the problem was and explain it face-to-face if you ask, afterwards, for more help.

Informal Methods

Assignment 1 detail

In Week 1's lecture we did together, in class,
a programming exercise based on an assignment
that you had last year. The two programs
we developed on the board looked like this:

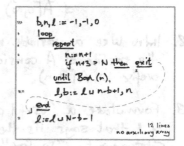

```
m := 0
for b := 0 to N-3 do
    if Bad(b) then B[m], m := b, m+1
l := 0
for i := 0 to m-1 do
    if i = 0 then l := l ∪ B[0] + 2
    else if i = m-1 then l := l ∪ N - B[i] - 1
    else l := l ∪ B[i+1] - B[i] + 1
                              12 lines
                        and an auxiliary array
```

```
b, n, l := -1, -1, 0
loop
    repeat
        n := n+1
        if n+3 > N then exit
    until Bad(n),
    l, b := l ∪ n - b+1, n
end
l := l ∪ N - b - 1
                              12 lines
                        no auxiliary array
```

They were each about 12 lines long. Our first
attempt used an auxiliary array, but was very
straightforward — though a bit tricky in the
small details. In our second attempt we got rid
of the auxiliary array by using a flow chart to
help us introduce a more sophisticated control
structure.

We think both programs are correct: but we aren't sure.

In this assignment you will find an answer to this
programming problem that is shorter and simpler
than either of the above and you will be able to
explain why it is correct.

But how ?

Fig. 11. Example of marked assignment with colour conventions.

Here's how.

See next page for footnotes.

1. We make some useful definitions: say that a subsegment $A[s,f)$[1] of $A[0,N)$ is Good just when it contains no Bad() triples. Our programming problem then becomes

$$l := \text{"length of a longest Good subsegment of } A[0,N).\text{"}[2]$$

2. Introduce a variable n whose meaning is "the prefix of A considered so far". That prefix is $A[0,n)$.[3]

3. Formulate a "useful property" — an invariant — of l that says it's the length of a longest Good subsegment "so far":

Inv1 is   "l is the length of a longest Good subsegment of $A[0,n)$."

4. Now think of our program skeleton like this:

Note! Not N.

```
l,n := ?,?
{Inv1 is true}
While n ≠ N do
    {Inv1} l := ? {Inv1 "for A[0,n]"}       A[n] as well
    n := n+1
    {Inv1}                    Hard part
end
{Inv1 ∧ n = N}
```

Fig. 11. (*continued*)

5. Introduce a new variable e, and a new invariant for it:

$$\text{Inv2 is } \text{``}A[e,n) \text{ is a longest Good suffix of } A[0,n).\text{''}$$ [3]

6. Refine our program to this:

```
ℓ,n,e := ?,?,?
{Inv1 ∧ Inv2}
while n ≠ N do
      {Inv2}
      if n-2 ≥ 0 ∧ ? then e := ?
      {Inv2 "for A[0,n]"}

      ℓ := ?  // Use e to help with this.
      { (Inv1 ∧ Inv2) "for A[0,n]" }

      n := n+1
      {Inv1 ∧ Inv2}
end
{Inv1 ∧ n = N}
```

---

[1] Start is s, (one more than) finish is f.

[2] There might be several "longest" — but they will all have the same length.

[3] A[s,f) is a prefix of A[0,n) when s=0; it's a suffix when f=n.

Fig. 11. (*continued*)

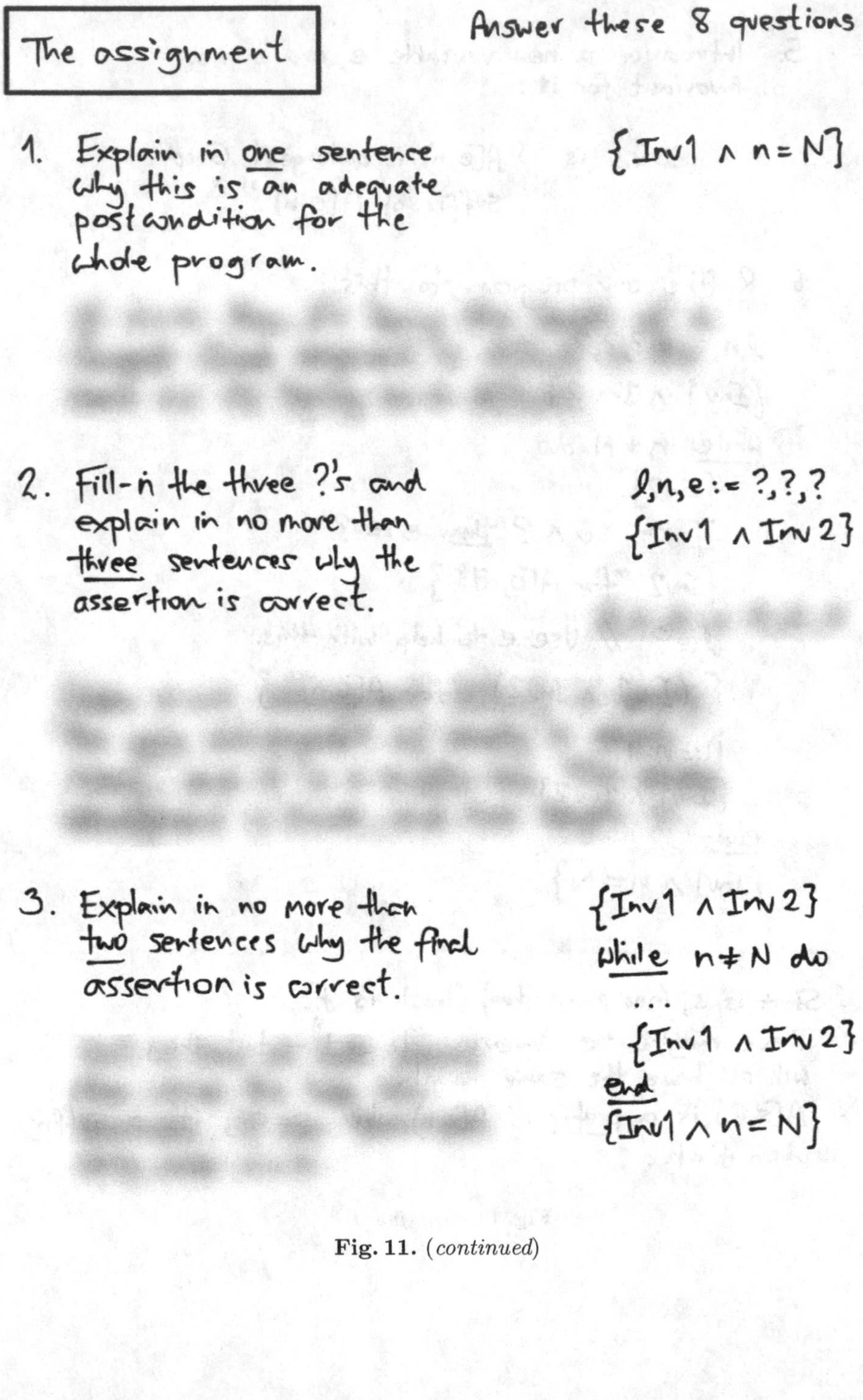
The assignment
Answer these 8 questions
1. Explain in one sentence why this is an adequate postcondition for the whole program.
{Inv1 ∧ n = N}
2. Fill-in the three ?'s and explain in no more than three sentences why the assertion is correct.
l, n, e := ?, ?, ?
{Inv1 ∧ Inv2}
3. Explain in no more than two sentences why the final assertion is correct.
{Inv1 ∧ Inv2}
while n ≠ N do
...
{Inv1 ∧ Inv2}
end
{Inv1 ∧ n = N}

Fig. 11. (*continued*)

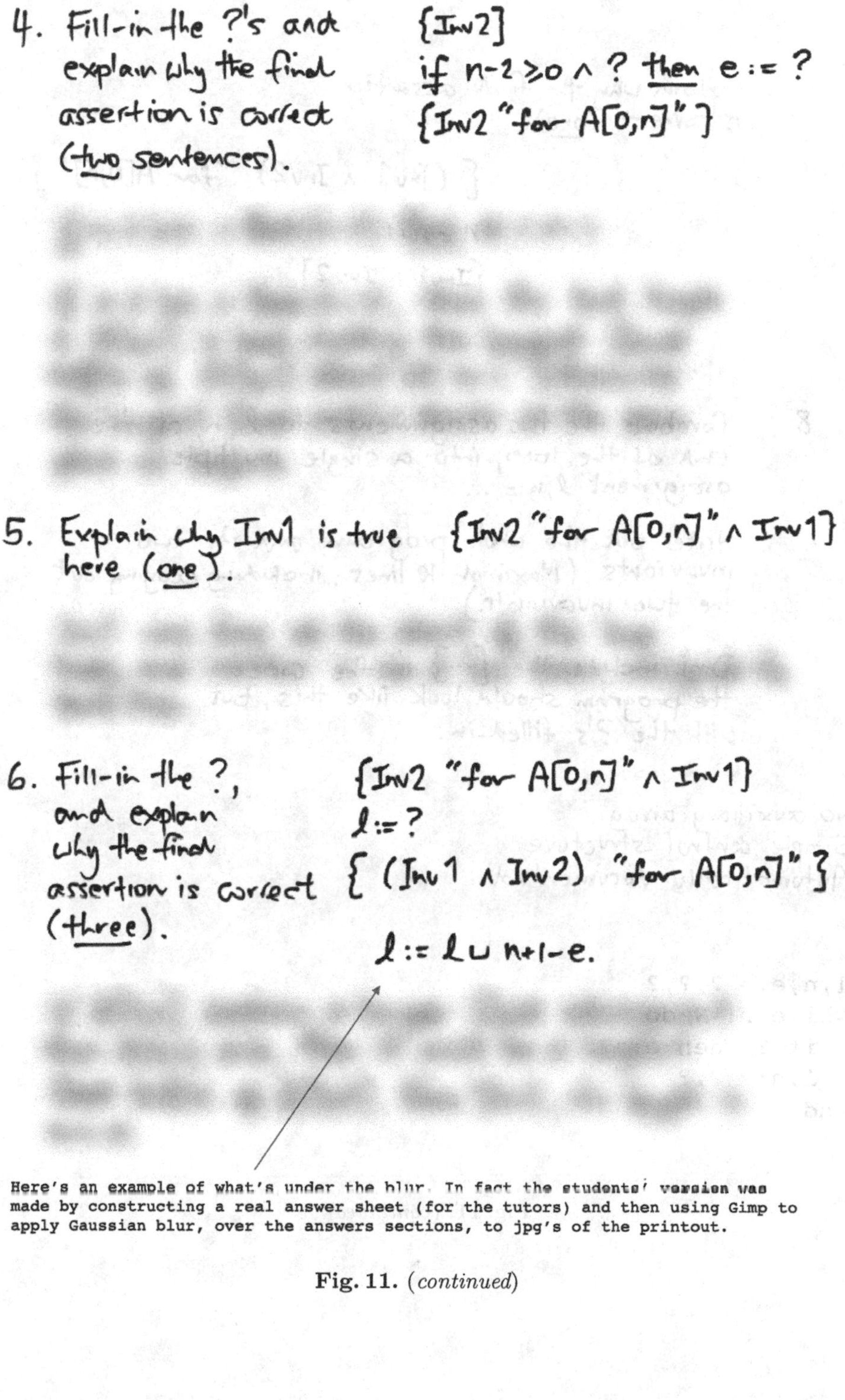
4. Fill-in the ?'s and explain why the final assertion is correct (two sentences).

{Inv2}
if n-2 ≥ 0 ∧ ? then e := ?
{Inv2 "for A[0,n]"}

5. Explain why Inv1 is true here (one).

{Inv2 "for A[0,n]" ∧ Inv1}

6. Fill-in the ?, and explain why the final assertion is correct (three).

{Inv2 "for A[0,n]" ∧ Inv1}
l := ?
{ (Inv1 ∧ Inv2) "for A[0,n]" }

l := l ⊔ n+1-e.

Here's an example of what's under the blur. In fact the students' version was made by constructing a real answer sheet (for the tutors) and then using Gimp to apply Gaussian blur, over the answers sections, to jpg's of the printout.

Fig. 11. (*continued*)

7. Explain why the final assertion is correct (one).

$$\{ (Inv1 \land Inv2) \text{ "for } A[0,n]\text{" } \}$$
$$n := n+1$$
$$\{Inv1 \land Inv2\}$$

8.   Combine the two assignments to l, n, at the end of the loop, into a single multiple assignment $l, n := \ldots$

Write out the whole program and its two invariants. (Maximum 10 lines, including copying out the two invariants.)

Don't include the $\{\ldots\}$ in the code: the program should look like this, but with the ?'s filled-in.

No auxiliary array
Simple control structure
Automatically documented

```
l,n,e:= ?,?,?
while n!=N do
   if ? then e:=?
   l,n:= ?,?
end
```

Fig. 11. (*continued*)

Informal Methods Session 1 YYYY
Assignment 1
Jack SPRAT   **Need to say -why- it's the right invariant** | 18/30 |
#1234567   **and -why- it's the right loop guard.**   0/2

Answer 1: Inv1 must be true since it establishes the purpose of the program; it starts and
remains true (hence invariant) and n=N is true because it means the end of the array has
been reached and the program should terminate.

Answer 2: l,n,e:= 0,0,0 3   **This is just repeating the question.**
Inv1 and Inv2 must be correct at the start for the program to execute, given the initialised
values of l,n,e. Inv1 is correct at the start since the array has not been scanned yet.
Similarly, Inv2 is correct since A[0,0) is the longest good suffix of an empty array.   4/7

Answer 3: Inv1 must be true at the end to ensure the program has achieved its purpose, since
l has now been set and also because the invariant doesn't change. Also n=N must be correct
since the entire array has been scanned and the end has been reached, thus ending the   2/3
program.   1   0.5   0.5

Answer 4: if n-2 >= 0 and Bad(n-2) then e:= n-1   2
Since Inv2 is the length of the longest good suffix, it must be true over the segment A[0,n)
until a bad triple is encountered (which is what the if statement checks), which changes the
value of e and thus restarts the length of the longest good suffix from n-1. Inv1 remains
true but not necessarily for A[0,n) because l is greater than or equal to the length of the
longest good suffix and has not yet been updated.   **It can never be greater.**   0.5   2.5/5

Answer 5: Inv1 was true previously and since no other variables changed and the invariant
doesn't change, it must be true afterwards here.   **You can't say the invariant hasn't changed**
Answer 6: l:= max(l,n-e+1)   **"because it's invariant".**   1.5/2
Inv2 was already true from the previous assertion and since no variables affecting it have
changed, it remains true. Also the value of l has been updated to reflect the change in the
length of the longest good suffix. Therefore, Inv1 is now also true for A[0,n], making the
assertion correct.   **You don't say why t's the right change.**   2/3

Answer 7: Inv1 and Inv2 are true after each iteration and must remain true for the loop to
continue.
                    This seems to be saying that they have to be true because the program is correct.   0/2
Answer 8:
Inv1: "l is the length of a longest good sub-segment of A[0,n)."
Inv2: "A[e,n) is a longest good suffix of A[0,n)."

```
l,n,e:= 0,0,0
while n!=N do
     if n-2 >= 0 and Bad(n-2) then e:= n-1
     l,n:= max(l,n-e+1), n+1                    6/6
end
```

Fig. 11. (*continued*)

C   Dafny Versions of Introductory Assertion-Exercises

```
method Page1() {
    {var x:int; assume x==1;   x:= x+1; assert true;}
    {var x:int; assume x==2;   x:= x/2; assert true;}
    {var x:int; assume x==3;   x:= x/2; assert true;}
    {var x:int; assume false; x:= x/2; assert x==1;}

    {var x,y:int; ghost var A,B:int; assume x==A && y==B; x:= y; assert true;}
    {var x,y:int; ghost var A,B:int; assume x==A && y==B; x:= y; y:= x; assert true; }

    {var x,y:int; ghost var A,B:int;
        assume x==A && y==B;
        x:= x+y; y:= x-y;
        assert true;
    }
    {var x,y:int; ghost var A,B:int;
        assume x==A && y==B;
        x:= x+y; y:= x-y; x:= x-y;
        assert true;
    }
    {var x,y,t:int; ghost var A,B:int;
        assume x==A && y==B;
        t:= x; x:= y; y:= t;
        assert true;
    }
    {var x,y,z,t:int; var A,B,C:int;
        assume x==A && y==B && z==C;
        t:= x; x:| x==A; y:| y==C; z:| z==A;
        assert x==B && y==C && z==A;
    }
    {var x,y:int; assume false; y:= x*x - 2*x + 1; assert y==0;}
    {var x,y:int; assume false; y:= x*x - 3*x + 2; assert y==0;}
}
```

Fig. 12. First part of assertion exercises

```
function abs(x:int):int {if (x>=0) then x else -x}
function method max(x:int,y:int):int {if (x>=y) then x else y}
function method min(x:int,y:int):int {if (x<=y) then x else y}
var minInf:int; var maxInf:int; // Infinities.

method Page2() {
    {var x:int; ghost var A:int;
        assume x==A;
        if (x<0) {x:= -x;}
        assert true;
    }
    {var x,y:int; ghost var A,B:int;
        assume x==A && y==B;
        if (x<y) {x,y:= y,x;}
        assert true;
    }
    {var x,y:int; ghost var A,B:int;
        assume x==A && y==B;
        if (x<=y) {x,y:= y,x;}
        assert true;
    }
}
```

Fig. 13. Second part of assertion exercises

```
{var s,x,y,z:int;
    s:= x;    assert true;
    s:= s+y; assert true;
    s:= s+z; assert true;
    assert true;
}
{var p,x,y,z:int;
    p:= x;    assert true;
    p:= p*y; assert true;
    p:= p*z; assert true;
    assert true;
}
{var s,x,y,z:int;
    s:= 0;    assert true;
    s:= s+x; assert true;
    s:= s+y; assert true;
    s:= s+z; assert true;
    assert true;
}
{var p,x,y,z:int;
    p:= 1;    assert true;
    p:= p*x; assert true;
    p:= p*y; assert true;
    p:= p*z; assert true;
    assert true;
}
{var m,x,y,z:int; var minInt:int;
    m:= x;              assert m==x;
    if (m<y) {m:= y;} assert m==max(x,y);
    if (m<z) {m:= z;} assert true;
    assert true;
}
{var m,x,y,z:int; var minInt:int;
    assume minInt<=x;
    m:= minInt;        assert m==minInt && minInt<=x;
    if (m<x) {m:= x;} assert true;
    if (m<y) {m:= y;} assert true;
    if (m<z) {m:= z;} assert true;
    assert true;
}
}
```

Fig. 14. Third part of assertion exercises

```
function maxSeq(A:seq<int>,n:int): int
    reads this; // To access minInf.
    requires 0<=n<=|A|;
{ if n==0 then minInf else max(A[0],maxSeq(A[1..],n-1)) }

ghost method maxLast(A:seq<int>,n:int)
    requires 0<=n<|A|;
    ensures max(maxSeq(A,n),A[n])==maxSeq(A,n+1);
{ if (n!=0) { maxLast(A[1..],n-1); } }

function sumSeq(A:seq<int>,n:int): int
    requires 0<=n<=|A|;
{ if n==0 then 0 else A[0]+sumSeq(A[1..],n-1) }

ghost method sumLast(A:seq<int>,n:int)
    requires 0<=n<|A|;
    ensures sumSeq(A,n+1) == sumSeq(A,n)+A[n];
{ if (n!=0) { sumLast(A[1..],n-1);} }

function prodSeq(A:seq<int>,n:int): int
    requires 0<=n<=|A|;
{ if n==0 then 1 else A[0]*prodSeq(A[1..],n-1) }

ghost method prodLast(A:seq<int>,n:int)
    requires 0<=n<|A|;
    ensures prodSeq(A,n)*A[n]==A[0]*prodSeq(A[1..],n);
{ if (n!=0) { prodLast(A[1..],n-1);} }
```

Fig. 15. Fourth part of assertion exercises

```
method Page3() {

    // Maximum of x,y,z.
    {var m,x,y,z:int;
        m:= minInf;
        m:= x; assume minInf<=x; // Property of minInf assumed.
        assert m==x;
        m:= max(m,y); assert m==max(x,y);
        m:= max(m,z); assert m==max(x,max(y,z));
        assert m==max(x,max(y,z));
    }

    // Minimum of x,y,z.
    {var m,x,y,z:int; var maxInt:int; assume maxInt>=x;
        m:= maxInt;
        m:= x; assume maxInf>=x; assert m==x; // Property of maxInf assumed.
        m:= min(m,y); assert m==min(x,y);
        m:= min(m,z); assert m==min(x,min(y,z));
        assert m==min(x,min(y,z));
    }
```

Fig. 16. Fifth part of assertion exercises

```
// Maximum of A[0,N).
{var A:seq<int>; var m,n:int;
    m,n:= minInf,0;
    while (n!=|A|)
        invariant 0<=n<=|A|;
        invariant m==maxSeq(A,n);
    {   maxLast(A,n); // Lemma needed: definition is foldr but program is foldl.
        m,n:= max(m,A[n]),n+1;
    }
    assert m==maxSeq(A,|A|);
}

// Sum of A[0,N).
{var A:seq<int>; var s,n:int;
    s,n:= 0,0;
    while (n!=|A|)
        invariant 0<=n<=|A|;
        invariant s==sumSeq(A,n);
    {   sumLast(A,n);
        s,n:= s+A[n],n+1;
    }
    assert s==sumSeq(A,|A|);
}

// Product of A[0,N).
{var A:seq<int>; var p,n:int;
    p,n:= 1,0;
    while (n!=|A|)
        invariant 0<=n<=|A|;
        invariant p==prodSeq(A,n);
    {   prodLast(A,n);
        p,n:= p*A[n],n+1;
    }
    assert p==prodSeq(A,|A|);
}

// Maximum of A[0,N) when N>=1.
{var A:seq<int>; var m,n:int; assume |A|>=1;
    assume minInf<=A[0]; // Only place where minInf's being smallest is necessary.
    m,n:= A[0],1; // Start with the first element instead of minInf.
    while (n!=|A|)
        invariant 0<=n<=|A|;
        invariant m==maxSeq(A,n);
    {   maxLast(A,n);
        m,n:= max(m,A[n]),n+1;
    }
    assert m==maxSeq(A,|A|);
}
}
```

Fig. 17. Sixth part of assertion exercises

D   Stepwise Development in Dafny

In this appendix we give explicitly the stages through which one develops "from the outside in" a verified implementation of Binary Search. The virtues of this were explained in Sect. 8.

In Fig. 18 we have the *specification* of Binary Search given in the requires/ensures clause(s) just after the method header.

Then the method body sets n to an arbitrary value nondeterministically, via n:= * and, immediately afterwards, with assume statements forces that arbitrary value to be one that satisfies the very same ensures clauses as are above. Thus this "implementation" simply achieves the postcondition by setting n to a value that... satisfies the postcondition.

This extreme caution is brought about by experience: sometimes Dafny cannot prove that a universal quantification implies itself: in broad terms, that is because its general strategies for proving universal quantifications are sometimes confounded by simple instances. Here we are making sure at the very beginning that this won't happen to us here.

And what do we do if Dafny fails even this simple first step? In that case, we look for another way to specify what we want the program to do.

```
// Step 0: Write the body as a single step that
//         satisfies the requires/ensures trivially.

method BinarySearch0(A:seq<int>,a:int) returns (n:int)
    requires forall i,j:: 0<=i<j<|A| ==> A[i]<=A[j];
    ensures 0<=n<=|A|;
    ensures forall i:: 0<=i<n    ==> A[i]<a;
    ensures forall i:: n<=i<|A| ==> a<=A[i];
{   n:= *;
    assume 0<=n<=|A|;
    assume forall i:: 0<=i<n    ==> A[i]<a;
    assume forall i:: n<=i<|A| ==> a<=A[i];
}
```

Fig. 18. BinarySearch0.dfy

In Fig. 19 we make our first refinement step, preparing to replace the simple assignment by a loop that keeps most of the postcondition as an invariant, but splits one conjunct off to be established by the negation of the loop guard. We introduce the variables low and high, and anticipate a loop whose effect is to make them equal.

Note this does not mean that, when you do this yourself, you have to type in the whole program again. Copy the method BinarySearch0; paste the copy in and rename it to BinarySearch1; then alter its body. Then verify them both together. (For a larger program, you might use separate files to avoid constant verifying of the earlier steps; but for a small program like this one, it's so fast it makes no difference.)

```
// Step 1: Re-write the body as the specification of a loop
//         that maintains the first three asumptions as a invariants
//         and establishes the fourth assumption on loop-exit.

method BinarySearch1(A:seq<int>,a:int) returns (n:int)
    requires forall i,j:: 0<=i<j<|A| ==> A[i]<=A[j];
    ensures 0<=n<=|A|;
    ensures forall i:: 0<=i<n   ==> A[i]<a;
    ensures forall i:: n<=i<|A| ==> a<=A[i];

{   var low,high:= *,*;
    assume 0<=low<=high<=|A|;                          // Inv1
    assume forall i:: 0<=i<low     ==> A[i]<a;         // Inv2
    assume forall i:: high<=i<|A| ==> a<=A[i];         // Inv3
    assume low==high; // Negation of loop-guard
    n:= low;
}
```

Fig. 19. BinarySearch1.dfy

In Fig. 20 we insert a loop skeleton: its invariant and guard are as advertised in the previous step (Fig. 19). But at this stage, with **decreases** *, we indicate that we are not yet interested in proving that the loop terminates. (Experiment by commenting out the **decreases** clause.)

```
// Step 2: Add a loop that satisfies the post-condition given in the previous step,
//         with the loop body to be filled-in.
method BinarySearch2(A:seq<int>, a:int) returns (n:int)
     requires forall i,j:: 0<=i<j<|A| ==> A[i]<=A[j];
     ensures 0<=n<=|A|;
     ensures forall i:: 0<=i<n   ==> A[i]<a;
     ensures forall i:: n<=i<|A| ==> a<=A[i];
     decreases *; // Declare that the method (for now) is allowed not to terminate.

{    var low,high:= 0,|A|;
     while (low!=high)
         invariant 0<=low<=high<=|A|;
         invariant forall i:: 0<=i<low   ==> A[i]<a;
         invariant forall i:: high<=i<|A| ==> a<=A[i];
         decreases *;
     {   low,high:= *,*; // arbitrary values that re-establish the invariant
         assume 0<=low<=high<=|A|;
         assume forall i:: 0<=i<low   ==> A[i]<a;
         assume forall i:: high<=i<|A| ==> a<=A[i];
     }
     n:= low;
}
```

Fig. 20. BinarySearch2.dfy

In Fig. 21 we add the variant function that will guarantee loop termination. In this case it is that the variables `low` and `high` must move strictly closer together. First their current values are captured, and then the "set such that" statement requires that the difference has decreased.

With this done, a `decreases high-low` will be accepted by `Dafny`. But in many cases (including this one), `Dafny` can guess the loop variant itself: provided you code actually decreases some variant, `Dafny` will often figure out what variant that is.

```
// Step 3: Make progress towards termination by reducing the search,
//         in the loop body, to a strictly smaller portion of the sequence.
//         Note the "decreases *" is no longer needed.
//         Dafny figures out "decreases high-low" for itself.

method BinarySearch3(A:seq<int>,a:int) returns (n:int)
    requires forall i,j:: 0<=i<j<|A| ==> A[i]<=A[j];
    ensures 0<=n<=|A|;
    ensures forall i:: 0<=i<n   ==> A[i]<a;
    ensures forall i:: n<=i<|A| ==> a<=A[i];

{   var low,high:= 0,|A|;
    while (low!=high)
        invariant 0<=low<=high<=|A|;
        invariant forall i:: 0<=i<low    ==> A[i]<a;
        invariant forall i:: high<=i<|A| ==> a<=A[i];
        // decreases high-low; // Dafny figures this out for itself.
    {   var oldLow,oldHigh:= low,high;
        low,high:| high-low < oldHigh-oldLow;
        assume 0<=low<=high<=|A|;
        assume forall i:: 0<=i<low    ==> A[i]<a;
        assume forall i:: high<=i<|A| ==> a<=A[i];
    }
    n:= low;
}
```

Fig. 21. BinarySearch3.dfy

In Fig. 22 we implement the strategy "Choose some new variable `mid` to lie between `low` and `high`, and use it to change one or the other of those two variables." We don't know which, yet; but the decrease of the variant forces us even so to choose assignment right-hand sides that will have that strict-decrease effect. (Experiment by replacing the `mid+1` with just `mid`.)

Note the nondeterministic `if` statement whose both-`true` guards allow either of its two branches to be executed. At the moment, the `assume` statements further below live up to their name: they "assume" that the nondeterminism in the `if` statement has been resolved correctly, i.e. in a was that preserves the invariant. What will force us to code that up into "real" tests is that the `assume`'s are not allowed to be in our final program: in the *Refinement Calculus* it would be said that they are "not code".[38]

```
// Step 4: Introduce binary chop, so that termination is guaranteed.
//         But how do we chop?

method BinarySearch4(A:seq<int>, a:int) returns (n:int)
    requires forall i,j:: 0<=i<j<|A| ==> A[i]<=A[j];
    ensures 0<=n<=|A|;
    ensures forall i:: 0<=i<n   ==> A[i]<a;
    ensures forall i:: n<=i<|A| ==> a<=A[i];

{   var low,high:= 0,|A|;
    while (low!=high)
        invariant 0<=low<=high<=|A|;
        invariant forall i:: 0<=i<low    ==> A[i]<a;
        invariant forall i:: high<=i<|A| ==> a<=A[i];
    {   var mid:| low<=mid<high; // 1824: Set mid to anything that satisfies.
        if { // 1826: Which do we choose? Figure that out in the next step.
            case true => low:=  mid+1; // 1826.
            case true => high:= mid;   // 1826.
        }
        // 1824: The earlier assumption here is no longer necessary.
        assume forall i:: 0<=i<low    ==> A[i]<a;
        assume forall i:: high<=i<|A| ==> a<=A[i];
    }
    n:= low;
}
```

Fig. 22. BinarySearch4.dfy

---

[38] Carroll Morgan. *Programming from Specifications. Prentice Hall* 1994. Ralph-Johan Back, Joachim von Wright. *Refinement Calculus: A Systematic Introduction.* Springer 1998.

In Fig. 23 we have replaced the **true** guards with actual tests; and, having done that, we can remove the **assume**'s. Rather than **Dafny**'s *assuming* that they hold, it can now prove that they do.

Note however that we still have a nondeterministic statement choosing the value of **mid**. And yet the program is correct. What that means is that this program works *however* we choose **mid** strictly between **low** and **high**. That is, the "binary chop" step, which we are about to implement, is a matter of efficiency, not of correctness.

```
// Step 5: Make careful choices so that the loop invariant is maintained,
//         and the assumptions can be removed.

method BinarySearch4(A:seq<int>, a:int) returns (n:int)
    requires forall i,j:: 0<=i<j<|A| ==> A[i]<=A[j];
    ensures 0<=n<=|A|;
    ensures forall i:: 0<=i<n   ==> A[i]<a;
    ensures forall i:: n<=i<|A| ==> a<=A[i];

{   var low,high:= 0,|A|;
    while (low!=high)
        invariant 0<=low<=high<=|A|;
        invariant forall i:: 0<=i<low    ==> A[i]<a;
        invariant forall i:: high<=i<|A| ==> a<=A[i];
    {   var mid:| low<=mid<high;
        if {
            case A[mid]<a  => low:=  mid+1;
            case a<=A[mid] => high:= mid;
        }
        // All assumptions gone.
    }
    n:= low;
}
```

Fig. 23. BinarySearch5.dfy

Finally, in Fig. 24 we choose **mid** to lie somewhere approximately in between **low** and **high** and, finally, we have the traditional Binary Search.

Note though that by choosing **mid** differently (yet still in between), we end up with a linear search.

```
// Step 6: Choose binary chop specifically, by picking mid somewhere in the middle.

method BinarySearch6(A:seq<int>, a:int) returns (n:int)
    requires forall i,j:: 0<=i<j<|A| ==> A[i]<=A[j];
    ensures 0<=n<=|A|;
    ensures forall i:: 0<=i<n   ==> A[i]<a;
    ensures forall i:: n<=i<|A| ==> a<=A[i];

{   var low,high:= 0,|A|;
    while (low!=high)
        invariant 0<=low<=high<=|A|;
        invariant forall i:: 0<=i<low   ==> A[i]<a;
        invariant forall i:: high<=i<|A| ==> a<=A[i];
    {   var mid:= (low+high)/2;
        if { // We strengthen the guards.
            case A[mid]<a  => low:= mid+1;
            case a<=A[mid] => high:= mid;
        }
    }
    n:= low;
}

// But we could also do a linear up-search by choosing mid:= low .
method Search6Up(A:seq<int>, a:int) returns (n:int)
    requires forall i,j:: 0<=i<j<|A| ==> A[i]<=A[j];
    ensures 0<=n<=|A|;
    ensures forall i:: 0<=i<n   ==> A[i]<a;
    ensures forall i:: n<=i<|A| ==> a<=A[i];

{   var low,high:= 0,|A|;
    while (low!=high)
        invariant 0<=low<=high<=|A|;
        invariant forall i:: 0<=i<low   ==> A[i]<a;
        invariant forall i:: high<=i<|A| ==> a<=A[i];
    {   var mid:= low;
        if {
            case A[mid]<a  => low:= mid+1;
            case a<=A[mid] => high:= mid;
        }
    }
    n:= low;
}

// Or a linear down-search by choosing mid:= high-1. Try it!
```

Fig. 24. BinarySearch6.dfy

E   Assignment 4: Real-World Programming

The assignment follows, adapted for this article. Footnotes in italics have been added in this text; footnotes in normal font were in the original.[39]

(In-)Formal Methods
Fourth assignment

Real-World Programming: A circular I/O buffer

E.1   Why "Real World" Programming?

With the programming techniques taught in this course, you will be able to develop code more quickly than before, and it will have far fewer errors than is normal in the *IT* industry.[40] And your code will be more easily maintained as well.

For that to happen, you must learn to apply our "perfectionist" techniques in an imperfect world, where systems have imprecise or incomplete specifications, and where most programs are too large and detailed to allow assertion-based reasoning by hand alone. *We need tools to help.*

The UNIX-style copy command (cp simplified) is our example, using (almost) the real UNIX system calls. We abstract the system calls' behaviour as Dafny requires/ensures specifications; and we will transliterate our Dafny programs into actual *C* code, and run it.

The remaining vulnerabilities are mainly that we have no real assurance that we have specified the UNIX calls correctly; and we have no assurance either that our transliteration into *C* of our own code did not itself introduce errors. The more-than-compensating strengths are that the algorithm is verified, that it

---

[39] In fact it was not possible to prepare for the assignment a fully "circular" buffer in the 2014 version of this course: getting the Dafny proof to go through proved too difficult to have prepared beforehand. But it was completed after the course, and the buffer will be fully circular next time.

[40] Is "Information Technology" a euphemism to disguise the fact that writing programs actually requires disciplined thinking and rigorous practices, more than just running spreadsheets, databases and word-processors? If so, it's good news for some: the people who *can* apply discipline and rigour, when it's required, will stand out from the pack. They'll be more valued, will have important projects and earn higher salaries. The rest of us will depending on them.

can easily be changed without introducing errors, and that its documentation is enforced (and, if necessary, updated) automatically — and all of these because *Dafny won't verify it otherwise.*

E.2   UNIX-Style Copying with a Single Buffer

In this section we take our first steps towards developing real code that copies standard input to standard output: it will be a scaled-down version of the UNIX command cp. For the moment, however, we abstract from UNIX by modelling the standard input, standard output and in-memory buffer all three as (Dafny) *sequences* rather than as actual files (input and output), or as a buffer-array with a pointer into it. That simplifies our initial sketch of the copying algorithm, so that we can see its overall structure.

The input-file sequence is fixed in value, modelling that in the real-life situation it is not being changed (by something else) as we read it; what does change as it is read is an *offset pointer* into the file that indicates the position from which the next read will occur. (UNIX stores that pointer as part of a "file descriptor" structure.) That pointer is initialised to 0 because the file is to be read from its beginning. The output-file sequence begins empty, modelling that we create a new file (rather than appending to an existing one); it is gradually extended by the buffer-loads of data that are successively written to it.

The effect of all this abstraction can be seen in the different answers required for the two questions marked by stars ★ below.[41] They refer to our Dafny code (Fig. 26) and its corresponding code in *C* (Fig. 25).

1. A simple *C* program for copying standard input to standard output is given in Fig. 25. It uses a single buffer of size BUF_SIZE which size, in your case, you will set to digits 1–3 of your student number. (In the example, the student number is z7654321.) It reads at most IN_MAX bytes of data at at time; you will set IN_MAX to digits 2–3 of your student number.
   Take the code of Fig. 25 and edit BUF_SIZE and IN_MAX to reflect your own student number as above: make it into a file cpA.c. Compile it using the command cc cpA.c -o cpA. Run it by typing ./cpA < cpA.c, and check that it correctly copies its own text to the standard output.
   Now change BUF_SIZE to 0, then re-compile and re-run your program.
   ★ *What error message do you get, and when?*
2. In Fig. 26 appears the Dafny program from which the *C* program of Fig. 25 was transcribed.[42] Make it into a file cpA.dfy and edit its constants as above; verify it using the command dafny cpA.dfy. (It should get no errors.) Now change the bufSize parameter to 0, and re-verify it.
   ★ *What error message do you get, and when?*

---

[41] Since the questions are based on an actual assignment, references such as "you" etc. are to the students.

[42] That is, the code in Fig. 26 was written *before* the code of Fig. 25. Unfortunately, Fig. 26 is normally not made at all.

```
// For read() and write().
#include <unistd.h>

#define STD_INPUT 0      // File descriptor for standard input.
#define STD_OUTPUT 1     // File descriptor for standard output.

#define BUF_SIZE 765
#define IN_MAX 65        // Maximum read length: requires 0<IN_MAX<=BUF_SIZE.

int main() {
    // Initialisation of STD_INPUT and STD_OUTPUT is done for us.

    char buf[BUF_SIZE]; // Note: Characters, not integers.
    int eof= 0;

    while (!eof) {
        int count= read(STD_INPUT,&buf,IN_MAX);
        if (count==0) eof= 1; else write(STD_OUTPUT,buf,count);
    }
}
```

Fig. 25. *C* code `cpA.c` transcribed from Fig. 26.

E.3   Unit Testing: Harnesses and Stubs

In the Dafny code of Fig. 26 there are "simulations" of the environment in which
our copy method is intended to run. The `read(...)` system-call is simulated
by

```
if (inputPos==|inputData|) { eof:= true; } else {
    var count:nat:| 0<count<=inMax && inputPos+count<=|inputData|;
    inputPos,buf:= inputPos+count,inputData[inputPos..inputPos+count];
}
```

where the declaration and initialisation of `count` is *nondeterministic* — the
symbols `:|` mean "...is given a value such that." And so the read system-call
guarantees to set `count` to a natural-number value satisfying

```
0<count<=inMax && inputPos+count<=|inputData|
```

but, beyond that, it makes no guarantee at all about which value that will be.
    Similarly, the `write(...)` system-call is simulated by

```
outputData:= outputData+buf;
```

where + is sequence concatenation.
    In both cases these simulations can be compared with the informal descrip-
tions given in the actual UNIX man-pages. (You can enter the UNIX commands
`man 2 read` and `man 2 write` if you want to see them.) The code-fragments
above are called *stubs* because they are not the real system calls. Similarly, the

```
// Input file, output file are sequences of integers.
var inputData:seq<int>,inputPos:nat;
var outputData:seq<int>;

method cpA(inMax:nat,bufSize:nat) modifies this;
    requires 0<inMax<=bufSize;
    ensures outputData==inputData;
{   inputPos:= 0; // Open inFile for reading.
    outputData:= []; // Open outFile for writing.

    var buf:seq<int>:=[]; var eof:=false;
    while (!eof) // Can't test file for EOF directly.
        invariant inputPos<=|inputData|;
        invariant outputData==inputData[0..inputPos];
        invariant eof ==> inputPos==|inputData|;
        decreases |inputData|-inputPos + (if eof then 0 else 1);

    {   // UNIX-style read() returns EOF-indicator only -after- you fail to read.
        if (inputPos==|inputData|) { eof:= true; } else {
            // Read "some" data into buf: set count "such that"...
            var count:nat:| 0<count<=inMax && inputPos+count<=|inputData|;
            inputPos,buf:= inputPos+count,inputData[inputPos..inputPos+count];

            // Write all data out from buf.
            outputData:= outputData+buf; // Here "+" is sequence concatenation.
        }
    }
}

method main() modifies this; {
    cpA(65,765);
}
```

Fig. 26. Dafny code `cpA.dfy` for simple UNIX-style read/write loop.

method-call `cpA(65,765)` is a simulation of what is using (rather than used by) our copy method: it is called a *harness*.

In both cases – in conventional program development – the simulations, the stubs and harnesses, are supposed to provide a great variety of behaviours typical of what the unit under test will encounter in practice, focussing particularly on the so-called "edge cases" where coding errors are likely to have occurred: when index-variables are smallest, or largest; when structures are empty, or full etc. Making an effective test environment requires <u>lots</u> of work.

With a modern software development method (such as we are now using) this work is much reduced and yet is <u>more</u> effective, as we now show.[43]

---

[43] Compare for example *our* read-stub to a traditional one in which nondeterminism is not available: then the stub would probably return one of three values for the number of characters read: the least, the greatest and one somewhere in between. Our approach here in effect tests *all* values, not just three of them.

```
method cpB(input:Input,output:Output,inMax:nat,bufSize:nat) modifies this;
    requires input!=null && output!=null; modifies input,output;
    requires 0<inMax<=bufSize; // This takes the place of the harness.
    ensures output.data==input.data;

{   input.open(); // Open inFile for reading.
    output.creat(); // Open outFile for writing.

    var buf:seq<int>; var eof:=false;
    while (!eof)
        invariant input.pos<=|input.data|;
        invariant output.data==input.data[0..input.pos];
        invariant input.eof ==> eof;
        invariant eof ==> input.pos==|input.data|;
        decreases    (|input.data|-input.pos)
                   + (|input.data|-|output.data|)
                   + (if eof then 0 else 1);
    {   if (input.pos==|input.data|) { eof:= true; } else {
            var data:=input.read(inMax); //1036: See Fig. 28.
            buf:= data;
            output.write(buf); //1036.
        }
    }
}
```

A note on documentation: the arbitrary number 1036 links several comment-points together; only one of them has text. The choice of number is supposed to be random, and is in fact just the time of day I typed it in: that reduces the risk of "randomly" choosing a number more than once.

Doing multiple-relevance comments this way means you have to write the comment itself only once, and it automatically applies consistently in all the other places even if you update the comment text in that one place.

If you find such a comment NNNN: Something. then a search with a text editor for NNNN. finds all the (other) places it applies. And if you find a comment NNNN. then a search for NNNN: will find the relevant comment text. All this keeps everything in step with a minimum of effort.

Fig. 27. "Unit test" cpB.dfy of method cpB, no stubs or harnesses: Part I.

First, we can remove the harness altogether: its function is taken over by the **requires** clause(s) of the copy method itself, which describes *all* of the things a harness for this program is allowed to do, including the edge-cases automatically. (A conventional harness can only implement *some* of those things, in general). In Fig. 27 the harness is no longer there; and your student number is no longer necessary for selecting "random" block-sizes.

Second, we can remove the stubs by replacing them by a *specification* of what they do; again, this describes *all* of their possible behaviours, not just some of them. In Fig. 28 there is no code for reading or writing.

```
class Input { // 0902.
    var data: seq<int>; // The data in the (input) file.
    var pos:nat; // The current reading position.
    var eof:bool; // Whether end-of-file has been indicated.

    // Open file for reading.
    method open() modifies this;
        ensures pos==0 && !eof && data==old(data);

    // Read up to len from current position.
    method read(len:nat) returns(justRead:seq<int>) modifies this; //1036.
        requires pos<=|data|; ensures pos<=|data|; // Datatype invariant.
        ensures data==old(data) && pos>=old(pos);

        requires len!=0; // Can't ask to read 0.
        requires !eof; // Can't ask to read if EOF is already signalled.

        ensures old(pos)!=|data| ==> justRead!=[];
        ensures justRead==data[old(pos)..pos];
        ensures |justRead|<=len;
        ensures eof <==> old(pos)==|data|;
}

class Output {
    var data: seq<int>; // The data in the (output) file.

    // Create a new, empty file.
    method creat() modifies this;
        ensures data==[];

    // Append to file.
    method write(toWrite: seq<int>) modifies this; //1036.
        requires |toWrite|!=0; // Can't ask to write nothing.
        ensures data==old(data)+toWrite;
}
```

These two classes take the place of the stubs; note they contain *no* executable code.

Fig. 28. "Unit test" cpB.dfy of method cpB: Part II.

★ *Our* **read(...)** *specification replaces the traditional "read-stub".
Describe very briefly in words the intention of the following four postconditions
of the specification of* **read** *in Fig. 28:*

(a) ensures old(pos)!=|data| ==> justRead!=[];
(b) ensures justRead==data[old(pos)..pos];
(c) ensures |justRead|<=len;
(d) ensures eof <==> old(pos)==|data|;

★ *Describe very briefly in words what (bad things) the* **read** *method could do to its calling copy method if each the following three postconditions of* **read** *in Fig. 28 had separately been left out, i.e. in a case, for each one, where the* **read** *method violates it:*

(a) `ensures old(pos)!=|data| ==> justRead!=[];`
(b) `ensures justRead==data[old(pos)..pos];`
(c) `ensures |justRead|<=len;`

★ *Explain the purpose of the term* `+ (if eof then 0 else 1)` *in the* decreases *clause of the copy method in Fig. 27.*

★ *Explain the different purposes of the Booleans* `input.eof` *within the class* Input *and* eof *within the main program* cp.

E.4 The Buffer as Array; Reading/Writing in Blocks

The sequence abstraction for buf is very convenient for specification, but sequences are expensive to implement in real applications — and that is why it is is not used in the actual UNIX cp program.[44] Instead, an array (in C) is allocated for the buffer; and so we will model that now with an array in **Dafny**.

Because an array (unlike a sequence) does not move around in memory once allocated, for efficiency reasons, our use of it will have to become more sophisticated: we will have start- and end pointers s,e into buf that indicate the part of it buf[s..e] that contains actual data. When the pointers get to the end of the buffer, we will reset them to the beginning.[45]

Having such pointers allows furthermore that input and output might have different preferred block-sizes, and that might be important depending on what the actual input- and output devices are. For example, if the input device prefers to deliver data in blocks of 100 elements but the output device prefers to receive data in blocks of 150 elements, again for efficiency reasons, then we should read *twice* into the buffer (200 elements) before we write once (leaving $200 - 150 = 50$ elements behind, which we should try not to write until we have read more).

---

[44] Sequences are expensive because they support so many convenient operations: concatenation, subsequencing etc. Arrays are much faster, but have fewer native operations.

[45] The circular-buffer version of this is more sophisticated.

Our more sophisticated `Dafny` code is given in Fig. 29; notice that it is written in the multiple-guard while-loop style, which is much less error-prone than the usual form.[46] (The updated stub-specifications are given in Fig. 30.)

★ *For* `cpC.dfy` *in Fig. 29, supply code for the missing portions according to the following hints.*

(a) `can write` Put a Boolean test here that ensures there is some data to write.

(b) `set n to how much to write` Put a "such that" assignment here to `n` that is as liberal as possible consistent with correctness of the program, but is not more than `outBlock`.

(c) `update s,e` Set `s,e` to the correct (new) values.

(d) `can read` Put a Boolean test here that ensures that an *EOF* indication has not already been received, and that there is room in the buffer for more data.

(e) `set n to how much to read` Put a "such that" assignment here to `n` that is as liberal as possible consistent with correctness of the program, but is not more than `inBlock`.

(f) `update e` Set `e` to the correct (new) value.

★ *Based on* `cpC.dfy`, *make a file* `MYcpC.dfy` *according to your answers above. Then verify it with* `Dafny`.

The C code corresponding to Fig. 31 is given in Fig. 31, where the `Dafny`-style multiple-guard `while` has been transliterated into a C-style

$$\text{while (1) } \{\text{if} \cdots \text{ else if } \cdots \text{ else break;}\}.$$

What's especially interesting is that in doing that transliteration we have had to decide which `if` comes first, so to speak the "read `if`" or the "write `if`". Our choice in Fig. 31 has taken the second option: it gives priority to writing in the sense that if both reading and writing are possible, then writing will be

---

[46] If a loop $\mathbf{do}\, G_1 \to S_1 \mid G_2 \to S_2\, \mathbf{od}$ were recoded as as a conventional while-loop, it would become

$$\mathbf{while}\ G_1 \vee G_2\ \mathbf{do}\ \ \mathbf{if}\ G_1\ \mathbf{then}\ S_1\ \mathbf{else}\ S_2\ \mathbf{fi}\ \ \mathbf{od},$$

which has the disadvantages that (1) it must repeat G_1 and (2) it is not obvious from the text what assertion holds at the beginning of S_2. (It is of course $(G_1 \vee G_2) \wedge \neg G_1$, that is G_2; but that might not be obvious if $G_1 \vee G_2$ itself has been simplified into some other form.)

So what we have written in Fig. 31 corresponds instead to

$$\begin{aligned}
&\mathbf{while}\ true\ \mathbf{do} \\
&\quad \mathbf{if} \qquad G_1\ \mathbf{then}\ S_1 \\
&\quad \mathbf{else\ if}\ G_2\ \mathbf{then}\ S_2 \\
&\quad \mathbf{else\ break} \\
&\mathbf{od},
\end{aligned}$$

which avoids both of those disadvantages. It still encodes a priority, however, favouring G_1 over G_2. To do the opposite, we would swap first two interior `if`-branches.

```
method cpC(input:Input,output:Output,inBlock:nat,outBlock:nat,bufSize:nat)
    modifies this;
    requires input!=null && output!=null; modifies input,output;
    requires 0<bufSize && 0<inBlock && 0<outBlock;
    ensures output.data==input.data;
{   input.open();
    output.creat();

    var buf:= new int[bufSize];
    var s:nat,e:nat:= 0,0; // Only buf[s..e] contains valid data.

    var eof:= false;
    while
        invariant input.data==old(input.data);
        invariant input.pos<=|input.data|;
        invariant s<=e<=bufSize;
        invariant e==bufSize ==> s!=e;
        invariant input.data[..input.pos]==output.data+buf[s..e];
        invariant input.eof ==> eof;
        invariant eof ==> input.pos==|input.data|;
        decreases  (|input.data|-input.pos)
                + (|input.data|-|output.data|)
                + (if eof then 0 else 1);

    {   case  can write   =>
            var n:nat;   set n to how much to write
            ghost var data0:= output.data;
            var count:= output.write(buf,s,n); // Write from buf starting at s.
            assert output.data==data0+buf[s..s+count];
            s:= s+count;
            if (s==bufSize) {  update s,e   }

        case  can read   =>
            var n:nat;   set n to how much to read
            ghost var buf0,pos0:= buf[..],input.pos;
            var count:= input.read(buf,e,n); // Read into buf starting at e.
            assert input.data[..pos0+count]
                ==input.data[..pos0]+input.data[pos0..pos0+count];
            if (count==0) { eof:= true; } else {  update e   }
    }
}
```

Fig. 29. Code cpC.dfy with array-buffer: reading/writing in blocks, Part I.

chosen. That is, the code of Fig. 31 reads _only_ when it can't write; even though the original Dafny code does not have that property. Technically that represents a "resolution of specification-time nondeterminism".

But we could have put the if's the other way, as in Fig. 32, in which case instead the code would write only when it couldn't read. _Both_ Figs. 31 and 32 are valid transliterations of Fig. 29, and we can choose whichever we want

```
class Input {
    var data: seq<int>,pos:nat,eof:bool;

    method open() modifies this;
        ensures pos==0 && !eof && data==old(data);

    method read(buf:array<int>,p:nat,len:nat) returns(count:nat) modifies this;
        requires pos<=|data|; ensures pos<=|data|;
        ensures data==old(data) && pos>=old(pos);
        requires len!=0 && !eof;
        modifies buf; requires buf!=null && p+len<=buf.Length;
        ensures old(pos)!=|data| ==> count!=0;
        ensures count<=len;
        ensures buf[p..p+count]==data[old(pos)..pos];
        ensures eof <==> old(pos)==|data|;
        // Change only the part of buf into which we have read.
        ensures buf[..p]==old(buf[..p]) && buf[p+count..]==old(buf[p+count..]);
}

class Output {
    var data: seq<int>;

    method creat() modifies this;
        ensures data==[];

        method write(buf:array<int>,p:nat,len:nat) returns(count: nat) modifies this;
            requires buf!=null && p+len<=buf.Length;
            requires len!=0;
            ensures 0<count<=len; // Different from UNIX.
            ensures data==old(data)+buf[p..p+count];
}
```

The UNIX manual page (man 2 write) does not state that write is guaranteed to write more than zero bytes; but in our specification above, we have added that feature. Otherwise we could not be able to prove that our copy code terminates.

Fig. 30. Code cpC.dfy with array-buffer: reading/writing in blocks: Part II.

depending on implementation issues (like which of reading or writing should be given priority in our particular application).

★ *Based on* cpC.c, *make* MYcpC.c *by filling-in the missing portions of Fig. 31 found in your verified* MYcpC.dfy. *Convert the* Dafny *such-that assignments to* n *to deterministic assignments in C that make* n *as big as possible consistent with the such-that's. Fill in the constants according to your student number.*

★ *Compile* MYcpC.c *with* cc MYcpC.c -o MYcpC.c *and run it using the command* ./MYcpC <yourFile 2>/dev/null *on a test file of your choice.*[47]

E.5   Refinement of Multiple-Choice Iterations

In Footnote 48 we saw the general form

---

[47] The 2>/dev/null merely hides the output of the fprintf's.

```
#include <unistd.h>
#include <stdio.h>
#define STD_INPUT  0    // File descriptor for standard input.
#define STD_OUTPUT 1    // File descriptor for standard output.

#define BUF_SIZE  76543 // The first five digits of your student number.
#define IN_BLOCK  7654  // The first four digits of your student number.
#define OUT_BLOCK 765   // The first three digits of your student number.

#define MIN(a,b) ((a)<(b)?(a):(b)) // C has no built-in MIN.

int main() {
    char buf[BUF_SIZE]; int eof= 0;
    int s= 0; int e= 0;
    fprintf(stderr,"BUF_SIZE=%d, IN_BLOCK=%d, OUT_BLOCK=%d.\n\n",
        BUF_SIZE,IN_BLOCK,OUT_BLOCK);

    while (1) {
        if  [can write]  {
            int n= [set n to how much to write (maximum allowed)]

            int count= write(STD_OUTPUT,&buf[s],n);
                s+= count;
            if (s==BUF_SIZE) [update s,e]
            fprintf(stderr, " Write: asked for %d, wrote %d and now s,e,e-s=%d,%d,%d.\"
                , n,count,s,e,e-s);

        } else if [can read]  {
            int n= [set n to how much to read (maximum allowed)]
            int count= read(STD_INPUT,&buf[e],n);
            if (count==0) eof= 1; else [update e] ;
            fprintf(stderr, "Read: asked for %d, read %d and now s,e,e-s=%d,%d,%d.\n"
                , n,count,s,e,e-s);

        } else break;
    }
}
```

Fig. 31. C code cpC.c corresponding to Fig. 29, with some fprintf's.

$$\textbf{do } G_1 \rightarrow S_1 \parallel G_2 \rightarrow S_2 \textbf{ od} \qquad\qquad (3)$$

of a multiple-guard iteration. It executes by first evaluating the *guards* G_1, G_2; if both are false, the loop terminates. If exactly one of G_1, G_2 is true, then the corresponding statement S_1, S_2 is executed. But if *both* G_1, G_2 are true, then *either* of S_1, S_2 can be executed. This is known as *nondeterminism*.

Nondeterminism might at first seem to make reasoning about programs harder. But in this form at least it actually makes it easier. What an alternative $G_i \rightarrow S_i$ says is that "if S_i is executed in a state where G_i holds, then it is guaranteed to maintain the invariant and to decrease the variant." It's that simple.

```
...
int main() {
...
    while (1) {
        if  can read  {
            ...
        } else if  can write  {
            ...
        } else break;
    }
}
```

Fig. 32. C code corresponding to Fig. 29, but with priority for reading. (cpC.c)

When the guards do overlap in this way, then it's possible in a refinement to alter the guards slightly in order to take implementation concerns into account. For example if we wanted a refinement in which the same overall effect was reached but, during the execution, the first guard was executed in favour of the second whenever both were ready, then we could use the modified loop

$$\mathbf{do}\ G_1 \to S_1 \parallel G_2 \wedge \neg G_1 \to S_2\ \mathbf{od},$$

in which the second guard G_2 has been strengthened to include "unless G_1". It is a refinement of (3). And the complementary $\mathbf{do}\ G_1 \wedge \neg G_2 \to S_1 \parallel G_2 \to S_2\ \mathbf{od}$ is also a refinement of (3), but one where we have given the priority to S_2 instead of to S_1.

The general refinement rule is that

$$\mathbf{do}\ G_1 \to S_1 \parallel G_2 \to S_2\ \mathbf{od} \quad \sqsubseteq \quad \mathbf{do}\ G_1' \to S_1 \parallel G_2' \to S_2\ \mathbf{od} \qquad (4)$$

when $G_1 \vee G_2 \equiv G_1' \vee G_2'$ and $G_1' \Rightarrow G_1$ and $G_2' \Rightarrow G_2$. In words, the conditions are that the two loops have the same overall guard, and that whenever S_i is executed in the more-refined loop, it must have been permissible to have executed it in the less-refined loop.

In our read/write loop of Fig. 29 in fact we have actual non-determininism whenever it is both possible to read (because there's some space left in the buffer) and to write (because there's some data in the buffer). In the C code of Fig. 31 we resolved that nondeterminism in favour of writing; and in Fig. 32 we resolved it in favour of reading.

★ *By examining the guards you added to Fig. 29, write down exactly, in terms of the program variables, the conditions in which nondeterminism is present, that is when both reading and writing are possible.*

★ *Alter your guards so that writing has priority over reading whenever a full* **outBlock** *elements can be written, but otherwise the priority is not determined.*

★ *Use the refinement rule in (4) to check that your new loop, with its limited*[48] *output priority, is a refinement of the original.*

Code up your altered read/write method in the style of Fig. 31 (with the fprint *'s included); call the file* cpD.c. *When you resolve any remaining nondeterminism (i.e. as you transliterate the multiple-guard loop into the form* if– else if–*else), give the priority to reading.*[49]

★ *Compile it, and run it on the input file* Ass4In,[50] *capturing its* fprint *output in a file* Ass4Out *using the commands*

```
cc cpD.c -o cpD
./cpD <~se2011/Ass4/Ass4In >/dev/null 2>Ass4Out
```

E.6   How This Assignment Will Be Marked

1. The written answers to "why this" and "why that" will be checked. They should be very short, and precise.
2. The Dafny codes will be checked, by running Dafny on them, to see whether they verify.
3. The C codes will be checked to see whether they appear correctly to transliterate the Dafny codes. They won't be marked for style (otherwise), since conceptually the Dafny is our source code, and the transliterations are our assembly code. We don't usually mark the assembly-code output of a compiler for style (unless we are evaluating the compiler itself).
4. The test-file Ass4In was specially constructed to allow errors easily to be seen, and it will be used to check for run-time errors. But what kind of errors will it find? If the Dafny verified, the program should be correct as far as functionality goes. Thus this check helps to uncover transliteration errors; but it also captures cases where the nondeterminism was not resolved in the way the question required.

Written answers will be marked in the usual way, with partial credit available for answers that are partly correct. However...

Full credit for Dafny code is given only if it is the same structure (essentially) as the (supplied) code from which it is supposed to be derived, and has no verification errors when checked with Dafny. If it *does* have verification errors, then only partial credit is given. However if the Dafny code does not verify

---

[48] By "limited" we mean as above that output has priority only when it can write a full outBlock elements; otherwise (above) the choice between reading/writing remains nondeterministic.

[49] Thus in this question you are resolving the *remaining* nondeterminism in favour of reading, and you are doing it by choosing the way you transliterate the Dafny while-loop into C.

[50] This was a huge file, so large that the students could not tell just by looking what correct program output should be. Thus their confidence had to be based on the verification. They had to submit the fprintf output only: just the blocksizes read and written were checked.

completely (that is, if it gets *even just a single error*), then <u>no credit</u> is available for the other two (remaining) files `MYcpC.dfy` and `Ass4Out`. That is, if your `Dafny` doesn't verify then your *C* code gets zero, even if it looks right. Even if it *is* right. Our *C* code cannot be guesswork.

If the `Dafny` code does verify completely, i.e. with zero errors, then the remaining answers are marked simply as either *correct* or *incorrect* (i.e. either full credit, or none). To get full credit, the *C* code should compile without error and must accurately copy the marker's (not merely the student's) test-data file. For the `printf` outputs, the output you get must be byte-for-byte what is expected (based on the student number and the test file `Ass4In`). If it differs in even a single byte, it will be marked zero.

F   Student Feedback: At Least Not a Failure

The comments below are verbatim, collected anonymously via UNSW's teaching-evaluation web-interface just after the course has ended. Any material about the lecturer personally, rather than about the course, has been omitted however. Otherwise they are complete.[51]

As remarked in Sect. 10, there is no sense in which student feedback in the short term can establish that a course has been successful: it indicates only what they thought of its style, delivery and content. In spite of that, for formal-methods related material especially, it's encouraging that none of these students felt the course was pointless or irrelevant.

F.1   From Second-Years in 2014

Best Features:

- The interactive and hands on approach of the teaching in the course, as well as the content itself.
- The content is relevant, lectures are interesting, tutorial is interesting.
- The assignments were an amazing learning experience, the lectures were helpful and so were the tutorials. The assignments eased you in and allowed me to learn a lot of the content while doing it.
- [This] course [was] interesting, challenging and overall awesome. The amount of content I learnt this semester in this course was huge. The structure of the course allowed a smooth transition for all students and the mentor sessions along with extensive notes provided allowed students to practice many examples before tackling the assignments.
- This course let us know how to design and plan[ning] to build a software which is really cool and interesting.
- [The] class room style teaching.

---

[51] That is, *all* the comments are included, not just the favourable ones. That is to give a fair picture of good vs. bad: there's no "cherry picking".

- Very easy to understand and interesting [...] Assignments were incredibly fascinating and were well thought out. Notes also aided in reinforcing knowledge.
- Encouraged thinking outside the box.
- Teaching methodology [...] and course content. The choice of tutors were mostly good. Structure of the course (except Project Management).
- [The] content was extremely interesting and useful.
- Clear [...] The relevance of content was made clear from the start to beginning. Very interesting course.
- Examples. Organisation.
- Relevance to past real world examples. Assignments were not testing as much but rather assessing through learning using ideas taught throughout the course. They were thought out and well constructed to make you think.
- [...] Interesting content. Challenging.

Suggested Improvements:

- Splitting the 3 h lecture slot into 2 time slots.[52]
- Nothing, it's already the best.
- Removing Assignment 4 and giving project management component an additional 2 weeks. I really enjoyed Assignments 1–3 but Assignment 4 seems somewhat repetitive (a summary of the other assignments in some ways). Also the invited guest speaker towards end of semester was also very interesting, I would love to see more in the future.
- No improvements needed.
- Iterating why it is important. I was not aware of how important proving correctness was until the guest speaker from NICTA visited.[53]
- More defined learning areas.
- Revise what Project Management requires and the aim of it.
- Better mentor sessions.
- Conducting better mentor sessions.
- Cover more content. We went a little slow at times.

F.2   From Fourth-Years in 2012

Best Features:[54]

- Encouraged a different way of thinking than I was used to, that makes much more sense. These concepts should be taught in first year.
- Teaching thinking method that I never use before.
- Subtlety, concurrency ..... No EXAM ..... Assignments.... Requirement to think in a different way.
- Everything. The content is amazing, very well structured, has a lot of interesting material and is well explained.

---

[52] Three 1-hour slots per week is best; but time-tabling forced one 3-hour slot in 2014.
[53] The guest speaker was June Andronick from NICTA.
[54] The course was not given at all in 2013.

- Good approach, but perhaps more appropriate for introducing people to programming properly than as a course numbered 6xxx which implies it should be taken later in the degree.[55]
- This course radically changed the way I view programming, and has certainly improved my programming skills immensely. This course should be compulsory for all Computer Science students, or have its content integrated into first year.
- The interesting problems and concepts presented. No other course makes you think like this, or presents methods of solving problems as this course does. Well structured and interesting topics. Assignments really helped to solidify lecture material.
- The subject matter, the way it was structured, and the way it was taught. One of the best courses offered at CSE.
- Fascinating content. Assignments were pitched at a good progression of difficulties. In general, the course was run extremely well.
- Made the abstract, theory side of computing very accessible, with clear practical applications. Not sure what determines the lecture times, but the one-hour-per-day split was very good.[56]

Suggested Improvements:

- It honestly could not be.
- Nothing actually. Maybe more students?
- Some lecture notes could [have] been released a week before the lectures so that you could have a better understanding of the content beforehand.
- Nothing.
- Having it in a room where you can hear from further back than the first row!
- Not much, maybe some of the concepts were a little too challenging, and that coupled with the new techniques of problem solving we were learning really sent your head into a spin. Although you set it out extremely logically, it can still become rather overwhelming.
- Not changing it in the slightest.

F.3   From Fourth-Years in 2011

Best Features:

- The subject matter [...] the interaction between the students and the lecturer, in short all of it.
- It changed my approach to programming in a way that I was then able to do better in my other subjects as well as in teaching programming.
- Very useful technique, impressive lecture.
- Class participation in lectures, interesting material.

---

[55] This comment is of course the thesis of this whole article.
[56] The courses in 2010–2 were taught in three 1-hour slots per week. In 2014 timetabling for second-years forced that to change to one 3-hour slot.

Suggested Improvements:

- Maybe some preview notes?
- More consistent marking. Although I now recognise and appreciate the difficulty in marking the assignments, disparity between marks for making the same mistakes seems odd.

F.4   From Fourth-Years in 2010

Best Features:

- Giving a thorough grounding to good programming techniques in computing through static reasoning.
- It was awesome, limited size group. I've benefited more from that course than from any other at UNSW. The best feature definitely is the informal style of the course, the high interaction between the lecturer and the students, the timetable (three times one hour instead of three hours in a row in most courses), and the fact that the teached material is actually quite a rare stuff.
- Interesting.
- Everything!!!
- The course content was really well thought out and prepared.
- The course content was extremely interesting.

Suggested Improvements:

- Better course notes.
- Hard to say really. I can't think of a simple way to improve it. But that doesn't mean there is no room for improvement!
- More time to do more stuff.
- A more concrete assessment schedule.

Program Refinement, Perfect Secrecy and Information Flow

Annabelle K. McIver(✉)

Department of Computing, Macquarie University, Sydney, NSW 2109, Australia
annabelle.mciver@mq.edu.au

Abstract. "Classical" proofs of secure systems are based on reducing the hardness of one problem (defined by the protocol) to that of another (a known difficult computational problem). In standard program development [1,3,14] this "comparative approach" features in stepwise refinement: describe a system as simply as possible so that it has exactly the required properties and then apply sound refinement rules to obtain an implementation comprising specific algorithms and data-structures.

   More recently the stepwise refinement method has been extended to include "information flow" properties as well as functional properties, thus supporting proofs about secrecy within a program refinement method.

   In this paper we review the security-by-refinement approach and illustrate how it can be used to give an elementary treatment of some well known security principles.

Keywords: Proofs of security · Program semantics · Compositional security · Refinement of ignorance

1   Introduction

The challenge of designing secure programs is controlling information in such a way that program execution achieves something useful without, in the process, divulging secrets. *Provable security* means that there is a sound mathematical argument demonstrating that executing a program incurs no such security breach. A crucial first step in provable security is to specify what the secrets are and how they may be accessed. But specifying security properties accurately is extremely difficult because it requires the specifier to be very precise about often informally understood but subtle concepts. Such concepts can often seem counterintuitive without a lot of experimentation and a high degree of proficiency in specialised logics.

   More recently researchers have explored an alternative approach to security verification based on a new notion of "refinement of ignorance" first described in

A.K. McIver — We acknowledge the support of the Australian Research Council Grant DP140101119.

© Springer International Publishing Switzerland 2016
Z. Liu and Z. Zhang (Eds.): SETSS 2014, LNCS 9506, pp. 80–102, 2016.
DOI: 10.1007/978-3-319-29628-9_2

Morgan's *Shadow semantics* [16]. Instead of proving rigorously that a given program "is secure", the analysis becomes comparative: we say "this program is more secure than that one", where the semantics provides the means to prove that such is the case. The refinement viewpoint focusses the technical scrutiny on information and access control, important ideas introduced by Denning [4], and later studied by Landauer [6] who suggested a lattice of information to provide the mathematical structure for comparing security of some deterministic programs.

The Shadow semantics is a significant generalisation of Landauer's work. It allows secret information to be updated, as well as supporting nondeterminism in the sense of underspecification. Those capabilities mean that protocols can be described very succinctly in terms of how information must change to achieve something useful, and what information must necessarily leak (and thus be "downgraded") in order to affect that change. In such a description, a security specialist can reflect on whether the security risk incurred by any unavoidable information leaks is balanced by the benefits the protocol brings to the particular application.

Although, in some sense, the Shadow semantics is unrealistic because it adopts an information theoretic approach to security, its clean treatment of information control provides a sound and straightforward basis on which to introduce fundamental principles of security. Teaching security principles to undergraduates in a formal way helps them to think critically and precisely about the control of information without them having to understand –at the same time– the complexities of cryptographic primitives used in real systems as an engineering device to implement those principles.

In this paper we review the Shadow semantics and use it to illustrate some well-known principles of secure communication. In particular we show how the refinement of ignorance approach supports straightforward algebraic proofs of intricate data access problems.

1.1 Notational Conventions

Throughout we use left-associating dot for function application, so that $f.x.y$ means $(f(x))(y)$ or $f(x, y)$, and we take (un-)Currying for granted where necessary. Comprehensions/quantifications are written uniformly, as $(Qx : T | R \cdot E)$ for quantifier Q, bound variable(s) x of type(s) T, range-predicate R (probably) constraining x and element-constructor E in which x (probably) appears free: for sets the opening "$(Q$" is "$\{$" and the closing "$)$" is "$\}$" so that e.g. the comprehension $\{x, y : \mathbb{N} | y=2^x \cdot yz\}$ is the set of numbers $z, 2z, 4z, \cdots$.

2 Principles of Non-interference

2.1 Review of the Shadow Semantics

The shadow model of security extends Goguen's classical model of non-interference security [5] by tracking the effect of observed information flows on correlations between variables. As with established methods for analysing information flow, the Shadow semantics is based on a partitioning of the state space into *high* and *low* security variables: an observer has full read access only of the low-security variables, and cannot read the high-security variables at all. The Shadow semantics is sensitive to "run-time" observations, such as the values of low-security variables and the program counter. This allows the attacker to infer *possible* values of the high-security variables even without the benefit of direct observation. These run-time observations of the low-security variables can be used in conjunction with a static analysis of the program source, possibly resulting in very accurate predictions of the values of high-security variables. We set out, more precisely, the threat model below at Sect. 2.3, but for now we give an informal description of the underlying principles, noting here that a fundamental feature of their design is to ensure *compositionality* of the related security-refinement order, also explained below.

We use types $\mathcal{V}$ and $\mathcal{H}$ respectively to distinguish between "visible" (i.e. low-security) variables and "hidden" (i.e. high-security) variables mentioned above. In traditional non-interference security, if the attacker cannot infer anything at all about the hidden variables by observing the visible variables then the program is deemed "Goguen-secure". Although an influential idea, this notion of security is normally not achievable in practical security protocols. This can be seen clearly in a password checker: if the correct password is entered then the observer deduces exactly what the password is, but even if he enters the incorrect password he learns what the password is not. Either outcome *necessarily* leaks some information.

The Shadow semantics provides support for analysing the extent to which an attacker can deduce the value of the hidden state. A program can still be deemed secure provided that the information revealed does not compromise a *specified level of secrecy*. In the password checker, leaking what the password is not is deemed an acceptable risk associated with the convenience of secure access control by password.

Consider the two programs set out at Fig. 1. Both have a single hidden variable h which is initialised to a value drawn from the set $\{0, 1, 2\}$, and a visible variable v initialised to a value drawn from $\{0, 1\}$. In standard program semantics we would be able to say that *ProgA* is refined by *ProgB*, since in *ProgB*, v's value is determined by that of h, whereas in *ProgA*, v's value is chosen arbitrarily in $\{0, 1\}$. However, in terms of non-interference, we will see that *ProgB* is actually *less secure* than *ProgA*, since it potentially can leak quite a lot of information about h. Taking that into account would force us to conclude that *ProgA* is not refined by *ProgB* after all.

To compare information-flow characteristics of programs we use **hid** and **vis** respectively as *visibility* declarations: these determine semantically how the state is divided between $\mathcal{V}$ and $\mathcal{H}$ (introduced above). Variables with the **vis** declaration mean that the observer has full "read access" at runtime, and these variables are mapped to $\mathcal{V}$. On the other hand variables with the **hid** declaration mean that the observer cannot see runtime updates, but can only infer values based on the program source and the observed state changes of visible variables. Variables with the **hid** declaration are mapped to $\mathcal{H}$ in the semantics.

ProgA	ProgB
vis $v{:}\in\{0,1\}$;	**hid** $h{:}\in\{0,1,2\}$;
hid $h{:}\in\{0,1,2\}$	**vis** $v := (h \bmod 2)$

A **vis** declaration means that the observer has full "read access" to v. A **hid** declaration means that he is not able to read directly the value of h.

Fig. 1. Similar output values but dissimilar information-flow characteristics

Now with these declarations, we can analyse the information about h leaked at run-time. We write $h{:}\in\{0,1,2\}$ to mean that the hidden variable h is set to any of the three possible values, but the observer's knowledge of the state cannot be any more precise than that. For visible variables the observer always has complete knowledge of the runtime values. When we write $v{:}\in\{0,1\}$, it means that from the source code alone the observer cannot predict which of 0 or 1 will be assigned to v; however he can observe at run-time exactly which value is selected. In particular ProgA of Fig. 1 is non-interference secure in the sense of Goguen, because whatever the run-time value of v is observed, the attacker is unable to use that information to determine the value of h more accurately than its initialisation set. An attacker observing ProgB on the other hand can deduce a great deal about the value of h by observing the run-time value of v. Since v's final value depends on the parity of h, if v is set to 1 it can only mean that h is also 1, since it is the only odd value in the set of values that h can have. If v is observed to be 0, then the attacker can rule out 1 as a possible value for h. Thus we can deduce that ProgB is not non-interference secure in the classical sense. However the Shadow semantics has given us a precise relationship between the visible state and the hidden state, rather than a single judgement of non-interference. This detailed relationship between the hidden state and visible behaviour can be used to compare the relative security of programs using a "security refinement" relation which takes both functional and non-interference security into account. We review this relationship next.

The basic "Shadow state" for programs is a pair (v, H) where v is the current state of the visible variables v, and H is a subset of *possible* values for the hidden state variable h that the attacker has deduced is consistent with his observations. Thus (v, H) should be thought of as pairing visible values together with "equivalence classes" of possible values for h which the attacker is able to infer from run-time observations and the source code.[1]

The Shadow semantics of a program is then a mapping from initial paired states to sets of paired states $\mathcal{V} \times \mathbb{PH} \rightarrow \mathbb{P}(\mathcal{V} \times \mathbb{PH})$, where the multiplicity of the result sets accounts for nondeterminism in the observations. In Fig. 2 we can see the final result sets for our examples at Fig. 1. In the case of ProgA there are two possible observations, depending on the nondeterministic setting

---

[1] Another way to think of the pairs (v, H) are abstractions of "prior"/"posterior" distributions in a full probabilistic semantics. See for example [12,13].

of visible variable v. However for each observation, no information about the possible value of the hidden variable is leaked, thus each visible state is paired with the set $\{0, 1, 2\}$ denoting that the attacker is unable to make any run-time deductions about the value of the hidden h by comparing what he knows before with what he knows after executing and observing the program's behaviour. In the case of *ProgB*, significant information about h is leaked at run-time, and this is taken into account by the different subsets paired with the observations, which the attacker can take advantage of when the program executes. For example if the attacker observes that v is 1 at run-time then he can deduce precisely the value of h, thus the singleton subset $\{1\}$ is paired with that observed state.

Shadow refinement of programs remains consistent with standard functional refinement, but prevents refinements which lead to inconsistent security properties between the specification and the implementation. As mentioned above, a standard semantics of *ProgA* and *ProgB* (i.e. one that ignores the visibility declarations) would imply that *ProgA* is actually "functionally refined" by *ProgB*, because the nondeterminism (in the final values of v) has been reduced in *ProgB*. However the security properties of *ProgB* are *worse* than those of *ProgA*, since, as explained above, information about h is leaked to the attacker. Thus with respect to *Shadow refinement ProgA* and *ProgB* are unrelated.

Two programs *are* in the Shadow refinement relation if *both* their functional and security properties are improved. The Shadow semantics incorporates assumptions in the threat model to ensure that secure refinement is *compositional*. "Compositionality" means that security (and functional) properties of a program can be determined by the corresponding properties of its components. To ensure compositionality in the Shadow semantics the attacker must have the following two important capabilities.

The first is "perfect recall", which means that previous information flows are carried forward, and can be used to make additional deductions when combined with subsequent run-time information flows. For example consider $ProgB; v := 0$ in Fig. 4, where *ProgB* first leaks information about h, and then resets the value of v. We see that, in spite of overwriting the visible variable, the effect of the information flow is sustained in the semantics, so that although the visible variables have the same value in the end, the control flow of (the original) *ProgB*, which leaks information about h, is preserved by the result set.

The second capability relates to the consistency of the observer's deductive powers. We say that the observer *cannot* deduce facts that are inconsistent with his observations, but can deduce facts that are. In particular if the observations imply that a value taken by h *could* be possible, then it must be included in some output (v, H). Similarly if the observations imply that a value taken by h could *not* be possible then it must be excluded by all outputs (v, H). We define observation consistency as follows.

Definition 1 *(Observation consistency).* Given a set of observations $\mathcal{O}_v$ associated with the same visible state v,

$$\mathcal{O}_v := \{(v, H_1), \ldots, (v, H_k)\},$$

we say that any observation (v, H') is *consistent with* $\mathcal{O}_v$ if there is some subset $\mathcal{U} \subseteq \mathcal{O}_v$ such that $H' = \bigcup_{(v,H) \in \mathcal{U}} H$. □

For example in $ProgB; v := 0$ the observer can deduce that $h \in \{0, 1, 2\}$, but can also deduce that $h \notin \{3, 4, 5\}$, thus $(0, \{0, 1, 2\})$ is consistent with all the observations, but $(0, \{0, 1, 2, 3\})$ is not. This is why the semantics Definition 2 (below) mandates the inclusion of all consistent observations in the result set.

In fact consistency is related to *union closure* on the H-component: we say that a set of observations $\mathcal{O}$ is union-closed for v if whenever (v, H_1) and $(v, H_2) \in \mathcal{O}$ then $(v, H_1 \cup H_2) \in \mathcal{O}$ as well. If a set of observations is union-closed for all v then any observation that the attacker can deduce is consistent with all observations in the set.

Definition 2 *(Shadow semantics).* The space of *Shadow programs* is given by $\mathcal{V} \times \mathbb{P}\mathcal{H} \to \mathbb{P}(\mathcal{V} \times \mathbb{P}\mathcal{H})$, where the result sets are union-closed for all v.[2]

Given two programs $P, Q : \mathcal{V} \times \mathbb{P}\mathcal{H} \to \mathbb{P}(\mathcal{V} \times \mathbb{P}\mathcal{H})$ we say that P is *secure refined by* Q, or $P \sqsubseteq Q$, provided that for all $(v, H) \in \mathcal{V} \times \mathbb{P}\mathcal{H}$ we have $P.(v, H) \supseteq Q.(v, H)$. □

Definition 2 we can now see that in fact $ProgA; v := 0$, with the nondeterminism in v now removed by the final assignment, is a refinement of $ProgB; v := 0$, i.e.

$$ProgB; v := 0 \sqsubseteq ProgA; v := 0.$$

The refinement tells us that any observation that the attacker can deduce about $ProgA; v := 0$ is something that can also be deduced about $ProgB; v := 0$. In other words, the attacker can deduce fewer properties about the secrets of $ProgA; v := 0$ than he can about the secrets of $ProgB; v := 0$.

2.2   Semantics of a Simple Programming Language

In Fig. 3 we set out the semantics of a small programming language for describing straight-line programs. The semantic brackets $[\![\cdot]\!]$ take a program text and map it to a function of type $\mathcal{V} \times \mathbb{P}\mathcal{H} \to \mathbb{P}(\mathcal{V} \times \mathbb{P}\mathcal{H})$ as described in Definition 2.

The general principle for keeping track of the correlations between the observed behaviour of the program is to form "equivalence classes" of the hidden state consistent with the observables. The formulae given in Fig. 3 express the division into equivalence classes of the Shadow variables once the information flow and the state updates have been carried out. For example when the visible state is set according to an expression that depends on the hidden state, the

---

[2] For simplicity we do not consider the empty set, i.e. outputs of the form $(v, \{\})$.

$$\llbracket ProgA \rrbracket.(\mathsf{v}, H) \qquad\qquad \llbracket ProgB \rrbracket.(\mathsf{v}, H)$$

$$\{\ (0, \{0, 1, 2\})\ , \qquad\qquad \{\ (0, \{0, 2\})\ , $$
$$(1, \{0, 1, 2\})\ \} \qquad\qquad (1, \{1\})\ \}$$

We use (v, H) to stand for an arbitrary initial paired state, and the semantic brackets $\llbracket \cdot \rrbracket$ maps program texts to functions $\mathcal{V} \times \mathbb{P}\mathcal{H} \to \mathbb{P}(\mathcal{V} \times \mathbb{P}\mathcal{H})$; the subsets denote the final values of the paired states after executing the programs in Fig. 1.
Full details of the semantic function $\llbracket \cdot \rrbracket$ are given at Fig. 3.

Fig. 2. Final result sets

Program P	Semantics $\llbracket P \rrbracket.(\mathsf{v}, H)$
Assign to visible $v := \phi(v, h)$	$\{\mathsf{v}' : \phi(\mathsf{v}, H) \cdot (\mathsf{v}', \ \{\mathsf{h} : H \mid \phi(\mathsf{v}, \mathsf{h}) = \mathsf{v}' \cdot \mathsf{h}\})\}$
Assign to hidden $h := \phi(v, h)$	$\{(\mathsf{v}, \ \{\mathsf{h} : H \cdot \phi(\mathsf{v}, \mathsf{h})\})\}$
Choose visible $v :\in S.v.h$	$\{\mathsf{v}' : S(\mathsf{v}, H) \cdot (\mathsf{v}', \{\mathsf{h}' : H \mid \mathsf{v}' \in S.\mathsf{v}.\mathsf{h}' \cdot \mathsf{h}'\})\ \}$
Choose hidden $h :\in S.v.h$	$\{\mathsf{h}' : S(\mathsf{v}, H) \cdot (\mathsf{v}, \{\mathsf{h}' : H; \mathsf{h}'' : S.\mathsf{v}.\mathsf{h}' \cdot \mathsf{h}''\})\ \}$
Composition $P_1 ; P_2$	$\mathsf{lift}.\llbracket P_2 \rrbracket.(\llbracket P_1 \rrbracket.v.h.H)$
Demonic choice $P_1 \sqcap P_2$	$\llbracket P_1 \rrbracket.(\mathsf{v}, H) \cup \llbracket P_2 \rrbracket.(\mathsf{v}, H)$
Conditional **if** $\phi(v, h)$ **then** P_t **else** P_f **fi**	$\llbracket P_t \rrbracket.(\mathsf{v}, \{\mathsf{h}' : H \mid \phi(\mathsf{v}, \mathsf{h}') = \textbf{true} \cdot \mathsf{h}'\})\ \bigcup$ $\llbracket P_f \rrbracket.(\mathsf{v}, \{\mathsf{h}' : H \mid \phi(\mathsf{v}, \mathsf{h}') = \textbf{false} \cdot \mathsf{h}'\})$

For an expression ϕ that formally is evaluated on variables v and h, on the right-hand-side, we write $\phi(\mathsf{v}, \mathsf{h})$ for the value that is produced when v has value v and h has value h. Similarly, we write $\phi(\mathsf{v}, H)$ for the set of values $\{\mathsf{h} : H \cdot \phi(\mathsf{v}, \mathsf{h})\}$ that could arise by varying over H.
The function $\mathsf{lift}.\llbracket P_2 \rrbracket$ applies $\llbracket P_2 \rrbracket$ to all paired states in its set-valued argument, un-Currying each time, and then takes the union of all results.
The extension to many variables $v_1, v_2, \cdots$ and $h_1, h_2, \cdots$, including local declarations, is straightforward [15, 16].

Fig. 3. Semantics of non-looping commands

original set H then becomes divided into equivalence classes depending on the visible value observed. In Figs. 1 and 2, *ProgB* illustrates this. A similar situation can occur when the hidden state is set according to the value of the visible state. For example $h := v$ implies that after the assignment to h, the Shadow variable corresponds to a singleton.

The conditional always releases information depending on whether it resolves to **true** or not. We note also that non-determinism in the assignments to the visible variables can arise through information flows whenever the uncertainty in the hidden state becomes resolved through a definite observation. For example the statement $v := (h \bmod 2)$ can lead to a non-deterministic setting of v when the incoming uncertainty of H allows the possibilities that h could be both odd and even.

$[\![ProgA; v:=0]\!].(\mathsf{v}, H)$	$[\![ProgB; v:=0]\!].(\mathsf{v}, H)$
$\{\ (0, \{0, 1, 2\})\ \}$	$\{\ (0, \{0, 2\})\ , (0, \{1\})\ ,$ $(0, \{0, 1, 2\})\ \}$

Setting the final value of v to 0 preserves the prior information leaks — in effect the attacker has perfect recall. Union-closure allows functionally equivalent programs with better security properties to be possible refinements.

Fig. 4. Perfect recall and refinement

2.3   Refinement of Ignorance

We can understand the secure refinement in Definition 2 in terms of increasing ignorance (of the observer) as programs become more refined. The more refined a program, the less definite is an observer's knowledge concerning the value of the hidden variables at run-time. We use a "possibility modality" to express degrees of observer ignorance. Let ϕ be an ordinary expression in the program variables. Given a paired state (v, H) we say that it *possibly satisfies* ϕ, or $(\mathsf{v}, H) \models P(\phi)$ provided that:

$$(\exists \mathsf{h} \in H \mid \phi(\mathsf{v}, \mathsf{h})), \tag{1}$$

where we write $\phi(\mathsf{v}, \mathsf{h})$ for ϕ with the free occurrences of v and h replaced by the corresponding values v and h.

Similarly, given a set S of paired states, we say $P(\phi)$ is satisfied for S provided that all (proper) paired states in S possibly satisfy ϕ, that is:

$$S \models P(\phi) \quad \textit{iff} \quad (\forall (\mathsf{v}, H) \in S \mid (\mathsf{v}, H) \models P(\phi)). \tag{2}$$

For example if ϕ is "*h is even*", then $(0, \{0, 1, 2\}) \models P(\phi)$, but $[\![ProgB]\!].(\mathsf{v}, H) \not\models P(\phi)$, since for $(1, \{1\}) \in [\![ProgB]\!].(\mathsf{v}, H)$ there is no possibility that the final value of h is even. Thus, if for some property ϕ, program $Prog$ and initial state (v, H), if $[\![Prog]\!].(\mathsf{v}, H) \models P(\phi)$, then the attacker is unable to distinguish any of the outputs of $Prog$ in respect of ϕ. This feature is preserved by refinement.

Lemma 1 (*Ignorance refinement [16]*). If $Prog \sqsubseteq Prog'$ then for any expression ϕ in the program variables, and initial state (v, H),

$$[\![Prog]\!].(\mathsf{v}, H) \models P(\phi) \quad \Rightarrow \quad [\![Prog']\!].(\mathsf{v}, H) \models P(\phi).$$

$\square$

2.4   Summary of the Non interference Threat Model

We end the review of the Shadow semantics by summarising the operational principles underlying the threat model.

An observer:

1. **Has complete knowledge of the source code.**
   This implies that the attacker can perform a static analysis to make informed predictions about possible correlations between the hidden and visible state.

2. **Is able to observe run-time control flow.**
   By making run-time observations the attacker is able to rule out some of the static predictions made at step 1, thus significantly improving his current knowledge of the secret.

3. **Has perfect recall.**
   This means that once information about the value of a hidden variable has leaked, there is no way to cover it up except by re-setting the value.

4. **Is able to make logical deductions.**
   This means that the attacker can put together all the basic facts from the analyses mentioned above, including static and run-time analysis, to draw additional logical facts about the secret data.

5. **Is unable to guess or prove the actual value of the hidden state** more precisely than that which is implied by the above forms of information flow.
   This is an important limitation on the accuracy of his knowledge of the secrecy: it says that if there is no *logical evidence* to suggest that the value of the secret *is not in* some set H, then the attacker cannot improve his guess further.

6. **Can use refinement in context.**
   If $S \sqsubseteq I$, then any property which the attacker can deduce about S can also be deduced about I. This last property imposes "compositionality" for reasoning, and makes secure refinement useful in practice.

3   The Reveal Statement

It is often useful to analyse exactly what the adversary can deduce at various stages of the program execution; to do this we introduce a program statement, additional to the language constructs at Fig. 3. The statement **reveal** ϕ, where ϕ is an expression in the program variables v and h, is an explicit publication of a value. It does so without changing any variables. Semantically it is equivalent to publishing the value $\phi(v, h)$ in a (local) visible variable.[3]

---

[3] Equivalently it can be done by publishing the value in any visible variable and then overwriting that variable with its former value, leaving perfect recall to retain the information revealed.

Definition 3 *(Reveal Statement)*. Let ϕ be an expression involving program variables v and h. The program **reveal** ϕ publishes the value of ϕ based on the current actual value of the variables:

$$[\![\textbf{reveal } \phi]\!].(\mathsf{v}, H) \quad := \quad \{\mathsf{G} : \mathcal{G} \cdot (\mathsf{v}, \quad \{\mathsf{h} : H \mid \phi(\mathsf{v}, \mathsf{h}) = \mathsf{G} \cdot \mathsf{h}\})\},$$

where $\mathcal{G}$ is the set of distinct values taken by $\phi(\mathsf{v}, \mathsf{h})$ as h ranges over possible values in H. $\qquad\square$

We can use the reveal statement in two ways when analysing a program. The first is as a specification statement because it separates very clearly the overall effect of a program in terms of how variables are updated, and which facts about those variables are known to the attacker. For example, the program $ProgB; v := 0$ is equivalent to a more straightforward one that sets the variables and then publishes a property about the hidden state:

$$\begin{aligned}
&\textbf{hid } h{:}\in \{0, 1, 2\}; \\
&\textbf{vis } v := 0; \\
&\textbf{reveal } (h \bmod 2).
\end{aligned} \qquad (3)$$

Second, we can use the **reveal** statement to prove information flow properties. Since the **reveal** statement is only concerned with information flow and not state updates, it satisfies a number of simple but powerful algebraic laws, and these can be used in conjunction with the programming language to deduce information flows about programs which do include state updates.

Theorem 1 *(Reveal properties [9, 10])*. Let $Prog, Prog'$ be programs with visible variable v and hidden variable h, and let ϕ, ψ be expressions in those program variables. The following properties hold.

1. **reveal** $\phi \quad \sqsubseteq \quad$ **skip**;

2. **reveal** ϕ ; **reveal** $\psi \quad = \quad$ **reveal** ψ ; **reveal** ϕ;

3. $v := \psi(v, h)$; **reveal** $\phi =$ **reveal** ϕ ; $v := \psi(v, h)$, whenever ϕ does not depend on v;

4. $v := \phi(v, h) \quad = \quad$ **reveal** ϕ ; $v := \phi(v, h)$;

5. $v := \phi(v, h)$; $v := \psi(v, h) \quad = \quad$ **reveal** ϕ ; $v := \psi(\phi(v, h), h)$; $\qquad\square$

Theorem 1(1) says that only revealing information, without changing any variables, is always an anti-refinement of **skip**. Theorem 1(2) says that information can be revealed in any order. In fact we define a useful shorthand for multiple reveals:

$$\textbf{reveal } (\psi, \phi) \quad := \quad \textbf{reveal } \phi \text{ ; } \textbf{reveal } \psi. \qquad (4)$$

Next, Theorem 1(3) says that revealing information about h that is independent of the visible state can occur before or after updates to the visible state.

Theorem 1(4) says that if an assignment to a visible variables already reveals information then making an explicit reveal of that information before the update is redundant.

Theorem 1(5) allows two updates to v to be combined provided the information flow of the first update is recorded in a reveal statement.

To illustrate reasoning with **reveal** we consider $ProgB; v:= 0$:

$$
\begin{aligned}
&\quad ProgB; v := 0 \\
&= \quad \textbf{hid } h{:}\in \{0,1,2\}; \textbf{vis } v := (h \bmod 2); v := 0 &\text{``Fig. 1''} \\
&= \quad \textbf{hid } h{:}\in \{0,1,2\}; \textbf{reveal } (h \bmod 2) \; ; \textbf{vis } v := 0 &\text{``Thm. 1(5)''} \\
&= \quad \textbf{hid } h{:}\in \{0,1,2\}; \textbf{vis } v := 0; \; \textbf{reveal } (h \bmod 2), &\text{``Thm. 1(3)''}
\end{aligned}
$$

demonstrating the asserted equality between (3) and $ProgB; v := 0$.

3.1   Reveal Statements as Tests for Information Leaks

Theorem 1(4) suggests a testing interpretation for reveal statements. If

$$
Prog \; ; \; \textbf{reveal } \phi \;\; = \;\; Prog,
$$

then $Prog$ already reveals a relationship between v and h through publication of ϕ, since following it by the explicit reveal incurs no further information leak. When two programs are functionally equivalent, but differ in their Shadow semantics it is because one reveals different information than the other. We can capture these differences using reveal statements.

Definition 4 *(Test for information leaks).* A *test for an information leak* is any program T such that $T \sqsubseteq \textbf{skip}$. We say that it is possible that a program $Prog$ can *leak* information expressed by T provided $Prog; T = Prog$.   □

The program **skip** is a very weak test because all programs satisfy $Prog; \textbf{skip} = Prog$, and indeed **skip** expresses no relationship between observations and the hidden state. More demanding is the test given by **reveal** $(h \bmod 2)$ — programs whose results remain unchanged after this explicit reveal already leak the parity of h.

For example $ProgB; \textbf{reveal } (h \bmod 2) = ProgB$, but $ProgA; \textbf{reveal } (h \bmod 2) \neq ProgA$.

4   The Shadow Semantics and Information-Theoretic Security

In 1949 Claude Shannon [20] set out the principles and properties of encryption schemes which guarantee perfect secrecy. In this section we review those definitions in terms of the Shadow semantics, illustrating some of those principle's consequences using algebraic reasoning set out above.

Let E represent an "encryption mechanism" described by Shannon consisting of a mapping from $\mathcal{M} \times \mathcal{K} \to \mathcal{E}$, where $\mathcal{M}$ is the set of possible messages, $\mathcal{K}$ is the set of possible keys and $\mathcal{E}$ is the set of possible encryptions. For any key $k \in \mathcal{K}$ the mapping $m \mapsto E.m.k$ must be injective, so that any given encryption $E.m.k$ can be decrypted with key k. Shannon studied *information theoretic* security in which an attacker is accorded unlimited computational power; in such a model the notion of perfect secrecy means that if a secret is chosen uniformly at random from $\mathcal{M}$, and the key is chosen uniformly at random from $\mathcal{K}$, then the encryption $E.m.k$ is perfectly secure provided that whatever the value $E.m.k$ observed by the attacker, he cannot guess the message m with probability greater than $1/|\mathcal{M}|$.

Shannon proved an important limitation of perfect security: that the set of keys must be the same size as the set of messages.

Theorem 2 *(Perfect security [20]).* Let $E : \mathcal{M} \times \mathcal{K} \to \mathcal{E}$ be a perfectly secure encryption mechanism. Then the set of possible keys $\mathcal{K}$ must be at least as big as the set of possible messages $\mathcal{M}$. □

Theorem 2 suggests a definition of a "generic perfectly secure" encryption mechanism using the Shadow semantics: revealing $E.m.k$ leaks nothing about the precise value of m or k, if neither are known initially.

Definition 5 *(Perfect encryption).* Let $E : \mathcal{M} \times \mathcal{K} \to \mathcal{E}$ be an encryption mechanism, where $\mathcal{M}$ is set of possible messages, $\mathcal{K}$ is a set of encryption keys and $\mathcal{E}$ the set of possible encryptions. We say that E corresponds to a *perfect encryption mechanism* if:

$$\begin{array}{ll} \textbf{hid } m{:}\in \mathcal{M}; & \\ \textbf{hid } k{:}\in \mathcal{K}; & = \quad \begin{array}{l} \textbf{hid } m{:}\in \mathcal{M}; \\ \textbf{hid } k{:}\in \mathcal{K} \end{array} \\ \textbf{reveal } E.m.k & \end{array}$$

□

As an example, consider a "one time pad" implemented with the "exclusive-or" operator denoted $\oplus$. If we define $E : \mathsf{Bool} \times \mathsf{Bool} \to \mathsf{Bool}$ as $E.b.b' := b \oplus b'$ then it can be shown directly [11] that E satisfies Definition 5, validating the method of "masking" key bits with randomly chosen values.

4.1 The Encryption Lemma

We state Morgan's encryption lemma for perfectly secure encryption schemes.

Lemma 2 *(Encryption Lemma [16]).* Let $E : \mathcal{M} \times \mathcal{K} \to \mathcal{E}$ correspond to a perfectly secure encryption mechanism as set out at Definition 5. If m is a hidden variable, and k is a fresh, hidden variable, then:

$$\begin{array}{ll} \textbf{hid } k{\cdot}\in \mathcal{K}; & - \quad \textbf{skip}, \\ \textbf{reveal } E.m.k; & \\ \textbf{skip}_{\mathcal{M}} & \end{array}$$

where $[\![\textbf{skip}_{\mathcal{M}}]\!].(\mathsf{v}, \mathsf{H}) := \{(\mathsf{v}, \mathsf{H}_{\mathcal{M}})\}$ and $\mathsf{H}_{\mathcal{M}}$ is the projection of $\mathsf{H} \subseteq \mathcal{M} \times \mathcal{K}$ onto $\mathcal{M}$. □

Although Lemma 2 is equivalent to Definition 5, stated in this way, it is a concise representation of how much information about h is released by publishing the result of the encryption. When E is a perfectly secure mechanism then it reveals no more information about h than was known before.

4.2 The Decryption Lemma

Shannon's analysis says that, even when the key and message sets are the same size, then for the mechanism to be perfectly secure it must be very like a one-time pad. The next theorem summarises this idea.

Theorem 3 *(Perfect secrecy [20])*. Let $E : \mathcal{M} \times \mathcal{K} \to \mathcal{E}$ be a perfectly secure encryption mechanism such that $|\mathcal{M}| = |\mathcal{K}| = |\mathcal{E}|$. Then the following must hold:

1. Each key must be chosen with probability $1/|\mathcal{K}|$;
2. For every message $m \in \mathcal{M}$ and cipher text $\mathsf{E} \in \mathcal{E}$ there is a unique k such that $E.m.k = \mathsf{E}$. □

Given Theorem 3 we can now prove a property similar to Shannon's Theorem 3(2), saying that if the attacker has knowledge of both the secret and the cipher text, then he can deduce the key.

Lemma 3 *(Decryption Lemma)*. Let $E : \mathcal{M} \times \mathcal{K} \to \mathcal{E}$ be a perfectly secure mechanism known to the observer such that $|\mathcal{M}| = |\mathcal{K}| = |\mathcal{E}|$. Then

$$\mathbf{reveal}\ (m, E.m.k) \quad = \quad \mathbf{reveal}\ (m, k). \tag{5}$$

Proof: Theorem 3(2) states that for every $m \in \mathcal{M}$, if $E.m.k = E.m.k'$ then $k = k'$. Hence if the observer knows both m and $E.m.k$ for some k then he must be able to infer the value of k exactly. □

Lemma 3 expresses a second limitation of perfectly secure encryption systems, that both the cipher text and the message must be kept secret for the encryption not to leak anything.[4]

5   Modelling Protocols Between Multiple Agents

Most security protocols involve several participants, each with different security concerns, and each with different accessibilities to the information content within the system. The security proofs of such systems must ensure that each participant's (individual) specified security objectives are met. Thus far we have described a semantics which can handle a simple scenario of a single attacker; in this section we review how to adapt it so that we can describe security protocols with multiple participants, where we treat each participant as a potential observer of all the others.

---

[4] This abstract algebraic property also captures the capability of a "known plain text attack". An encryption mechanism is susceptible to a known plain-text attack if, given the message m and the encryption $E.m.k$ is able to work out the key k. If such an attack succeeds against an encryption method then we would say that the encryption mechanism satisfies (5).

5.1   Multiple Agents and Their Potential Attackers

A typical security protocol involves a communication between at least two "agents". Typically both agents have their own secret information which is private to them individually. The objective of a security protocol between the agents might be to share some secret information without leaking it to a third party, or to convince each other that they really are who they claim to be. To implement the protocol means sharing some part of their private data, but in a constrained manner so that they do not reveal too much.

The simplest example of such a "multi-party" protocol is publishing the conjunction of two secret bits, described informally as follows.

Two agents A and B each have a private bit held in variables a and b respectively. They wish to compute the conjunction $a \wedge b$ without either one telling the other the actual value of their own bit, and without releasing any more information than can be deduced from knowing $a \wedge b$.

The objective of this protocol is to publish *only* the value $a \wedge b$, but without revealing any more than that, even to each other. This, of course, necessarily involves some information flow but, depending on the actual value of $a \wedge b$, some uncertainty can still remain. If the value of $a \wedge b$ is 1, then indeed publishing this will reveal exactly that $a = b = 1$. However if $a \wedge b$ is 0 then there are several different scenarios which could lead to this result: either both a and b are 0 or exactly one is 0. By publishing the value of $a \wedge b$ in this case, there should be no distinction between relevant scenarios from the point of view of any participating agent or third party observer. In particular if a is 0, then agent A should not know whether b is 0 or 1.

We adapt the simple semantics described above so that it can be used to take into account each "agent's viewpoint", and the individual constraints on information access required by protocols such as this.

Elsewhere we introduced agent viewpoints [11] into the system by embellishing the declaration of each variable to include a list of agents which treat the variable as an observable. In detail we use the following declarations to classify various explicit visibility relationships between agents.

- **var** means the associated variable's visibility is unknown or irrelevant.
- **vis** means the associated variable is visible to all agents.
- **hid** means the associated variable is hidden from all agents.
- **vis**$_{list}$ means the associated variable is visible to all agents in the (non-empty) list, and is hidden from all others (including third parties).

For example in the case of the secure conjunction protocol, we can use the visibility declarations to include which agents can observe which parts of the state. The formal protocol is set out at Fig. 5. First A and B each choose (at random) a secret bit and save it to their respective private variables. Those variables are declared with a visibility that makes explicit that only A can observe a, and only B can observe b directly. Of course A and B each have a "copy" of the source code. Finally the universally visible variable c (visibility declaration **vis**) is set to the value $a \wedge b$.

$$\mathbf{vis}_A \ a{:}\in \{0,1\}; \qquad \leftarrow A \ chooses \ a \ secret \ bit$$
$$\mathbf{vis}_B \ b{:}\in \{0,1\}; \qquad \leftarrow B \ chooses \ a \ secret \ bit$$
$$\mathbf{vis} \ c{:=}\, a \wedge b \qquad \leftarrow Their \ conjunction \ is \ published \ in \ c.$$

$\mathbf{vis}_A$ and $\mathbf{vis}_B$ are visibility declarations placing constraints on which part of the state is visible to which agent.

Fig. 5. Specification of the secret conjunction

5.2 Interpreting Agent Viewpoints

The state of the small program at Fig. 5 is defined by the values of the variables a, b and c but, given the visibility declarations summarised above, each agent has a very different perspective when we take into account which variables they can read at runtime. We adapt the simple semantics of variable classified as either hidden or visible by treating each agent individually via their *viewpoint*.

Definition 6 *(Viewpoint).* Let program *Prog* with named agents $A, B, \dots$. We write $Prog_W$ for agent W's viewpoint of *Prog*, where all declarations $\mathbf{vis}_{list}$ become **hid**, if W does not appear in *list* and **vis** otherwise. All **hid**, **var** and **vis** declarations remain unchanged.
    The semantics of agent W's viewpoint of *Prog* is given by $[\![Prog_W]\!]$. □

Given the visibility declarations at Fig. 5, we define A's viewpoint to be the Shadow semantics of the program at Fig. 6, where all declarations in which A is on the list are set to **vis** and all declarations where A is not on the list are set to **hid**.
    Similarly agent B has a viewpoint similar to agent A's except that b is declared visible and a is declared hidden. We use a special universal agent called U to represent a third-party observer who is never included on any visibility list so that all variables except those with the **vis** declaration are hidden from U. Agent U's viewpoint of secret conjunction therefore has both a and b declared hidden, and c declared visible.
    In Fig. 7 we summarise the semantics for each agent's viewpoint for secure conjunction. Observe that the implications of the visibility declarations are to set the Shadow sets. In the case of agent A, the observables are derived from variables a and c, and so in the result sets, the triples are of the form $(\mathsf{a}, \{\mathsf{b}, \mathsf{b}'\}, \mathsf{c})$, with the uncertainty in variable b captured as a set of possible values in the second position of the triple correlated with the observation. For agent U, the uncertainty is over variables a and b, and so its viewpoint result sets are of the form $(\{(\mathsf{a}, \mathsf{b}), (\mathsf{a}', \mathsf{b}')\}, \mathsf{c})$, since its Shadow sets are drawn from $\mathcal{A} \times \mathcal{B}$.
    We define refinement of multiagent systems as follows.

Definition 7 *(Multiagent Refinement).* For specification S and implementation I, involving named agents $A, B, \dots$, and universal agent U, we say that $S \sqsubseteq I$ provided that $S_W \sqsubseteq I_W$ for all agents W, where S_W, I_W denote the corresponding viewpoints of agent W with respect to S and I. □

vis $a :\in \{0, 1\}$;   ← *A chooses a secret bit*
hid $b :\in \{0, 1\}$;   ← *B chooses a secret bit*
vis $c := a \land b$ ← *Their conjunction is published in c.*

Fig. 6. Agent A's viewpoint for secret conjunction

	Agent A	Agent B	Agent U
vis	a, c	b, c	c
hid	b	a	a, b
Shadow sets contained in	$\mathcal{B}$	$\mathcal{A}$	$\mathcal{A} \times \mathcal{B}$
Result sets	$\{ (0, \{0, 1\}, 0) , (1, \{0\}, 0) , (1, \{1\}, 1) \}$	$\{ (\{0, 1\}, 0, 0) , (\{0\}, 1, 0) , (\{1\}, 1, 1) \}$	$\{ (\{(0, 1), (1, 0), (0, 0)\}, 0) , (\{(1, 1)\}, 1) \}$

The state of each viewpoint is derived from triples of variable values a, b, c. In each case the shadow sets are determined by the visibility declarations so that the structure of split states is to group equivalence classes of triples together. For clarity we keep the order of the triples as $\mathcal{A} \times \mathcal{B} \times \mathcal{C}$ with the hidden part of the state indicated by braces. For example elements in agent A's final result sets are of the form $(\mathsf{a}, \{\mathsf{b}, \mathsf{b'}\}, \mathsf{c})$ indicating that A can observe the first and last item of the triple but not the middle item. Similarly B's final result sets are of the form $(\{\mathsf{a}, \mathsf{a'}\}, \mathsf{b}, \mathsf{c})$, and agent U's result sets are of the form $(\{(\mathsf{a}, \mathsf{b}), (\mathsf{a'}, \mathsf{b'})\}, \mathsf{c})$ since U cannot observe either of the first two components in the triple.

Fig. 7. Semantics for each agent's viewpoint for secret conjunction Fig. 5

We note that visibility declarations can be thought of as placing access restrictions on variables rather than proscribing that an agent can never deduce the value of variables not on his visibility list: that depends on the code. For example, hidden h is published once the statement $v := h$ has been executed, and this knowledge is available to all agents. Visibility declarations do however have an impact on which refinements will be judged ultimately to be valid.

For example the following refinement fails, because although nothing has changed with regards agents A, B, for agent U, the program on the left reveals strictly less information than the program on the right.

$$\begin{array}{ccc}
\mathbf{vis}_A \ a :\in \{0, 1\}; & & \mathbf{vis}_A \ a :\in \{0, 1\}; \\
\mathbf{vis}_B \ b :\in \{0, 1\}; & \not\sqsubseteq & \mathbf{vis}_B \ b :\in \{0, 1\}; \\
\mathbf{vis}_{A,B} \ c := a \land b & & \mathbf{vis} \ c := a \land b
\end{array} \qquad (6)$$

5.3   Agent Viewpoint of Knowledge

Within a multiagent system, it is useful to be able to prove what individual agents know. We recall a special reveal statement $\mathbf{reveal}_{list}\,\phi$ introduced elsewhere [9], which behaves like **reveal** ϕ from the perspective of any agent viewpoint if that agent is on the list *list*, and **skip** otherwise.

Definition 8. *We say that an expression ϕ is effectively list-visible at a point in a program just when putting a statement $\mathbf{reveal}_{list}\phi$ there would not alter the program's meaning.*

For example in the program on the left at (6), the expression $a \wedge b$ is effectively $\{A, B\}$-visible, but is not effectively $\{U\}$-visible, since the Universal agent cannot observe the conjunction of a and b, and so following it with $\mathbf{reveal}_U \ a \wedge b$ will change its information flow properties and hence its meaning.

6 Elementary Impossibilities Using the Shadow

One of the basic concerns of secure communication is to establish a shared secret between agents in the system. If the agents are able to communicate already over a private channel, then they can continue to share secrets between each other via that private channel. If they do not have a private channel then they must transmit messages encrypted over a public channel.

Shared secrets are important because they provide the basis for secret communication using an efficient encryption mechanism known as "symmetric encryption". But how do two agents establish any shared secret in the first place if they don't already share a secret channel?

There is a well-known "folk theorem" which describes a limitation of symmetric encryption mechanisms for establishing a shared secret, namely that they cannot do so if they are only able to use a symmetric encryption mechanism. The fact that this general impossibility result exists is the reason why more complicated forms of encryption are used for setting up shared secrets, e.g. Shamir's secret sharing protocol [19]. In this section we review the symmetric encryption folk theorem as an exercise in using algebraic specification and reasoning in the Shadow semantics.

An encryption mechanism is *symmetric* if the decryption key is the same as the encryption key, or can be feasibly calculated from it. In the Shadow semantics that is the same as saying that knowing both the key and the encrypted message is the same as knowing both the key and the message in plaintext.

Definition 9 *(Symmetric encryption).* An encryption mechanism E is *symmetric*, if for any key k and message m we have

$$\mathbf{reveal}(E.m.k, k) \quad = \quad \mathbf{reveal} \ (k, m).$$

$\square$

In the context of the Shadow semantics we can also apply the Decryption Lemma which, when put together with Definition 9, implies we have for any m, k, and a symmetric encryption mechanism E that:

$$\mathbf{reveal}(E.m.k, k) \quad = \quad \mathbf{reveal}(k, m) \quad = \quad \mathbf{reveal} \ (m, E.m.k). \qquad (7)$$

This says that within the threat model for the Shadow semantics, for any symmetric encryption mechanism E, if the observer knows *any two* of k, m or $E.m.k$ then he can deduce the remaining value. Recall that the Decryption Lemma is also implied by a "known plain text attack", thus our reasoning also applies for symmetric encryption mechanisms known to have this weakness.

With (7) we can demonstrate the folk theorem in an elementary way using program algebra.

6.1   Symmetric Encryption and the Folk Theorem

A secret sharing protocol consists of two agents A and B who can send messages to each other over a public channel using a given encryption mechanism E. Once a message is transmitted via the channel then the contents of the file are considered to be observable by any agent, even the universal agent U. We assume that all values are created by either A or B, and respectively stored in variables private to the creator. Values can be chosen at random, or calculated from existing values using E. The system is defined by the operations set out at Fig. 8. The operations model the capacity for each agent to choose a secret value, and to encrypt or decrypt values using the mechanism E. They communicate with each other by sending values over a publicly observable channel. One way to model this is to introduce an explicit channel variable *chan*, which takes values from one of the agents and then passes them to the other. For example, if B sends a value stored in b to A, we could write:

$$\textbf{vis } chan := b; \textbf{vis}_A \ a := chan.$$

However considering only the information flow concerning the variables declared by agents A and B, this is equivalent to

$$\textbf{reveal } b; \textbf{vis}_A \ a := b \quad = \quad \textbf{vis}_A \ a := b \ ; \textbf{reveal } b.$$

In Fig. 8 we use the latter formulation because we are interested in information flow, and using **reveal** statements directly will simplify our reasoning.

- $\textbf{vis}_A \ a_i :\in \mathcal{A}$ — Agent A chooses privately a random value drawn from set $\mathcal{A}$.
- $\textbf{vis}_B \ b_j :\in \mathcal{B}$ — Agent B chooses privately a random value drawn from set $\mathcal{B}$.
- $\textbf{vis}_A \ a_l := E.a_j.a_k$ — Agent A encrypts or decrypts a value from known values stored in variables a_j and a_k .
- $\textbf{vis}_B \ b_l := E.b_j.b_k$ — Agent B encrypts or decrypts a value from known values stored in variables b_j and b_k .
- $\textbf{vis}_A \ a := Z; \textbf{reveal } Z$ — Agent B sends agent A a value Z over the public channel.
- $\textbf{vis}_B \ b := Z; \textbf{reveal } Z$ — Agent A sends agent B a value Z over the public channel

Fig. 8. Computation steps in a secret sharing protocol

We model a *secret sharing protocol* between A and B as any sequence of the above statements described in Fig. 8. An example of such a protocol is:

$\mathbf{vis}_A\ a{:}\in \mathcal{A};$ $\leftarrow$ *A chooses a random value*
$\mathbf{vis}_A\ a'{:}\in \mathcal{A}$ $\leftarrow$ *A chooses another random value*
$\mathbf{vis}_B\ b{:=}E.a.a';\mathbf{reveal}\ E.a.a'$ $\leftarrow$ *A sends B variable a encrypted with a'*

We say that a value Z is *generally known* after executing P if

$$P;\mathbf{reveal}\ Z\ =\ P. \tag{8}$$

In the above protocol, provided that neither $\mathcal{A}$ nor $\mathcal{A}'$ are singleton sets then neither a nor a' is generally known; in fact these values are also not known to agent B.

Learning a Value. Given any secret sharing protocol P, the agents only know the value of a variable if either they created it for themselves, or they were sent it, or they were able to decrypt it using E with values they already knew. For example, if agent B knows two values X and Y after executing P, and the last action was to receive value X from agent A, then either he knew Y before receiving X from A, or he was able to use X to decrypt $E.X.Y$, which value he already knew. We capture this "learning event" with the following property:[5]

$$P;\mathbf{reveal}_B(Y,X) = P \Rightarrow$$
$$P';\mathbf{reveal}_B\ Y = P' \lor P';\mathbf{reveal}_B\ E.Y.X = P', \tag{9}$$

where $P = P';\mathbf{vis}_B\ b{:=}X;\mathbf{reveal}\ X$.

6.2   The Folk Theorem

We state the folk theorem as follows:

Theorem 4 *(Symmetric Encryption Folk Theorem).* Let P be a secret sharing protocol between agents A and B using symmetric encryption method E. Any value X that is known by both A and B after executing P is also known generally, i.e.

$$P;\mathbf{reveal}_A\ X\ =\ P\ \land\ P;\mathbf{reveal}_B\ X\ =\ P$$
$$\Rightarrow\quad P;\mathbf{reveal}\ X\ =\ P. \tag{10}$$

Proof. We use structural induction. For simplicity we also assume that all variables are initialised at most once, to avoid questions of definability.

The base case is when $P = \mathbf{skip}$, and the result follows since we assume initially that all secrets known to both A and B are generally known.

We next consider $P = P';Q$, where Q is one of the statements in Fig. 8. We assume by the inductive hypothesis that P' satisfies the theorem. We assume

---

[5] We prove in the Appendix Sect. A.1 that this property holds for E implemented with $\oplus$, exclusive-or.

also that $P;\mathbf{reveal}_A\ Y = P;\mathbf{reveal}_B\ Y = P$ for some value Y. We must show, for each case of Q, that $P;\mathbf{reveal}\ Y = P$ also.

Suppose Q is the action "Agent A sends value X to Agent B on the public channel". i.e. $P = P';\mathbf{vis}_B\ b := X;\mathbf{reveal}\ X$. We have the following facts:

(i) Agent A knew value X already after P':

$$P';\mathbf{reveal}_A\ X = P'$$

(ii) Agent A knew value Y already after P':

$$P';\mathbf{reveal}_A\ Y = P'$$

(iii) Definition 7 for Agent A:

$$P';\mathbf{reveal}_A\ E.X.Y = P'$$

(iv) Assumption:

$$P;\mathbf{reveal}\ Y = P$$

Fact (i) is assumed since Agent A sends value X to Agent B. Fact (ii) follows from (i) since:

$$
\begin{aligned}
&\ P';\mathbf{reveal}_A\ Y \\
=&\ P';\mathbf{reveal}_A\ X;\mathbf{reveal}_A Y && \text{``(i) above''} \\
=&\ P';\mathbf{reveal}_A X && \text{``Assumption: } P';\mathbf{reveal}_A\ (X,Y) = P';\mathbf{reveal}_A\ X\text{''} \\
=&\ P'. && \text{``(i) above''}
\end{aligned}
$$

Using the above facts, we can now reason as follows that value Y is also known generally after P.

We begin with (9) because after Agent B receives value X, then either he knew Y already, or he learned it. We treat each case separately.

Case 1: Suppose first that $P';\mathbf{reveal}_B\ Y = P'$. (Agent B knew Y already.) By (ii) and structural induction on P', we deduce immediately that Y was generally known after P', i.e. $P';\mathbf{reveal}\ Y = P'$.

Perfect recall then gives us immediately that $P;\mathbf{reveal}\ Y = P$.

Case 2: Suppose instead from (9) that $P';\mathbf{reveal}_B\ E.X.Y = P'$. But we also have by (iii) that $P';\mathbf{reveal}_A\ E.X.Y = P'$, and so by structural induction we deduce that $P';\mathbf{reveal}\ E.X.Y = P'$.

Thus by perfect recall we must have that $P;\mathbf{reveal}\ E.X.Y = P$. We put this together with (4) and (7) to deduce in fact that $P;\mathbf{reveal}\ Y = P$, as required.

The other cases for Q, when it represents a local assignment by either A or B to local variables, does not transfer new knowledge of the other agent, and so there is nothing to prove.

$\square$

7   Conclusions and Outlook

This paper reviews refinement of ignorance and how it applies to the analysis of information flow. The Shadow semantics is based on ideas originally due to Mantel [8], Leino [7] and Sebelfeld [17]. Mantel's emphasis is on events and traces, whilst Leino and Sabelfeld concentrate on information flow with respect to the (initial) values of the secret. The Shadow semantics is concerned with the final state, with the shadow variable H in an observation (v, H) acting as a digest of all information flows relating to the current value of the secret variable h.

Our treatment of the folk theorem is inspired by Schmidt *et al.* [18] who also provide some mechanical support to determine whether protocol designs based on a given equational theory are able to establish a shared secret.

Variations on the Shadow semantics include probability and this line of work has resulted in connections to the channel model of information flow [2,13], allowing the amount of information flowing to be quantified thus giving a better understanding of the degree to which programs leak information.

A   Some Proofs

A.1   Learning a Value

We prove (9) for the special case where E is the exclusive-OR, $\oplus$. We re-state (9) here for $\oplus$.

$$P; \mathbf{reveal}_B(Y, X) = P \Rightarrow$$
$$P'; \mathbf{reveal}_B \ Y = P' \vee P'; \mathbf{reveal}_B \ X \oplus Y = P', \quad\quad (11)$$

where $P = P'; \mathbf{vis}_B \ b := X; \mathbf{reveal} \ X$.

Assume that B has (private) variables $b_1, b_2, \ldots b_k$, and that A has (private) variables $a_1, a_2 \ldots a_m$. We also assume that each variable is assigned exactly once and then never changed.

B's knowledge of the state after executing P' can be summarised as follows:

1. B knows the values of all its own variables $b_1, b_2, \ldots b_k$.
2. B knows the values of any encrypted value sent over the public channel. Each of those values is of the form

$$a_{i_1} \oplus a_{i_2} \oplus \cdots \oplus a_{i_n},$$

   for some selection of variables drawn from $a_1, a_2 \ldots a_m$.
3. B can learn new facts by using the facts he already has and computing new values using $\oplus$. Let $\mathcal{K}$ be the set of facts so-computed using $\oplus$.

Notice that whenever a value $\alpha \in \mathcal{K}$ we have that $P'; \mathbf{reveal}_B \ \alpha = P'$.

Assume that $Y \notin \mathcal{K}$, but that when B learns X then he can deduce Y. We will show that $X \oplus Y$ is contained in $\mathcal{K}$.

Since $Y \notin \mathcal{K}$, this means that $Y = X \oplus \alpha$ for some fact $\alpha \in \mathcal{K}$. But with this we reason:

$$Y = X \oplus \alpha$$
$$\Rightarrow \quad X \oplus Y = X \oplus X \oplus \alpha$$
$$\Rightarrow \quad X \oplus Y = \alpha, \qquad\qquad\qquad\qquad\qquad \text{``Property of } \oplus\text{''}$$

implying that $X \oplus Y$ (i.e. $E.Y.X$ as at (9)) is contained in $\mathcal{K}$.

References

1. Abrial, J.-R.: The B Book: Assigning Programs to Meanings. Cambridge University Press, New York (1996)
2. Alvim, M.S., Chatzikokolakis, K., Palamidessi, C., Smith, G.: Measuring information leakage using generalized gain functions. In: Proceedings of the 25th IEEE Computer Security Foundations Symposium (CSF 2012), pp. 265–279, June 2012
3. Back, R.-J.R.: Correctness preserving program refinements: proof theory and applications, Tract 131, Mathematisch Centrum, Amsterdam (1980)
4. Denning, D.: Cryptography and Data Security. Addison-Wesley, Boston (1983)
5. Goguen, J.A., Meseguer, J.: Unwinding and inference control. In: Proceedings of the IEEE Symposium on Security and Privacy, pp. 75–86. IEEE Computer Society (1984)
6. Landauer, J., Redmond, T.: A lattice of information. In: Proceedings of the 6th IEEE Computer Security Foundations Workshop (CSFW 1993), pp. 65–70, June 1993
7. Leino, K.R.M., Joshi, R.: A semantic approach to secure information flow. Sci. Comput. Program. **37**(1–3), 113–138 (2000)
8. Mantel, H.: Preserving information flow properties under refinement. In: Proceedings of the IEEE Symposium Security and Privacy, pp. 78–91 (2001)
9. McIver, A.K.: The secret art of computer programming. In: Leucker, M., Morgan, C. (eds.) ICTAC 2009. LNCS, vol. 5684, pp. 61–78. Springer, Heidelberg (2009)
10. McIver, A.K., Morgan, C.C.: A calculus of revelations. Presented at VSTTE Theories Workshop, October 2008. http://www.cs.york.ac.uk/vstte08/
11. McIver, A.K., Morgan, C.C.: *Sums and Lovers*: Case Studies in Security, Compositionality and Refinement. In: Cavalcanti, A., Dams, D.R. (eds.) FM 2009. LNCS, vol. 5850, pp. 289–304. Springer, Heidelberg (2009)
12. McIver, A., Meinicke, L., Morgan, C.: Compositional closure for bayes risk in probabilistic noninterference. In: Abramsky, S., Gavoille, C., Kirchner, C., Meyer auf der Heide, F., Spirakis, P.G. (eds.) ICALP 2010. LNCS, vol. 6199, pp. 223–235. Springer, Heidelberg (2010)
13. McIver, A., Morgan, C., Smith, G., Espinoza, B., Meinicke, L.: Abstract channels and their robust information-leakage ordering. In: Abadi, M., Kremer, S. (eds.) POST 2014 (ETAPS 2014). LNCS, vol. 8414, pp. 83–102. Springer, Heidelberg (2014)
14. Morgan, C.C.: Programming from Specifications, 2nd edn. Prentice-Hall, Upper Saddle River (1994). http://web.comlab.ox.ac.uk/oucl/publications/books/PfS/
15. Morgan, C.C.: The shadow knows: refinement of ignorance in sequential programs. In: Uustalu, T. (ed.) Math Prog Construction. Springer, vol. 4014, pp. 359–378. Springer, Treats Dining Cryptographers (2006)
16. Morgan, C.C., Knows, T.S.: Refinement of ignorance in sequential programs. Sci. Comput. Program. **74**(8), 629–653 (2009). Treats Oblivious Transfer

17. Sabelfeld, A., Sands, D.: A PER model of secure information flow in sequential programs. High.-Ord. Symbolic Comput. **14**(1), 59–91 (2001)
18. Schmidt, B., Schaller, P., Basin, D.: Impossibility results for secret establishment. In: Proceedings of the 23rd IEEE Computer Security Foundations Symposium (CSF), pp. 261–273 (2010)
19. Shamir, A.: How to share a secret. Commun. ACM **22**(11), 612–613 (1979)
20. Shannon, C.E.: Theory of secrecy systems. Bell Syst. Tech. J. **28**, 656–715 (1949)

The Z Notation: Whence the Cause and Whither the Course?

Jonathan P. Bowen[1,2,3]($\boxtimes$)

[1] Department of Informatics, School of Engineering,
London South Bank University, Borough Road, London SE1 0AA, UK
[2] Israel Institute for Advanced Studies,
The Hebrew University of Jerusalem, Jerusalem, Israel
[3] Museophile Limited, Oxford, UK
jonathan.bowen@lsbu.ac.uk
http://www.jpbowen.com

Abstract. The Z notation for the formal specification of computer-based systems has been in existence since the early 1980s. Since then, an international Z community has emerged, academic and industrial courses have been developed, an ISO standard has been adopted, and Z has been used on a number of significant software development projects, especially where safety and security have been important. This chapter traces the history of the Z notation and presents issues in teaching Z, with examples. A specific example of an industrial course is presented. Although subsequent notations have been developed, with better tool support, Z is still an excellent choice for general purpose specification and is especially useful in directing software testing to ensure good coverage.

1 Whence the Cause?

"Mathematical reasoning may be regarded rather schematically as the exercise of a combination of two facilities, which we may call intuition and ingenuity."

– Alan M. Turing
The Purpose of Ordinal Logics (1938)

1.1 History

The computing pioneer Alan Turing (1912–1954) [13,22] and the physicist Albert Einstein (1879–1955), who died only a year after Turing although after a considerably longer lifespan, are two of the western scientists who are celebrated with busts on the campus of Southwestern University in Chongqing, China (see Fig. 1). Einstein is of course extremely well-known internationally, but Turing has been less well-known until more recently when his achievements have become increasingly visible to the public. He is considered by many to be the founding father of modern computer science with his 1936/7 paper on the *Entscheidungsproblem* ("decision problem" in German), establishing what is computable

© Springer International Publishing Switzerland 2016
Z. Liu and Z. Zhang (Eds.): SETSS 2014, LNCS 9506, pp. 103–151, 2016.
DOI: 10.1007/978-3-319-29628-9_3

Fig. 1. Busts of Alan Turing and Albert Einstein on the campus of Southwest University, Chongqing, China. (Photographs by Jonathan Bowen.)

through the theoretical computing device that has become known as a Turing Machine [42]. This is an abstract model of a computing machine that is useful for demonstrating what is and what is not computable. This astoundingly novel approach has had a profound effect on the theory of computation subsequently, effectively founding the field of theoretical computer science.

Turing produced what is considered by many as the first paper on proving a program correct [43]. However, sadly this short paper had little impact on the development of formality in computing until it was rediscovered and evaluated in its historical context much later [34]. Instead, Tony Hoare's much later 1969 paper on an axiomatic basis for computer programming, introducing Hoare logic and assertions, was a turning point in providing a formal approach to program proving [29].

Formal methods [18] emerged during the 1970s as a mathematically-based approach to software development. Jean-Raymond Abrial's 1974 paper on data semantics [1] was in hindsight a seminar paper leading to the development of the Z notation for the formal specification of computer-based systems. In the early 1980s, Abrial visited the Programming Research Group (PRG) in the Oxford University Computing Laboratory (OUCL) and sowed the seeds for the development of the Z notation there. A Z course was established for both academics and industry. Projects such as the Distributed Computing Software Project used Z to specify network services at OUCL [15,24]. A series of Z User Meetings was established, first in Oxford from 1986, with written proceedings from 1987 [5], then around the UK from 1992 [36], and finally internationally from 1998 [14].

A "Z Reference Manual" (ZRM) was published as a book originally in 1989, with a second edition in 1992, and further revisions online in 2001 [39]. This was and even remains a *de facto* standard, with an associated type-checker, fUZZ [40]. However, an ISO/IEC standard with a formal semantics written in the Z notation itself was issued in 2002 [32]. The development of a formal semantics revealed some issues in Z that were clarified in the final semantics in the ISO/IEC standard [27].

Turing is associated with Cambridge University and later Manchester University. There is no known record of him ever having even visited Oxford University. However, Turing did liaise with Christopher Strachey (1916–1975), at one time a teacher at Harrow School, but also an expert early programmer. His program for the game of draughts impressed Turing. Strachey went on to found the Programming Research Group at Oxford in the 1960s, where he developed denotational semantics with colleagues there. Strachey's untimely death in 1975 led to the appointment of Tony Hoare as the next head of the PRG. It was Hoare who fostered a suitable environment at Oxford for the Z notation to emerge and flourish in the 1980s and 1990s.

1.2 Background

The Z notation is an industrial-strength formal specification notation based on typed set theory and first order predicate logic, used in the specification of discrete computer-based systems [10,39]. As well as standard mathematical operators, Z also includes a number of additional operators that have proved to be useful for specifications in practice, using more specialised sets such as relations, functions, and sequences. In addition to the mathematical notation, Z also includes a schema notation that collects the mathematical description into schema boxes containing declarations and predicates. These schemas may be combined to form larger specifications using schema operators that largely match logical operators, aiding the structuring of large specifications at an industrial scale.

This chapter includes a description of an industrially used course that covers the mathematical and schema notation of Z. Delivery of the course is in the form of lectures interspersed with paper-and-pencil exercises. The course is based around an ongoing case study example and finished with a further example for study. Previous experience of standard mathematical set theory and predicate logic is helpful although not essential.

1.3 Brief Survey

Formal methods are useful for improving software engineering where high integrity is desirable or required [18,19,28]. Examples of real industrial use are available [2,3,25]. There are a number of formal methods available with various strengths – and weaknesses – depending on the situation in which they are applied. See http://formalmethods.wikia.com for a wiki with information on formal methods in general and the Z notation in particular. Z's strength is its use as a general purpose specification language in a human-readable form, interspersed with informal text, that can be scaled up to an industrial level. A weakness is its lack of good tools.

Z can be used for formal specification with the aim of designing and documenting mainly software but also hardware systems [6]. For example, Z has been used to specify microprocessor instruction sets [4]. It can also be used to specify software tools [7] and even window-based user interfaces [8].

Z is not executable in the general case, although an executable semantics for Z has been explored [20]. It is possible to embed Z within other formal systems. For example, see a shallow embedding of Z in HOL (Higher Order Logic) [16].

Z has good type-checking support, notably the fUZZ type-checker [40] based on the Z Reference Manual [39]. This is based around the LaTeX document preparation system, widely used in academia. There are a number of style files available to allow formatting of the Z symbols and schema structures. These include zed.sty (the original style file), fuzz.sty (designed for use with fUZZ), zed-csp.sty (also including support for CSP [30]), and oz.sty (supporting the object-oriented extension of Z, Object-Z [38]). All these styles are essentially compatible with the core parts of the Z notation. This chapter has been formatted using zed-csp.sty, mainly because it is very comprehensive for the Z glossary in Appendix A.

LaTeX is not widely used in industrial, where Word is much more common. There is a *Z Word Tools* plug-in for Word that allows Z symbols and schemas to be written in Word using an additional menu entry [26]. It also integrates the fUZZ type-check to allow convenient type-checking of Z from within Word. Z has the potential to allow proofs, either at an informal level, or with tool support. Leading Z proof tools include Z/EVES [37] and ProofPower [33]. However, learning to use such a tool effectively requires a significant amount of time and effort, longer than is normally available on an industrial project,

Despite the issues of proof support for Z, a Z specification is still extremely useful for another important part of the development process in industrial-scale projects. It can be used to aid much more effective and comprehensive testing of a software artefact [21,23,31,41], helping to ensure more complete coverage of branches in a program for example. It can even be used to specify testing criteria, which are often defined in a rather loose way, in a more precise manner [44,45].

1.4   Overview of Z Structuring

The Z notation includes mathematics based on logic and set theory (see a glossary in Appendix A) together with the schema box structuring notation. It is the latter than makes Z powerful and useful for very large specifications (potentially consisting of thousands of pages) as well as small specifications, as typically presented by academics for didactic purposes. In this section we present some of the important basic aspects of a Z specification, especially with respect to structuring using schemas.

All Z specifications have the set of integers ($\mathbb{Z}$) included by default as a given set, with the standard arithmetic operators available. Additional given sets (or basic types) may be specified as needed, providing distinct types of sets from which more complex abstract data structures can be constructed. For example, to declare given sets X and Y, the following could be included at the start of a Z specification:

$[X, Y]$

A Z schema has the form of a name (used to reference it later in the specification), a declaration part, and a predicate part that optionally relates components that have been declared in the schema (defaulting to *true* if omitted). For example, the following simple schema T declares an integer n with no constraints on its value:

$$\begin{array}{|l}\hline T \\\hline n : \mathbb{Z} \\\hline\end{array}$$

It is possible to include a schema within another schema. For example, the following schema S includes the declarations and predicates of T. It also declares an additional set x and constrains the value of n to be the size of the set (an "invariant" predicate for the state schema S):

$$\begin{array}{|l}\hline S \\\hline T \\ x : \mathbb{P}X \\\hline n = \#x \\\hline\end{array}$$

Note that $\mathbb{P}$ indicates a power set (the set of all subsets of X in this case). x is drawn from this set (i.e., it is some subset of X, possibly the empty set $\emptyset$, possible the full set X, or somewhere in between). The complete version of S if the included schema T is expanded is as follows:

$$\begin{array}{|l}\hline S\_expanded \\\hline n : \mathbb{Z} \\ x : \mathbb{P}X \\\hline n = \#x \\\hline\end{array}$$

Schemas may be "decorated" with appended subscripts and superscripts. The most normal decoration is the prime (or "dash", $'$), used by convention to indicate the "after state" of an operation schema (with a matching unprimed "before state"). All the components of the schema S' are also renamed with an appended prime (i.e., n' and x' in this simple example). Thus S' expands to:

```
┌─ S'_expanded ─────────────────────────────────────
│  n' : ℤ
│  x' : ℙX
├───────────────────────────────────────────────────
│  n' = #x'
└───────────────────────────────────────────────────
```

In a state-based Z specification, the system is modelled as a series of operations (with related before and after states) that change the state of the system. For the system to start in the first place, there needs to be an initial state that is the system state, but normally together with some initial constraints (specified as predicates). Since this is the state *after* initialisation, it is normally specified in terms of an after state, namely S' in this example:

```
┌─ InitS ───────────────────────────────────────────
│  S'
├───────────────────────────────────────────────────
│  n' = 0
└───────────────────────────────────────────────────
```

The constraint that n' is zero means that the size of x' is also zero and thus x' is empty. The predicate $x' = \emptyset$ could equally well have been used.

For an operation schema in Z, a before state (undecorated) and an after state (decorated with primes) are related together. The most general operation, where the after state may take on any arbitrary value with respect to the before state, can be specified using schema inclusion as follows with the example S state schema:

```
┌─ ChangeOfState ───────────────────────────────────
│  S
│  S'
└───────────────────────────────────────────────────
```

This expands to:

```
┌─ ChangeOfState_expanded ──────────────────────────
│  n, n' : ℤ
│  x, x' : ℙX
├───────────────────────────────────────────────────
│  n = #x
│  n' = #x'
└───────────────────────────────────────────────────
```

Note that predicates on separate lines in a schema are joined with logical conjunction by default.

Most operation schemas in Z will include this general change of state together with further constraining predicates relating the after-state components (here n' and x') with the before-state components (here n and x). Since the *ChangeofState* schema above is likely to be useful in a number of operation schemas in practice and since a real Z specification may specify operations on a number of sub-states that can later be combined into a complete system, there is a convention that a schema named ΔS (in the case of the S schema for example) is automatically available for the specification, with the same meaning as *ChangeOfState* above.

For the specification of operations, typically these may have inputs and outputs as well as the change of state. Inputs and outputs are conventionally indicated with an appended "?" and "!" respectively. So, as an example, consider an operation to add an input element $e?$ to the set x:

$$
\begin{array}{|l}
\underline{\quad AddOp \quad\quad\quad\quad\quad\quad\quad\quad\quad\quad\quad\quad} \\
\Delta S \\
e? : X \\
\hline
e? \notin x \\
x' = x \cup \{e?\} \\
\end{array}
$$

Here there is a "precondition" predicate that $e?$ is not already a member of the set x, There is also a "postcondition" predicate meaning that the set x' is the original set x with the element $e?$ added to it. Note that the value of n' has not been specified explicitly, but implicitly it has a value of the size of the set x' due to the invariant predicate in S'. The full expanded version of *AddOp* is as follows:

$$
\begin{array}{|l}
\underline{\quad AddOp\_expanded \quad\quad\quad\quad\quad\quad\quad\quad\quad\quad} \\
n, n' : \mathbb{Z} \\
x, x' : \mathbb{P}X \\
e? : X \\
\hline
n = \#x \\
e? \notin x \\
n' = \#x' \\
x' = x \cup \{e?\} \\
\end{array}
$$

Sometimes operation schemas do not actually change the state of the system, for example in status operations where part of the state is returned as an output. Z includes a convention similar to the Δ convention, with matching before and after states where the values of the matching before and after components maintain their value. For example in this case:

```
┌─ NoChangeOfState ──────────────────────────────────────
│ ΔS
│ ──────────────────────────
│ n' = n
│ x' = x
└────────────────────────────────────────────────────────
```

Similarly to the Δ convention described earlier, there is a convention that a schema named ΞS (again for example) is automatically available within the specification, having the same meaning as *NoChangeOfState* above. So in the running example, for a status operation that returns, using the output $n!$, the size of the set x (which is always constrained to be the same is n), the following status operation scheme could be specified:

```
┌─ SizeOp ───────────────────────────────────────────────
│ ΞS
│ n! : ℤ
│ ──────────────────────────
│ n! = n
└────────────────────────────────────────────────────────
```

This could be expanded as:

```
┌─ SizeOp_expanded ──────────────────────────────────────
│ n, n' : ℤ
│ x, x' : ℙX
│ n! : ℤ
│ ──────────────────────────
│ n = #x
│ n' = #x'
│ n' = n
│ x' = x
│ n! = n
└────────────────────────────────────────────────────────
```

As can be seen, there is much clutter in the expanded version of the schema that obscures its actual purpose. Thus the use of schema inclusion is a very important part of the structuring techniques used by Z in practice, making the specification much shorter, less repetitive, and more readable.

There are further features for combining schemas, using operators that match the logical operators, but the introduction above should be sufficient for non-experts in Z to follow the example questions and answers in the next section.

2   Whither the Course?

"Teaching to unsuspecting youngsters the effective use of formal methods is one of the joys of life because it is so extremely rewarding."

– Edsger W. Dijkstra (1930–2002)
A. M. Turing Award winner in 1972

There have been many Z courses over the years, since the original one at Oxford University started in the 1980s, initially inspired by Jean-Raymond Abrial (see Fig. 2) and later developed as a course for academic and industry, as well as being presented on the Masters degree course on Computation at the Programming Research Group there. Subsequently many universities incorporated Z into their undergraduate Computer Science degree programmes [35]. and it continues to be used for teaching, especially in software engineering courses, to this day.

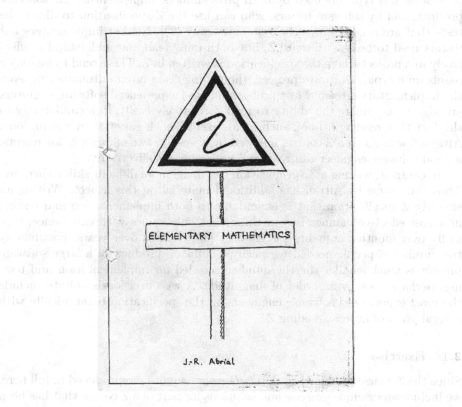

Fig. 2. The front page of the hand-written notes on the Z course during the 1980s at the Programming Research Group, Oxford University. (Drawing by Ib Sørensen, from an idea by Bernard Sufrin.)

In addition to academic courses on Z, industrial courses have also developed for training practitioners in software engineering. On of these was at Praxis (later Altran Praxis and now Altran UK). The course, written in the *troff* document markup language of UNIX, is in use to this day. It has been presented by the author at Altran Praxis in Bath, UK, and more recently in abbreviated form, with some additional material, at the Summer School on Engineering Trustworthy Software Systems (SETSS) held at Southwest University, Chongqing, China, in September 2014. The course is proprietary and copyright by Altran so cannot be published publicly in full. However extracts are including in Appendix B to give a flavour of the material. The course is normally presented intensively over a period of around four days, with lectures together with paper-and-pencil exercises intermingled.

An interesting feature is that the course is actually really two courses, one for "readers" of Z and one for "writers" of Z. In practice, many more engineers must learn to read Z on a particular project and far fewer are needed to write Z. This is because Z is typically used by both programmers, implementing the software product, and by software testers, who can use the Z specification to direct the tests that are needed in a very systematic way [23]. Neither implementers nor testers need to be able to write Z, but both must read and understand Z effectively in a project where the specification is written in Z. These tend to be major teams on a typical software project, the testing team often outnumbering even the implementation team. Most professional and experienced software engineers are able to assimilate the ability to read Z relatively easily, in a similar way to the fact that reading a book such as a novel is much easier than writing one. After a few day's on a Z course, followed by a week or two of using Z documents, a good software engineer can read and understand Z effectively.

In contrast, writing a Z specification is a much more difficult skill to acquire. Thus the course by Altran has additional material on this aspect. Writing an effective Z specification that is amendable to both implementation and testing in a cost effective manner is something that only comes with experience, typically over months, arguably for greatest effectiveness over years. Fortunately the number of people needed to specify a software product on a large software project is much smaller the the numbers needed for implementation and testing, perhaps even by an order of magnitude. A wise decision is only to include the most experienced software engineers on the specification team, ideally with several years of at least reading Z.

2.1   Exercise

Since the Z course produced by Altran/Praxis cannot be reproduced in full here, we include an example exercise and solutions for part of a Z course that has been delivered as a component of the final year of an undergraduate degree programme in Computer Science at Birmingham City University.

We use, as an example, a simplified air traffic control system. The questions are informal in nature and the task is to write Z that formally specifies the informal description in the questions. This emulates the task of a software specifier on a real project, where some informal requirements written in a natural language such as English, perhaps augmented with some diagrams, need to be formalised in a more rigorous and mathematically-based notation such as Z.

One issue of learning a notation like Z is that there are often examples of a completed specification available, but there is very little indication of how to reach that specification [11]. An example has previously been given of a simple invoicing system specified using a number of different notations, including Z [12], where the questions that should be answered as the specification is developed are explicitly stated. Here we first present the questions and then example solutions with an indication of how these can be derived mentally.

2.2   Questions

The following are questions on a simple air traffic control system that need to be answered using Z notation. A comprehensive glossary of the Z notation is available in Appendix A for reference.

Question 1: An air traffic control system involves a number of airspace sectors and a number of planes. Define two given sets to model these.

Question 2: The airspace consists of a number of sectors. Each sector may have a number of adjacent sectors, which are then related to each other. Note that the adjacency relation is symmetric; i.e., if a sector is adjacent to another sector, then the reverse is also true. Sectors cannot be adjacent to themselves (i.e., sectors cannot map to themselves in the adjacency relation). In addition, all sectors in the airspace have adjacent sectors. Define a state schema that models sectors and a relation indicating which sectors are adjacent, with appropriate constraining predicates. Note that id X in Z is a one-to-one function that maps all elements in X to themselves.

Question 3: Each sector may contain a number of planes at any given time. Extend the previous state schema with a function that models planes in sectors. Planes can only be in valid sectors within the airspace.

Question 4: In each sector, some of the planes may be queued to leave the sector, in a sequence of planes. Extend the state schema in Question 3 to include a function that models the queued planes in each sector. Such queues can only be in valid sectors in the airspace. In addition these queues can only include a subset of the planes that are in each sector.

Question 5: There is more than one sector in the airspace. Initially there are no planes in the airspace. Define an initialisation schema that ensures these conditions.

Question 6: Define operations for the following, assuming success in each case, but including preconditions as needed:

1. Have a new plane added to one of the sectors (both specified as inputs), but not in the queue for the sector (e.g., after taking off from an airport or arriving from another airspace).

2. Queue an existing plane (specified as an input) that is not yet in a queue. The plane should be added to the last position of the queue in its sector.
3. Remove the plane at the head of a queue in a specified sector from the airspace (e.g., land at an airport or be transferred to another airspace). Output the plane involved.
4. Have the plane at the head of a queue in a sector move to an adjacent sector. Both sectors should be specified as inputs and the plane should not be included in the queue of the new sector.

Question 7: (optional)

1. Extend your answers in Question 6 to handle errors and provide total operations, with appropriate error messages.
2. Informally describe and formally specify further operations (e.g., changing airspace sectors).

2.3   Answers

Here for each question in the previous subsection we present the thought processes that lead to a solution, together with an example model answer in Z.

Answer 1: In Z, "given sets" (or "basic types") are potentially infinite sets with no implicit structure on which the specification is going to operate. Z is typed so these sets are non-overlapping and are not compatible with standard set operations (e.g., union ∪ or intersection ∩). The question suggests two such sets, which we could name *SECTOR* to model all the possible airspace sectors in the system and *PLANE* for all the possible airplanes in the system. Obviously these are two different types of entity, so comparing them, subsets of them, or elements of them in any way (e.g., with equality =) is not correct and in Z would produce a type error if the specification is mechanically type-checked.

In our simple example, we can define these two given sets in Z at the beginning of a specification as follows:

$$[SECTOR, PLANE]$$

Note that a convention (but not a requirement) in Z is to use all upper case name for given sets. This is not required, but it does make identifying them easier in a specification and is widely used in practice.

Answer 2: Once we have some given sets in Z, we can start to use these to build up more complex structures. Typically we do this with "schema" boxes, that collect together mathematical objects such as sets, relations, functions, sequences, etc. A feature of Z is that all these are modelled as various types of set, so many Z operators can be reused on more specific structures. For example, standard set operators like union and intersection can be used on all these more refined set-based structures if desired. In addition, further more specific operators are available in Z that can be applied only to restricted forms of sets (e.g., relations). Schemas in Z are often used to specify abstract state structures on which operations can perform changes to those structures.

In thisquestion, we require a number of sectors. We can do this by defining a set *sectors* (for example) to be drawn from a set of subsets of *SECTOR* (a "power set" $\mathbb{P}$ *SECTOR*). In the declarations below, ":" is much like that used in many programming languages to declare variables. In Z, it can be considered as meaning "is a member of" a set (written as $\in$ when used in predicates (in the lower half of a schema box) rather than the declaration part (the upper half of the schema box). So $x : X$ can be thought of as $x \in X$. Further, a declaration of the form $x_1 \in \mathbb{P} x_2$ can be considered as meaning $x_1 \subseteq x_2$ (i.e., x_1 is a subset of x_2). So below, *sectors* $\subseteq$ *SECTOR* holds. This is because we wish to model the airspace is a number of sectors, which are a subset of all the possible sectors (the set *SECTOR*).

Another property of airspace is that some sectors are adjacent to each other. I.e., it is possible for airplanes to fly directly between them. We model this as pairs of sectors that are considered to be next to each other. Adjacent sectors have a number of properties that always hold for all configurations of sectors in the airspace. For example, if a sector is adjacent to another sector, then the second sector is also adjacent to the first sector (i.e., it is symmetric, *adjacent*$^{\sim}$ = *adjacent*). Sectors cannot be adjacent to themselves, so the intersection of adjacent sectors and sectors mapped to themselves is empty (*adjacent* $\cap$ id *sectors* = $\emptyset$). All sectors in the airspace have at least one adjacent sector (i.e., the domain of the adjacent sectors is the same as the set of sectors in the airspace, *sectors* = dom *adjacent*). This means that the range of the adjacency relation is also the same as all the sectors in the airspace (*sectors* = ran *adjacent*) since this relation is symmetric. So in all, the following holds:

$$
\begin{array}{|l}
\_\_ \textit{Airspace0} _____ \\
\textit{sectors} : \mathbb{P} \, \textit{SECTOR} \\
\textit{adjacent} : \textit{SECTOR} \leftrightarrow \textit{SECTOR} \\
\hline
\textit{adjacent}^{\sim} = \textit{adjacent} \\
\textit{adjacent} \cap \text{id} \, \textit{sectors} = \emptyset \\
\textit{sectors} = \text{dom} \, \textit{adjacent} \\
\end{array}
$$

Answer 3: All planes in the airspace are in one of the sectors. We can model this as a partial function from airplanes to sectors. (*planes* : *PLANE* $\nrightarrow$ *SECTOR*). The sector for each plane must be one of those that is in the airspace (ran *planes* $\subseteq$ *sectors*). We can augment the state space by adding this information to the existing airspace *Airspace0* (an "included" schema with all the information in that schema too) as follows:

$$
\begin{array}{|l}
\text{\_\_} \textit{Airspace}1 \text{_____} \\
\textit{Airspace}0 \\
\textit{planes} : \textit{PLANE} \nrightarrow \textit{SECTOR} \\
\hline
\text{ran } \textit{planes} \subseteq \textit{sectors}
\end{array}
$$

Answer 4: Within each sector there is a queue of planes (possibly empty) waiting to leave the sector, again modelled as a partial function, this time from sectors to an injective sequence of airplanes ($queues : SECTOR \nrightarrow$ iseq $PLANE$). Being injective meane that the planes in the sequence are all different. Queues of planes waiting to leave each sector. Each sector in the airspace has a (possibly empty) queue associated with it (dom $queues = sectors$). What is more, the planes in the queues within each sector are a subset of the planes in that sector ($\forall s : sectors \bullet \text{ran}(queues\ s) \subseteq planes^\sim$ $(\!|\ \{s\}\ |\!)$). Some planes in the sector may not (yet) be waiting in the queue for that sector. Again we can augment the state space to create our complete abstract state scheme $Airspace$:

$$
\begin{array}{|l}
\text{\_\_} \textit{Airspace} \text{_____} \\
\textit{Airspace}1 \\
\textit{queues} : \textit{SECTOR} \nrightarrow \text{iseq } \textit{PLANE} \\
\hline
\text{dom } \textit{queues} = \textit{sectors} \\
\forall\, s : \textit{sectors} \bullet \text{ran}(\textit{queues } s) \subseteq \textit{planes}^\sim (\!|\ \{s\}\ |\!)
\end{array}
$$

Answer 5: The airspace at initialisation has more than one sector in it ($\#sectors' > 1$) and no planes ($planes' = \emptyset$). Thus the state *after* initialisation, indicated with a postpended prime ($'$) by convention in Z, is as follows:

$$
\begin{array}{|l}
\text{\_\_} \textit{InitAirspace} \text{_____} \\
\textit{Airspace}' \\
\hline
\#\textit{sectors}' > 1 \\
\textit{planes}' = \emptyset
\end{array}
$$

Note that the prime appended with the *Airspace* schema means that all its components (in this case *sectors*, *adjacent*, *planes*, and *queues*) all have primes appended to them as well (i.e., *sectors'*, *planes'*, etc.).

In formulating the state at initialisation, we should consider all the state components. However it is normal for there to be invariant predicates relating some of these components. It is often the case that specifying one state component to be empty implies that one or more other related state components are restricted in some appropriate way, typically to be empty too. For example in this case, because there are no planes in the airspace initially, the queues in each sector (modelled by the *queues* state component) are restricted by the universally quantified predicate in *Airspace* to be empty too since a subset of an empty set can only be the empty set too. Note that nothing specific has been said about the *adjacent* state component apart from the constraints that are already in the predicate part of the *Airspace0* schema since there is no additional predicate involving *adjacent'*.

Answer 6: Below are various operations on the airspace, specified as schemas with a "before state" (with "unprimed" state components) and a matching "after state" (with "primed" state components, postfixed with the prime symbol '). $\Delta Airspace$ indicates both a before state *Airspace* and an after state *Airspace'* where the prime ' filters through to the names of all the components parts of the state in the schema too.

1. A plane entering the airspace can be specified as follows:

$$
\begin{array}{l}
\_\_NewPlane _____ \\
\Delta Airspace \\
\Xi Airspace0 \\
p? : PLANE \\
s? : SECTOR \\
\hline
p? \notin \text{dom } planes \\
planes' = planes \cup \{p? \mapsto s?\} \\
queues' = queues
\end{array}
$$

The $\Xi Airspace0$ is similar to $\Delta Airspace0$ but with all the primed state components in $Airspace0'$ constrained to be the same as the unprimed equivalents in *Airspace0*. In this case, the state components in *Airspace0* are *sectors* and *adjacent*. Inputs to operation schemas (with before and after states) are appended with a question mark (?) by convention to differentiate them from state components. Here there are two inputs, $p?$ for the plane that is entering the airspace and $s?$ for the sector that it enters.

Next the predicates for the schema need to be formulated. First consider the *precondition* for the operation to be valid, only dealing with the before (unprimed) state and inputs. The plane $p?$ must not be one of the planes already in the airspace. It is worth considering especially if there are any limitations on inputs for the operation to be successful. This is very often the case and it is helpful to specify this explicitly even if it is implied indirectly by other predicates. The implementer will find it useful and it will help in testing the implementation later too if the specification is used to direct the tests.

Now consider the *postcondition* for the operation. I.e., how are the after state and outputs related to the before state and inputs? The plane $p?$ is added to the sector $s?$ that it enters. It is not in the queue to leave the sector initially so the queues are unchanged. The rest of the airspace state is also unchanged. It is important to explicitly specify when the after state is the same as the before state in a specification of an operation if this is what is required. Otherwise the after state may take on any value. It is important to go through all the after-state components and outputs in an operation and ensure that they are specified in some way. It is unusual to allow an after state or output to take on any value. This is easy for the implementer, but normally not very useful or desirable for the customer. Similarly, it is normally for all the inputs to be used in some way in the predicate part of the schema and all the outputs to be set in some useful way,

Here $\Xi Airspace0$ ensures that the rest of the otherwise unmentioned state components remain the same after the operation. This is a technique often used in Z to "frame" operations on selected parts of the state of interest in a particular set of operations. It helps in structuring the specification when there are several similar operations where much of the state is unchanged but a particular part is changed in a different way for individual operations. In this case, $\Xi Airspace0$ in the declaration part of the schema acts as a short form for the predicate $sectors' = sectors \wedge adjacent' = adjacent$, which would become repetitive if needed in multiple operations and would also obscure the important predicates in the operations.

2. Queueing a plane to leave a sector can be specified as follows. The plane starts at the back of the queue.

$$
\begin{array}{|l}
\hline \textit{QueuePlane} \\
\Delta Airspace \\
\Xi Airspace1 \\
p? : PLANE \\
\hline
p? \in \mathrm{dom}\ planes \\
\forall s : sectors \bullet p? \notin \mathrm{ran}(queues\ s) \\
queues' = queues \oplus \\
\quad \{planes\ p? \mapsto queues(planes\ p?) \frown \langle p? \rangle\} \\
\hline
\end{array}
$$

In this case, $\Xi Airspace1$ is used to specify the fact that all the state components $sectors$, $adjacent$, and $planes$, remain the same. It is only $queues$ that changes, in fact only one queue in one particular sector. $p?$ is the input plane that is to be queued.

Again, for the predicate part, we consider the precondition first. The plane $p?$ is in the airspace but it is not in any of the queues in all of the sectors in the airspace. In considering the postcondition, only one individual queue is changed. All of the rest of the state remains the same since the sector where the plane is located does not change. The plane $p?$ is added to the end of the queue for the sector in which it is located. The overriding operator ($\oplus$) is one that is commonly used in Z when a small part of a relation, often a function, is to be change to have a different value in the range associated with a particular element in the domain.

The use of $\Xi\,Airspace1$ in the declaration part of the schema above ensures that other state components apart from *queues* remain the same, so only *queues* needs to be considered explicitly for the postcondition.

3. The plane at the head of the waiting queue in a given sector leaves the airspace (e.g., comes in for landing or passes to another airspace).

$$
\begin{array}{l}
\underline{\quad RemovePlane \quad\quad\quad\quad\quad\quad\quad\quad\quad\quad\quad\quad\quad\quad\quad} \\
\Delta Airspace \\
\Xi\,Airspace0 \\
s? : SECTOR \\
p! : PLANE \\
\hline
queues\ s? \neq \langle\rangle \\
p! = head(queues\ s?) \\
planes' = \{p!\} \lhd planes \\
queues' = queues \oplus \{s? \mapsto tail(queues\ s?)\} \\
\end{array}
$$

Here there is an input $s?$ to specify the sector to which the operation applies and an output $p!$ giving the plane at the head of the queue that is leaving the sector. An appended exclamation mark (!) is used to indicate an output by convention in Z.

As a precondition, the queue for the sector $s?$ must be non-empty. This is an important precondition since at least one plane is needed in the queue to allow one to be removed. The plane $p!$ is the one at the head of the queue. It is removed from the overall airspace. It must also be removed from the queue for the specified sector $s?$.

4. The plane at the head of the waiting queue in a given sector moves from that sector to an adjacent sector.

$$
\begin{array}{l}
\underline{\quad MovePlane \quad\quad\quad\quad\quad\quad\quad\quad\quad\quad\quad\quad\quad\quad\quad} \\
\Delta Airspace \\
\Xi\,Airspace0 \\
s1?, s2? : SECTOR \\
\hline
queues\ s1? \neq \langle\rangle \\
s1? \mapsto s2? \in adjacent \\
planes' = planes \oplus \{head(queues\ s1?) \mapsto s2?\} \\
queues' = queues \oplus \{s1? \mapsto tail(queues\ s1?)\} \\
\end{array}
$$

Two sectors are declared as inputs, $s1?$ for the sector where the plane at the head of the queue is to be moved and $s2?$ for an adjacent sector where it is to be moved.

Again, a precondition is that the queue for the sector $s1?$ must be non-empty. Another precondition is that the sector $s2?$ must be immediately adjacent to the sector $s1?$. A postcondition is that the plane is moved from sector $s1?$ to sector $s2?$. It is also removed from the queue in sector $s1?$. Note that it is not added to the queue in sector $s2?$.

Answer 7: (optional)

There are a variety of answers possible for this part. It is designed to be more open-ended for the better students to tackle. Only those aiming for top marks are likely to attempt this question.

2.4   Z Course

The Z course produced by Altran is a commercial course and as such the copyright is owned by the company. Thus some extracts are included as Appendix B of this chapter to give a sample of the style of the course. Full model answers are also available, but these are not reproduced here for obvious reasons.

The following is a timetable for a typical four-day *Z Readers Course*. There are normally four sessions each day, two in the morning and two in the afternoon, with breaks between the sessions. These sessions are typically of 90 min duration. Lectures are interspersed with exercises, normally at the end of sessions.

Day 1
    Session 1: General Introduction
    Session 2: Case Study Introduction
    Session 3: Underlying Mathematics: Sets
    Session 4: Case Study (continued) and Relations

Day 2
    Session 1: Relations (continued)
    Session 2: Functions
    Session 3: Case Study (continued)
    Session 4: Underlying Mathematics: Logic

Day 3
    Session 1: Introduction to Schemas
    Session 2: Case Study Operations
    Session 3: Schema Calculus
    Session 4: Analysing Specifications

Day 4
    Session 1: Schemas as Types
    Session 2: Alternative Case Study
    Session 3: Syndicate Exercise
    Session 4: Syndicate Exercise (continued)

The *Z Writers Course* is longer than the *Z Readers Course*. In particular, more time is allocated to actually writing a Z specification, e.g., as a mini-project in small groups.

3   Conclusion

This chapter has presented the formal specification language Z, including information on an industrial Z course and some example Z questions and answers, with commentary on how to approach developing a formal Z specification from an informal description. A glossary of Z is included in Appendix A and parts of an industrial Z course are included in Appendix B, with some commentary,

Z is now a mature formal specification language with an ISO standard. It is still lacking in good industrial-strength tools but despite this deficiency it has been used in significant industrial projects involving teams of more than a hundred engineers and associated personnel. Research in Z has now slowed but that is an indication of its maturity. It is likely to continue to play an important part of safety and security-related projects when high integrity is essential. It can play an important part in a safety case, especially with respect to its use in improving the efficacy of testing. To paraphrase a well-known quotation by Winston Churchill, reports of Z's death are greatly exaggerated!

Acknowledgements. Material for the Z course was kindly made available by Altran UK (formerly Altran Praxis), a software engineering company based in the United Kingdom with extensive experience of the industrial use of formal methods in general and the Z notation in particular. The extracts of the Z course included in Appendix B are copyright Altran UK and are reproduced here with permission. I am very grateful to Jonathan Hammond of Altran UK for his help and advice in this matter. Thomas Lancaster of Birmingham City University invited me to contribution to a Z course for final year undergraduates. The questions and answers on an example air traffic control system as presented here were originally developed as a result.

The Z notation in the main part of this chapter has been formatted using the LaTeX style file zed-csp.sty and type-checked using the ƒUZZ type-checker [40]. It is believed that the drawing in Fig. 2 is by Ib Holm Sørensen (who died in 2012), from an idea by Bernard Sufrin.

Many thanks to my good colleague, Prof. Zhiming Liu, for inviting me to present at the Summer School on Engineering Trustworthy Software Systems (SETSS) at Southwest University in Chongqing, China, during September 2014, and thank you to all at Southwest University for a very pleasant and well organized visit, together with financial support. I am grateful too for financial support from Museophile Limited.

Finally, very many thanks to the Israel Institute for Advanced Studies at the Hebrew University of Jerusalem, who funded me as a Visiting Scholar for a Computability Research Group during the completion of this chapter and provided a very supportive academic environment in which to do it.

APPENDICES

A   Glossary of Z Notation

A comprehensive glossary of the Z mathematical and schema notation as used in this chapter is included here for easy reference. Earlier versions of this Z glossary have been distributed to students on Z courses delivered by the author and others. These have also been made available online and in published form [9]. The notation is only explained in summary form. For more detailed information on the formal meaning of Z constructs, see [32,39].

Z Glossary

Names

a, b	identifiers
d, e	declarations (e.g., $a : A;\ b, \ldots : B \ldots$)
f, g	functions
m, n	numbers
p, q	predicates
s, t	sequences
x, y	expressions
A, B	sets
C, D	bags
Q, R	relations
S, T	schemas
X	schema text (e.g., $d,\ d \mid p$ or S)

Definitions

$a == x$	Abbreviation definition
$a ::= b \mid \cdots$	Free type definition (or $a ::= b \langle\!\langle x \rangle\!\rangle \mid \ldots$)
$[a]$	Introduction of a given set (or $[a, \ldots]$)
$a\_$	Prefix operator
$\_a$	Postfix operator
$\_a\_$	Infix operator

Logic

$true$	Logical true constant
$false$	Logical false constant
$\neg\, p$	Logical negation
$p \wedge q$	Logical conjunction
$p \vee q$	Logical disjunction
$p \Rightarrow q$	Logical implication ($\neg\, p \vee q$)
$p \Leftrightarrow q$	Logical equivalence ($p \Rightarrow q \wedge q \Rightarrow p$)
$\forall X \bullet q$	Universal quantification
$\exists X \bullet q$	Existential quantification
$\exists_1 X \bullet q$	Unique existential quantification
let $a == x;\ \ldots \bullet p$	Local definition

Sets and expressions

$x = y$	Equality of expressions
$x \neq y$	Inequality ($\neg\, (x = y)$)
$x \in A$	Set membership
$x \notin A$	Non-membership ($\neg\, (x \in A)$)
$\emptyset$	Empty set
$A \subseteq B$	Set inclusion
$A \subset B$	Strict set inclusion ($A \subseteq B \wedge A \neq B$)
$\{x, y, \ldots\}$	Set of elements
$\{X \bullet x\}$	Set comprehension
$\lambda X \bullet x$	Lambda-expression – function
$\mu X \bullet x$	Mu-expression – unique value
let $a == x;\ \ldots \bullet y$	Local definition
if p then x else y	Conditional expression
$(x, y, \ldots)$	Ordered tuple
$A \times B \times \ldots$	Cartesian product
$\mathbb{P}\,A$	Power set (set of subsets)
$\mathbb{P}_1 A$	Non-empty power set
$\mathbb{F}\,A$	Set of finite subsets
$\mathbb{F}_1 A$	Non-empty set of finite subsets
$A \cap B$	Set intersection
$A \cup B$	Set union
$A \setminus B$	Set difference
$\bigcup A$	Generalized union of a set of sets

$\bigcap A$	Generalized intersection of a set of sets	$\mathbb{N}_1$	Set of non-zero natural numbers $(\mathbb{N} \setminus \{0\})$
$first\ x$	First element of an ordered pair	$m + n$	Addition
$second\ x$	Second element of an ordered pair	$m - n$	Subtraction
		$m * n$	Multiplication
$\#A$	Size of a finite set	$m\ \mathrm{div}\ n$	Division
		$m\ \mathrm{mod}\ n$	Modulo arithmetic
		$m \leq n$	Less than or equal
		$m < n$	Less than
		$m \geq n$	Greater than or equal

Relations

$A \leftrightarrow B$	Relation $(\mathbb{P}(A \times B))$
$a \mapsto b$	Maplet $((a, b))$
$\mathrm{dom}\ R$	Domain of a relation
$\mathrm{ran}\ R$	Range of a relation
$\mathrm{id}\ A$	Identity relation
$Q \mathbin{{}_9^8} R$	Forward relational composition
$Q \circ R$	Backward relational composition $(R \mathbin{{}_9^8} Q)$
$A \lhd R$	Domain restriction
$A \ntriangleleft R$	Domain anti-restriction
$R \rhd A$	Range restriction
$R \ntriangleright A$	Range anti-restriction
$R(\!| A |\!)$	Relational image
$iter\ n\ R$	Relation composed n times
R^n	Same as $iter\ n\ R$
$R^\sim$	Inverse of relation (R^{-1})
R^*	Reflexive-transitive closure
R^+	Irreflexive-transitive closure
$Q \oplus R$	Relational overriding $((\mathrm{dom}\ R \lhd Q) \cup R)$
$a\ \underline{R}\ b$	Infix relation

Functions

$A \nrightarrow B$	Partial functions
$A \rightarrow B$	Total functions
$A \nrightarrowtail B$	Partial injections
$A \rightarrowtail B$	Total injections
$A \ntwoheadrightarrow B$	Partial surjections
$A \twoheadrightarrow B$	Total surjections
$A \twoheadrightarrowtail B$	Bijective functions
$A \nrightarrow\!\!\!\!\to B$	Finite partial functions
$A \nrightarrowtail\!\!\!\to B$	Finite partial injections
$f\ x$	Function application (or $f(x)$)

Numbers

$\mathbb{Z}$	Set of integers
$\mathbb{N}$	Set of natural numbers $\{0, 1, 2, \ldots\}$

$m > n$	Greater than
$succ\ n$	Successor function $\{0 \mapsto 1, 1 \mapsto 2, \ldots\}$
$m \mathinner{.\,.} n$	Number range
$min\ A$	Minimum of a set of numbers
$max\ A$	Maximum of a set of numbers

Sequences

$\mathrm{seq}\ A$	Set of finite sequences
$\mathrm{seq}_1 A$	Set of non-empty finite sequences
$\mathrm{iseq}\ A$	Set of finite injective sequences
$\langle\rangle$	Empty sequence
$\langle x, y, \ldots\rangle$	Sequence $\{1 \mapsto x, 2 \mapsto y, \ldots\}$
$s \frown t$	Sequence concatenation
$\frown/s$	Distributed sequence concatenation
$head\ s$	First element of sequence $(s(1))$
$tail\ s$	All but the head element of a sequence
$last\ s$	Last element of sequence $(s(\#s))$
$front\ s$	All but the last element of a sequence
$rev\ s$	Reverse a sequence
$squash\ f$	Compact a function to a sequence
$A \upharpoonright s$	Sequence extraction $(squash(A \lhd s))$
$s \upharpoonright A$	Sequence filtering $(squash(s \rhd A))$
$s\ t$	Sequence prefix relation $(s \frown v = t)$
$s\ t$	Sequence suffix relation $(u \frown s = t)$

s in t — Sequence segment relation $(u \frown s \frown v = t)$

disjoint A — Disjointness of an indexed family of sets

A partition B — Partition an indexed family of sets

Bags

bag A — Set of bags or multisets $(A \nrightarrow \mathbb{N}_1)$

$[\![\,]\!]$ — Empty bag

$[\![x, y, \ldots]\!]$ — Bag $\{x \mapsto 1, y \mapsto 1, \ldots\}$

$count\ C\ x$ — Multiplicity of an element in a bag

$C \sharp x$ — Same as $count\ C\ x$

$n \otimes C$ — Bag scaling of multiplicity

x in C — Bag membership

$C \sqsubseteq D$ — Sub-bag relation

$C \uplus D$ — Bag union

$C \uplus D$ — Bag difference

$items\ s$ — Bag of elements in a sequence

Schema notation

Vertical schema.

$$\begin{array}{|l}\hline S \underline{} \\ d \\ \hline p \\ \hline \end{array}$$

New lines denote ' ; ' and '∧'. The schema name and predicate part are optional. The schema may subsequently be referenced by name in the document.

Axiomatic description.

$$\begin{array}{|l}\hline d \\ \hline p \\ \hline \end{array}$$

The definitions may be non-unique. The predicate part is optional. The definitions subsequently apply globally in the document.

Generic constant.

$$\begin{array}{|l}\hline [a] \underline{} \\ d \\ \hline p \\ \hline \end{array}$$

The generic parameters are optional. The definitions must be unique. The definitions subsequently apply globally in the document.

$$\begin{array}{|l}\hline S[a] \underline{} \\ d \\ \hline p \\ \hline \end{array}$$

Generic schema.

Generic version of schema definition.

$S \mathrel{\widehat{=}} [X]$ — Horizontal schema

$[T; \ldots \mid \ldots]$ — Schema inclusion

$z.a$ — Component selection (given $z : S$)

θS — Tuple of components

$\neg\, S$ — Schema negation

pre S — Schema precondition

$S \wedge T$ — Schema conjunction

$S \vee T$ — Schema disjunction

$S \Rightarrow T$ — Schema implication

$S \Leftrightarrow T$ — Schema equivalence

$S \setminus (a, \ldots)$ — Hiding of component(s)

$S \upharpoonright T$ — Projection of components

$S \fatsemi T$ — Schema composition (S then T)

$S \gg T$ — Schema piping (S outputs to T inputs)

$S[a/b, \ldots]$ — Schema component renaming (b becomes a, etc.)

$\forall X \bullet S$ — Schema universal quantification

$\exists X \bullet S$ — Schema existential quantification

$\exists_1 X \bullet S$ — Schema unique existential quantification

Conventions

$a?$ — Input to an operation

$a!$ — Output from an operation

a — State component before an operation

a' — State component after an operation

S — State schema before an operation

S' — State schema after an operation

ΔS — Change of state (normally $S \wedge S'$)

ΞS — No change of state (normally $[\Delta S \mid \theta S = \theta S']$)

B   Altran Z Course Description and Extracts

Here an overview of the material is given, together with sample pages from the Altran Z Course, which are reproduced with permission as examples of the style of the course material. The examples are intersperse with some commentary on the various parts of the course. Note that all the material reproduced from the Z course itself in this Appendix is Copyright © Altran. The sample pages are designed to give a feel for the style of the course. For the full Z course and its delivery, contact Altran UK.

Altran has two overlapping Z courses for Z "readers" and a longer course for Z "writers". The extracts included here are from the more widely delivered *Z Readers Course*. Introductory slides on questions such as what is a specification, what is a formal specification, what is a Z specification, and what is taught during the main part of the material are presented at the start of the course.

The course starts with a gentle introduction to specifications in general, followed by formal and Z specifications in particular. In summary, a specification covers *what* a system does as opposed to *how* it does it. The specification documentation provides an interface between the specification team and the implementation team. A "black-box" specification concentrates on the external behaviour, as visible from outside the system. A specification must cover how the system affects its environment. Of course, the specification can only cover the immediate environment relevant to and controlled by the system.

The system being specified needs a model of the environment. This system can use information within the model and also change the model's state. This model is an abstract view of the actual world environment. It is an engineering judgement to decide what model is reasonable and appropriate for a given system. It should include all the relevant features of the real world in a simplified manner, but not so simple that pertinent information is not included in the model.

A formal specification is based on mathematics. This is useful because of various properties of mathematics, such as the ability to abstract, its power to specify in a simple and universal way with the soundness that mathematics can provide, enabling formal reasoning for example. One widely used approach is "model-based" specification. Formal notations and methods appropriate for a model-based approach include ASM, B, VDM, Z, etc. [17]. This type of approach includes a mathematical model of the state associated with the system and operations that change the state of that system. This in operation, there is an initial state, followed by the first operation, a modified state after that operation, another possibly different operation, yet another modified state, and so on.

Such a specification covers functional attributes of the systems behaviour. Non-functional aspects such as availability of the system, performance, reliability, usability, size aspects, etc., are normally covered in alternative ways. More implementation-oriented aspects such as features like concurrency and real-time issues, may not be covered by all formal notations in a convenient manner. This is certainly true of the Z notation, which is a general purpose specification language. A formal specification does not normally cover design aspects of the system. In fact, it is quite possible to produce a specification that cannot be implemented in practice (by introducing *false* into the specification, typically through some incompatible logic, e.g., $P \wedge \neg P$), obviously something to avoid in a real engineering situation.

The Z notation is normally used in a model-based style, although this is by convention and for convenience rather than being a built-in aspect of the notation. A Z specification includes mathematics (logic and set theory), a structuring approach (using the schema box notation), some conventions for the model-based aspects, and accompanying interleaved natural language text (typically English). Typically the informal description is of a similar length to the formal specification, providing an aid to the understanding of the mathematics and emphasising the connection with the real world.

The mathematics employed by Z is relatively simple, being based on first-order predicate logic and set theory. The sets in Z are strongly typed with basic sets (also known as given types) and simple constructors. More complex sets can be created, such as relations (normally sets of pairs), functions (relations where at most one element in the range is associated with each element in the domain) and sequences (modelled as finite functions mapping a contiguous set of natural numbers from one upwards to the elements in the sequence). All of these are thus modelled as sets in Z. Many Z operators can be applied across these different set structures.

Both infinite and finite sets may be specified in Z, although practical implementations of the specification will be finite of course. The Z notation has a relatively few number of constructs that are fundamental to the language. There is a library (a "toolkit" [39]) of generally useful notation that is formally defined in Z. Additional constructs can be formally defined for a particular specification in a similar way if desired.

The mathematical notation of Z alone would be adequate for a very small specification but a structuring technique is needed for a specification of any size. Z has such a mechanism in the form of schemas, which use a box-like visual notation to encapsulate the mathematical description. Schema boxes have names and can thus be referenced later in the specification. Common fragments of specification can be formulated and explained once, then used through reference to their schema name subsequently. This allows partial specifications to be formulated and then combined by including schemas within other schemas and also using a calculus of schema operators that match the logical operators in Z. Conjunction for building up specifications and disjunction for dealing with error cases are the most useful operators in practice.

There are a number of conventions in Z that make both writing and reading Z easier once they are understood. These conventions are used in the naming of both variable components and schemas. They aid in the concise specification of operations with state changes and also the identification of inputs and outputs for such operations.

B.1   Approach Sequencing Case Study

The Altran Z course includes an extended case study for approach sequencing of aircraft for an airport. This is gradually developed with features to introduce aspects of the Z notation in a measured manner. Initially sets and their associated operators are introduced.

First the informal requirements are presented, using an English description covering messages that can be sent and simple diagrams, such as a system context diagram to aid in analysing the requirements and an entity-relationship diagram to help in modelling the world under consideration. Next the operations that the system must perform are considered. Once a list of operations has been formulated, it is possible consider a formal specification of the system in terms of an abstract state and operations on that state. Each operation has inputs, a starting state, a finishing state, and outputs.

To formulate any specification in Z, sets are needed, so the course first introduces the simplest form of sets available, with no internal structure. Venn diagrams are used to introduce the standard set operators of union ($\cup$), intersection ($\cap$), set difference ($\setminus$). The concept of the size of a set using the "#" operator is also introduced. In Z, the set of integers ($\mathbb{Z}$) is assumed to exist for all specifications. Additional basic sets can also be introduced (e.g., $[X]$ to introduce a set called X). More complex sets can be constructed using sets of sets ($\mathbb{P}$ for infinite sets, $\mathbb{F}$ for finite sets, and $\mathbb{F}_1$ for finite sets with the empty set excluded), sets of pairs (using $\times$), and also schemas for more complex internal structure where needed. Sets can contain sets themselves, and so on in a nested manner if desired.

Using simple sets, a system state is specified, with a specific initial state for the system when it starts. Operations with before and after states, as well as inputs, are also defined. The conventions for schema operations are introduced informally (e.g., Δ for change of state schemas, ' appended for after-state components, and ? appended for inputs).

Altran   Z Course   Reference N056.111.140
                Lecture notes for Approach Sequencing Case Study   Issue 1.6
                                                        Page 3

1   INTRODUCTION

This case study is intended to show how and why to write a specification in Z. It is not a real example but it is, very loosely, based on a real system that was formally specified and developed. The structure of the study follows an alternating pattern: an aspect of Z is introduced, and then used to specify part of the system. An important aim is to show some of the benefits of writing a formal specification, in particular:

1. The modelling power of Z allows a more expressive description of the system state.

2. The ability to define operations allows the behaviour of the system to be specified, as well as its static structure.

3. The formality of Z helps to detect and eliminate ambiguities and inconsistencies in the informal statement of requirements.

4. The ability to reason about the specification allows the discovery of unexpected behaviour and assurance that the specification has the properties that are expected.

Chapter 2 is an informal statement of the problem, and an introductory analysis using a structured method. Chapter 3 introduces the overall structure of the Z specification. The specification is then built up incrementally. Chapter 4 introduces the *sets* and shows how they can be used to build a simple model of parts the system. Chapter 5 introduces *relations* and *functions* and uses them to represent properties of the objects in the model. Chapter 6 describes a special kind of function, the *sequence* and completes the framework of the specification. Chapter 7 describes the logical language that is used within Z and shows how it is used to write unambiguous specifications and to express and think about conjectures regarding the proper behaviour of the system. Chapter 8 shows how the formal nature of the specification can be used to reason about its correctness and completeness, leading to the early identification of errors and to a high level of assurance in the reasonableness of the final specification.

Although all the notation used in the specification is introduced and described, it is not expected that the reader will immediately learn all the notation presented, nor follow the details of all the reasoning. However, it is hoped that enough detail is given to make the steps of specification and analysis plausible. To help the reader, a summary of all the notation used is included as an appendix.

B.2   Relations and Functions

Sets are the most basic form of structuring abstract data in Z. For more structure where pairs of elements are associated with each other, relations are available, with further specific operators available for handling them. Elements in the domain and range of a relation may be related in arbitrary ways (i.e., a many-to-many mapping). Functions are a special sort of relation in Z where elements in the domain map to at most one element in the range (i.e., a many-to-one mapping). This allows standard function application for example in the form $f(x)$ (or even just $f\,x$ in Z), where f is a function and x is an element in the function's domain. Care must be take if f is a partial function (i.e., the entire domain is not necessarily mapped) to ensure that x is in the domain of f (formally, $x \in \operatorname{dom} f$). Otherwise $f(x)$ will be undefined, resulting in an arbitrary value in the two-state (*true/false*) logic of Z.

Pairs of elements using the Cartesian product operator ($\times$), together with the "maplet" notation ($\mapsto$) are introduced. Relations ($\leftrightarrow$) are explained using simple diagrams with a domain("dom"), range ("ran"), and mappings between elements in the domain and range. Additional operators that only apply to relations are introduced, such as domain restriction, $\lhd$), domain subtraction (or anti-restriction ($\lhd\!\!\!-$), range restriction ($\rhd$), and range subtraction (or anti-restriction, $\rhd\!\!\!-$), are covered. These operators are not so common in standard set theory, but have been found to be useful for manipulating relations in practical Z specifications so are included as part of the standard language. The use of infix relational operators (such as $\in$ and $\subset$) in Z is explained.

Next functions, a special sort of relation in Z, are covered, including function application (e.g., $f(x)$). Relational overriding ($\oplus$), often used with functions, is also explained. This operator is another more unusual feature of Z, but is very useful in cases where a function needs a part of it modifying in some way.

With some basic aspects of relations and functions covered, the course material continues with the case study, adding a state component that uses a partial function ($\rightharpoonup$), using schema inclusion, which is also explained. The concept of a state invariant (a predicate in a state schema that applies to all possible states in the system), is introduced. The initial state and operations schemas previously defined using sets are augmented with the newly defined partial state schema using schema inclusion, together with additional inputs and predicates as needed.

130   J.P. Bowen

5   RELATIONS AND FUNCTIONS

5.1   Introduction

So far we have considered sets whose members have no internal structure, unless they are themselves sets. This allows us to model sets of entities such as flights, but it does not help to relate things together. We can't talk about the attributes of a flight such as its ETA or the relationship between an approach sequence and the flights in it. To do this we need a new way of building sets, by making them out of *pairs* of objects. For example we could make a set whose members were *(flight, eta)* pairs. In Z such sets are called *relations*. A *function* in Z is just a special kind of relation.

5.1.1   Pairs and Cartesian Product Operator

To declare a variable which represents the single pair of a flight with its ETA, we need the set which contains all possible pairs of flights with ETA. This is the *Cartesian product* of FLIGHT with $\mathbb{N}$ and is written

FLIGHT $\times \mathbb{N}$

So if we declare

flightEta : FLIGHT $\times \mathbb{N}$

then *flightEta* can take a value like

BAW001 $\mapsto$ 1005

(where $\mapsto$ is a Z symbol used to represent a pair)

$X \times Y$ is pronounced "Cartesian product of X with Y" or "set of pairs from X and Y"

For example,

$\{a, b\} \times \{c, d\} = \{a \mapsto c, a \mapsto d, b \mapsto c, b \mapsto d\}$

5.1.2   What a relation is

A relation is a new set composed of pairs of elements from two other sets.

A relation R between two sets X and Y is made up of elements of the form

$x \mapsto y$

where

$x \in X$ and $y \in Y$

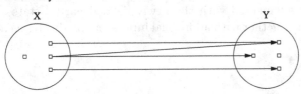

A binary relation R can be thought of as a many-many mapping, relating elements of one set to

Approach Sequencing

B.3   Sequences

Sequences in Z are modelled as a special sort of function where the domain consists of natural numbers from one up to the size (length) of the sequence. Further operators are available specifically for sequences, notably concatenation of two sequences to form a new sequence.

The sequence notation of Z ("seq" and "$\langle \ldots \rangle$") is introduced and an example is presented. Injective sequences ("iseq"), in which all the elements of the sequence are different, are also covered. Sequences can be concatenated ($\frown$). It is also possible to select from (or filter) a sequence using a set of elements that may be in the sequence ($\upharpoonright$), resulting in a new sequence with potentially fewer elements in it.

The state for the case study example is augmented with an injective sequence, related to an existing state component with an invariant predicate.

There are a significant number of further operators for use with sequences in Z, as listed in Appendix A. Perhaps the most useful are the functions *head* for returning the first element in a non-empty sequence, *tail* for returning all except the head of a sequence as a new sequence, *last* for returning the last element in a non-empty sequence, and *front* for returning all but the last element of a sequence as a new sequence. In addition, *rev* can be used to reverse any sequence, even the empty sequence.

A further but less-used feature of Z is a "bag" (also known as a multiset), which is like a set but used where multiple copies of the same element are needed. This is modelled in Z as a partial function from the type of the elements in the bag (e.g., X), to strictly positive natural numbers ($\mathbb{N}_1$, i.e., all natural numbers except zero), indicating the number of elements in the bag. If this number as always one, the bag would act like a normal set. There are various built-in operators in Z for handling bags, as listed in Appendix A. Some of these have counterparts with operators on standard sets, such as bag membership, the sub-bag relation, bag union, and bag difference, but need different definitions to handle the multiplicity of elements appropriately.

Most of the operators used in Z are defined formally within Z using generic definitions, as part of a mathematical "toolkit" [39]. It is often the case for large specifications that some additional operators will also be specified in this way, to enable a shorter and more understandable specification overall. Some could be deemed generally useful and form the basis for an augmented toolkit at an organisation that produces many Z specifications.

6   SEQUENCES

Now all the information about flights had been modelled, it was time to look at the approach sequence itself. When he tried to model this, John immediately got stuck. He could model it just like the entity relationship model, of course, by introducing a type [APPROACH_SEQUENCE]. And he could talk about what flights were related to the approach sequence by having a partial function from FLIGHT to APPROACH_SEQUENCE. But he felt sure there was more to it than this. For example, he thought he ought to be able to model the *order* of flights in the sequence. The Z construct needed for this is the *sequence*.

6.1   The Z Model of Sequences

A sequence is an ordered collection of objects. The items in a sequence are numbered from 1 to n.

In Z, a sequence of FLIGHTs is just a function from the natural numbers to FLIGHT, where the domain of the function is the numbers from 1 to the length of the sequence.

You can write

sas : seq FLIGHT

which is like writing

sas : $\mathbb{N} \nrightarrow$ FLIGHT

with the extra constraint on the domain of the function.

6.1.1   Notation

There is a special notation provided as a convenient way to write sequences.
Angle brackets are used to display sequences:

<a,b,c>

is a sequence of three items numbered 1 to 3

which could equally be displayed without sequence notation as

$\{1 \mapsto a, 2 \mapsto b, 3 \mapsto c\}$

The empty sequence is written <>.

A simple book with one chapter might have the following contents:

<   preface,
        introduction,
        contents,
        chapter,
        index   >

B.4   Logic

As well as sets in Z, first order predicate logic is also used as the main form of detailed specification, with standard logical operators on predicates. Note that the logic of Z is two-valued, with only *true* or *false* possible. There is no "undefined" logical value, unlike some other logics. If any expressions are undefined in a predicate, Z handles this by allowing the predicate to take either a *true* or *false* value. This is normally something that is not desirable in real specifications, so it is avoided in practice through careful formulation of the specification, with appropriate error handling where needed.

The course initially introduces propositional logic in which statements are *true* or *false*. The standard logical connectives of negation ("not", $\neg$), conjunction ("and", $\wedge$), disjunction (inclusive "or", $\vee$), implication ("implies", $\Rightarrow$), and equivalence ("equivalent", $\Leftrightarrow$) are introduced using truth tables. The binding powers (strongest binding first in the list above) and use of brackets to override this if needed are explained. An example of a truth table for a more complex expression is also presented.

Next predicate logic is covered, in which variables are also included. In Z, variable components are typed, so predicates and expressions in them must respect this typing. Existential quantification ($\exists$), universal quantification ($\forall$), and the nesting of quantifications are introduced. All quantified variables in Z must be declared with a type when introduced since Z is a typed language. Selective quantification is explained, in which a predicate is included after the declaration part (separated by "|") to restrict the quantified variables further before the main predicate of the quantification (separated by "•") is stated.

Next, set comprehension (of the form $\{\ldots \mid \ldots \bullet \ldots\}$) is explained, with a number of examples. This has a similar form to quantification in Z. Set comprehension can always be used to define a set in Z if there is no other more convenient way to do it.

The case study is then used to demonstrate an axiomatic description that introduces a global constant to the specification, a typical use of this construct. Then a concept of time is introduced to the state, using a natural number that increases as time progresses. Next an illustration of how a quantified predicate may be determined and added as an invariant for the state is explained, as several possible candidate invariants. An operation to model time passing is presented, including a change of state to the system that may occur as time passes. This is an operation that the user cannot directly control, but will be interleaved with other user operations.

The schema operations are augmented to handle the additional state now being modelled in the system. The complete state, and initial state, and final versions of the operations are presented.

7   LOGIC

In Z, properties of a system are described in the language of logic.

In fact, John has already been using some of this language. Everything that appears below the line in a schema is in fact a collection of logical statements called predicates. So far he has used only simple predicates like

$$eta' = eta \oplus \{flight? \mapsto newEta?\}$$

or

$$ran\ sas \subseteq flights$$

However, to express the rules about the SAS he will have to use more complex logical expressions.

7.1   Propositional Logic

A proposition is a statement which is either True or False.

$$1 + 1 = 2$$

$$1 \in \{0, 1, 2\}$$

$$2 + 2 = 5$$

elephants are mammals

Many sentences are *not* propositions:

Are you happy?

Go away

Add 2 to 4

B.5   Analysing the Specification

Once a specification has been formulated, it is possible to reason about it. This may be informally in the head of the engineer or more formally. The former if most typical in industrial use of Z. The Altran Z course illustrates some of the thought processes and the techniques that are helpful in such reasoning.

Proofs associated with a specification can check a number of properties. Firstly an initial state must exist for the system to be able to start at all. Then preconditions of operations can be checked. If they are not *true*, it is normal to add schemas to cover the error conditions (the negation of the precondition for the successful operation) so a complete "total" operation can be produced that has an overall precondition of *true* and typically an output that indicates if an error occurred. Any invariant predicates are consistently applied to the state are all times. If these or other predicates reduce to *false*, operations may not be implementable.

Finally, challenge theorems demonstrating desirable properties are beneficial when checking a specification. If true, they increase confidence in the specification since our understanding is compatible with the mathematical description. If false, it indicates a possible misunderstanding and may necessitate a change in the specification. Even with all these checks, the specification may still not be "correct" with respect to informal notions of what the system should do. For that, engineering judgement, expertise, and experience is needed.

The course material provides examples of checking these issues using the case study specification. It also includes its own summary of the Z notation.

Altran   Z Course   Reference N056.111.140
                  Lecture notes for Approach Sequencing Case Study   Issue 1.6
                                                                      Page 43

8   ANALYSING THE SPECIFICATION

One of the benefits of a formal notation is that we can actually prove that a specification has the properties we expect. If we are using a notation formally, rather than just to develop ideas, then we have certain proof obligations. If we discharge these obligations by proving the required theorems then we guarantee at least some desirable properties of our specification.

8.1   Proofs in Specification

Proof obligations occur in the following areas:

- consistency of state invariants;
- existence of initial state;
- preconditions of state operations;
- totality of state operations;
- demonstration of desired properties.

The first four types of proof obligation guarantee that the specification of our system is not nonsense. If the state invariant is inconsistent, the set of states of the model is the empty set (ie there's no state which can satisfy the state invariant) and this is not a useful specification. Given that the initial state exists, we must then show that each operation on a legal state can produce a legal finishing state.

If all these proof obligations are met, the model is a sensible one. This doesn't necessarily imply that the model encapsulates the *required* behaviour; it merely means that the model is sufficiently well-constructed to exhibit *some* behaviour!

The ultimate user of the system being specified may be concerned about issues such as safety or security. A specification of a large complex system may not demonstrate the desired properties in an obvious manner and it may thus be necessary to derive proofs of such properties from the specification. Note that these proofs are not really proof obligations insofar that such proofs do not give us any more reassurance that the model is sensible; however they do reassure us that general requirements of interest are satisfied by the specification.

B.6   Exercises

On the following page is part of a sample exercise from the Altran Z course. Matching model answers are also available for both presentation by the course teacher once the exercises have been attempted by students and also distribution to the students after that have tackled the questions.

Exercises cover sets, relations, functions, propositional logic, and predicate logic. The exercise on sets includes questions on the understanding of enumerated sets, the use of set operators in expressions, predicates involving sets, and the selection of given sets for a specification. The exercise on relations covers the understanding of notation relevant to relations, expressions using relations, and the understanding of a small specification involving a relation. The exercise on functions includes questions on the difference between a relation and a function, followed by the understanding of a small specification involving a number of functions.

The exercise on logic has questions on propositional logic and predicate logic. Propositional logic questions include determining the truth value of propositions, choosing a value to make propositions true, explicitly adding brackets to complex logical statements, and producing truth tables for logical statements. Questions on predicate logic cover rewriting logical statements using quantifiers, determining if quantified predicates are true or false, and expressing informal sentences as formal quantified predicates.

1   RELATIONS: EXERCISES

1. What set is denoted by the set-product $X \times Y$?

2. Explain how $X \times Y$ and $X \leftrightarrow Y$ are related.

3.

    a. Describe, in your own words, what is meant by:
        [PERSON]
        PERSON $\leftrightarrow$ PERSON
        IsParentOf : PERSON $\leftrightarrow$ PERSON

    Assume the definition of IsParentOf in the following questions.

    b. On the assumption that the following are all names of people, which of the
        following could be members of IsParentOf?

        i.   Anne $\leftrightarrow$ Mary

        ii. Anne $\mapsto$ Mary

        iii. John $\times$ Jenny

        iv. Mary

        v.   John $\rightarrowtail$ David

        vi. John $\mapsto$ Mary

4. Imagine you are designing a new hospital. One task of the designer is to decide how to
    juxtapose various facilities so that the smoothest running of the hospital may result. It is
    not sensible to place certain facilities adjacent to certain others.

    The hospital specification includes the given set [FACILITY] and the relation

    CannotJuxtapose : FACILITY $\leftrightarrow$ FACILITY which models the property "cannot be
    adjacent".

    A particular aspect of a design deals with those facilities that are actually adjacent to one
    another, that is, models facilities that the architect has placed adjacent to one another in
    his or her design. Suppose there is a relation called "design" modelling the facilities in
    the architect's design that are actually next to one another:

    design : FACILITY $\leftrightarrow$ FACILITY

    Given this definition of the relation "design" say what is meant by the following
    expressions.

    a.   design $\cap$ CannotJuxtapose = { }

    b.   CannotJuxtapose \ design = CannotJuxtapose

B.7   Introduction to Schemas

This part of the Z course covers the schema as a structuring concept, schemas in use as abstract state, schema inclusion enabling the building up of a specification, and schemas as operations involving relating a before state with an after state.

First the idea of schemas is introduced informally. A schema box has a name, a declaration part, and a predicate part (which may be omitted if the predicate is *true*):

```
┌─ Name ──────────────────────────────────────────────────────
│  Declaration part...
│ ─────────────────
│  Predicate part...
└─────────────────────────────────────────────────────────────
```

Some examples of schemas are explained, based around the well-known "Birthday Book" example in Z [39]. A schema can specify the abstract state of a system and this is explained in terms of the state components and invariant predicates that can constrain those components, normally by relating them together in some way.

Generic schemas are also introduced briefly, although these are less used within Z in practice. Next the important concept of schema inclusion is covered, explaining how declarations are merged (especially if component names match) and how predicates are conjoined.

As well as being used for specifying state, schemas can also be used to specify operations, with both a before state and a matching after state (in which the components are decorated with primes, $'$). In fact schemas can be decorated with arbitrary subscripts and superscripts if desired, but the use of primes for decoration is but far the most common style of decoration with Z schemas in typical specifications.

An example of schema inclusion is given, including the expansion of the overall schema to include all the constituent state components. It is important to be able to do this mentally when using Z, so an understanding of schema inclusion is critical when reading most Z specifications. The technique is a key part of Z and may be used to specialise an existing partial specification for a particular specification, potentially multiple times even in a single overall specification.

As well as specifying abstract state, an important use of Z schemas in practice is to specify a change of state (with before and after states), in which typically some state components change their values and others remain the same. The standard naming convention for state components in an operation schema is that undecorated state components are in the before state, matching primed (or "dashed") components ($'$) are in the after state, inputs have a "?" appended, and outputs have a "!" appended to their names. These conventions are extremely common in Z specifications in the standard model-based style. Subscripts and superscripts can also be used for decoration if desired for a special purpose, although this is less common in practice.

An operation schema will typically have a number of predicates conjoined together (often implicitly on separate lines). Normally preconditions are included first and postconditions afterwards, but the order is logically immaterial since logical conjunction ($\land$) is commutative and conjunction is assumed between lines of predicates by default if no other logical operator is included since it is the most common connective for predicates in Z specification in practice.

Preconditions are constraining predicates that only involve before-state unprimed components and inputs. Postconditions also include after-state primed components and outputs. It is normally very important to check that all after-state components and outputs are constrained in some way since it is unusual for these to be allowed to take on any value after an operation has been performed.

Often an after-state component is constrained deterministically in terms of a function involving the matching before-state component (e.g., $x' = \ldots x \ldots$). If no change of state is required, this must be explicitly specified (e.g., $x' = x$), although often it is possible to do this conveniently using the Ξ convention with included schemas that adds this constraint for all the components in the relevant schema.

It should be noted that it is possible to include hidden preconditions in what appear to be postconditions. For example, $x' \in xs$ implicitly assumes that $xs \neq \emptyset$ (i.e., xs is not an empty set), which is thus a precondition if this is included in an operation. Thus, formally the precondition in a schema should be calculated (by existentially quantifying all the after-state components and outputs), although in practice this can often just be done mentally.

The important Δ and Ξ conventions for state schemas are covered. Δ may be prefixed to a state schema name to produce a schema with a before state and matching primed after state. Ξ is similar, but adds the constraint that all the after-state components have the same value as the matching before-state components (e.g., $x' = x$, etc.).

There are associated exercises with questions on schemas, together with model answers. Aspects of schemas covered include understanding of the purpose of schemas, their constituent parts, and conventions associated with schemas. Example state and operations schemas are provided and questions explore their meaning and use. Finally, a more advanced question covers the use of a generic schema. These are less used in simple Z specifications, but can be more useful in larger specifications, as found in industrial-scale examples.

Altran   Z Course   Reference N056.111.35
                 Introduction to Schemas: Lecture Notes   Issue 3.6
                                                               Page 5

2.5   Writing Schemas

A schema can be written in one of two forms:

BirthdayBook
$$\begin{array}{|l}
\hline
known : \mathbb{P}\ NAME \\
birthday : NAME \nrightarrow DATE \\
\hline
known = dom\ birthday \\
\hline
\end{array}$$

or

$BirthdayBook \triangleq$
          $[known : \mathbb{P}\ NAME;$
          $birthday : NAME \nrightarrow DATE\ |$
          $known = dom\ birthday]$

The types used in the declaration part must be declared somewhere above the schema.

The predicates in the predicate part constrain the values which the declared variables may take.

Here is a specific example of a birthday book which satisfies the constraints imposed by the schema:

$known = \{Joe, Mary, Dennis\}$

$birthday = \{Joe \mapsto Apr27, Mary \mapsto Jan16, Dennis \mapsto Aug07\}$

© Altran 2013   INTRODUCTION TO SCHEMAS

B.8   Schema Calculus

There are matching logical operators on schemas such as conjunction ($\land$) and disjunction ($\lor$) that allow larger specifications to be constructed from earlier schemas. This is a very important aspect of Z that allows large specifications, potentially thousands of pages long, to be created and used effectively. If only the mathematical aspects of Z were available, it would not be possible to use it on an industrial scale.

First the most used schema operator, namely schema conjunction ($\land$), is introduced and explained. This is used for building up specifications from constituent schemas that have specified part of the overall system. Declarations are merged and predicates are logically conjoined, in a similar way to schema inclusion.

If schema components have the same name and are type-compatible, they map on top of each other. This is a useful feature but some care is needed because Z declarations can and often do include additional constraints as well as type information. If the component is declared in exactly the same way, the issue is easy. However, say there is a declaration of $x : \mathbb{N}$ (a natural number of zero or more) in one schema and $x : \mathbb{Z}$ (an integer of arbitrary value) in another. These are type-compatible since $\mathbb{N}$ is a subset of $\mathbb{Z}$ but when logically conjoined, the value of x must be a natural number, not an arbitrary integer.

Thus an important aspect of combining schemas using schema operators (or schema inclusion) is the normalisation of the types of components. In the example above, $x : \mathbb{N}$ is normalised to $x : \mathbb{Z}$ with the constraining predicate that $x \in \mathbb{N}$. The same issue applies to functions, which are a constrained form of relation. Thus $f : X \nrightarrow Y$ normalises to $f : \mathbb{P}(X \times Y)$, for example, with the constraint that $f \in X \nrightarrow Y$, assuming that X and Y are given sets and thus already normalised. Remembering that $X \leftrightarrow Y$ is the same as $\mathbb{P}(X \times Y)$ is a useful fact to memorise to understand typing in Z.

Components with the same name must be type-compatible (i.e., have the same normalised types) for the specification to be meaningful. Components with different names are just merged in the declaration part of the new schema. Note that component declaration order is immaterial in a schema. A common mistake is to try to relate two schema components in the declaration part, but this is invalid since the declarations are only meaningful in the predicate part of the schema, which is where such relationships should be specified.

Schema disjunction ($\lor$) is covered next since this is also an important way that schemas can be combined, especially when dealing with error cases. The declarations are combined in exactly the same way as for schema conjunction, with the same normalisation of types needed when combining components with the same name. However in this case the predicates of the two schemas are combined using logical disjunction.

Robust (or "total") operations can be produced using disjunction to give an overall precondition of *true*. Typically if there is a precondition P in a successful operation schema (e.g., Op), an error schema (e.g., Err) with a precondition $\neg\, P$ can handle the error case, and $Op \lor Err$ gives a total operation schema with a precondition of *true*. If an operation schema has two preconditions $P \wedge Q$, there can be two error schemas with preconditions $\neg P$ and $\neg Q$, and so on.

Typically error schemas output an error result of some sort (e.g., *report!*). For example, the successful operation schema could output $report! = ok$ (perhaps specified once is a single schema, e.g., *Success*, for reuse later) and the error schema could output $report! = error$. Further error reports can be introduced as needed. A robust total operation (*TotalOp* in this case) could be specified in the form of combined schemas as follows:

$$TotalOp \mathrel{\hat{=}} (Op \wedge Success) \vee Err$$

In a typical Z specification with total operations, there would be a number of such total operations specified in this form.

There is also a schema negation operator ($\neg$), although this is less used in practice. However it is included for completeness and is covered by the Z course. Again, the schema is first normalised with respect to all the declarations and then the entire predicate part is logically negated, including any predicates introduced through normalisation. For example, if the declarations in a schemas S included $x : \mathbb{N}$, the negated schema $\neg S$ would include a declaration of $x : \mathbb{Z}$ and a predicate of $\neg x \in \mathbb{N}$ (or $x \notin \mathbb{N}$). Thus the x component in $\neg S$ would be constrained to be a negative integer ($x < 0$). An example of schema negation is included in the course. A schema normalisation example where a similarly named component has different but compatible declarations in the two schemas that are to be combined (using disjunction) is also included.

Z includes a facility to rename individual schema components if needed. If a schema S includes a component variable *old*, it is possible to create a new schema T with that component renamed to *new* as follows:

$$T \mathrel{\hat{=}} S[new/old]$$

This is not used much in small specifications, but can be useful in industrial-scale specifications, allowing reuse of a schema in a different context. Several component variables can be renamed simultaneously and renaming can also be combined with a generically defined schema for even more possibilities of reuse. An example is given in the course material.

Again, there are associated questions on schema calculus with model answers. These include a general question on schema operators and their use. An example of schema disjunction is given for explanation. A more complex example with schema conjunction and disjunction must also be understood and explained informally.

Altran   Z Course   Reference N056.111.55
                  Schema Calculus I: Lecture Notes   Issue 2.5
                                                        Page 4

2   LOGICAL OPERATORS

Schemas can be composed using disjunction, conjunction, and negation in Z.

This is useful in building complex systems from simpler components.

One logical operator is conjunction: in the simplest case this is just like schema inclusion.

SimpleFilofax $\hat{=}$
        BirthdayBook $\wedge$ AddressBook

┌─ SimpleFilofax ──
│
│   BirthdayBook
│   AddressBook
│
└──

2.1   Merging of Declarations

In order to combine two schemas with a logical operator, or include one schema within another, their declarations must be mergeable.

This is easy if there are no variable names common to any of the sets; the merged set is then just the union of the sets of declarations.

If a variable name is shared, however, the sets of declarations are mergeable only if the base type of the common variable is the same in each set. Just one of the duplicated declarations is retained in the merged set.

A declaration of a variable in a schema may include information in addition to its base type. This information must sometimes be made explicit when using logical operations on schemas.

2.2   Signatures and Declarations

The signature of a variable is the name of the variable together with its underlying type.

A signature is introduced by a declaration.

The declaration may also include additional predicates. The operation of **schema normalisation** makes such predicates explicit:

┌─ BirthdayBook ───
│
│   known : $\mathbb{P}$ NAME
│   birthday : $\mathbb{P}$ (NAME $\times$ DATE)
│ ──
│
│   birthday $\in$ NAME $\nrightarrow$ DATE
│   known = dom birthday
│
└──

Here the declaration of birthday defines its base type. The extra information that it is a function (and not a general relation) is left to the predicate part of the schema.

The more usual style is the one we have already introduced, where the declaration includes the

SCHEMA CALCULUS I

B.9   Schemas as Types

Z is a typed language and standard types are built up from basic types (or given sets) that are unstructured. Of course, relations, functions, sequences, etc., can be specified as well. For more complex structuring, the use of schemas as types is helpful. Schemas can be used somewhat like records in many programming languages, with the named state components in the schema identifying different parts of the structure.

An example of a simple schema being used in a type declaration is explained. It should be noted that the ordering of declarations in schemas is unimportant, unlike a Cartesian product where the ordering is meaningful. Even if two schemas have different predicates, they can still be type-compatible since it is the normalisation of the schema components that matters.

If a component variable has a schema type, components in that schema can be selected. For example, with a declaration of $s : S$ where S is a schema with components x and y in its declaration, $s.x$ and $s.y$ can be used to refer to those components. With two variables declared using type-compatible (or identical) schema types, they can be made equal in a predicate. E.g., with declarations $s, t : S$ using a schema S, the predicate $s = t$ is valid.

If the variables of S are in scope within a schema (e.g., it has been included in another schema), then θS is an instance of the schema type S with all the components have the values in the current context. The schema may be decorated, so $\theta S'$ is also meaningful. This is especially useful in specifying the meaning of ΞS (for example) formally:

$$\Xi S \mathrel{\widehat{=}} [S;\ S' \mid \theta S' = \theta S]$$

The technique of schema promotion is also covered. This is very important in larger specifications since it allows a smaller specification to be embedded in a larger specification in a convenient manner, especially if the rest of the larger system is to remain unchanged while the smaller subsystem is updated in some way. An example of this approach is provided by the course. The approach is particularly useful in industrial-scale Z specifications. First the course material explains a specific example and then this is generalised. The template can be used in many real examples of the specification of large systems and solves the framing problem of dealing with a small update of a large system in a convenient manner in the context of Z.

Associated questions and model answers are available. Firstly a schema is provided and the compatibility of this with other schemas when used as a schema type must be determined. This especially checks schema normalisation skills. Then a more complex example is presented including two schema component variables declared using schema types with a complex predicate relating the two. The relationship that this conveys must be explained in English.

146   J.P. Bowen

2   SCHEMAS AS TYPES

Using Schemas in Declarations

The structure of a schema type

The meaning of a schema type

Component selection

Equality

Constructing instances

2.1   Using Schemas in Declarations

A schema reference can be used as the expression on the right hand side of the colon in a declaration. The declared variable is then an instance of the schema type.

If we write

b : BirthdayBook

we mean that b is an instance of a birthday book. It is an object (called a *binding*) which associates the identifier *known* with a particular set of NAMEs and the identifier *birthday* with a particular function from NAME to DATE, subject to the condition that the set *known* is the domain of the function *birthday*.

2.2   The Structure of a Schema Type

littleRedBook : BirthdayBook

The type of littleRedBook is *unordered* and *named*.

Hence BirthdayBook is NOT the type

$\mathbb{P}$ NAME $\times$ $\mathbb{P}$ (NAME $\times$ DATE)

Nor is BirthdayBook the same type as:

DateOfBirthBook

known : $\mathbb{P}$ NAME
dateOfBirth : NAME $\nrightarrow$ DATE

known = dom dateOfBirth

But it is the same as

BookBirthday

birthday : NAME $\nrightarrow$ DATE
known : $\mathbb{P}$ NAME

SCHEMAS AS TYPES

B.10 Syndicate Exercise

An extended Z specification is available for students to learn how to discuss and use a more realistic formal specification. This is an optional but useful part of the course, taking around half a day. Example questions are provided, but this part of the course is more open-ended and the course teacher can lead a discussion with students on the course once they have studied the case study material.

The specification is provided with Z and associated English explanation in a way that is typical for a Z specification. A number of operations are covered. The example questions start with detailed technical issues, why certain features have been selected in the Z specification, and what effect these have in practice. The questions become more general as they proceed, allowing more discussion. Further questions could easily be formulated and discussed either by the course leader or by more able participates on the course.

Those participants who are able to provide sensible input to the discussions on this specifications are the ones that are likely to be more productive in reading Z specification on a real project. This could be helpful in deciding the roles of participants subsequently on a subsequent project involving Z specification.

Altran   Z Course   Reference N056.111.82
             Syndicate Exercise for 'Understanding Z' Course   Issue 1.2
                                                                  Page 3

1   SPECIFICATION FRAGMENT

1.1   Introduction

This specification describes a distributed system called CASE. CASE supports a number of practitioners working on a common project. Central to the operation of a CASE project is its logical division into Individual Machines, used by the practitioners, and a Project Machine, which is not used directly by anyone but serves as a repository of project-wide information and a processor for project management and checking. The specification here defines how a CASE project is configured given a collection of CASE servers and workstations.

The CASE practitioner deals entirely at the level of Individual and Project Machines. Login, for example, is to a particular Individual Machine, not to a workstation.

The state of the machine subsystem contains:

1. the underlying hardware

2. a Project Machine and a number of Individual Machines

3. information defining how the Project and Individual Machines are mapped onto the hardware

4. information defining which users are allocated to which Individual Machines

1.2   Machine Subsystem Specification

1.2.1   Given sets

The following sets are assumed to be given, and their internal structure is either irrelevant or described only informally:

[WORKSTATION, SERVER, IM, USER]

WORKSTATION This is the set of workstations. A workstation must have storage, a processor and user interface devices, but that is not formally specified.

SERVER   This is the set of machines suitable for use as Project Machines. Notice that a CASE server is completely distinct from a workstation, even though it may be implemented on the same piece of hardware.

IM   This is the set of all Individual Machines. (Note that there is no need for a set PM of Project Machines, because there is only one per project.) The set IM can be thought of as the "system names" for the Individual Machines, generated when the Individual Machines are created.

USER   This is the set of all CASE users on this project.

1.2.2   The state of the machine subsystem

At any time the machine subsystem contains a set of workstations and CASE servers - at least one workstation and one CASE server. It must contain exactly one Project Machine and at least one Individual Machine. The Project Machine must be allocated to a CASE server, and Individual Machines must all be allocated to workstations. The project may have a set of CASE servers, and the Project Machine may be moved from one to another, but only one CASE server is in use at a time. Note that a workstation can have more than one Individual Machine on it. All this is expressed in the schema MachineSys1.

B.11 Summary

As well as material for distribution to students on the Altran Z course, there are also matching teaching notes with an expanded form of the material. Slides are available with reduced material for presentation by the course teacher on a screen during lectures. The exercises have full associated model answers in general.

An expanded version of the *Z Readers Course* is available, the *Z Writers Course*, designed for people who are going to need to write specifications. On a typical industrial project using Z, the number of people who need to be able to read Z vastly outnumbers the team needed to write Z. Typically the Z specification may be used to guide the software tests that are undertaken, by partitioning the specification for the various tests that are required. It will always be used to guide the implementation by programmers. Both these large teams only require engineers that are able to read Z, a much easier task than writing good Z specifications.

For more information on Altran, see http://www.altran.com. For specific information on "Formal Computing" from Altran, see:

http://intelligent-systems.altran.com/technologies/software-engineering/
formal-computing.html

References

1. Abrial, J.R.: Data semantics. In: Klimbie, J.W., Koffeman, K.L. (eds.) IFIP TC2 Working Conference on Data Base Management, pp. 1–59. Elsevier Science Publishers, North-Holland, April 1974
2. Bagheri, S.M., Smith, G., Hanan, J.: Using Z in the development and maintenance of computational models of real-world systems. In: Canal, C., Idani, A. (eds.) SEFM 2014 Workshops. LNCS, vol. 8938, pp. 36–53. Springer, Heidelberg (2015)
3. Boulanger, J.L. (ed.): Formal Methods: Industrial Use from Model to the Code. ISTE, Wiley, London (2012)
4. Bowen, J.P.: Formal specification and documentation of microprocessor instruction sets. Microprocessing and Microprogramming **21**(1–5), 223–230 (1987)
5. Bowen, J.P. (ed.): Proceeding of Z Users Meeting, 1 Wellington Square, Oxford. Oxford University Computing Laboratory, Oxford, December 1987
6. Bowen, J.P.: Formal specification in Z as a design and documentation tool. In: Proc. 2nd IEE/BCS Conference on Software Engineering, pp. 164–168, No. 290 in Conference Publication. IEE/BCS, July 1988
7. Bowen, J.P.: POS: formal specification of a UNIX tool. IEE/BCS Softw. Eng. J. **4**(1), 67–72 (1989)
8. Bowen, J.P.: X: why Z? Comput. Graph. Forum **11**(4), 221–234 (1992)
9. Bowen, J.P.: Glossary of Z notation. Inf. Softw. Technol. **37**(5–6), 333–334 (1995)
10. Bowen, J.P.: Formal Specification and Documentation Using Z: A Case Study Approach. International Thomson Computer Press, London (1996)
11. Bowen, J.P.: Experience teaching Z with tool and web support. ACM SIGSOFT Softw. Eng. Notes **26**(2), 69–75 (2001)
12. Bowen, J.P.: Z: A formal specification notation. In: Frappier, M., Habrias, H. (eds.) Software Specification Methods: An Overview Using a Case Study, chap. 1, pp. 3–20. ISTE (2006)

13. Bowen, J.P.: Alan Turing. In: Robinson, A. (ed.) The Scientists: An Epic of Discovery, pp. 270–275. Thames and Hudson, London (2012)

14. Bowen, J.P., Fett, A., Hinchey, M.G. (eds.): ZUM'98: The Z Formal Specification Notation. LNCS, vol. 1493, pp. 24–26. Springer, Heidelberg (1998)

15. Bowen, J.P., Gimson, R.B., Topp-Jørgensen, S.: Specifying system implementations in Z. Technical Monograph PRG-63, Oxford University Computing Laboratory, Oxford, February 1988

16. Bowen, J.P., Gordon, M.J.C.: A shallow embedding of Z in HOL. Inf. Softw. Technol. **37**(5–6), 269–276 (1995)

17. Bowen, J.P., Hinchey, M.G.: Ten commandments ten years on: lessons for ASM, B, Z and VSR-net. In: Abrial, J.-R., Glässer, U. (eds.) Rigorous Methods for Software Construction and Analysis. LNCS, vol. 5115, pp. 219–233. Springer, Heidelberg (2009)

18. Bowen, J.P., Hinchey, M.G.: Formal methods. In: Gonzalez, T.F., Diaz-Herrera, J., Tucker, A.B. (eds.) Computing Handbook, vol. 1, 3rd edn., chap. 71, pp. 1–25. CRC Press (2014)

19. Bowen, J.P., Hinchey, M.G., Janicke, H., Ward, M., Zedan, H.: Formality, agility, security, and evolution in software development. IEEE Comput. **47**(10), 86–89 (2014)

20. Breuer, P.T., Bowen, J.P.: Towards correct executable semantics for Z. In: Bowen, J.P., Hall, J.A. (eds.) Z User Workshop, Cambridge 1994. Workshops in Computing, pp. 185–209. Springer, London (1994)

21. Ciancarini, P., Cimato, S., Mascolo, C.: Engineering formal requirements: an analysis and testing method for Z documents. Ann. Softw. Eng. **3**, 189–219 (1997)

22. Copeland, J., Bowen, J.P., Sprevak, M., Wilson, R.J., et al.: The Turing Guide. Oxford University Press (to appear 2016)

23. Cristia, M., Hollmann, D., Albertengo, P., Frydman, C., Monetti, P.R.: A language for test case refinement in the test template framework. In: Qin, S., Qiu, Z. (eds.) ICFEM 2011. LNCS, vol. 6991, pp. 601–616. Springer, Heidelberg (2011)

24. Gimson, R., Bowen, J.P., Gleeson, T.: Distributed computing software project. In: 2nd Workshop on Making Distributed Systems Work, pp. 1–3. ACM, September 1986

25. Gnesi, S., Margaria, T.: Formal Methods for Industrial Critical Systems: A Survey of Applications. IEEE Computer Society Press, Wiley, Chichester (2012)

26. Hall, J.A.: Z word tools. SourceForge (2008). http://sourceforge.net/projects/zwordtools/. Accessed 28 September 2015

27. Henson, M.C., Reeves, S., Bowen, J.P.: Z logic and its consequences. CAI. Comput. Inform. **22**(4), 381–415 (2003)

28. Hinchey, M.G., Jackson, M., Cousot, P., Cook, B., Bowen, J.P., Margaria, T.: Software engineering and formal methods. Commun. ACM **51**(9), 54–59 (2008)

29. Hoare, C.A.R.: An axiomatic basis for computer programming. Commun. ACM **12**(10), 576–580 (1969)

30. Hoare, C.A.R.: Communicating Sequential Processes. Series in Computer Science. Prentice Hall International, London (1985)

31. Hörcher, H.M.: Improving software tests using Z specifications. In: Bowen, J.P., Hinchey, M.G. (eds.) ZUM'95: The Z Formal Specification Notation. LNCS, vol. 967, pp. 152–166. Springer, Heidelberg (1995)

32. ISO: Information technology - Z formal specification notation - syntax, type system and semantics. International Standard 13568, ISO/IEC, July 2002

33. Jones, R.B.: ICL ProofPower. BCS-FACS FACTS Series III **1**(1), 10–13 (1992)

34. Morris, F.L., Jones, C.B.: An early program proof by Alan Turing. IEEE Ann. Hist. Comput. **6**(2), 139–143 (1984)
35. Nicholls, J.E.: A survey of Z courses in the UK. In: Nicholls, J.E. (ed.) Z User Workshop, Oxford 1990. Workshops in Computing, pp. 343–350. Springer, Heidelberg (1991)
36. Nicholls, J.E. (ed.): Z User Workshop, York 1991. Workshops in Computing. Springer, London (1992)
37. Saaltink, M.: The Z/EVES system. In: Till, D., Bowen, J.P., Hinchey, M.G. (eds.) ZUM 1997. LNCS, vol. 1212. Springer, Heidelberg (1997)
38. Smith, G.: The Object-Z Specification Language, Advances in Formal Methods, vol. 1. Springer, Heidelberg (2012)
39. Spivey, J.M.: The Z Notation: A reference manual. Series in Computer Science, Prentice Hall International (1989/1992/2001). http://spivey.oriel.ox.ac.uk/mike/zrm/
40. Spivey, J.M.: The fuzz type-checker for Z. Technical report, University of Oxford, UK (2008). http://spivey.oriel.ox.ac.uk/mike/fuzz/
41. Stocks, P., Carrington, D.: A framework for specification-based testing. IEEE Trans. Softw. Eng. **22**(11), 777–793 (1996)
42. Turing, A.M.: On computable numbers with an application to the Entscheidungsproblem. Proc. London Math. Soc. **2**(42), 230–265 (1936/7)
43. Turing, A.M.: Checking a large routine. In: Campbell-Kelly, M. (ed.) The early British computer conferences, pp. 70–72. MIT Press, Cambridge (1949/1989)
44. Vilkomir, S.A., Bowen, J.P.: Formalization of software testing criteria using the Z notation. In: Proceeding 25th Annual International Computer Software and Applications Conference (COMPSAC 2001), Chicago, pp. 351–356. IEEE Computer Society Press, 8–12 October 2001
45. Vilkomir, S.A., Bowen, J.P.: From MC/DC to RC/DC: formalization and analysis of control-flow testing criteria. Formal Aspects Comput. **18**(1), 42–62 (2006)

Model-Driven Design of Object
and Component Systems

Zhiming Liu[1]([⊠]) and Xiaohong Chen[2]

[1] Centre for Software Research and Innovation,
Southwest University, Chongqing, China
`zhiming.liu88@gmail.com`
[2] Singapore University of Technology and Design, Singapore, Singapore
`xiaohong_chen@sutd.edu.sg`

Abstract. The notion of software engineering implies that software
design and production should be based on the types of theoretical foundations and practical disciplines that are established in the traditional
branches of engineering. The goal is to make development of complex
software systems more *predictable* and the systems developed more *trustworthy - safe, secure and dependable*. A number of theories have been
well developed in the past half a century, including *Abstract Data Types*,
Hoare Logic, *Process Calculi*, and *I/O automata*, and those alike. Based
on them, techniques and tools have been developed for software specification, refinement and verification.

However, the theoretically sound techniques and tools have not been
seamlessly integrated in practical software development, and their impact
upon commonly-used software systems is still far from convincing to software engineering practitioners. This is clearly reflected by the challenges
of their applications in engineering large-scale systems, including Cyber-
Physical Systems (CPS), Networks of Things and Cloud-Based Systems,
that have multi-dimensional complexities. Indeed, students are not often
shown how the theories, and their underpinned techniques and tools, can
better inform the software engineering they are traditionally taught. The
purpose of this course to demonstrate such an effort.

We present a *model-driven design* framework for *component-based and
object-oriented* software systems. We identify a set of UML notations and
textual descriptions for representing different abstractions of software
artefacts produced in different development stages. These abstractions,
their relations and manipulations all have formalisations in the rCOS formal method of component and object systems. The aim is to allow the
advantage of using precise models for development better appreciated.
We organise the lecture notes into three chapters, each having a title
page but all the references to literature are given at the end of Part III.

Keywords: Component-based architecture · Object-oriented design ·
Interfaces · Contracts · Design patterns · rCOS · UML

© Springer International Publishing Switzerland 2016
Z. Liu and Z. Zhang (Eds.): SETSS 2014, LNCS 9506, pp. 152–255, 2016.
DOI: 10.1007/978-3-319-29628-9_4

1   Part I: Introduction

1.1   Background and Organisation

This chapter is organised based on the materials that have been taught since 1998 at the University of Leicester, United-Nations University – International Institute for Software Technology (UNU-IIST[1], Macau) and Birmingham City University. The materials have also been adapted to and taught at training schools similar to the Summer School on Engineering Trustworthy Software Systems (SETSS) held in Chongqing in August 2014. Furthermore, these materials and the feedbacks from students have influenced the development of the *rCOS method*, which is a formal model-driven method of object and component systems. With the insight developed through research in the rCOS method, we taught the students how to prepare themselves for effective study and application of formal techniques and tools in software design and program verification.

Our aim is and has consistently been to show that in order to apply formal techniques, models and tools to software development projects, the requirements and the design, together with their models must first be developed. We demonstrate an informal process of requirements gathering and analysis as well as design patterns can be used to develop models that are formalisable. Thus they are a basis for reasoning about and verifying desired properties. We believe this will contribute to bridging the gap between formal techniques and their application in practical software development.

We focus on the requirements gathering and analysis, component-based architecture design and object-oriented design of components. The theme of the approach is model-driven development of component-based architectures, their interface-based decomposition and composition and detailed object-oriented design. Component-based architectures (or systems of systems architecture) with techniques and tools of interface-based composition, evolution and integration are seen as key to dealing with modern complex software systems, including cloud-based systems, internet of things (IoT), smart cities and cyber-physical systems (CPS).

Organisation. We divide this chapter into three parts in order for the reader to select different sections from each parts. Part I contains a brief introduction to the background and organisation in Sect. 1.1, a historical account of software engineering in Sect. 2, that is followed by a discussion of the basics of model driven development in Sect. 3. Though software development process models are not a focus topic of this chapter, the concepts of modelling, analysis and design activities and the artefacts they produce are useful for understanding the technical discussions, and thus they are introduced in Sect. 5. The technical discussion throughout the chapter is based on a case study described in Sect. 4.

Part II is on use case driven object-oriented requirements gathering, modelling and analysis. Section 6.1 discusses about use cases, their identification,

---

[1] It is now renamed to UNU-CS.

description and decomposition. Section 7 is about object-oriented modelling of the domain structure through identification of classes, their attributes and associations. Section 8 moves into understanding, modelling and analysis of functional behaviour of the requirements, followed by a summary of this part in Sect. 9.

Part III presents the techniques and models for component-based architecture design in Sect. 10.1, and for object-oriented design of the architecture components in Sect. 11. The component-based architecture model emphases on the contracts of the component interfaces, provides the basis of the object-oriented design of the components using design patterns for responsibility assignments to objects. Section 12 gives an overall summary of the chapter and discusses possible future developments.

At the end of each technical section, we relate the informal techniques to the rCOS formal method with references to publications. The materials in the textbook of Larman [42] are a major source of the knowledge and ideas in the discussion, developed through all the versions of the course notes, from the first version used at University of Leicester, through the tailored versions taught at the international schools, to the version used for the Software Design module at Birmingham City University.

2   Software Engineering

For a long time there was no authoritative account of when "software engineering" first appeared in the literature, but it is now widely accepted that the term was first coined by Anthony Oettinger in 1966, ACM President between 1966 and 1968, in his "letter to the ACM membership" [71], and then used by Hamilton [1,80] while working on the Apollo guidance software. The term was used in 1968 in the title for the world's first conference on software engineering, sponsored and facilitated by NATO [67]. The motivation for the conference was the so-called "software crisis", characterised by the symptoms of late delivery, over budget, product failing to meet specified requirements, and inadequate documentation [67]. The notion of software engineering was meant to imply that software design and production should be based on the types of theoretical foundations and practical disciplines that are established in the traditional branches of engineering. This meaning and aim of the term, though its content was yet to be defined, was clearly reflected in the discussions on development processes and cycles at the first conference, and the discussions on the notion of program correctness appeared as a key issue at a followup conference in 1969 [78].

2.1   Software Complexity

Though there are disputes about if there is a "software crisis", software development is hugely complex, and the source of the so-called crisis is just the inherent complexity of software development. Fundamental understanding of software complexity has contributed to the formation of major areas of software engineering and advances in these areas. In particular, complexity of software development is characterised by the following four fundamental attributes of software [6,8,9]:

1. the complexity of the domain application,
2. the difficulty of managing the development process,
3. the flexibility possible to offer through software, and
4. the problem of characterising the behaviour of software systems.

Complex systems are open to total breakdowns [73], and consequences of system breakdowns are sometimes catastrophic and very costly, e.g., the famous Therac-25 Accident 1985–1987 [44], the Ariane-5 Explosion in 1996 [81], and the Wenzhou High Speed Train Collision[2] in 2011. Also the software complexity attributes are the main source of *unpredictability* in software development projects. Software projects fail due to our failure in mastering the complexity [35]. Advances in software engineering have been largely driven by understanding of and seeking solutions to handle the different attributes of software complexity.

The first attribute, the complexity of the domain application, is the main cause of the difficulty of capturing and specifying the requirements. Imagine the requirements of the Apollo guidance software in the 1960s [1,80], and the software systems used nowadays in air traffic control and hospital information systems. A major challenge comes from the fact that it is not realistic to expect a software engineer to understand the domain thoroughly, or a domain expert to come up with a design for the software. Solutions to this problem are in the scope of the sub-discipline of (*Software*) *Requirement Engineering*, which includes specification/modelling languages (together with their semantic theories), techniques and tools for requirements specification, validation and verification [69]. The aim is to master the complexity of requirements capture, definition, validation and documentation. These constitutes elements of *requirements specification and analysis* in a *software development process* [40].

The second attribute, the difficulty of managing the development process, concerns the difficulty to define and manage a development process that has to deal with complex and changing requirements and constraints. A software project typically involves a large team of software engineers and domain experts, possibly in different geographical places. The process has to identify the software technologies and tools that support collaboration of the team in working on shared software artefacts. Roughly speaking, a development process defines in the development when, who, does what work or tasks, uses what techniques and tools, and produces what artefacts. Tasks include work management and artefacts management, and techniques and tools should also support the ways of collaboration of the team. Research, education and practice of solutions to this challenge form the area of *Software Project Management* [86].

The third attribute, the flexibility possible to offer through software, is about the problem of making sound design decisions among a wide range of possibilities

---

[2] http://en.wikipedia.org/wiki/Wenzhou_train_collision.

that have conflicting features. This includes the design of the software architecture, and the design and reuse of software components, algorithms and communication networks. For the same requirements, different decisions lead to different software products. In particular, the decision making involves the best practice of the fundamental engineering principles of (a) *separation of concerns*, (b) *divide and conquer*, and (c) *use of abstraction* through information hiding (in different design stages). The notions of *modularity* and *interfaces* discussed at the 1968 NATO Software Engineering Conference [67], and the later developed *structured design* [84], *object-oriented design* [6], *component-based design* [25,28,61,88] and *service-oriented architecture* [5] all aim to support the practice of these three engineering principles. These three principles also apply to other software development activities including requirements analysis, verification and validation, and software project management. Model-driven architecture (MDA) [70], that recently has become a main stream approach, aims at a seamless integration of the above approaches in a unified development process, such as the Rational Unified Process (RUP) [40].

The final attribute, the problem of characterising the behaviour of software systems, pinpoints the difficulty in understanding and modelling the dynamic behaviour of software, for analysis, validation and verification for correctness, as well as reliability assurance. The dynamic behaviour of a program is defined in terms of all possible changes of states of the program. A *state* is a mapping from the program variables to their value space, representing the values that the variables take (stored in the memories allocated to the variables) at a point of the program execution. The variables include the program variables defined by the programmer and those which controls the program execution flow, such as program or process counters. A program is (functionally) correct if its dynamic behaviour conforms to its specification. For a large program with a big number of variables, especially a large scale concurrent and distributed software system, the dynamic behaviour has a great scale of complexity. This poses a great challenge for (a) writing the right requirements specification that identifies the correct state changes allowable by the application, and (b) verifying that the behaviour of the program is correct with respect to the specification. It is well-know that finding bugs in a program which may cause its behaviour to violate the program requirements is hard and costly. Seeking solutions to these challenges is the background motivation for *formal methods* of software development, that include mathematical theories of modelling and programming languages, including their syntaxes and semantics, techniques and tools for design (such as correctness preserving refinement), logical reasoning about and verification of program correctness.

2.2   Chronic Complexity of Modern Software

The characteristic attributes of software complexity still hold for modern and future software, but their extensions are becoming increasingly wider, due to the increasing power of computers, here we quote

"The major cause of the software crisis is that the machines have become several orders of magnitude more powerful. To put it quite bluntly: as long as there were no machines, programming was no problem at all; when we had a few weak computers, programming became a mild problem, and now we have gigantic computers, programming has become an equally gigantic problem."

– Edsger Dijkstra
The Humble Programmer, Communications of the ACM [20]

Now computers are everywhere and networked, executing programs anywhere and any time, which share data and communicate and collaborate with each other. New buzz-words are introduced for these different kinds of networked computing systems, *Cloud Computing*, *Internet of Thing* (IoT) [48], *Smart Cities* [83], and *Cyber-Physical Systems* (CPS) [43]. Application, control and monitoring programs [89] are being developed and integrated into these systems, which we see in our everyday life in transportation, health, banking and enterprise. These systems provide their users with a large variety of *services* and *features*. They are becoming increasingly *distributed*, *dynamic* and *mobile*. Their components are *deployed* over large networks of *heterogeneous platforms*. In addition to the complex functional structures and behaviours, modern software systems have complex aspects concerning *organisational structures* (i.e., *system topology*), *adaptability*, *interactions interoperability*, *safety*, *security*, *real-time* and *fault-tolerance*.

It is even more challenging when a networked system supports collaborative workflows involving many different kinds of stakeholders and end-users across different domains. The system is open to ever changing requirements during the development of the software and when it is in operation. Typical cases are health-care applications, such as telemedicine, where chronic conditions of patients on homecare plans are monitored and tracked by different healthcare providers. The openness makes it much more difficult to do requirements modelling and analysis, software design, system validation and verification, and management of the development. Furthermore, it imposes challenges to *software maintenance*.

This chapter focuses on handling software complexity through component-based modelling, decomposition, refinement and verification. The next section summarises the state of the art of software engineering and motivate model-driven and component-based software engineering, and formal methods.

3   Model-Driven Software Engineering

For the discussion in this section and technical discussions in the later sections, some concepts related to software engineering were clarified.

3.1   Basic Concepts in Software Engineering

Textbooks and websites have numerous definitions for *computer software*. For examples

- a collection of *computer programs* and related *data* that provide the instructions for telling a *computer* what to do and how to do it.
- a set of *computer programs* or *procedures*, and associated documentation concerned with the operation of a *data processing system*.
- one or more *computer programs* and *data* held in the storage of the *computer* for some purposes.

For developing a systematic understanding, we first give a rather abstract description of the related concepts of *computation, computer*, a *data process system*, and *programs* as follows:

1. a *computer* carries out a *computation* by executing a *program*;
2. a *program* defines of a number of variables and a sequence of *commands*;
3. when a computer executes the program, the variables are allocated in memories (storage) of the computer to hold data values at any moment of time, called the *state* of the program execution at that moment of time;
4. at the beginning of the execution, the computer receives *input values* for the variables (to set up the *initial state* of the execution);
5. during the execution, the commands are carried out according to the flow of control defined by the sequence of commands and the execution of each command changes the current state to the next state defined by the *semantics* of the command; and
6. at the end of the execution (if the execution terminates), an *output* is produced that is determined by the final state of the program in the execution.

Note that the same program can be executed repeatedly with different inputs (i.e., initial states) to generate different outputs (i.e., final states). The fifth and sixth statements above imply that the semantics of a program command, thus that of a whole program can be mathematically defined as a *relation between program states* (see later in this Subsection for further clarification). This relational semantic model is the theoretical foundation of the method we study in this chapter.

The above discussion on computation, computers and programs is easy to comprehend when we think of sequential programs running on uni-processor computers. For example, given any initial value x_0 and y_0 to variable x and y, i.e., from the initial state $s_0 = \{(x,y) \mapsto (x_0, y_0)\}$, the execution of command (program) $x := x + y + 1$ changes the value of x from x_0 to the value $x_0 + y_0 + 1$, i.e., the execution changes from the initial state s_0 to final state $s_1 = \{(x,y) \mapsto (x_0 + y_0 + 1, y_0)\}$.

The semantics of the program, denoted by $[\![x := x + 1]\!]$ is defined to be the relation $\{(s_0, s_1) \mid x_0 \in T_x \wedge y_0 \in T_x\}$, where T_x and T_y is the value spaces of x and y, say the set of integers. The semantics of the composite commands can be defined using operations on relations, and recursive or iterative commands by fixed points of recursive equations in relational algebra [32]. The following examples give the flavour of the calculation of the semantics of composite commands:

$$[\![x := x + y + 1; y := x]\!]$$
$$= [\![x := x + y + 1]\!]; [\![y := x]\!]$$
$$= \{((x,y) \mapsto (x_0, y_0), (x,y) \mapsto (x_0 + y_0 + 1, y_0)) \mid x_0 \in T_x \wedge y_0 \in T_y\};$$
$$\{((x,y) \mapsto (x_1, y_1), (x,y) \mapsto (x_1, y_1)) \mid x_1 \in T_x \wedge y_1 \in T_y\}$$
$$= \{((x,y) \mapsto (x_0, y_0), (x,y) \mapsto (x_0 + y_0 + 1, x_0 + y_0 + 1)) \mid x_0 \in T_x \wedge y_0 \in T_y\}$$

where in the above formulas we overloaded ";" for both the sequential composition of program commands and for the composition of relations in relational algebra. Another example illustrates the conditional command, where $C_1 \lhd B \rhd C_2$ denotes the conditional choice **if** B **then** C_1 **else** C_2:

$$[\![x := x + y + 1 \lhd x < y \rhd y := x + y + 1]\!]$$
$$= [\![x := x + y + 1]\!] \cap [\![x < y]\!] \cup [\![\neg(x < y)]\!] \cap [\![y := x + y + 1]\!]$$
$$= \{((x,y) \mapsto (x_0, y_0), (x,y) \mapsto (x_0 + y_0 + 1, y_0)) \mid x_0 \in T_x \wedge y_0 \in T_y \wedge x_0 < y_0\}$$
$$\{((x,y) \mapsto (x_0, y_0), (x,y) \mapsto (x_0, x_0 + y_0 + 1)) \mid x_0 \in T_x \wedge y_0 \in T_y \wedge y_0 \leq x_0\}$$

where $[\![B]\!] = \{(s, s') \mid B \text{ holds in } s\}$, thus $x < y$ hold for state $(x,y) \mapsto (x_0, y_0)$ if $x_0 < y_0$. The semantics of an iterative command **while** B **do** C, algebraically denoted as $B * C$, is defined to be the "smallest" solution [32,68,87] to the recursive equation $[\![B * C]\!] = [\![C; B * C]\!] \lhd B \rhd \textbf{skip}$, where **skip** is the identity relation that define the semantics of the program whose execution does not change the state.

The above discussions on computation, computers and programs can be generalised to models of modern computer systems, including networks of data processing systems (cf. the second definition of computer software), and other programming paradigms such as object-oriented programs, concurrent and distributed programs [32].

An extension of the notion of "computer software" is *software systems* which are a "collection of programs" and the associated "data", which are interrelated in an architecture and the 'work' together when being running on a computer. Here, "computer" refers to any device or system with the power of processing and transmitting data. We thus define a **software system** to consist of set of architected programs and data that tell a set interrelated computers what to do and how to it. Computers include all devices with programmable processing capacity, all kinds of "smart devices" as well as "computers", that now affects all aspects of daily life.

We take the general view that **software engineering** is about the application of a systematic, disciplined, quantifiable approach to the development, operation, and maintenance of software systems, and the study of these approaches. This is to say software engineering is about the application of *engineering* to manufacture of software systems, and software engineering has a significant foundation in mathematics, computer science and has practice that have strong origins in engineering. In more concrete terms software engineering is about development, study and application of *theories, techniques and tools* for requirements analysis, design, implementation, correctness validation and verification (including testing and simulation), and maintenance of software systems.

A **software engineering method** consists of a theory, a set of techniques developed based on the theory, and a suit of tools that support systematic applications of the techniques to requirements analysis, software design, implementation, validation and verification, and maintenance in software systems development. The systematic application of a method to software development relies on well-defined *software development processes*. Examples of software engineering methods include *structured software development*, *object-oriented design*, *component-based design*, and *model-driven development* (or *MDA - model-driven architecture*), that have overlapping theories, techniques and tools support. Software engineering has to help in mastering software complexity. Therefore, the theory, techniques and tools have to support effective handling of software complexity. This means they need to define mechanisms of separation of concerns, divide and conquer and information hiding for abstraction. A model-driven software engineering method represents the state of the art of software engineering methods with regard to these aspects.

3.2   Model-Driven Development

All well established engineering branches rely on the use of *models* to represent different *viewpoints* and *concerns* of the *artefacts* constructed at different stages of the engineering process. All models are representations of the views with details that are not relevant to the present concern being excluded. Model-driven software engineering methods [70,88,89], propose the same approach to engineering software systems. That is, a software system is manufactured through building system models in all stages of the development. A particular model-driven method is called *Model-Driven Architecture* (MDA), launched as a standard model-driven software engineering method by Object Management Group[3].

Example. Consider an application case in the context of smart cities. One can imagine a street lightening system has different stakeholders, each having different views and concerns. The city council is concerned about the conveniences of the citizens when walking in the night; the police office on the other hand has an interest in the relation of the street lightning with crimes; and further the electricity company is concerned about power consumption as readings on meters and bills. These different views are represented as models of the requirements, the interfaces of services to these stakeholders, and the program implementations of the services. These different models are at different levels of abstraction, but they are closely related and can all be built based on a common model of the configurations and dynamic behaviour of the lights.

MDA supports the principles of divide and conquer with its component-based architectures, in which an architectural component is hierarchical and can be divided into subcomponents. The architectural components inside a (composite) component interact and communicate with each other through their interfaces, according to explicitly specified *contracts*, and work together to realise the interface contract of the whole composite component. For example, a buffer of

---

[3] http://www.omg.org.

capacity one has an interface for a user to "put" a data item and for another user to "get" the data item stored in the buffer. Then a two-place buffer can be composed from two one-place buffers by employing a connector. The user puts a data item using the 'put' of one-place buffer and get a data item out using the "get" of the other. The connector moves the data item out of the first one-place buffer using its "get" and puts it into the second one-place buffer using its "put". This is shown in Fig. 1.

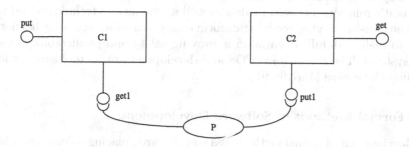

Fig. 1. Composite component

MDA supports *separation of concerns* by providing notations for representing different viewpoints of a component. These include the static component and class views using UML component and class diagrams, interaction views by UML sequence diagrams, and dynamic behavioural views by UML state machine diagrams. The models of different views of architectural models are important when defining and managing a development process [53]. However, a serious consistency problem arises in both of its theoretical foundation and its practical application in software system development, caused by the large number of UML models that are constructed in different notations possibly by different members of the project team.

The consistency problem is mainly due to first the lack of clear defined development process that defines the models to be sued and their relations, and secondly the omission of a unified semantics of these models for the project. Therefore, integration and transformation of models are mostly syntax-based, having no provable semantic correctness. Hence, the tools developed to support model integration and transformation cannot immediately be integrated with tools for verification of semantic correctness and correctness preserving transformations [60]. For MDA to support a seamless development process of model decomposition, integration, and transformation, there is a need of formal semantic relations between models of different viewpoints at the same level of abstraction, and between models of the same viewpoint at different levels of abstraction. The relations for the former are to deal with consistency among models of different views for correct integration [12,51,52], and the relations for the models at different levels are the refinement/abstraction relations [15,27,52,91]. We do not promote a single unified semantics for UML, but a unified semantics of the models used in a project should be defined.

Most MDA techniques and tools focus on transformations between models of the same view, such as class models or state-based behaviour, but built with different notations and tools. Also, there are plenty of techniques and tools for transformations between PSMs. There is, however, very little support for transformations between PIMs at different levels of abstraction, except for some design patterns directed model transformations [63]. This is actually the reason why MDA has yet to convincingly demonstrate its potential advantages of *separation of concerns*, *divide and conquer* and *incremental development*. This lack of semantic relations between models as well as the lack of techniques and tools for semantics-preserving model transformations is also an essential barrier for MDA to realise its full potential in improving safety and predictability of software systems. The research in rCOS and development of its tool support focus on filling these gaps [4,47,90,91].

3.3   Formal Methods of Software Development

The development of formal methods is a step towards placing software and hardware development on a sound engineering discipline so that appropriate mathematical analysis is possible [7]. A formal method is about the uses of a broad range of theoretical computer science fundamentals to solve problems in software and hardware specification and verification. These fundamentals include logic calculi, formal languages, automata theory, and program semantics, but also type systems and algebraic data types. We say a *formal method of software engineering* consists of a semantics theory, a body of techniques and a suite of tools for the *specification*, *development*, and *verification* of software systems of a certain programming paradigm, such as procedural sequential programming or object-oriented programming, concurrent and distributed programming and component (or service) based programming. The semantic theory of a formal method is developed based on the fundamental theories of *denotational semantics* [87], *operational semantics* [75], or *axiomatic semantics* (including algebraic semantics) [19,30] of programming. As they are all used to define and reason about behaviour of programs, they are closely related [68], and indeed, they can be "unified" [27,32].

A specification is an abstract model of the program or the specification of desirable properties of the program in a formally defined notation. In the former case, the specification notation is also called a modelling language though a modelling language usually includes graphic notations (e.g., Petri Nets [74]). There are now a large number of well-known formal modelling/specification languages, including CSP [31], CCS [66], the Z-Notation [85], the B-Method [2,3], VDM [36], UNITY [10], and TLA+ [41]. In the latter case, desirable properties are defined on a computational model of the executions of the system and specified in a formal logic. Well-known examples include the *labelled transition systems* and the *linear temporal logic* (LTL) of Manna and Pnueli [65] and the *branching temporal logic* (or CTL), which are also used in verification tools like Spin [33] and Uppaal.[4]

In the past half a century or so, a rich body of formal theories and techniques have been developed. They have made significant contributions to understanding the behaviour of programs. Recently there has been a growing effort in development of tool support for verification and reasoning. However, these techniques and tools, each of which each has its own community of researchers, have been mostly focusing on models of individual viewpoints. For examples, type systems are used for data structures, Hoare Logic for local and static functionality, process calculi (e.g., CSP and CSS) and I/O automata [64] for interaction and synchronisation protocols. While process calculi and I/O automata are similar from the perspective of describing the interaction behaviour of concurrent and distributed components. The former is based on the observation of the global behaviour of interaction sequences, and the latter on the observation of local state transitions caused by interaction events. Processes calculi emphasise algebraic reasoning, and automata are primarily used for algorithmic verification techniques model checking [18,77].

The impact of these theories, techniques and tools on the improvement of qualities of the daily used software systems is yet to become convincing to software engineering practitioners for their industry adoption. The gap between the development of formal methods and the advances in software technologies is not becoming narrower. More precisely, the relation between formal methods and software technologies is not well understood yet. This is clearly reflected by the challenges in engineering current large-scale systems, including CPS, IoT and cloud-based systems, that have multi-dimensional complexities. The experience, e.g., in [34], and investigation reports on software failures, such as those of the Therac-25 Accident in 1985–1987 [44] and the Ariane-5 Explosion in 1996 [81], show that a simple mistake can lead to catastrophic consequences. *Ad hoc* application of the above methods to specification and verification of programs will not be enough or feasible to detect and remove these causes. Different formal techniques that deal with different concerns more effectively have to be systematically and consistently used in all stages of a development process, along with safety analysis that identifies the risks, vulnerabilities, and the consequences of the risk incidents. There are applications that have concerns of extra functionalities, such as real-time and fault-tolerance constraints [57]. Studies show that models with these extra functionalities can be obtained and treated by model transformations of models without these concerns [22,56,57]. But this is yet to be better understood by software engineering practitioners.

4   Case Study: A Trading System

We will use this example to demonstrate the attributes of software complexity, motivate the problems in our discussion, as well as to understand the fundamental concepts and techniques of the model driven method.

---

[4] http://www.uppaal.org.

This case study describes a *Trading System*. It was used as the Common Component Modelling Example (CoCoME) in a comparative modelling exercise using different methods. The problem description and the solutions developed by the participants were presented at the two GI-Dagstuhl Research Seminars [79]. A team from UNU-IIST led by the first author used the rCOS method in the exercise [13]. The case study is an extension of the Point of Sale System (POST) described in the textbook of Larman [42].

This version of the Trading System focuses on the functionalities in terms of *use cases*, related to processing sales in a supermarket. This restriction obviously is related to the limited space. However, it also reflects a fundamental engineering principle that MDA, object-oriented design and component-based design provide effective support [6,27,91] for dealing with complexity. That is,

'start with a small and simple system and get it work; then let the system evolve by adding new features and/or functionalities'.

The description of this case study plays the role of a client's requirements document as if it were provided to the software development team by a business company in the reality. Therefore, the description is potentially imprecise, incomplete and even inconsistent, as it has to go through the requirements analysis by the developer. The Trading System is used in handling sales in a supermarket including the processes at a Cash Desk (or a Point of Sale). For example

1. a Casher *scans* or *types in* the Products being purchased using a Bar Code Scanner or a Keyboard, then the Customer *pays* for the Sale by a Credit Card, or
2. by Cash and receive the Change.

Notice the italic verbs and capitalised nouns, which in later stages of analysis and specification might be formalised as "operations" and "objects" (or "classes"), respectively. These processes of a business task, e.g., handling sales, will be defined as *use case scenarios*, and all the use case scenarios of a task form an abstract *use case*. The Trading System is also used for various administrative tasks, such as reordering various products or generating reports. The following subsection gives a brief overview of the Trading System and its hardware parts. The required use cases will be presented in the subsections to follow. The description is based on Chap. 1 [29] and the rCOS solution [13] of the final workshop proceeding [79].

4.1   The Hardware Components

Software components run on or controls hardware components and their interactions. The Cash Desk is the place where a Sales Assistant/Cashier scans the product items which a customer wants to purchase and where the payments (either by credit card or cash) are carried out. Furthermore it is possible to switch to an express checkout mode which allows only costumers with a few

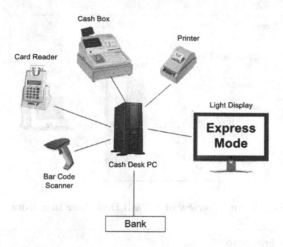

Fig. 2. Hardware components of a single Cash Desk.

items and cash payments to speed up the checkout process. To manage the processes at a Cash Desk a lot of hardware devices are necessary (See Fig. 2).

Using the Cash Box, which is available at each cash desk, a sale can be processed from the start to the end, *through the interactions between the Cashier (a human actor) and the customer (a human actor), and between the Casher and the system under design.* The cash payment process needs to involve the cash box. To handle payments by credit card, a Card Reader is used. In order to identify all product items the Customer are purchasing the Cashier uses the Bar Code Scanner. At the end of the process a receipt is produced using a Printer. Each cash desk is also equipped with a Display to let Customer know if this cash desk is in the express checkout mode or not. The central unit of each cash desk is the Cash Desk PC which interfaces to all the hardware components. This PC also runs the software which is responsible for handling the sale process as well as communication with the Bank for credit payment authorisation.

A single Cash Desk might be enough for the management of a small retail shop. In general, a larger Store has several cash desks in a Cash Desk Line. The cash desk line is connected to a Store Server which itself is also connected to a Store Client as shown in Fig. 3. The store client can be used by the manager of the store to view reports, order products or to change prices of goods. A Store Server is also needed to hold the inventory of the corresponding store.

The Trading System can have even more components. Consider an enterprise with a chain of supermarkets/stores. Then, the cash desk lines of the stores can be connected to a server, called Enterprise Server. With the assistance of an Enterprise Client the Enterprise Manager is able to generate several kinds of reports. The enterprise system of a Store Chain is shown in Fig. 4.

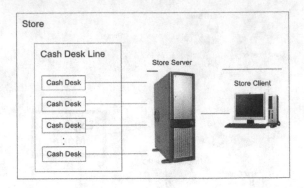

Fig. 3. An overview of a Cash Desk Line in a store.

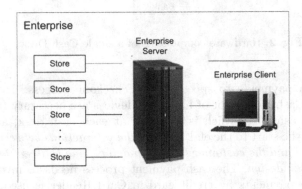

Fig. 4. The Enterprise of a Store Chain with an Enterprise Server and an Enterprise Client.

4.2   Functional Requirements and Use Cases

We describe the functional requirements using the very important notion of *use cases*, though their precise definitions and systematic discussions will be left to Sect. 6.1 in Part II. To show a moderate scale of complexity of the Trading System, we introduce five use cases[5] though we will not present the analysis and design of all of them. In what follows, we present brief and informal descriptions of these use cases.

UC 1 - Process Sale

Overview: A customer arrives at the Cash Desk with the product items to purchase. The payment - either by credit card or cash - is performed. Involved Actors includes Customer, Cashier, and Bank[6].

---

[5] CoCoME [29] has eight use cases.

[6] In the CoCoME problem description [29], the hardware devices, such as Printer, Card Reader, Cash Box, Bar Code Scanner, and Light Display, are also modelled as actors that the software has to interact with. In our approach, they are separated from the application logic and treated as a separate embedded system.

Process: The normal courses of interactions between the actors and the system are described as follows.

1. When a Customer comes to the Cash Desk with her items, the Cashier initiates a new sale.
2. The Cashier enters each item, either by scanning in the bar code or by some other means; if there is more than one of the same item, the Cashier can enter the quantity. The system records each item and its quantity and calculates the subtotal. When the Cash Desk is operating in express mode, only a predefined maximum number of items can be entered.
3. When there are no more items, the Cashier indicates the end of entry. The total of the sale is calculated. The Cashier tells the Customer the total and asks her to pay.
4. The Customer can pay by cash, check, or credit card. If by cash or check, the amount received is entered. The system records the cash payment amount or the check and calculates the change; operating the Cash Box to put cash or the check in and take cash out. If by a credit card, the card information is entered. The system sends the information to the Bank for authorisation. The payment succeeds only if a positive validation reply is received. In express mode, only cash payment is allowed. After the payment is made, the inventory of the store is updated and the completed sale is logged.

Alternative Courses of Events: There are exceptional or alternative courses of interactions, e.g., if the entered bar code is not known in the system, the Customer does not have enough money for a cash payment, or the authorisation reply is negative. A system needs to provide means of handling these exceptional cases, such as cancel the sale or change to another way of paying for the sale.

In many books and papers, e.g., the chapter [29], use case descriptions include *preconditions* and *postconditions*. However, no clear definitions are given to preconditions and postconditions, or the definitions are confusing, specially sometimes the preconditions are confused with the notion of "guards". Guards are conditions for control flow and synchronisation. In our method, we do not have preconditions and postconditions for use cases. Instead, we introduce notions of preconditions, postconditions and guards of *use case operations* in Sect. 8 of Part II. Examples of use case operations include "initiate new sale", "enter item", "make cash payment". We will give details on use case operations in Sect. 8 of Part II.

UC 2 - Manage Express Checkout Mode

Overview: The Cashier should be able to switch the checkout mode between "express mode" and "normal mode" by pressing a button at his Cash Desk. Involved Actors includes Cashier only.

Process: The normal courses of interactions between the actors and the system are informally described as follows.

1. Depending on the current mode of the check out, the Cashier switches the mode to "express" if it is currently "normal".

Notice this is a one-step process. Unlike the description given in [29] where automatic control of checking model is considered, we leave the decision of changing mode to the human actor, Cashier. To automatically control this operation, the human operator would be replaced by a digital operator triggered by a certain condition. In this chapter, automatic control of hardware devices is not considered.

UC 3 - Order Products

Overview: For the purpose of inventory control in a store, products should be ordered when the stock becomes low (determined by a threshold value). There are two actors involved: Store Manager and Product Suppliers.

Process: The normal process of interactions of Store Manager and the Trading System is as follows.

1. The Store Manager makes an Order (of Products).
2. The Store Manager enters the identities of the products, their amounts and the identities of the corresponding suppliers to the system, one product at a time.
3. The Order is saved in the system and the order is sent to Suppliers.

UC 4 - Receive Delivery of Ordered Products

Overview: When a delivery of ordered products arrives at the Store, the Store Manager checks the correctness and completeness (compared to the order), and then the inventory is updated. The Store Manager is the involved actor.

Process: The normal course of interactions is:

1. A Delivery of ordered products arrives at the Store.
2. The Store Manager checks the delivery against the order for correctness and completeness.
3. The Store Manager updates the inventory of all the received products.

Alternative Courses of Events:

- Step 1: if the delivery is not correct (either the delivery contains products not ordered, or larger amounts of some products delivered than ordered), exception handling is needed.
- Step 2: if the delivery is not complete (either there are omissions of products ordered or not enough amounts of some ordered products have delivered), exception handling is needed.

UC 5 - Product Exchange Among Stores. Consider an enterprise of a chain of stores. If a store runs out of certain products and these products are not available from their suppliers, it is possible for this store to ask the enterprise management to check whether those products are available in some other stores. If there is such a store, called a Providing Store, it will ship the requested products to the store that asked for them. Notice that this use case involves interactions among Requesting Server (i.e., the server of the requesting store), Enterprise Server and Providing Server (i.e., the server of the providing store).

Overview: The Requesting Store Manager makes a query (similar to a Product Order) at her Store Server. This Store Server sends the query to the Enterprise Sever. The Enterprise Server then looks for a Providing Store, through interaction with the other servers at the stores of the enterprise. Once a Providing Store is found, the product query is passed on to the Providing Store Server. The Providing Store Server generates a delivery according to the product query and send to the Requesting Store Server. The Providing Store ships the products to the Requesting Store.

Process: The normal course of interactions is described as follows.

1. The Requesting Store Manager makes a query.
2. The Requesting Store Manager enters the identities and amounts, one at a time, in the query.
3. After entering the last item, the Requesting Store Manager indicates the Requesting Store Server to save the query and sends it to Enterprise Server.
4. Enterprise Server looks for a Providing Store through interactions with the other Store Servers.
5. The Providing Store Server generates a delivery according to the query.
6. The Providing Store Server sends the delivery to the Requesting Store Server.

Alternative course of interactions:

- Step 2. If product identity is not known, raise exception handling.
- Step 3. If Enterprise Server is not available (in terms of communication and system failures), exception handling (keep trying for example), raise exception handling.
- Step 4. If no providing stores is available, exception handling, including communication failures in finding a providing store, raise exception handling.
- Step 5. The delivery fails to be received by the Requesting Store Server (communication error), raise exception handling.

Remarks

1. The enterprise server needs to realise a distributed algorithm to find a providing store. The algorithm should be efficient in terms of space and time complexity, and implements a strategy that this economically optimal.
2. There is a use case for each store server to be designed and implemented to receive the shipment of the goods against the delivery received from the providing store server.

3. The requirements description does not have to start with such a use case involving interactions between a number of subsystems. We could instead write use cases Prepare Query, Look for Providing Store, and Prepare for Delivery. Then we analyse and design them in separation. We can then compose (or integrate) them together with middleware.

In the CoCoME functional requirements description [29], three more use cases are introduced. They are *Show Stock Reports*, *Show Delivery Reports* and *Change Price*. These use cases are quite simple by themselves. However, they introduce significant complexity to system integration. We also notice the descriptions of the use cases involve hardware devices, such as printers, lights and cash boxes as actors. However, in our approach we treat these hardware devices as an embedded system separated from the application logic. They can be represented as variables to be changed by the use case operations, such as "switch light" and "print sale".

The discussion of use cases in this section is rather ad hoc. Thus, it is impossible to carry out systematic analysis and design. In the sections to follow, we will introduce a definition of use cases, their presentations, and compositions for requirements analysis.

5   Software Engineering Process in Brief

The model-driven approach we present combines object-oriented design and component-based design. Although its principles and techniques of modelling, analysis and design can be used in general software processes, this approach supports especially seamlessly the use case driven Rational Unified Process [40].

5.1   Software Development Processes

Recall the view of software engineering introduced in Sect. 2 as being concerned with the theories, methods and tools which are needed to develop software systems. Its aim is the production of dependable software, delivered on time and within budget, that meets the user's requirements. For all life cycles of the software, that is reliable installation, operation and maintenance as well for the development cycles, software development not only produces a working software system, but also documents such as those of the requirements specification, system design, user manual, and so on. For the development of a software system of a certain scale of complexity, there is a need for an *engineering process* which allows techniques and tools of software methods to be used effectively and systematically (See Sect. 2 about the 2nd attribute of software complexity).

All engineering is about how to produce products in a disciplined process. In general, an *engineering process* defines who is involved in the process, which products is being produced, what and when activities of the process happens, and which and when techniques and tools are being used for the production of what artefacts. A process to build a software system and its documents or to enhance an existing one is called a **software development process**. A software development process is thus often described in terms of a set of activities needed to transform the user's (or client's) requirements into a software system. At the highest level of abstraction, a development process is in general an iterative of activities that can be depicted in Fig. 5.

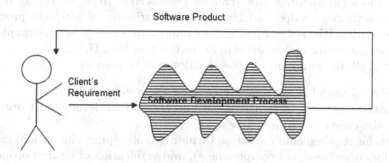

Fig. 5. Software development process

The *client's requirements* define the goal of the software development. They are prepared by the client (sometimes with the help from a software engineer) to set out the services that the system is expected to provide, e.g., the functional requirements of the Trading System described by the sue cases in Sect. 4. Apart from functional requirements, a client may also have non-functional constraints they would like to place on the system, such as the required response time or the use of a specific language standard. In this chapter, we are mainly concerned with functional requirements.

We must bear in mind about the following facts, as demonstrated in the description of the Trading System, which make the requirements capture and analysis very difficult:

- The client's requirements are often incomplete.
- The client's requirements are usually described in terms of concepts, objects and terminology that may not be directly understandable to software engineers (cf. first attribute of software complexity discussed in Sect. 2).
- The client's requirements are usually unstructured and they are not supposed to be rigorous, without redundancy, vagueness, and inconsistency.
- The client's requirements may not be feasible, as one cannot expect a client to know as well as software engineers, about theories of computability and computational complexity, and about state of the art of computer technologies.

Therefore, any development process must start with the activities of capturing and analysing (part of) the system requirements based on the client's requirements. These activities and the associated results form the first phase (or sub-process) of the process called *requirements gathering and analysis*.

5.2 Requirements Gathering and Analysis

This phase is to develop a good understanding of the application domain and capture the right requirements for the system to design. It is the first step aiming the development towards an adequate system[7]. The goal is to produce the artefact called the *requirements specification*. The whole scope of requirements capture and analysis forms *requirements engineering*. Here, we briefly discuss the main activities needed and the essential attributes of artefacts produced by the activities. We study object-oriented and component-based techniques for requirements capture and analysis in Sects. 6.1–8 in Part II.

First of all, the requirements specification will be used as

1. a fairly full model of the requirements for the system to design;
2. a contract agreed between the client and the system development organisation, also called the *project developer*;
3. a basis for requirements validation including prototyping, simulation, reasoning (for correctness and completeness), and verification of desired properties of the specification;
4. a basis for design and system verification:
   – test cases should be made against the specification, and
   – test cases should be designed to cover all the crucial services required;
5. a basis for system evolution.

To produce a requirements specification with the above attributes, requirements analysts need notations, techniques and tool support to carry out the following highly iterative interrelated activities, involving discussions and collaborations with the client, the application domain experts, and the potential system users.

– **Domain understanding.** The analysts must develop their understanding of the application domain. Therefore, the concepts are explored and the clients' requirements are elicited.
– **Requirements capturing.** The analyst must have a way of capturing the clients' needs so that they can be clearly communicated to everyone involved in the project. Skills of abstraction are important to capture the essence and ignore the accidental details.
– **Classification.** This activity takes the unstructured collection of requirements captured in the earlier phases and organises them into coherent clusters, and then prioritises the requirements according to their importance to the client and the users.
– **Validation.** This is to check if the requirements are consistent and complete, and to resolve conflicts between requirements.
– **Feasibility study.** This is to estimate whether the identified requirements may be satisfied using the software and hardware technologies, and to decide if the proposed system will be cost effective.

---

[7] There can be a number of adequate systems, as discussed in Sect. 2 about the 3rd attribute of software complexity.

There are no rigid rules on when requirements analysis is completed and the development process proceeds into the next phase. It is helpful, however, to ask the following questions before the development progresses moving into the next phase:

- Has the system requirements been understood by the clients, end-users, and the developers?
- Has a fairly complete model of the requirements been built? This model specifies what the system must do in terms of
  - available functions (or services),
  - inputs and outputs, and
  - necessary data.
- Are the functions and data correct and complete, and how are they related? To check this, fast prototyping for validation is often used.

Precise and systematic statements of these questions and development of their answers require notations for requirements description and techniques and tools for their analysis. In Sects. 6.1–8 of Part II, we will introduce these notations and techniques, and demonstrate how they are used in the requirements analysis of the Trading Systems. They are largely based on the notion of use cases and structures of conceptual classes, the UML notations and tool support. Rigorous requirements specification and analysis (i.e., mathematical based analysis) fall into the scope of *formal requirements specification and analysis*. In summary, we make two remarks on requirements analysis:

- The requirements specification is the official statement of what is required of the system to be developed. It is not a design document and it must state what to be done rather than how it is done. It must be in a form which can be taken as the starting point for the software development. For this, specification languages, including graphic notations, are often used to describe the requirements specification.
- The requirements capture and analysis phase is important, as an error which is not discovered at the requirements analysis phase is likely to remain undiscovered, and the later it is discovered, the more difficult and more expensive is it to fix.

5.3   System Design

After the requirements specification is produced through requirements analysis[8], it undergoes iterative cycles of *architectural design* and *detailed design*. In the architecture design of a cycle, part of the requirements are partitioned into interconnected *components* which are specified in terms of their *interfaces* and the *contracts of the interfaces*. This results in an *architectural design document*. Then each component undergoes its *detailed design*, to decide how each component does what it is required to do by the contracts of its interfaces. The

---

[8] It is not necessarily for the overall requirements analysis to be completed before design activities can start.

architectural design is in general an abstract and implementation independent high level platform independent (PIM), defining the functionality and interface of each component. The detailed design is a low level PIM and it is desirable that an implementation can be generated once the programming language and system platform are given.

In Sect. 10.1 of Part III, we show how the architecture design is derived from the use case analysis and decomposition. The artefact produced there is the architectural design document called an *architectural model*, consisting of some component-based diagrams and the models of component interface contracts. In Sect. 11 of Part III, each component is designed using five design principles of responsibility assignments to objects [42], resulting in a detailed design model. The model of the system at this level is a low level PIM and it can be seen as a template program modules.

Correctness of Detailed Design. Verification of the design of the architectural components should be in general done against the specification of the components in the system architectural model. There are few effective techniques and tools for this correctness assurance if the model of the architecture and the models of the detailed designed components are informal. In formal methods, the verification of a low level design model can to some extend be done by logic reasoning, and automatically checking the low level model satisfies specified properties of the high level model using *model checking* techniques and tools.

Implementation and Unit Testing. After the design of the system architecture and the (detailed) design of the architectural components, each of the designed components is realised as a program unit. Each unit then must be either tested against its specification obtained in the design stage - *unit testing*, or formally verified using techniques and tools of automatic *static analysis*, *dynamic analysis*, and model checking.

System Integration and System Testing. The individual program units representing the components of the system are combined and tested as a whole to ensure that the software requirements have been met. When the developers are satisfied with the product, it is then go through acceptance testing. This phase ends when the product is accepted by the client. System testing plan must be made and test cases must be designed according to the system requirements specification.

Operation and Maintenance. This phase starts with the system being installed for practical use, after the product is delivered to the client. It lasts till the beginning of system's retirement phase, which we are not concerned in this chapter. Maintenance includes all changes to the product once the client has agreed that it satisfied the specification document. Traditionally, corrective maintenance (or software repair) and enhancement (or software update) are the main concerns. Corrective maintenance involves correcting errors which were not discovered in earlier stages of the development process while leaving the specification unchanged.

Modern software systems, however, are ever evolving, as their operation environments are constantly changing. Evolutionary changes include legacy components being upgraded or removed, and new components being integrated. These different components are often implemented and deployed on different platforms, and are interacting via different communication technologies and networks. Therefore, the maintenance process of modern systems now become different cycles of requirements analysis, design, implementation and integration. The method that we will introduce in later sections is characterised as use case driven and component-based design, with interfaces as a first concepts. This method provides effective support to the development of modern evolutionary software systems.

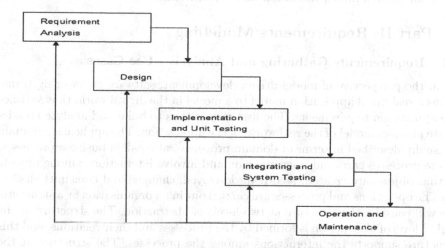

Fig. 6. Software development process

Waterfall Model of Development Process. According to the software development activities discussed in the earlier subsections, a development process is often organised into the so-called "waterfall model" depicted in Fig. 6. However, variants and extensions of the waterfall model are used in practical software system development, such that

- The stages in the waterfall model overlap and feed information to each other: during design, problems in requirements are identified; during coding, design problems are found and so on. Therefore, the development process is not a simple linear model but involves a sequence of iterations of the development activities.

- Sometimes it is quite difficult to partition the development activities in a project into these distinct stages.
- The waterfall model is often extended with validation and/verification activities/phases which are often inserted between two consecutive steps of the water fall model, and this extension model is called the *V-model* of development process [76].

The waterfall model can be used for some statistic studies about the software development. It mainly serves us for organisation and terminology of the discussions of the development activities and models of artefacts.

Our approach, being as the background motivation for and the informed practical approach by the development of the rCOS formal methods, supports the principle of *correct by construction* and improved assurance by validation and verification. Also, the construction identifies the obligations of validation and verification. In this chapter, we focus on model construction without the space for enough model validation and verification.

6   Part II: Requirements Modelling

6.1   Requirements Gathering and Analysis - Use Cases

From the perspective of model-driven development, software engineering transforms a real world application model to a model in the digital world that satisfies the application requirements. The first step is thus to build and analyse an adequate abstract model of the real world of the application. The application domain is usually described in terms of domain processes, also called business processes. These processes carry out operations on and involve interactions among objects so that objects are created, recorded, destroyed, changed and transmitted.

The operations and processes are carried out in an organisation or a structure. We will consider the structure at two levels of abstraction. The structure at the higher level of abstraction is formed by the processes and their relations, and this structure supports the interactions among the processes. The structure at the lower level supports the interaction among the objects involved in the execution of operations. The structures for processes interactions are component-based; and the structures for object interactions are object-oriented, are formed by objects and their relations.

We study an approach to build models for analysis, design and verification with these two kinds of structures and their relations. Thus, our approach is a combination of object-oriented and component-based modelling and analysis, driven by the domain processes. The main ideas are to model domain processes by use cases, and real world concepts and objects by classes and with relations between classes as associations. The classes and their associations will form a conceptual class model of the domain. The structure of the domain processes is represented by a component-based model of the architecture. The main points discussed in this section are: *use case descriptions* of domain processes, and *use case diagrams* for representing relations between use cases as well as *actors* and between use cases.

6.2 Use Cases

A key point in *object-oriented analysis* is decomposition by classification of the domain objects and their relations. An important technique to help in identifying and understanding domain concepts and objects and their relations is to inspect the domain processes. We use a *use case* for a narrative description of a domain process in terms of interactions between the users and the system. Domain processes that are required to be automated by the software must be done no matter which software requirements engineering approach is used in a software project. For example, the concept of use cases is similar to *viewpoints* in structured software requirements analysis.

Roughly speaking, a **use case** is a story board that tells how users carry out a business process (or a task). Here a 'system' does not have to be a digital system. It can be, for example, a paper based manual system. A 'user' does not have to be a human actor either. It can be, for example, a device or a digital system. More precisely, a **use case** describes possible *sequences of interactions* by *some types of users* using *some of the system functionality* to complete a process. Such a type of user is called an **actor**. An **interaction** is an happening of an *operation* by a user on the system or a *message* from the system to an actor.

A given user may have several roles and thus be different actors when interacting with the system. For example, a Store Server can act as a Requesting Store Server or as a Providing Store Server. On the other hand, several individual users may act as different instances of the same actor. For example, there can be many individual Cashiers. Therefore an actor represents a coherent role in using the system, rather than representing a particular individual or entity. In other words, an actor represents a type of users of the system. Actors are external to but interacting with the system. A use case is always initiated by some possible **initiator actor**. The actors that directly interact with the system are **direct actors**.

An actor interacts with the system by *sending messages* to and *receiving messages* from the system. For examples, a Cashier sends a message to record an item, and the system sends a request to actor Bank for authorising a credit payment. We make the following remarks on use cases.

- Use cases describe functional requirements of the system from the actors' perspective, stating what the actors do to use the system for realising application tasks.
- Each use case uses part of the functionalities of the system, providing a natural divide and conquer strategy and helping to identify system components.
- Actors form the *external environment* of the application; they define the boundary of the system under design. This offers a basis for *interfaced-oriented design of ever evolving systems*, such as cloud-based systems, IoT, and CPS [39, 43].

These features show that the use case driven approach is consistent with David Parnas' Four Value Model[9], and share the similar philosophical thinking to Michael Jackson's Problem Frames[10].

Identifying Use Cases. It is not in general easy to capture the use cases for an application. This obviously needs close collaboration between the requirements analyst and the domain expert. There are two approaches to find use cases, and they are often used together in practice.

1. **Actor-based**
   (a) identify the actors related to the system in the organisation, i.e., look at which users in the organisation will use the application and which other systems must interact with it; and
   (b) for each actor, identify the processes they initiate or participate in by reviewing how the actor communicates/interacts with the application.
2. **Event-based**
   (a) identify the external events that a system must respond to, and
   (b) relate the events to actors and use cases.

For example, in the Trading Systems the five uses case are easily identified through the actors Customer, Cashier and Store Manager. On the other hand, a use case for automatic checking the inventory of products and generating an alert to Store Manager can be identified by the alert and then this event is related to a "timer" as the initiating actor.

To identify use cases, we need to read the existing requirements from an actor's perspective and interact with those who will act as actors. It is necessary to think and discuss questions like:

- what are the main tasks of the actor?
- which of these tasks can be automated, and with what added values?
- will the actor have to read/write/change any of the system information?
- will the actor have to inform the system about outside changes?
- does the actor wish to be informed about changes?

6.3   Incremental Use Case Analysis

Capturing, understanding and describing use cases go hand in hand, and in an incremental manner. Taking the example of the Trading System introduced in Sect. 4 in Part I. Customer and Cashier are obviously associated with an use case Process Sale. After the identification of these actors and this use case, we can write down our initial understanding of this process as an overview below.

Use Case: Process Sale
Actors: Customer, Cashier

---

[9] http://en.wikipedia.org/wiki/DavidParnas.
[10] https://en.wikipedia.org/wiki/Problem_frames_approach.

Process of Interactions:
  1. Customer arrives at the Cash Desk with items to purchase.
  2. Cashier records the purchase items and collects payment.
  3. On completion, Customer leaves with the items.

This *overview* is a rather abstract description, but it contains significant information about what this use case does as well as the what actors are involved.

Consider, as another example, a software system used in a university library. An actor Librarian is easily identified in the application, and then another actor, Member (of the library) that defines the people who use the library. A possible use cease is to register a member. We write the following overview of the use case.

Use Case: Register Member
Actors: Member, Librarian
Process of Interactions:
  1. Member arrives at the reception desk with identification.
  2. Librarian records the personal details and issues a card.
  3. On completion, the Customer leaves with the card.

In the same way, we can identify more use cases and their actors for both the Trading System. A use case is a *complete course of interaction events described from the users' perspective*. This is a very important property of use cases, avoiding writing partial business processes as use cases or arbitrarily combining use case.

To support incremental development of use case documentation, we use the following structured format proposed in Larman's textbook [42] for writing overviews of use cases.

Use case:	**Name of use case** (use a phrase starting with a verb)
Actors:	List of actors
Purpose:	Intention of the use case
Overview:	A brief description of sequence of events in the process
Cross References:	Relations to other use cases and artefacts for **traceability**

Example. As an example of incremental use case analysis, we first consider a simpler version of Process Sale of the Trading System, which handles sales with cash payment.

Use case:	**Process Sale with Cash Payment**
Actors:	Customer (initiator), Cashier (direct actor)
Purpose:	Capture a **sale** and its **cash payment**
Overview:	A **customer** arrives at the **cash desk** with **items** to purchase. The **cashier** *records* the purchase **items** and *collects* the **cash payment**. On completion, the Customer leaves with the items
Cross References:	Restricted case of use case Process Sale

Notice in the above representation, the nouns that represent important concepts and objects in the domain are written in bold so that they will be identified as classes later when we develop the *class model* of the domain. This approach is suggested to adopt in practical project development. Also, some important verbs are emphasised, such as *records* and *collects*. They indicate possible interaction events.

The above high level overview use case, with only a couple of significant concepts (nouns) and interactions (verbs), does not contain sufficient information for identifying enough interaction events, concepts and objects. Further analysis of a high level use case through meeting with domain experts and end users are needed to refine it to a detailed use case, called an **expanded use case** in [42]. The refinement focuses on details about the interaction actions between the actors and the system and information about:

- input data an actor provides to the system when performing an interaction,
- data that an actor receives after an interaction,
- what the system does when an actor performs an interaction action, e.g., what objects are created, data updated, checked or read[11],
- the main course of actions and the time when exceptions may occur and how to handle them, and
- invariant properties that are preserved by the actions, including specific safety properties of the business process.

For expanded use cases, we also follow the structured format for their documentation proposed in Larman's textbook [42], which extends a high-level use case with a section of typical course of events and a section of alternative courses of events (or exceptions), respectively. The typical course of events is presented in an style of a conversation between the (direct) actors and the system.

Expanded Use Case Process Sale with Cash Payment

Use case:	**Process Sale with Cash Payment**
Actors:	Customer, Cashier
Purpose:	Capture a **sale** and its **cash payment**
Overview:	A **customer** arrives at the **cash desk** with **items** to purchase. The **cashier** *records* the purchase **items** and *collects* the **cash payment**. On completion, the Customer leaves with the items
References:	Restricted case of use case Process Sale

---

[11] This is the basis for identification of postconditions of an operation in Sect. 8.

Typical Course of Events

Actor Action	System Response
1. This use case begins when the **Customer** arrives at **Cash Desk** with **items** to purchase.	
2. Cashier starts a new sale.	**3.** Creates a new sale.
4. Cashier *records* the **identifier** for each **item**.	**5.** Determines the **item price** and *adds* the **item information** to the **running sale transaction**.
If there is more than one item, the Cashier may enter the **quantity** as well.	The **description** and **price** of the current **item** are presented.
6. On completion of item entry, the Cashier ends item entry is completed	**7.** Calculates and presents the *sale total*.
8. Cashier tells the Customer the total.	
9. Customer gives a **cash amount**, possibly greater than the sale total.	
10. Cashier *records* the **cash amount received amount**.	**11.** Shows the **balance** due back to the Customer. Generates a **receipt**.
12. Cashier deposits the cash received and extracts the amount back. Cashier gives the balance owing and the printed receipt to the Customer.	**13.** Logs the **completed sale**.
14. Customer leaves with the items purchased.	

Alternative Courses

– Line 4: Invalid identifier entered. Indicate error.
– Line 9: Customer didn't have enough cash. Cancel sales transaction.

This is slightly different from the use case "Buy Items with Cash" in Larman's book [42]. There, there are no steps **2** and **3** to start a new sale. Instead, these two steps and the following steps **4** and **5** are combined into the following step of interaction.

| **2. Cashier** records the **identifier** for each **item**. | **3.** If it is a new sale creates a sale. Determines the **item price** and *adds* the **item information** to the **running sale transaction**. |

This shows that a business process can be represented by use cases with different sequences of interactions. The decision on which one should be selected in the requirements specification needs to be made by the client and the project enveloper together. For complex cases, validation, say by prototyping or scenario plays, should be conducted to help the decision making. Experience from teaching shows that our slightly longer use case description is easier to formulate, and there is a general pattern that a use case often has a 'start' operation by a direct actor. For example, 'start to register a new customer', and 'start to make a new order'. On the other hand, after one use case is described and understood, it may be changed into another acceptable by further decomposing interactions or combining interactions[12].

Remarks. A use case description always implies, explicitly or implicitly, assumptions on the functionalities of the use case. Significant assumptions are better to be stated clearly for the sake of further refinement. The above stated Process Sale with Cash Payment makes the following assumptions:

- there is only one cash desk;
- there is no inventory management;
- no tax calculations (that is needed in the U.S.) or coupons;
- no record maintained of customers (some important business analysis or analysis of customer's buying habits (related to big data));
- no control of the cashbox;
- name and address of store are not shown on the receipt; and
- Cashier ID and CashDesk ID are not shown on receipts.

The given simplified Process Sale with Cash Payment can be refined step by step by adding more details to remove these restrictions. This can either be done at the requirements gathering and analysis phase, or in another cycle after the design, or even after the implementation, of this simplified use case.

Writing a good use case description requires experience, but we do not have the luxury of space for more examples. Readers can practise on the other use cases of the Trading Systems, use cases of a Library System, or an ATM system. For example, one can identify and describe the use cases of Check Balance, Deposit Money, Withdraw Money, and Transfer Money. More examples of us ceases can be founded in textbooks on use-case driven development processes [40].

---

[12] Though the use case of Process Sale with Cash Payment and the use case of Buy Items with Cash [42] are both adequate, one is not a *refinement* of another by formal theory of refinement or process simulations.

6.4   Use Case Diagrams

A use-case diagram represents a set of use cases, actors, and their relationships. In a use case diagram, as the one shown in Fig. 7, an oval represents a use case, a stick figure represents an actor, a line between an actor and a use case represents that the actor initiates and/or participates in the process[13]. The diagram shows three simple use cases of the Trading System.

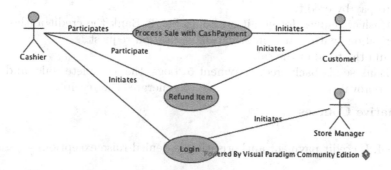

Fig. 7. An example of a use case diagram

We are not going to give the full definition of the syntax of the UML use case diagrams, as they can be found in many books and on many websites. We focus on the use of the modelling notation, thus we introduce the syntactic features that we need along with our discussion. Use case diagrams offer a means of organising use cases into groups such that the use cases in a group are logically related in the application domain. In Sect. 10.1 in Part III, each use case is modelled as a component that can be further decomposed into subcomponents. Also the components of the use cases in a use case diagram can be composed into a composite component.

6.5   Use Case Composition

Composition is essential in incremental development, just as decomposition is essential for divide and conquer. Now we show how to decompose large use cases into compositions of smaller ones. As an example, it is not difficult to see that the sequence of actions from steps **9** to **13** in the use case Process Sale with Cash Payment can be treated as a (sub-)use case, which we call Pay by Cash. In the same way as we identify and describe Pay by Cash, we can have two more use cases Pay by Credit and Pay by Check, both in addition to Cashier and

---

[13] The diagram, as many of the other UML diagrams in this chapter, is produced by using Visual Diagram www.visual-paradigm.com/features/uml-and-sysml-modeling.

Customer involving actor Bank for payment authorisation. We write the typical course of events and alternative courses of Pay by Credit as follows.

Typical Course of Events

Actor Action	System Response
1. Customer tells Cashier she wants to pay by credit.	
2. Cashier request for credit authorisation with card information and the total of the sale.	3. Sends Bank the credit authorisation request.
4. Bank sends back credit payment approval.	5. Logs the complete sale and generates the receipt.

Alternative Courses

– Line 4. If credit payment authorisation is denied raise exception.

This example also shows tricky decisions on the levels of abstraction. In the above description, the credit payment is decomposed into two phases of interactions: Cashier asks the system to enter a state for credit authorisation with the required input data, the system sends the authorisation request to Bank, Bank sends back the approval to the system and the system completes the payment and logs the sale. If PIN is required for the authorisation, Customer should also be a direct actor, and more interactions are required. One can also decide that the action of the sending the requests by the system to Bank for the credit authorisation will return a value that can be seen by Cashier. In this case, step 4 is changed to *Cashier indicates the system to complete the payment*. One can also decide to make the credit payment as one atomic step of interaction as follows.

Typical Course of Events

Actor Action	System Response
1. Customer tells Cashier she wants to pay by credit.	
2. Cashier records the credit payment information.	3. Sends the credit payment to Bank for authorisation. If the request is approved, it completes the payment. Logs the complete sale, and generates receipt.

Alternative Courses

– Line 2. If credit payment authorisation is denied, raise exception.

We will later see these different decisions also lead to different models of use case sequence diagrams, state machine diagrams, and contracts of the interaction operations. They also encounter theoretical problems. For example, the contract of the above 'big' operation of "records the credit payment" is hard to define as its execution involves calling for services, and the precondition relies on the result of the authorisation request from Bank.

Now we can use the three use cases for handling payments to form the general **Process Sale** use case, for which the typical course of actions is as follows.

Typical Course of Events

Actor Action	System Response
1. This use case begins with a Customer arrives at the Cash Desk checkout with items to purchase.	
2. Cashier indicates the system to start a new sale.	3. Creates a new sale.
4. Cashier records the identifier from each item.	5. Determines the item price and adds the item information to the running sales transaction.
If there is more than one of the same item, Cashier can enter the quantity as well.	The description and price of the current item are presented.
6. On completion of the item entry, Cashier indicates to the CashDesk that item entry is completed.	7. Calculates and presents the sale total.
8. Cashier tells Customer the total	
9. Customer chooses a payment method: (a) If cash payment, **initiate** *Pay by Cash*. (b) If credit payment, **initiate** *Pay by Credit*. (c) If cheque payment, **initiate** *Pay by Cheque*.	
	10. Logs the completed sale. And prints a receipt.
11. Cashier gives the printed receipt to the Customer.	
12. Customer leaves with the items purchased.	

A composite use case can be represented in a use-case diagram as shown in Fig. 8.

Remarks. About use case composition and decomposition.

1. In general, a use case may contain decision points. If one of these decision paths represents the overwhelming typical case, and the others alternatives

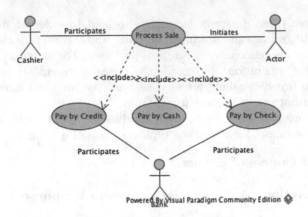

Fig. 8. Use case diagram for composite use cases

are rare and exceptional, then the typical case should be the only one in the Typical Course of events, and the alternatives should be in the Alternative Courses section. However, if the decision points represent alternatives which are all relatively common, then they appear as individual use cases in the main use case, such as Process Sale.

2. A use case represents a complete business process. It is not right to break a use case into arbitrary sequences of interactions. Neither is it right to compose arbitrary use cases to form a bigger one. For example one should not put Process Sale and Refund Item together to form a use cases.

3. Later, we will represent each use case as a *component* to provide services (interfaces) to it actors, and a composite use case corresponds to a component composed of the components of the sub-use cases. However, use case diagrams do not model interfaces of components. We introduce component diagrams in Sect. 10.1 of Part III.

6.6   Use Case Analysis in Development Process

The key steps for capturing and describing use cases are as follows.

1. Identify actors and use cases according to business (or domain) processes.
2. Carry out incremental use case analysis: from abstract high level to expanded versions with data to input, output, store and update.
3. Decompose and compose use cases.
4. Analyse and document the explicit and implicit assumptions made by each use case.
5. Rank use cases for project planning.
6. Present use case diagrams to group use cases belonging to business processes.

Write the expanded version most critical, influential and risky use cases to better understand and estate the nature and size of the problem.

The Significance of Use Cases Analysis

- Use cases answer the question what the system should do it in terms of what the system should do for each user/actor. They therefore identify the functionalities/services that the system provides to its users, and help to remove functionalities that do not have added values.
- Use cases identify relations among the system services/functionalities, as well as the required system services/functionalities. Therefore, services and functionalities are related in the processes to which they contribute.
- Use cases also relate functionalities and services to concepts and objects in the application domain. As illustrated in the next section, these concepts and objects are essential in modelling the structure of the system, and are later in the design realised as software classes and objects.
- Use cases are also used as "placeholders" for non-functional requirements (now widely called *extra functionality*), such as performance, availability, timing constraints, accuracy, and security requirements that are specific to a use case. Consider the use case Pay by Credit: It may be required that the authorisation result will be received in 30 s after the cashier makes the authorisation request. We will not discuss non-functional requirements in this chapter.

Relation to the rCOS Formal Method: The use case descriptions are purely textual and the use case diagrams are only a static organisation of the use cases. The analysis and description are not direct related to any formal techniques for requirements analysis. However, the conversational style presentations of the expanded use cases form the basis for obtaining the use case sequence diagrams in Sect. 8, and the use case diagrams will be further refined into component-based architecture models in Sect. 10.1. Both sequence diagrams and component-based model of architectures can be formalised in rCOS. However, we refer the reader to the paper [49,59] on a model of formal and use case-driven requirements analysis in the UML.

7 Requirements Modelling and Analysis – Conceptual Class Model

An important activity in object-oriented requirement analysis is to identify the domain concepts and their relations to create a *conceptual class model* of the domain[14]. The term "domain" covers the application area, e.g., the supermarkets in the Trading System case study. This section introduces the principles and techniques for identifying concepts which are meaningful in the problem domain, and the notation for representing them as a conceptual class model. The main objectives of this section are to

---

[14] A "conceptual model" is also called a "domain model". A conceptual model can also be seen as an *ontology model* does in information systems, but it is the part of the ontology model that contains only the concepts and relations relevant for the requirements of the system under design.

- understand the concepts of classes, associations and attributes;
- identify classes, their attributes and associations in the problem domain;
- understand the defining properties of objects that are important for distinguish objects from attributes of objects;
- define class diagrams and their use;
- understand the relevance and consistency relation between the conceptual
  model and the use cases model of a project.

The artefact that domain concept analysis produces is the conceptual class model
mainly formed by packages of *conceptual class diagrams*.

7.1 Concepts in Conceptual Models

Object-orientation supports divide and conquer by dividing the problem domain
in terms of interrelated individual concepts and their objects. These concepts and
objects are meaningful in the application domain and they are relevant to the
required business process.

A concept is an idea, a thing, or a set of objects. More formally, a **concept** is considered in terms of three defining elements: **symbol**, **intension** and
extension[15]:

- A **symbol**, in the form of words (or images) is used to refer to the concept
  when communicating and discussing about the concept.
- The **intension** is the definition of the concepts, this is, what the concept
  intents to define.
- The **extension** consists of the individual examples or instances to which the
  definition of concept applies.

From now on, we use **instance** or **object** to refer an individual example of a
concept. We also use *use cases* and *business process* as synonyms, though the
latter is more often used in the context of the domain discussion.

Considering the realisation of "business processes" involves "objects" in the
application domain and their "interactions", the above understanding of the
term "concept" is fundamental to object-oriented modelling and analysis. For
example, in the descriptions of Process Sale with Cash Payment, the concepts of
"Store", "Sale", "Product Item", and "Cash Payment" are used. This implies that
some instances of these concepts are involved in the execution of the process
represented by this use case. The concepts which have instances involved in the
realisation of a business process are said to be *relevant* to the use case. For
another example, in the student management system of a university, the symbol
Module is used to refer to the concept that has

- the intension to "represent a course offered as part of a degree in that university" with a code, title, and number of credits;
- the extension of all the individual modules being offered in the university.

---

[15] This is similar to *intentional* and *extensional* definitions of sets in mathematics.

Consider the concepts of "university" and "degree". Instances of "module" are parts of instances of "degree", and instances of "degree" are parts of instances of "university". Concepts and objects are defined in terms of other concepts, thus objects have hierarchical structures. Concepts also have **attributes** and concrete values of an attribute define a property of an individual instance. For examples, "Student" has name and age, and Module has code, title and credit; and a student with name John Smith and age 19. Actions in a use case may create (say when a student is enrolled) or destroy (say if a student is expelled from the university) instances of relevant concepts, as well as changing properties of existing instances.

Also, concepts are related to each other so that their instances can interact with each other in a use case execution. In the student management of a university, for example, Student and Module are related by a relation "Student Takes Module". The relation between concepts also defines a means for navigating from one object to the other. For example from a student instance, one can find about the modules that the student "takes". The attributes of relevant concepts of a use case are called *relevant attributes* to the use case if they are maintained, manipulated and transmitted in the use case, and relations among the relevant concepts that supports the interactions in the use case execution are the *relevant relations*.

Concepts can have numerous attributes and relations, abstraction is about to only include the relevant concepts, attributes and relations, excluding anything irrelevant. This is a general object-oriented principle of modelling and design known as "the need to know principle".

In modelling requirements and designs, it is important to differ *attributes* of classes from *associations* between classes, and *properties* (values of attributes) of objects from *relations* (links of associations) between objects models. Attributes in general take simple values, instead of relating complex domain objects. It is common in object-oriented programming languages that associations are represented as attributes by pointers or references that have object types. However, associations do not have to be implemented by pointers or references, e.g., in relational databases.

7.2 Classes and Class Diagrams in the UML

UML proposes a graphic modelling notation for **class diagrams** that models concepts as **classes**, e.g., in Fig. 9a, their conceptual attributes as **class attributes** (also called **members** in object-oriented programming languages), and relations between concepts as **associations**, e.g., in Fig. 9b.

Objects. Each instance in the extension of a concept is modelled as an **object** of the class that models the concept. The notions of classes and objects are interwoven as any object belongs to a class. The differences are: an object is a concrete entity exists in space and time (persistence property of objects); a class

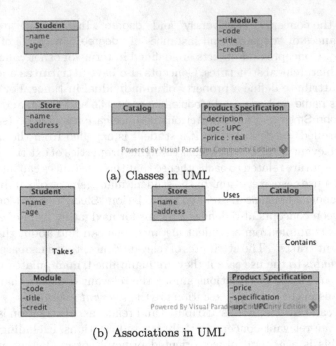

(a) Classes in UML

(b) Associations in UML

Fig. 9. UML classes, attributes and associations

is a model or type for a set of objects. In the UML, an object is represent[16], as in Fig. 10.

The UML definition of a class is a description of a set of objects that share the same attributes, operations, methods, relationships, and semantics. This is the notion of **type correctness** of an object with respect to its class, covering classes used at all stages in an object-oriented development process, including classes in object-oriented programs. For requirements analysis, we focus on the classes, their attributes and relations for modelling the conceptual structure of the domain. The operations of the classes, which are more closely related to the functionalities of the use cases, are designed latter after further analysis of the behaviour of the use cases.

Fig. 10. Objects in UML

---

[16] The UML Visual Paradigm tool does not support object-diagrams in the way that we want to use them. Here we abuse the Visual Paradigm class diagram by prefixing the class name with (optionally) a name followed a colon ':' to represented the fact that the instance has type of the class, and giving values to the attributes.

The following characteristics of objects are important for identifying concepts and objects, and for distinguishing between concepts and attributes.

- **Object identity:** Every object is distinguishable from every other object. This is true even if two objects have exactly the same properties. For example, two instances of Student may have the same name, age, doing the same degree, in the same year, taking the same courses, etc. This means "complete properties" of an object are not enough to identify an object.
- **Object persistence:** Every object has a life-time from it is created to it is destroyed, and this characteristic implies the static nature of the system.
- **Object's behaviour:** An object has dynamic behaviour and may act on other objects and/or may be acted on by other objects. That is, the properties of an object keep changing during its life-time. For example, a **Sale** object can be created, it creates **SaleLineItems** objects, and it also creates its related **Payment** object.
- **Object state:** An object may be in different state at different time and may behave differently in different states. For example, the **Sale** instance can be paid only when it is in the state "complete".

An object in the real world can have many kinds of behaviour. For example, a car can be made, repaired, driven, and stolen; carry passengers and carry objects. However, only the behaviour that is exhibited in the required use cases is relevant.

From the defining characteristics of objects we can see that, in the Trading Systems for example, **Product Item** is a class but its attribute "price" is not, as the properties of identity does not apply to prices (e.g., identical prices are not distinguishable in the conceptual domain). Similar, one can identify the concept of "Receipt". It is subtle to decide if it should be modelled as an object or an attribute. It should not be an object if it is not required in any use case to be checked and/or changed. It should, however, be modelled as an object if receipts carry details of information to be checked and changed, for example when they are used for a **Refund Item** use case.

Identifying Concepts from the Application Domain: A central difference between object-oriented analysis and structured analysis is decomposition by concepts (objects) rather than by functions. Concepts and objects are gathered from the client requirements documents and most importantly from the use case descriptions. In concept and object identification, a useful and simple technique is to identify the *nouns* and *noun phrases* in the textual descriptions of a problem domain, and consider them as candidate concepts or attributes. Larman suggests in his book [42] to use category lists of concepts to identify classes. This is quite effective for experienced analysts. However, care must be applied when these methods are used; mechanical noun-to-concept mapping is not possible. Different nouns can represent the same concept, and different occurrences of a noun in different context may on the other hand refer to the same concepts (a fundamental interoperability issue in information systems). Also, nouns can be about attributes, events, or operations, none of which should be modelled as classes. The defining characteristics of objects are always important in analysis for deciding on concept candidates, and these should be considered in relation to the use cases. This is the general principle of *"the need to know"* to follow in modelling requirements, so as to identify the relevant concepts.

Concept Candidates in the Trading System: Following the principles of conceptual modelling discussed above, the table of concept candidates in Fig. 11, are (very likely) related to Process Sale with Cash Payment.

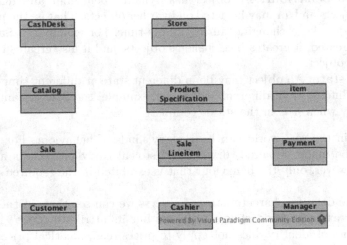

Fig. 11. Concept candidates for Process Sale with Cash Payment

The initial set of candidates may be incomplete and redundant. In later stages of analysis and design of use case behaviours, these candidates of concepts and the conceptual class models obtained need to go through a number of iteration steps of refinement to add and remove classes, attributes and associations. This relation between conceptual class models and use cases is formalised in rCOS [27,55]. This relation is in principle the same as the "completeness of program variable declarations with respect to the program body", where omission of variables could be detected by the compiler.

7.3   Associations

As shown earlier in Fig. 9, concepts are related, and object needs to be related so as to interact with each other when involving in computations. A conceptual model with only totally independent classes is useless.

In UML, an association is a relation between two classes that specifies how instances of the classes can be linked to work together. Associations and classes are at the type level of abstraction while, like objects being instances of classes, links are at the level of instances classes. An instance of an association is a **link** between objects of the two associated classes. Therefore, objects in the same class share the same relationships. For example, in Fig. 9, the association **Takes** relates classes **Student** and **Module**. An individual student, whose **name** is for example John Smith is linked with a particular module, which has the **code** MC206 if this student **John Smith** takes **Module** MC206. This is represented by an object diagram as shown in Fig. 12.

Fig. 12. Link between objects

The notion of **type correctness of a link** for an association can be defined as for the type correctness of an object with respect to a class.

Multiplicities of Associations. For an association between classes, an important information is about how many objects of one class can be associated with one object of the other. We use **multiplicity** to represent this information. Figure 13 shows the most often used multiplicity expressions and their meanings.

Determining multiplicities often exposes hidden constraints built into the model. For example, whether **Works-for** association between **Person** and **Company** in Fig. 14 is one-to-many or many-to-many depends on the application. A tax collection application would model the case when a person works for multiple companies. On the other hand, a workers' union maintaining member records may consider second jobs irrelevant. Therefore, multiplicities represent part of the business rules of the application. More examples of associations are shown in Fig. 15.

There can be more than one association between two classes, and there can be associations on a class itself. Whether an association is useful or not depends on whether it provides a means for providing the objects with links to interact with each other in the computations relevant to the use cases, i.e., "the need to know principle". In general, a link denotes the specific association through which one object (the client) calls for the services of another object (the supplier). Figure 16 shows a partial class diagram for Process Sale with Cash Payment.

Roles of Associations. In a class diagram, each association connects two classes, one at each end. They are called the **roles** of the association, which may have **role names**. Naming a role in a conceptual model is sometimes useful, especially for an association on a class itself. As shown in Fig. 17 for example, the role names '**boss**' and '**worker**' distinguish two employees who work for a

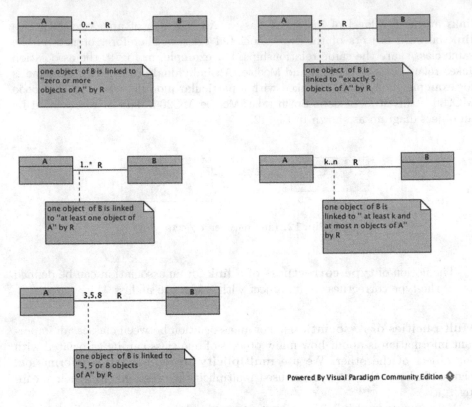

Fig. 13. Multiplicities

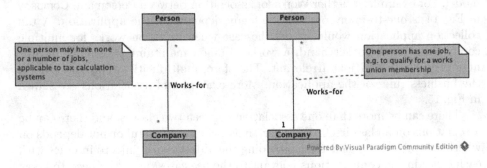

Fig. 14. Multiplicities depend on applications

company and participate in the **Manages** association. When we come to the design and implementation of the system, roles provide a way of viewing an association as a traversal from one object to the set of associated objects. In Java, a role name is the reference to the instance of the class, as shown below for role 'employer' of 'Company' in the association 'Works-for' of Fig. 17:

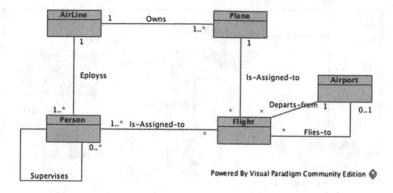

Fig. 15. Example of class diagram

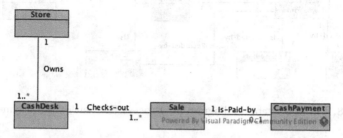

Fig. 16. Partial conceptual class diagram for Process Sale with Cash Payment

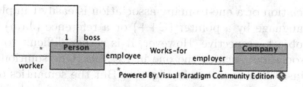

Fig. 17. Roles of an association

```
Class Person {
    Company employer;
    Person boss;
    }
```

Through identification of concepts, associations and their multiplicities, roles and using the UML notations, we build an initial conceptual class diagram for the use case Process Sale with Cash Payment shown in Fig. 18. The associations and multiplicities all represent assumptions on functionalities. For example, the one-one association Is-Used by between Catalog and Store rules out the possibility of a Catalog being shared among stores. The completeness and correctness will be further analysed along with the behaviour analysis of the use cases. Formalisation of the semantics of conceptual class diagrams are important for rigorous checking [27,55].

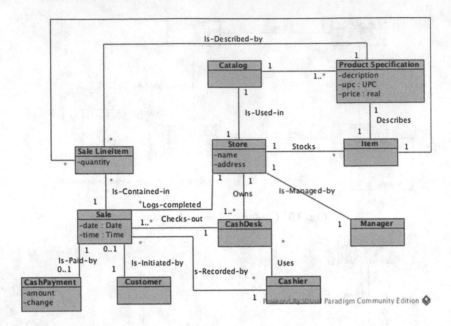

Fig. 18. Initial conceptual diagram for Process Sale with Cash Payment

7.4   Association Classes

A one-one association or a one-to-many association is easily t implemented in a programming language by a pointer (C++) or a reference (Java) to an object or a container object, respective. However, it is rather difficult to implement a many-many association, such as the one in Fig. 19a. One solution is to use an **association class**. This is shown in Fig. 19b. But the semantics of association classes is rather difficult to define in the same way as for the other classes. We thus propose to decompose a many-many association into a one-to-many association and a many-to-one association as shown in Fig. 19c. Another example is that we can decompose the many-many association **Student Take Module** into a one-to-many association **Student Takes Registration'** and a many-to-one **Registration Is-on Module**. This is analogous to normalisation in relational data bases.

7.5   Aggregation Association

A special kind of relation between objects is the "part-of" relation, which share important common properties. We call a "part-of" relation between two classes an **aggregation**. For example, a "finger" is part of a "hand", thus class **Hand** aggregates class **Finger**. Similarly, a bicycle has as parts a frame, two wheels and up to two lights. For most aggregations, the multiplicity at the composite end may be at most one, and in this case the aggregation is called a **composition**. In the UML, an aggregation is represented with a "diamond" at the end of the aggregating class.

(a) A many-many association

(b) An association class

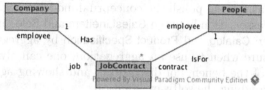

(c) Decomposition of a many-many association

Fig. 19. Many-many association and association class

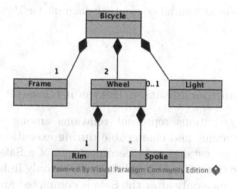

Fig. 20. Examples of composition

In some textbooks, **shared aggregation** is also introduced to model an aggregation where the multiplicity at the composite end may be more than one. Shared aggregation seldom (if ever) exists in the real world. We suggest to use general association to represent shared aggression if encountered in a project.

It is important to note two important proportios of aggregation, which are useful for identifying and designing aggressions:

- *Antisymmetry:* states that if an object o_1 is related to an object o_2 by an aggregation, it is not possible for o_2 to be related to o_1 by the same aggregation. That is, if o_2 is a part of o_1 then o_1 cannot be a part of o_2;

– *Transitivity:* states that if o_1 s related to o_2 by an aggregation link, and o_2 is related to o_3 by the same aggregation, then o_1 is also linked to o_3.

These properties imply that the composition hierarchies are organised in forms of trees as shown in Fig. 20. The following requirements analysis patterns are useful when identifying aggregations in models of requirements.

– The lifetime of the part is within the lifetime of the whole - there is a create-delete dependency of the part on the whole.
– There is an obvious whole-part physical or logical assembly.
– The whole is a collection of the parts.

Using these patterns, we can polish the conceptual model in Fig. 18 by replacing the **Is-Contained-in** association between **SalesLineItem** and **Sale**, and the Contains association between **Catalog** and **Product Specification** by aggregations as shown in Fig. 21. If not sure when to use an aggregation, one can always use a plain association. Most of the benefits of discovering and showing aggregation relate to the phases of designing the software solution.

Fig. 21. Compositions in the initial conceptual diagram for Process Sale with Cash Payment

7.6   Generalisation-Specialisation Between Classes

Associations and aggregations represent relations among classes. The corresponding links are dynamic and changeable during executions of use cases. For example, a **SaleLineItem** instance only becomes part of a **Sale** instance after the item is entered by the **Cashier**, and a **Sale** instance is only linked through **Is-Paid-by** a **CashPayment** instance only after the **Sale** is completed and the **CashPayment** is handled and recorded by the **Cashier**.

There is another kind of relations between classes. Such a relation is called a **generalisation-specialisation** or **is-a** relation. We say a class A is a **generalisation** (or a **superclass**) of a class B if every object of B *is an* object of class A. In this case, class B is also called a **specialisation** (or a **subclass**) of A. A generalisation-specialisation structure gathers the common properties and behavioural patterns of different classes into a more general class, and specialisations partition a class into subclasses which share some common properties or behavioural patterns. Therefore, instances in a subclass **inherits** all the properties of its super class, but each of them **extends** the superclass with possible more properties. A generalisation-specialisation relation is a static relation between two classes that is not changed by operations of use cases.

Generalisation-specialisation provides a mechanism of **reuse** through inherence, that properties modelled in a supperclass can be reused, and *abstraction* by partitioning a general class into a number of subclasses. In Java, a specialisation (or sub-class) A of a class B is written as

```
Class A extends B {
    T x; U:u; V v;
    }
```

In this, certain attributes and methods, called *protected attributes* and *protected methods* of A are inherited by B, but B declares the addition attributes x, u, v (similar methods can also be declared).

However, in a programming language, specialisation introduces **polymorphism** when properties and methods of the superclass are redefined in the subclasses. Polymorphism provides flexibility of reusing attributes and methods of the super class, but it can be troublesome for verification of program correctness. A subclass is **refinement** of a superclass when all the properties and functionality of the superclass are preserved by the subclasses, and in this case the specialisation is also called **subtyping**. Specialisations identified from the application domain are usually subtyping (or refinement).

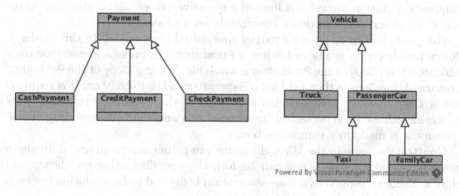

Fig. 22. Generalisation-specialisation hierarchy

An example of generalisation-specialisation in the Trading Systems is shown in the diagram on the left in Fig. 22. When all the instances of the superclass in a generalisation-specialisation relation is fully partitioned as the union of the instances of its subclasses, the superclass is called an **abstract class** and its identifier is signified in *italic* in UML. For example Payment will be an abstract class if only CashPayment, CreditPayment and CheckPayment are allowed in the Trading System, and in that case we would use "*Payment*" in the diagram. In Java, an abstract class is declared, for example, as follows

```
public abstract class Payment {
  }
Class CashPayment extends Payment {
  }
Class CreditPayment extends Payment {
  }
Class CheckPayment extends Payment {
  }
```

When a class is a specialisation of two or more different general classes, we say *multiple inheritance* occurs. For example, **Mammal** and **Winged Animal** are both specialisations of **Animal**, and **Bat** is a specialisation of both **Mammal** and **Winged Animal**. Java does not allow multiple inheritance from classes, but C++ do. Multiple inheritance introduces troubles when defining the semantics of the models, and programming languages. We do not exclude multiple inheritance in our models, though we do not have more examples of this.

7.7   Comments in Diagrams for Additional Constraints

We have discussed how multiplicities of associations are used for specification constraints, representing domain properties and business rules. However, a diagrammatic notation always has limited expressive power. UML provides "comments" for describing additional constraints on a model.

For example, Fig. 23 shows a partial conceptual class model. In this model, a library member who wants to borrow a **Publication** can make a **Reservation** on a **Publication** if no **Copy** of the **Publication** is available. When a **Copy** of the **Publication** is returned, the **Copy** is then held for a **Reservation** of the **Publication**. It is required that a **Copy** held for a **Reservation** is a **Copy** of the **Publication** reserved. This constraint cannot be represented by associations and multiplicities only. Thus, a comment is made in a comments box.

Constraints made in the UML diagrams are rather scattered and difficult to understand and manage. They can be formally specified using set theory and relation algebra, respectively, if an association is defined to be a relation between two sets, each defining a class [55].

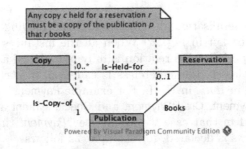

Fig. 23. Comment

$\forall c \in Copy \forall r \in Reservation \cdot (c\ Is\text{-}Held\text{-}for\ r \Rightarrow \exists p \cdot (r\ Books\ p \wedge c\ Is\text{-}Copy\text{-}of\ p))$
$Is\text{-}Held\text{-}for \circ Books \subseteq Is\text{-}Copy\text{-}of$

We thus define a **conceptual class model** to be a UML class diagram that may contain textual comments. Comments are part of the UML language definition, and they can be specified using the Object Constraint Language (OCL) analogous to the predicate above.

7.8   Relating Conceptual Class Models and the Use Case Models

As what we said earlier, the conceptual class model defines the domain structure for the use cases. A conceptual model is **adequate for a use case** if its classes, attributes and associations, together with the multiplicities and constraints imposed by the comments, support the behaviour specified by the use case. A conceptual class model is **adequate** for a use case model if it is adequate for all the use cases in the use case model.

Consider the two class diagrams in Fig. 14, the model on the left in the figure is adequate for all use cases that the class diagram on right of the figure is adequate for. Consider the two conceptual models in Fig. 24 for banking applications, that we call **Small Bank** and **Big Bank**, respectively. The only difference in the two diagrams is the multiplicities of the association "Has". The small bank only allows a **Customer** to have one **Account** and no **Account** is shared among **Customers**. On the other hand, the big bank allows one **Customer** to have up to 5 **Accounts**, and up to 3 **Customers** can share one **Account**. The small bank can support use cases "open an account", "deposit money", "check balance", and "withdraw money". The big bank on the other hand can support "transfer money" between two **Accounts** of the same **customer** as well.

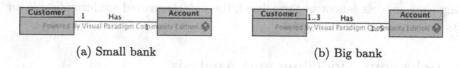

(a) Small bank   (b) Big bank

Fig. 24. Conceptual class diagrams

We say a conceptual class model $\mathcal{C}$ is a **structural refinement** of $\mathcal{C}_1$ if $\mathcal{C}$ is adequate for any use case that $\mathcal{C}_1$ is adequate for. Intuitively we have the proposition *that refactoring a conceptual model $\mathcal{C}_1$ in each of the following way generates a refinement of $\mathcal{C}_1$*:

- adding a class,
- adding an attribute to a class,
- adding an association between two classes,
- increasing the multiplicity of a role of an association (that is equivalent to adding attributes at the level of program code),

– promoting an attribute of a subclasses to its superclass, and
– promoting an association of a subclass to its superclass.

Obviously, structural refinement is reflexive and transitive. We say two class models are **equivalent** if they refinement each other.

At the current level of informal descriptions of use cases, we are not able to give rigorous definitions and checks the adequacy of a conceptual class model with respect to a use case model. We will come back to this topic in the next section when the specification of the behaviour of use cases is given in terms of contracts of use case operations. There, the contracts are defined by the change of the objects states of the class model.

7.9   Relation to the rCOS Formal Method

The conceptual class model focuses on what domain concepts and objects are, what structure the objects and concepts have, and what attributes the concepts have, for executing the required use cases. The use case description is very important for the incremental development of a good conceptual class model. The classes may not be complete for the execution of the use cases, and the missing classes will be discovered in later stage analysis and design. The class model may also contain classes that are not needed later, but they are useful for the domain understanding. For example, class Customer in the Trading System will not be implemented as a software class if information about customers does not need to be maintained or transmitted in the system.

Formal semantics of conceptual class models and their relations to use cases, and the design models (discussed in later sections) are give in our rCOS related publications, e.g., [27,49,55]. Incrementally adding classes, associations and attributes to a class model is also formalised in the sound and complete rCOS object-oriented refinement calculus [27,91]. Therefore, though the process of creating these models cannot be formalised, the models created are formalisable for verification.

8   Behaviour Modelling and Analysis

The process of identifying and describing the use cases and the activities of finding the concepts and building the conceptual class model is not in a linear order. Instead, they are interleaved, incremental and iterative, feeding back to each other. The conceptual model can be formalised, but the use case descriptions and use case diagrams remain informal. It is impossible to check formally the completeness and consistency of the conceptual class model with respect to the realisation of the described use cases. To this end, further modelling and analysis need to transform them, step by step, to models in the programming world. We will see that the closer to the programming world a model is, the more symbolic and precise it is. For this, we introduce more precise modelling notations:

1. the possible interaction sequences between the actors and the system in the execution of use cases, and
2. the state changes of objects caused by these interactions.

The first are modelled by UML *use case sequence diagrams*, and the latter by *contracts* of *use case operations* and UML *state machine diagrams* (a version *automata*). From these models, we define the concept of *components* and their *interfaces* in Sect. 10.1 in Part III. There, each use case is modelled as a component, and all use cases are combined to form a *component-based architecture*.

The key concepts of this section include *use case operations*, *use case sequence diagrams*, *object diagrams*, *object states*, *contracts of operations*, and *use case state machine diagrams*. The artefacts produced by this phase of analysis include the *use case sequence diagrams*, and use case state machine diagrams, *use case operations* and their *contracts*.

8.1 Use Case Operations

Recall that each expanded use case describes the patterns of interactions of its actors and the system under design, and interactions (communications) among actors. Each use case involves only a part of the functionalities required for the whole system, though different use cases may use some common functionalities. The first modelling decision we make is to treat a use case as a system *component*. The interactions among actors in the use case decryption are for requirements understanding, but they are not part of the functionalities required to design. Our second modelling is to eliminate the actors that do not directly interact with the system under design, such as **Customer** in use case Process Sale[17], from the model of interactions. Looking at the typical and the alternative courses of interactions, a use case describes the interactions of the direct actors and the component in the following way.

– **Input operations.** An actor generates an **input event** to the component to request an operation to be carried out. An input event may have input parameters to pass values to the component and return parameters for receiving values from the component. In the Process Sale use case for example, **Casher** generates *startSale()* to start handling a new **Sale**; *enterItem(upc)* to record an **Item**, where *upc* is an input parameter for the Universal Product Code (UPC) of the item; *finishSale()* to indicate the end of item input; and *makeCashPay(amount)* to record the **CashPayment**.
– **Output operations.** The component generates an **output event** to an actor to require a service from the actor. This is usually the execution of an operation in response to an input operation, but sometimes a component may also actively trigger an actor for the purposes of control and coordination. An

---

[17] In a further system evolution, more software components can be developed to automate these interactions so some of the interactions among actors are not needed anymore. For example, if online shopping is to be supported a customer would be a direct actor for the Make Order use case.

output event may have input parameters carrying values to be passed to an actor and return parameters to receive values from the actor. For example, the component for the Process Sale use case generates *authoriseCredit*() to the actor **Bank** for authorising credit card payment. By convention, the return value, including prompting message and signal, of an input operation or an output operation is part of the result of the interaction, but not an interaction event.

– **Repetitive interactions.** The interaction process may repeat a sequence of interaction operations, just as iterative statements in programming languages. Process Sale needs to repeatedly use *enterItem*() to record all the items that the customer is purchasing, until the last item is entered.
– **Branches.** Alternative branches of interactions may happen either controlled by an actor or by the component. The former is an external choices and the latter is an internal choices, both studied in communicating process description languages, such as CSP [31,82]. Process Sale may go through Process Sale with Cash Payment, Credit Payment or Check Payment; and also it can go into exception handling if the identity of an item, such as its Universal Product Code (UPC), is not recognised when executing *enterItem(upc)*.

8.2   Use Case Sequence Diagrams

For precise modelling of the interaction patterns of a use case, we first introduce symbolic names to represent the input and output operations for each use cases. An input operation is called by actors and an output operation is called by the component as response to an actor. The patterns of the interactions of the actors and the use case are modelled as a UML sequence diagram. The diagram defines all the possible sequences of interaction events of all possible execution instances of the use case. Each instance execution of the use case is called a *use case scenarios*. For example, the sequence of events *startSale*(), *enterItem*(01000, 2), *enterItem*(01001, 3), *endSale*(), and *makeCashPay*(30) is a particular scenario. The understanding and analysis of a use case can start from the understanding of its significant scenarios.

We informally explain the syntactic elements of use case sequence diagrams, leaving the study of the syntax and semantics of use case sequence diagrams out of this chapter. A sequence diagram is formed with

– the use case components and actors life lines;
– messages that represent (a) input operations sent from actors to the use case component, and (b) output operations sent from the use case component to actors;
– the temporal order of messages is defined by the order in which they occur downwards along the life lines;
– "loop combined fragment" representing repeating sequences of interactions; and
– "alt. combined fragment" representing branching among sequences of interactions.

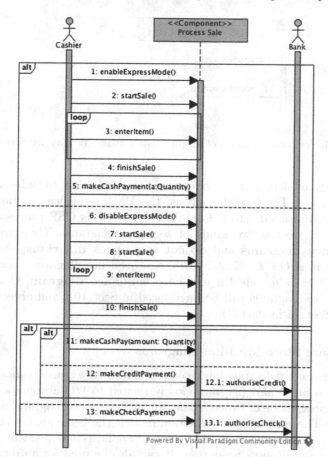

Fig. 25. Sequence diagram of Process Sale use case

Example. To illustrate the expressive power of use case sequence diagrams, we present the sequence diagram of the full use case of Process Sale in Fig. 25. Notice the nested choices, and the output operations of Process Sale. The sequence diagram becomes much simpler if express mode is disregarded, then only the bottom part starting from message 7:*startSale*() will be included. If we consider cash payment only, the component becomes closed and the sequence diagram will become the part from message 2:*startSale*() to message 5:*makeCashPayment*().

The interactions 11:*makeCreditPayment*() and 11.1:*authoriseCredit*() starts the sequence diagram for the Pay by Credit use case, but with the modelling decision that *makeCreditPayment*() treated as one atomic action. The use case sequence diagram for a different decision as discussed in Subsect. 6.5 is different, as shown in Fig. 26. Use case Pay by Check has the same design options to consider.

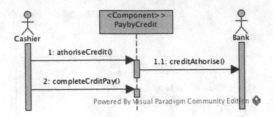

Fig. 26. Sequence diagram of an alternative model of **Pay by Credit**

Most UML modelling tools offer means of referring to sub-diagrams in complex diagrams. For formal analysis, the UML sequence diagrams can be automatically translated into a formal model, such as CSP processes [16,31]. In this chapter, we use two kinds of sequence diagrams. They are **component sequence diagrams** and **object sequences diagrams**, that are formally defined in rCOS [15,37,50]. A use case sequence diagram is a component sequence diagram, also called a **use case sequence diagram**. General component sequence diagrams will be introduced in Sect. 10.1 and object sequence diagrams in Sect. 11 in Part III.

8.3 Use Case State Machine Diagrams

The use case sequence diagram has a corresponding *state machine diagram* which is defined by a Statechart [24] and closely related to I/O automata [64]. If we ignore the express mode of Process Sale, we have the state diagram in Fig. 27 for Process Sale. The state machine diagram models the behaviour of the use case for verification (e.g., using model checking) of application dependent properties, such as safety and liveness properties. It can also be used for automatic generation of the interface control program. The states of a use case state machine diagram represents the conditions on the flow of control and synchronisation of the interaction processes when use case are being executed, thus they are called **control states**. A use case state machine diagram has a starting state, identifiable with a filled in circle. Most use case state machine diagrams also have final states, denoted by a circle with a black bullet inside, from which operations may stop. For example, an execution of Process Sale may stop after a sale is completed and paid, but it can also restart the execution to process a new sale.

The state machine diagram in Fig. 27 is consistent with the use case sequence diagram in Fig. 25. The transitions from state **completeSale** to the final state by the operations of *makeCreditPayment()*, *makeCreditPayment()/authoriseCredit()*, and *makeCheckPayment()*, *makeCheckPayment()/authoriseCheck()*, respectively. This models the input operations as single atomic operations with a *run to completion semantics* of method invocations. If we consider alternative models of these two input operations, such as the one shown in Fig. 26, the corresponding state machine diagram would be the one shown in Fig. 28.

However, different state diagrams can also model the same (observable) interaction behaviours. For example, the state machine diagram in Fig. 28 is

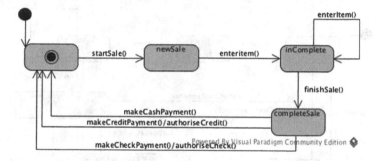

Fig. 27. State machine diagram of Process Sale

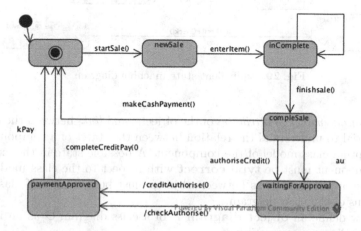

Fig. 28. An alternative state machine diagram of Process Sale

"equivalent" to the state machine diagram in Fig. 29. Consistency between the use case sequence diagram and the state machine diagram of a use cases can be formalised and automatically checked in rCOS. Equivalence between use case sequence diagrams and equivalence between state machine diagrams are studied in the formal theories of process refinement and simulation, such as CSP and CCS, and in theories of I/O automata and Statecharts.

8.4 Object Diagrams and Object States

Use case sequence diagrams do not have the concept of states and they only model interaction protocols. The states in a state machine diagram are symbolic and their names are insignificant, i.e., changing names of the states resulting in equivalent state machine diagrams. To design and implement a use case as a program component, we need to analyse and specify the *static functionality* of the interaction operations in terms of which *object state* changes they perform.

An **object state** of a component (or a use case or a system) is a snapshot at a particular time instant of the component execution, and it consists of the

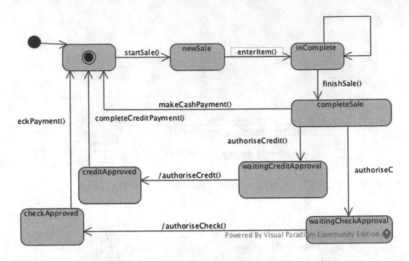

Fig. 29. Equivalent state machine diagram

existing *objects*, *values of attributes* of the objects, and *links* between the objects. It is essential to understand the relation between the states of a component and the conceptual class model of the component. A possible state in the execution of the component must be **type correct** with respect to the class model. This means, the objects and links between objects must be instances of classes and associations of the class diagram.

We now define an **object diagram** Γ of a class diagram Θ as an instance of the class diagram, consisting of

- a set of instances O, called **objects**, of some classes $\mathcal{C}$ in the class diagram,
- a set of instances L of some associations of the classes $\mathcal{C}$, which are **links** among the objects O, that satisfy the multiplicity and other (including the comments) constraints in class diagram Θ.

Example of Object Diagrams. Consider the conceptual class models of the small bank and big bank in Fig. 24. Figure 30(a) is an object diagram of both the small bank and big bank, but the object diagram in Fig. 30(b) is valid only for the conceptual class diagram of the big bank.

We call an object diagram of the class diagram of a component (or use case) an **object state** of the component. The **behaviour** of a component is the set of all possible sequences of state changes caused by the sequence of interactions between the actors and the component. We can equivalently define the behaviour of a component by the sequences of state changes caused by the operations defined by the state machine diagram. For example, consider a state in which the accounts related to **customer** Mrs. Mary Smith are shown in Fig. 30(b). Now Mrs. Mary Smith requests the big bank system to transfer 2000 GBP from her **account** $a2$ to **account** $a3$ that she shares with her son Mr. Bob Smith. After the execution of the transfer operation, denoted by *transfer*(), the system changes from the

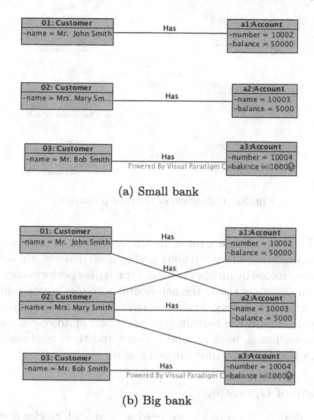

(a) Small bank

(b) Big bank

Fig. 30. Object diagrams

pre-state shown in Fig. 30(b) to the **post-state** shown in Fig. 31: the balance of $a2$, $a.balance$, is reduced by 2000 GBP, and the balance of $a3$, $a3.balance$, is increased by 2000 GBP. Notice that an operation, such as $transfer()$, only changes part of the state of the component, keeping the other accounts unchanged, for example.

In general, a use case operation can change a state in the following ways:

- create new objects (object creation), such as opening an account in a bank application;
- remove (destroy) existing objects in the current state (object deletion), such as closing an account;
- form new links between both existing and newly created objects (link formation), such as an operation (in the **Big Bank**) of registering Mr. John Smith on **account** $a3$ so as to allow him to access that account too;
- remove exiting links from the current state (link removal), such as deregistering Mrs. Mary Smith from **account** $a3$;
- modifies values of object attributes (attribute change), such as $transfer()$.

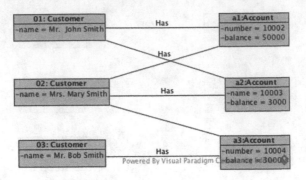

Fig. 31. Post-state of transfer operation

We describe the state change caused by an operation in an abstract way by stating what changes are made without saying how changes are made. A good analogy of a state change by an operation is a stage play performance. A snapshot on the of play on the stage shows the actors and actresses playing different roles, props, and background scenery, and their relations. Then the curtain is closed, changes are made behind the curtain (the execution of an operation) to change actors and actress, props, back ground scenery and their relations, then a new state is shown when the curtain is opened again.

8.5   Contracts of Operations

For systematic design of use cases, we need a clear and precise specification of the functionality of each use case operation, where the specification should define all the possible changes of states of the system. The specification of an operation $m()$ is called the **contract** of the $m()$, and it is formally defined to be a triple of the form

$$\{Pre\text{-}condition\}\ m()\ \{Post\text{-}condition\}$$

where

- *Pre-condition* is the condition that the states are assumed to satisfy before the execution of operation $m()$,
- *Post-condition* is the condition that the states have to satisfy when the execution of the operation terminates (if it terminates).

These triples are formalised in the well-known Hoare Logic [30] that is the foundation for formal program analysis and verification, and it is extended to object-oriented programs in rCOS [27,38,92]. Instead of introducing the formal specification of operation contracts in rCOS, we present a practical approach for informally stating these contracts. The advantage is that one does not need to have a background in formal logic, and these informal statements are yet formalisable for those who have the background. Also, the informal description of the contracts is a step that must be taken before further analysis, including formal analysis. We adopt the following format proposed by Larman [42].

Contract

Name:	Name of operation, and parameters.
Responsibilities:	An informal description of the responsibility this operation must fulfil.
Cross References:	Such as use cases.
Note:	Design notes, algorithms, and so on.
Exceptions:	Exceptional cases.
Pre-conditions:	As defined.
Post-conditions:	As defined.

Examples. We now write the contracts of the operations of Process Sale with Cash Payment, which are largely from Larman's book [42].

Contract

Name:	*startSale*().
Responsibilities:	Create a new sale and start the process.
Cross References:	Use case Process Sale with Cash Payment.
Exceptions:	If any of the precondition does not hold, indicate error.
Pre-conditions:	The objects Store, CaskDesk, Catalog exist and linked.
Post-conditions:	1. A new Sale was created.
	2. The new Sale was associated with the CashDesk.

Contract

Name:	*enterItem*(*upc:UPC, quantity:Integer*).
Responsibilities:	Enter an item and add it to the sale. Display item description and price.
Cross References:	Use case Process Sale with Cash Payment.
Note:	Use superfast database access.
Exceptions:	If *upc* is invalid, indicate an error.
Pre-conditions:	*upc* is valid, and Sale exists.
Post-conditions:	1. A LineItem was created.
	2. The LineItem.quantity was set to quantity.
	3. The LineItem was associated the Sale.
	4. The LineItem was associated with the Product Specification.

Contract

Name:	*finishSale*().
Responsibilities:	Indicates the end of item entry and get ready for make payment.
Cross References:	Use case Process Sale with CashPayment.
Pre-conditions:	The sale exists.
Post-conditions:	Attribute *isComplete* of Sale object was set to *true*.

Contract

Name:	$makeCashPayment(n : Quantity)$.
Responsibilities:	Record the payment and associate it to the sale, and log the completed sale.
Cross References:	Use case Process Sale with Cash Payment.
Note:	Use superfast database access.
Exceptions:	If the **Sale** is not completed.
Pre-conditions:	The **Sale** is complete.
Post-conditions:	1. A **CashPayment** object was created.
	2. The attribute *balance* of the **CashPayment** was set to the input value n.
	3. A the **CashPayment** object was associated to the **Sale**.
	4. The **Sale** was associated to the **Store** to log the completed **Sale**.

In informal specification of the contracts, it is hard to make sure the preconditions and postconditions are complete or consistent. The preconditions, in particular, are hard to assume complete and they also imply implicit assumptions. For example, the condition "*upc* is valid" implies the existence of **Catalog**, and "**Sale** exists" implies the existence of the **Store** and **CashDesk**. Some other conditions implied are even harder to see. For example, the existence of the link between **CashDesk** and **Store**, and link between **Store** and **Catalog**, etc. From this discussion, we see the need for logic formulation and reasoning.

8.6   Guarded Contracts

Another issue is related to the precondition "the **Sale** is complete" of operation $makeCashPayment()$. Preconditions need to be checked when an operation is executed, and if a precondition does not hold an exception should be thrown. For this, class **Sale** should have a boolean attribute, say *isComplete*. Attributes of this kind would be very hard to identify in an early stage of requirements analysis.

In fact this issue relates to more advanced modelling theory. Consider the above contracts of operations in relation to the state machine diagram Fig. 27, we notice that

- $startSale()$ can only be carried out in the starting state;
- operation $enterItem()$ can only take place in states *newSale* and *inComplete*;
- $finishSale()$ can only take place in state *inComplete*; and
- $makeCasPayment()$, $makeCreditPayment()$ and $makeCheckPayment()$ can only take place in state *completeSale*.

We introduce a boolean variable for each of the control states in the use case state machine diagram, for example, @*start*, @*newSale*, @*inComplete*, and @*completeSale*, which take the value true when and only when the state machine diagram is in the corresponding state. We then add to each contract a section of conditions called **guard conditions**. An operation can be executed only when all the gaud conditions hold. An attempt to execute (or call to) the operation is refused when the guard condition does not hold. An example of a **guarded contract** is given below, where the guard is emphasised.

Guarded Contract

Name:	*enterItem(upc:UPC, quantity:Integer)*.
Responsibilities:	Enter an item and add it to the sale. Display item description and price.
Cross References:	Use case Process Sale with Cash Payment.
Note:	Use superfast database access.
Exceptions:	If *upc* is invalid, indicate an error.
Guarded conditions:	*The system is in a state such that* @*newSale* *holds or* @*inComplete holds.*
Pre-conditions:	*upc* is valid, and **Sale** exists.
Post-conditions:	1. A **LineItem** was created.
	2. The **LineItem**.quantity was set to quantity.
	3. The **LineItem** was associated the **Sale**.
	4. The **LineItem** was associated with the Product Specification.
	5. *If in state* **newSale** *change to state* **inComplete**.

Note that the postconditions of a guarded contract may also change the control state. An error message (but not an exception) can be given when an operation is attempted when a guard is false.

8.7 Start Up Use Case

Before carrying any of the business processes of the application, the basic business infrastructure needs to be set up. This, for example, including the **Store**, the **Cash Desk**, and the **Catalog**. This is the operation *StartUp()*, that most system have. The contract of *StartUp()* for the Trading System is with on **Store** and one **Cash Desk** can be specified by the following postconditions:

1. **Store**, **CashDesk**, **Catalog** and **ProductSpecification** were created (instance creation).
2. **ProductSpecification** was associated with **Catalog**.
3. **Catalog** was associated with **Store**.
4. **CashDesk** was associated with **Store**.
5. **Catalog** was associated with **CashDesk**.

The creation of use case sequence diagrams, state machine diagrams and the specification of the contracts of the use case operations have been developed from the use case description and identification of conceptual class diagrams, and they together form a clear model of what the system under design is required to do. From these models, the development process is ready to move into the design phase.

8.8   Consistency Among the Models

The use case sequence diagrams, state machine diagrams, contracts of operations and the conceptual class model are models of the same system from different view-points. Their integration is the whole model of the applications requirements. Therefore, they must be consistent. The sequence diagram and state machine diagram of a use must be consistent so the sequence diagrams defines the same set of possible interaction sequences as those which are accepted by the state machine diagram.

The conceptual class model is required to be **adequate** for the definition of the contracts of the operations. This means that a conceptual class model is adequate for the operations of the use case model if it defines all the object states that are specified in the responsibilities, the preconditions and postconditions of all the operations. Clearly, this definition of the adequacy of a class model is a revised version of the adequacy of the conceptual class model for the use cases defined in Sect. 7. If a conceptual class model is adequate for an operation, so is its structural refinement.

Now we have a clearer and more precise definition of structural refinement: a conceptual model C is a **structural refinement** of C_1 if each type correct object diagram of C_1 is also a type correct object diagram of C. For example, the conceptual class model on the left of Fig. 14 is a structural refinement of the one on the right; and the conceptual model Big Bank in Fig. 24 is a structural refinement of the Small Bank.

8.9   Relation to the rCOS Formal Method

The development of rCOS [31, 82] shows that both use case sequence diagrams and state diagrams can be formally defined and analysed. In particular, they can be both translated to CSP process expressions for checking their consistency and for formal analysis and verification [14–17]. The informal descriptions of operation contracts are formalised in the rCOS extension [27] to UTP [32]; guarded contracts are presented in [11, 26]. The development of a complete and sound refinement calculus and its applications can be found in [15, 38, 91].

9   Summary of Requirements Modelling and Analysis

Sections 6.1 and 8 focus on notations, activities and models of requirements modelling and analysis. The emphasis of these is on understanding of the requirements, concepts, and operations related to the domain business processes for which automation by software is required. The investigation and analysis are often characterised as focusing on questions of what - what are the processes, concepts and objects, associations, attributes, and operations? We have the following models and descriptions for the answers to these questions with different levels of details and precision.

1. Use cases: high level and expanded descriptions and use case diagrams. They are from the application domain and for understanding the functional requirements (use cases can also used for non-functional requirements analysis) from the domain perspectives.
2. Conceptual class model: the concepts, objects and their relations that form the structure for the realisation of the use cases.
3. Use case sequence diagrams: identification of the interactions between actors and the system under design for the realisation of the use cases.
4. Use case operations and their contracts: specification the functionality of the interactions, that is what changes to the domain structure, that are modelled by changes of object states that interaction smay cause.

We use UML diagrams for the representation of the above models: UML use case diagrams, class diagrams, and use case sequence diagrams state machine diagrams, plus textual description of contracts of use case operations. The contracts are described in terms of pre-conditions and postconditions, that can be formalised in Object Constrain Language - defined as part of the UML. Our formal method of object-oriented and component-based design offers formal specification of contracts of methods [15, 27, 37] and formal semantics and relations of different UML models for requirements models and design [12, 25, 52, 55]. For the formal techniques and tools to be applied, the pre-formal activities should be carried out first to create the models with intuitive understanding of their meanings.

Through the above discussed modelling and analysis activities, and the creation of the models, the development team and the clients building a thorough understanding of the requirements. The UML models and the textual descriptions as a whole give a fairly clear model of requirements, including the architecture, the data model, and the static functionality. Further formal techniques and tools can also be applied for formal validation and verification. Therefore, it is fairly justifiable that after these activities and with the models built, the development can move into the next phase, that is the design phase to be discussed two sections to follow.

10 Part III: Component-Based and Object-Oriented Design

10.1 Component-Based Architecture Design

In Sect. 7 of Part II, the structure of the application domain is expressed in terms of conceptual class models and use case diagrams. It is not easy in these models to relate the functionalities of use case operations. For example, different use cases may perform some same operations, but these cannot be clearly represented. This section introduces the component-based modelling concepts of *components*, *interfaces* and *compositions*.

10.2 Components

A **component** C is a program unit with *encapsulated data states* and *explicitly specified* **interfaces**. In this presentation, operations are method invocations, and therefore a component in our framework can have two kinds of interfaces, **provided interfaces** for operations on data in the component and **required interfaces** for operations on other components. Syntactically an **interface** declares a set of method signatures of the form $m(in; out)$ with a method name m, a list of input parameters *in* and possibly an output parameter *out*.

In Java, interface are defined as shown in the following examples.

```
Interface pInterface_Process_Sale {
    startSale();
    enterItem(upc: UPC);
    finishSale();
    makeCashPayment(amount: Quantity);
    makeCreditPayment(cardInfo,amount);
    makeCheckPayment(cehckInfo,amount)
}

Interface rInterface_Process_Sale {
    authoriseCredit(cardInfo, amount);
    authoriseCheck(cardInfo, amount)
}
```

An interface is implemented by a class. For example,

```
Class CaskDesk implements pInterface_Process_Sale {
        startSale() {the contract of the operation to be coded};
        enterItem() {the contract of the operation to be coded};
        finishSale() {body to be designed};
        makeCashPayment(amount: Quantity) {the contract of
                        the operation to be coded};
        makeCreditPayment(cardInfo,amount) {the contract of
                        the operation to be coded};
        makeCheckPayment(cehckInfo,amount){the contract of
                        the operation to be coded}
    }
```

We use the UML graphic representations of interfaces, as for classes, and relate interfaces with class by the relation "a class implements an interface".

A component is **closed** if it does not have required interfaces, and it is **open** otherwise. We use the UML notation to represent classed and open components, as shown in Fig. 32, respectively. In the figure, C is a closed component that has a provided interface *pIFC* and D is an open components with a provided interface *pIFD* and a required interface *rIFD*.

Visual Paradigm does not show the encapsulated state variables and the declared methods of interfaces (except for those which only have a single method

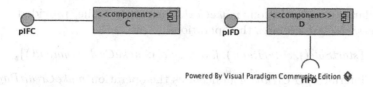

Fig. 32. Closed and open components

signature) of a component in the figure, but they can be specified with the textual editor and generated in the textual version. We define a component abstractly as a tuple $C = \langle X, pIF, rIF \rangle$, where X is the set of state variables, pIF and rIF are the provided interface and required interface, respectively. Each interface I is a set of method signatures, and we allow multiple provided interfaces and multiple required interfaces in diagrams but their unions are the provided interface and required interface in the abstract definition. The following examples show how use cases are modelled as components, and these are the initial components defined in the development.

Example. Consider the use cases Make Cash Payment, Process Sale with Cash Payment, Make Credit Payment, and Make CheckPayment, that can all be modelled as components in Fig. 33. The first two are closed components and the other two are open.

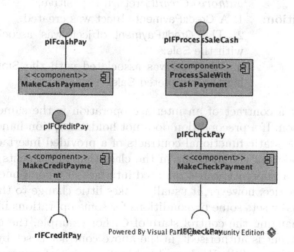

Fig. 33. Components of Process Sale

The input operations of a use case are declared in the provided interface of the component, and the output operations of the use case are declared in the required interface of the component. Provided interface *pIFCashPayment* only declares one operation $makeCashPayment()$, while provided interface $pIFProcessSaleCash$ declares the operations,

$$\{startSale(), enterItem(), finish\ sale(), makeCashPayment()\}.$$

Provided interface $pIFCreditPay()$ declares the operation $makeCreditPayment()$ and required interface $rIFCreditPay()$ declares $authoriseCredit()$; and provided interface $pIFCheckPay()$ declares $makeCheckPayment()$ and required interface $rIFCheckPay$ declares $authoriseCheck()$. The state variables of these components are the variables containing the **Store** object, **Catalog** object, **CashDesk** object, **Sale** objects and **Payment** objects, etc.

Neither a component diagram nor a tuple $C = \langle X, pIF, rIF \rangle$ specifies the functional behaviour of the component. We divide the specification of the behaviour of a component into two parts. First, the **static functional contract** of a component C is specified by the contracts of the operations declared in the provided interface pIF. The preconditions are assertions on the states variables, the input parameters of the operation; and the postconditions specify how the object states of the component are changed and what the value of the return parameter is. The contracts of the operations in $pIFProcessSaleCash$ are the same as those given in the contracts of the input operations of the use case. For an example of contracts of operations involving required operations, the contract of $makeCreditPayment()$ is

Pre-conditions: Sale.$isComplete$ is $true$
the credit payment is authorised, i.e., $authoriseCredit()$ return is positive.

Post-condition: 1. A **CreditPayment** object was created.
2. The **CreditPayment** object was associated with the **Sale**.
3. The **Sale** was associated with the **Store** to log the completed **Sale**.

The meaning of a contract of an interface operation is the same as that of a use case operation. If a precondition does not hold, exception handling needs to be designed. The static functional contracts of a provided interface are used to program the bodies of the methods in the class that implements the interface. The contract of an operation in a required interface of a component C is tricky in theory. In practice, however, it usually makes little change to the object state of C, and it usually sets some preconditions for some operations in the provided interfaces by changing the control state of C. For example, the condition that "the credit payment is authorised" in the above contract is set by the required operation $authoriseCredit()$. We leave further discussion of contracts of required operations out of this chapter.

In addition to the static functional contracts of the interfaces of the component, the flow of control for the protocol in which the interface operations can be executed should also be specified. This is called the **dynamic behaviour contract of the component** of the component, and it is modelled by a state machine diagram. For example, the state machine diagram in Fig. 27 of Part II is the dynamic

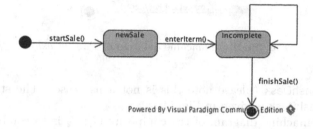

Fig. 34. State machine diagram of a finite component

behaviour contract of the component for Process Sale. Note that, the dynamic behaviour contract of a component can also be modelled by a sequence diagram, such as the sequence diagrams in Fig. 25 of Part II. The state machine diagrams, however, are easier to be associated with the static functional contracts of the component interfaces. We can associate assertions about object states to the control states of the state machine diagrams, for example, by adding comment boxes on the control states. The combination of the static functional contract and dynamic behaviour contract of a component are specified by the **guarded contract** of the interface operations, as defined in the previous section.

10.3   Composing Components

There is a need of mechanisms for components to be combined to form an architecture. For this purpose, the combinators known from concurrent and distributed program constructions, compositions for *sequencing, choices, parallel composition, service hiding* and *looping* (or *recursion*). Except for "plugging" to "link" provided operations to required operations, there are little UML tool support for these compositions. Here these compositions are defined as abstract operators, discuss their informal semantics, and then represented as special components called **connectors** in UML diagrams. Extending a UML tool to provide better support of component compositions, both their syntax and semantics could be an interesting student project.

Sequencing. Sequential composition is defined for "procedural components only", that is components that have terminating behaviour. For two components C_1 and C_2 whose required interfaces are disjoint with their provided interfaces, the sequentially composed components $C_1; C_2$ is defined if C_1 is terminating (or finite). When $C_1; C_2$ is defined, the provided and required interfaces of $C_1; C_2$ are the unions of the provided and required interacts, repetitively. The interaction behaviour of C_2 can start after that of C_1 terminates, i.e., the state diagram of C_1 enters a final state. Here C_1 is finite if its state machine diagram has a final state. Consider the behaviour from *startSale*() to *finishSale*() of the sequence diagram in Fig. 25 of Part II. We can model this part of Process Sale as a component

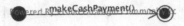

Fig. 35. State machine diagram of *PayByCash*

denoted by **CashDesk** (please note this is not a use case). The state machine diagram of **CashDesk** is given in Fig. 34.

The state machine diagram of the composite $C_1; C_2$ is to combine the final state of C_1 with the initial state of the C_2 into a new state so that the two state machine diagrams are composed. Consider the state machine diagram for component **PayByCash** for Pay by Cash use case as shown in Fig. 35. The state machine diagram of **CashDesk; PayByCash** is given in Fig. 36.

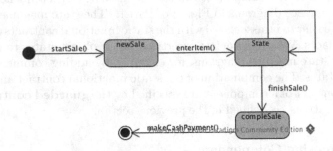

Fig. 36. Sequential composition of diagrams in Figs. 34 and 36

In a semantic theory, restrictions for $C_1; C_2$ to be defined are not needed. If C_1 and C_2 do not satisfy these conditions, it just make the behaviour of the composite component $C_1; C_2$ very complicated or even divergent. In practice, we would like to avoid these complicated cases when building our models. We use the **sequencing connector** component to represent the sequential composition. The sequencing connectors is shown in Fig. 37. It is easy to use the sequencing connector to realise **CashDesk; PayByCash** and this is the one iteration of Process Sale with Cash Payment.

Repeating. Similarly, the repeating composition is also defined for procedural components only. The **repeating operator** $*C$ is defined if C is finite and its behaviour is to repeat the behaviour of C as many times as possible (or as many times as the actors like). The state machine diagram of $*C$ is to combine the final state of the state machine diagram of C with its initial state.

The repeating connector is realised by the **repeating connector** component as shown by the diagram on the top of Fig. 38, and the combination use of the sequencing connector and repeating connector in forming the component **ProcessSaleWithCashPayment**, shown in the diagram at the bottom of Fig. 38. The state machine diagram of the composite component in Fig. 38 is given in Fig. 39.

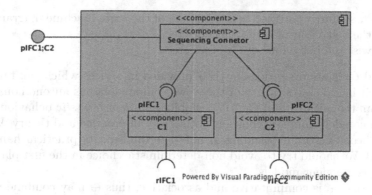

Fig. 37. Sequencing connector

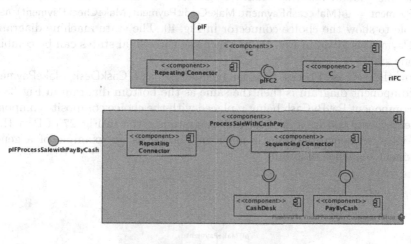

Fig. 38. Repeating connector

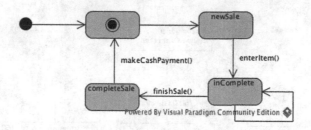

Fig. 39. State machine diagram of component ProcessSaleWithCashPayment

Choice. Given two components C_1 and C_2, the provided and required interfaces of $C_1 \oplus C_2$ are the unions of the provided interfaces and the required interfaces, respectively. The behaviour of component $C_1 \oplus C_2$ behaviour depends on the first move,

– if the first state transition is a transition of the state machine diagram of C_1, then the behaviour of C_1 is selected;
– otherwise the behaviour of C_2 is selected.

If C_1 and C_2 share operations in their provided interfaces which can take place from their initial states or one of these two components has autonomous transitions from the initial state, $C_1 \oplus C_2$ exhibits *non-deterministic* behaviour. Dealing with non-deterministic choice is both tricky in practice and theory. Without proper theoretical understanding of non-determinism, its practical handling is also hard. We should try to avoid non-deterministic choice in the first place when building component models.

Note that $\oplus$ is commutative and associative, thus $\oplus$ may combine an arbitrary number of components. We use the **choice connector** component to realise this general abstract choice operator. We consider the composition of MakePayment $= \oplus($MakecashPayment, MakeCreditPayment, MakeCheckPayment$)$ as an example to show the choice connector in Fig. 40. The state machine diagram of MakePayment is given in Fig. 41, in which the three final states can be combined into one state.

Now the use case Process Sale can be modelled as $*($CaskDesk; MakePayment$)$. The component diagram is then the same as the bottom diagram in Fig. 38 but with component PayByCash being replaced with the choice composite component MapkePayment, and its state machine diagram is given in Fig. 27 of Part II. Its component sequence diagram is given in Fig. 42, as an example of a general component sequence diagram.

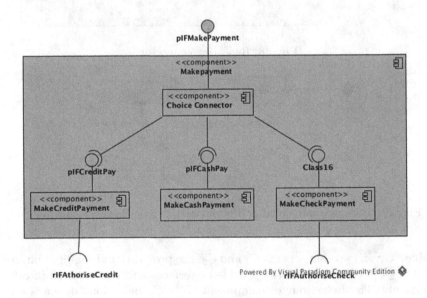

Fig. 40. Choice connector

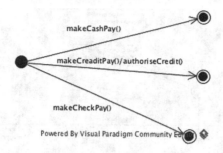

Fig. 41. State diagram of choice connector

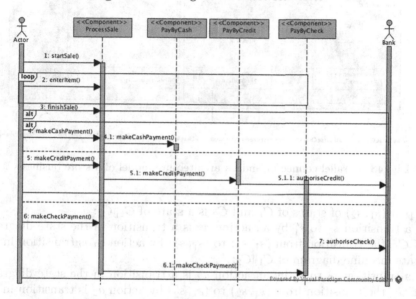

Fig. 42. General component sequence diagram

Parallel Composition. The parallel composition operator $C_1 \| C_2$ for general components C_1 and C_2 is complicated when the required interface of one component, say C_1, shares common operations with the provided interface of another. In this case, C_1 can use operations provided by component C_2 and the behaviour of the parallel composed component may suffer deadlocks and divergences. To handle this case in general, advanced semantic theory is needed. We restrict ourselves to the case when the provided interfaces of C_1 and C_2 do not contain operations in their required interfaces so that feedback method invocations are avoided. The provided interface and required interface of $C_1 \| C_2$ are the union of the provided interfaces and the union of the required interfaces of C_1 and C_2, respectively. The state machine diagram of $C_1 \| C_2$ is defined from the state machine diagrams of C_1 and C_2 as follows

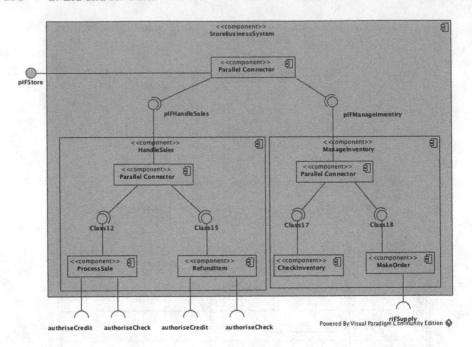

Fig. 43. Parallel connector and an architecture model of a store business

- a pair (s_1, s_2) of states of C_1 and C_2 is a state of $C_1 \| C_2$;
- if a transition s_1 to s'_1 by an action a_1 is a transition in the state diagrams of C_1, the transition from (s_1, s_2) to (s'_1, s_2) by action a_1 is transition in the state machine diagram of $C_1 \| C_2$;
- if a transition s_2 to s'_2 by an action a_2 is a transition in the state diagrams of C_2, the transition from (s_1, s_2) to (s_1, s'_2) by action a_2 is transition in the state machine diagram of $C_1 \| C_2$;
- if a transition s_1 to s'_1 by an action a is a transition in the state diagrams of C_1 and a transition s_2 to s'_2 by an action a is a transition in the state diagrams of C_2 the transition from (s_1, s_2) to (s'_1, s'_2) by action a is transition in the state machine diagram of $C_1 \| C_2$.

This definition is illustrated in Fig. 44.

Note that $\|$ is commutative and associative, thus it can be used to compose an arbitrary number of components, and $C_1 \| C_2 \| C_3$ can be written $\| (C_1, C_2, C_2)$. Consider use cases Process Sale, Refund Item, Make Order, and Check Inventory. The first two use case are about handling sales and the last two are about inventory management. A component HandleSales = ProcessSale∥RefundItem and a component InventoryManagement = CheckInventory∥MakeOrder. The (restricted version) StoreBusinessSsystem = HandleSales∥InventoryManagement can be defined. We introduce a component called **parallel connector** to represent the component diagram of a parallel composite component. The component diagram of StoreBusinessSsystem is shown in Fig. 43.

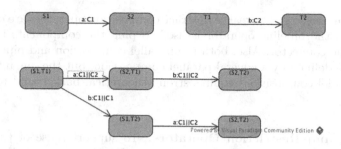

Fig. 44. Parallel composition of state diagrams

Pipeline Connector. Another often used composition of components is "plugging" an operation $m()$ provided by one component, say C_1, to a required interface of a component, C_2, which requires the operation "$m()$". For example, if Process Sale also causes changes to the stock of products, it can call an provided operation of the Managing Inventory use case instead of designing an operation in the component for Process Sale. Notice that Managing Inventory is mostly likely to operate on the Store database system. The **pipeline operator** is defined such that

- $C_1 >> C_2$ is defined if the provided interface of C_2 is disjoint with the required interface of C_1;
- when $C_1 >> C_2$ is defined, its provided interface is the union of the provided interfaces of C_1 and C_2 minus the required interface of C_2 (because any provided operations of C_1 that is also required operations of C_2 are plugged together) and its required interface is the union of the required interfaces of C_1 and C_2 minus the provided interface of C_1 (because any required operations of C_2 that are also provided operations of C_1 are connected);
- the behaviour $C_1 >> C_2$ is similar to the parallel composition $C_1 \| C_2$, but for a transition from s_1 to s'_1 by a provided operation a in C_1 and a transition from s_2 to s'_2 by $b/a \cdot tr$ that requires operation a in a required operation of C_2, there is a transition from (s_1, s_2) to (s'_1, s'_2) by the action b/tr that does not require any operation in $C_1 >> C_2$. Here tr is a sequence of required operations of C_1. This definition is illustrated in Fig. 45.

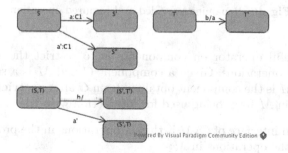

Fig. 45. Plugging state machine diagrams

The connectors used to realise abstract composition operators are open components and the pipeline operator is used to plug the components being connected to the connector. Also, both the parallel composition and pipeline operators can be defined by a general parallel composition, but the semantics of the general parallel composition requires strong theoretical background to comprehend.

Renaming and Restriction Operators. To support reuse of (models of) components, operations of interfaces often need to be renamed. For this, we define that two signatures $m(x; y)$ and $n(u; v)$ (syntactically) **matchable** if x and u are of the same type and y and v are of the same type. In this case the two signatures also called of the **same type**. Given a component C and an operation $n()$ that is of the same type of an operation $m()$, $C[m/n]$ is component obtained from C by replacing the interface operation $m()$ of C with $n()$. We call is a renaming function $[m/n]$.

In fact, renaming $C[m/n]$ does not required m to be an interface operation of C and in this case the renaming function has no effect and $C[m/n]$ is the same as C. The use of renaming includes avoiding conflicts of names when composing components, and in particular renaming a provided operation of C_1 with the name of a required operation of C_2 when plugging C_1 to C_2. In component diagrams, renaming connectors are shown in Fig. 46.

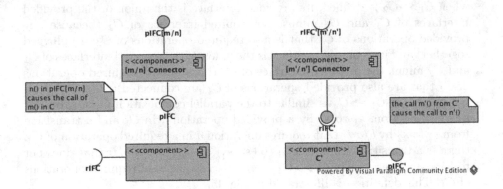

Fig. 46. Renaming provided and required operations

Another useful operator on components is to restrict the access to some of the provided operations. Given a component C and M is a set of operation signatures, $C \backslash M$ is the component obtained from C after **restricting** or **hiding** the operations in M from being used for interaction with the actors, that is

- The provided interface of $C \backslash M$ is the set operations in the provided interface of C minus the operations in M;
- The required interface of $C \backslash M$ is the required interface of C;

- The state machine diagram of $C \backslash M$ is obtained from that of C by removing all transitions made by operations in M.

Note that we do not restrict operations in required interfaces of components. We use a component called the **hiding connector** to realise the restriction operator, as shown in Fig. 47.

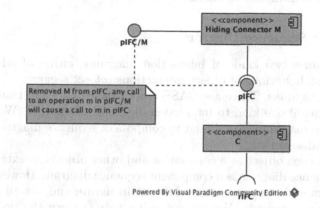

Fig. 47. Hiding connector

Relation to the rCOS Formal Method. Theoretical frameworks, such as CSP [31], CCS [66], I/O automata [64] and Statecharts [24] show the importance of the composition operators in concurrent and distributed computer systems, sound and complete algebraic theories are also developed, but they do not deal well with the complex issues in object-oriented, component based and interface contract driven development approach. We have spent quite some research effort in the development of the rCOS semantic theory [11,15,21,37,58,91], but large gaps still remain.

11   Object-Oriented Design of Components

The models discussed in Part II on requirements analysis focus on abstract, global and external functionality and behaviour. They are seen from the application domain point of view with a users' perspective. In Sect. 10.1, we transformed the use cases into *components* interrelated through their *interfaces*. The contract of an interface operation specifies what the operation does in terms of preconditions and postconditions, but it does not transformed how software objects are going work collectively to fulfil the contract. We need to transform the contracts into algorithms of object interactions and operations on object states. From the algorithms, program code can be easily developed or even automatically generated.

The essential technique is to decompose the functionality of interface operations into *responsibilities* of related objects, and design the object interactions by *assigning* (or delegating) the responsibilities to appropriate objects. This section studies the general principles for responsibility assignment which are called *design patterns for object responsibility assignment* (GRASP) [42]. Before we introduce the concept of object responsibility, we first discuss the UML diagrams for representing object interactions.

11.1   Object Sequence Diagrams

The UML defines two kinds of interaction diagrams, either of which can be used to express behaviour of object interactions: *object sequence diagrams* and *collaboration diagrams*. There are CASE tools to automatically translate interaction diagrams of one kind to interaction diagrams of another. We use object sequence diagrams, which are similar to component sequence diagrams (and use case sequence diagrams).

If we treat each object as a component and other objects as external actors, an object sequence diagram is a component sequence diagram. However, as show in [45], objects and components are different in nature and not all objects can be treated as components. We are not going to introduce the precise syntax of the UML object sequence diagrams using the UML meta model definition or the abstract syntactic definition in formal languages. Instead, we will show how different object-oriented decompositions mechanisms can be represented in object sequence diagrams.

Decomposition by Sequence of Object Method Invocations. We often need to decompose the functionality (i.e., the grand responsibility) of an operation specified by its contract into a sequence of method invocations to methods number of objects. These methods represent sub-functionalities (or partial responsibilities). We represent this form of decomposition by the object sequence diagram in Fig. 48. It shows that method $m(in; out)$ is decomposed into a sequence of operations.

```
Class B:: m(in;out) {c.m1(in1;out1); c.m2(in2;out2); c.m3(in3;out3)
                    }
```

In an object sequencing diagram, as commented in Fig. 48,

- **instances** of classes are written in boxes,
- a **directed link** between two objects represents an instance of an association between their classes and visibility,
- a **message** represents an invocation of a method of the target object (server) from the source object (client), and
- the messages are numbed to represent the order in which they are executed.

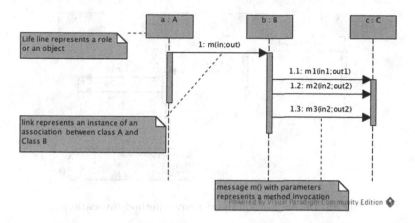

Fig. 48. Decomposition by sequence of method invocations

Note that

1. a message can be passed between two objects only when the two objects are linked in the current state, and
2. two objects can only be linked by an association of the classes of the objects - type correctness.

We also write a message *message(parameter:parameterType; return: returnType)* with a return parameter in a similar style to Java as follows:

```
return ' = message(parameter: parameterType): returnType
```

Recursive Method Invocation. It is often the case that an operation of a component or a method of an object is decomposed into recursive or nested method invocations as shown in Fig. 49, which represents the method decomposition.

```
Class B:: m() {o2.m1()
            }
Class C:: m1(){o3.n1();o3.n2()
            }
```

As an example, we decompose *makeCashPay(amount : Quantity)* in the way shown in the object sequence diagram in Fig. 50. The message *Create()* represents the call for the constructor of the target class. In an object-oriented programming language, such as Java, *makeCashPay(amount: Quantity)* is coded as

```
Class CashDsk::makeCashPay(amount:Quantity){s.makeCaskPay(amount)
                                            }
Class Sale::makeCashPay(amount:Quantity){p: =new CashPayment(amount)
                                            }
```

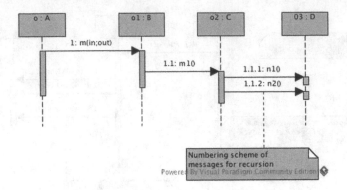

Fig. 49. Decomposition by recursive method invocations

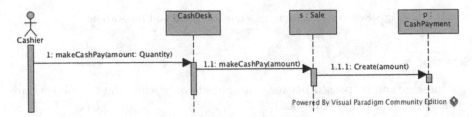

Fig. 50. A design of *makeCashPay* operation

As in component sequence diagrams, loops and choices are provided in object sequence diagrams, but only conditional choices are considered (to model case statements and **if-then-else** statements). However, here we need to discuss messages to **container objects**, which are also called **multiobjects**. The role of an association is modelled as a multiobject if its multiplicity in the association is more than one. For example, Figs. 18 and 21 in Sect. 7 of Part II show that a Sale instance aggregates a set of **SaleLineItem** instances. In the design, a **Sale** instance is linked to a multiobject of **SaleLineItem** by the aggregation associations. We use a stereotype ⟨⟨*Set*⟩⟩ to represent a multiobject.

Messages to Multiobjects. There are two kinds of messages to a multiobject. A message of the first kind is sent to the multiobject as a single object instead of a broadcast to each of the member objects contained in the multiobject. For example, if we want to check the size of a **Sale** instance, i.e.. the number of **SaleLineItem** instances in the Sale instance, we need to send the multiobject ⟨⟨*Set*⟩⟩ **Sale** a method call, say *size*(). This is shown in Fig. 51. In Java, a multiobject is often implemented by a variable of **vector type**.

When a method needs to be broadcast to each element in an multiobject, an iteration of a method call to the multiobject to extract links to each individual object, following by a message sent to each individual object using a temporary link (or reference/pointer in object-oriented programs). For example, when we

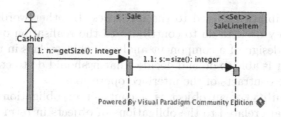

Fig. 51. Single message to a multiobject

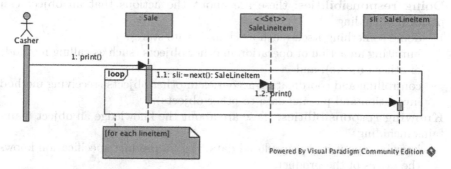

Fig. 52. Message to each element in a multiobject

print out a **Sale** instance, we need to print each **SaleLineItem** of the **Sale**. This is shown in Fig. 52.

Once the object sequence diagrams are created for all the interface operations of the architectural components, we actually have obtained a design model from which program code can be generated. Thus, the question is how we systematically constructed the object sequence diagrams from the model of the component-based architecture design. To this end, we introduce the design patterns for general principles in assigning responsibility (GRASP).

11.2   GRASP: Patterns of Assigning Responsibilities to Objects

Experienced object-oriented developers build up both general principles and idiomatic solutions called patterns that guide them in the creation of software. Design patterns are most popularly promoted by the Gang of Four in their book [23]. A **pattern** is a named problem/solution pair that can be applied to new context, with advice on how to apply it. We introduce five design patterns which are well-known as GRASP - General Responsibility Assignment Software Patterns (or Principles), consisting of guidelines for assigning responsibility to classes and objects in object-oriented design.

Responsibilities of Classes and Objects. Classes in the conceptual class models presented in Sect. 7 in Part II do not have methods. They have not been assigned responsibilities related to the use cases. In other words, we have not decided what they need to do to contribute to the realisation of the use cases. Object-oriented design of a component analyses what a class in the class model of the component is able to do and decide what it should do to contribute to the realisation of the contracts of the interface operations.

A **responsibility** of an object is a contract or obligation of the object. Responsibilities are related to the obligations of objects in term of their behaviour. There are in general two types of responsibilities:

1. **Doing responsibilities:** these are about the actions that an object can perform, including
   - doing something itself (such as changing its state),
   - initiating an action or operation in other objects (such as calling methods of other objects), and
   - controlling and coordinating activities in other objects (receiving method invocation and passing data to other objects).
2. **Knowing responsibilities:** these are about the knowledge an object maintains including
   - knowing about its encapsulated data. E.g., a product specification knows the prices of the product,
   - knowing about related objects, e.g., the **Catalog** knows all the product specifications and a student knows the modules he or she takes, and
   - knowing about things it can derive or calculate, e.g., if a **Student** knows his or her date of birth he or she knows his or her current age.

It is important to note that the knowing responsibilities of a class are clearly represented in the conceptual class model in terms of attributes of classes and associations between objects; and the doing responsibilities of a class are determined by its knowing responsibility, i.e., what an object can do depends on what it knows. Deciding the doing responsibilities of a class requires analysis and deduction, and thus is more challenging.

Object orientation supports the principle of information hiding, i.e., *data encapsulation*. All information in an object-oriented system is stored in its objects and can only be manipulated when the objects are asked to perform some actions. In order to use an object, we only need to know the interface that consists of the public methods and public attributes of the object.

The general steps to design the object sequence diagrams of a component is described as follows.

1. Start with the responsibilities which are identified from the use cases and conceptual models (knowing responsibilities), and the contracts of the interface operations of the component.
2. Assign these responsibilities to objects, then decide what the objects needs to do to fulfil these responsibilities in order to identify further responsibilities which are again assigned to objects.
3. Repeat these steps until the identified responsibilities are fulfilled and a object sequence diagram is completed.

For example, we may assign the responsibility of knowing the date of a **Sale** instance to the instance itself (a knowing responsibility), and the responsibility for printing a **Sale** instance to the instance itself (a doing responsibility).

Responsibilities of a class are implemented by programmed methods of the class which either acts alone or collaborates with other methods and objects. For example, the class **Sale** might define a method *print*() that prints an instance. To fulfil this responsibility, object **Sale** has to collaborate with other objects by sending a message to each of **SaleLineItem** objects contained in the **Sale** asking them to print themselves.

Using the UML, responsibilities are assigned to objects when creating an object sequence diagram, and the object sequence diagram represents both of the assignment of responsibilities to objects and the collaboration between objects for their fulfilment. For example, Fig. 52 in the previous subsection indicates that

1. **Sale** objects have been given the responsibility to print themselves, which is invoked with a message *print*() to **Sale**.
2. To fulfil this responsibility, **Sale** needs to collaborate with the **SaleLineItem** objects it contains, asking them to print themselves, thus each **saleLine** having a method *print*().

The Five GRASP Patterns: Each of these principles or solutions describes a problem to be solved and a solution to the problem. We follow the style of presentations of patterns see in Larman's textbook [42].

Pattern Name :	The name given to the patterns for easy reference.
Solution :	Description of the solution of the problem.
Problem :	Description of the problem that the pattern solves.

We now introduce the five patterns **Expert Pattern**, **Creator**, **Low Coupling**, **High Cohesion** and **Controller**. We will use some responsibilities of Process Sale use case as illustrating examples. Attention should be paid to how the conceptual class model and contracts component interfaces (or use case operations) are used in identification of responsibilities of classes.

Expert Pattern. We start with **Expert Pattern**

Pattern Name:	Expert.
Solution:	Assign a responsibility to the information expert - the class which has information necessary to fulfil the responsibility.
Problem:	What is the most basic principle by which responsibilities are assigned in object-oriented design.

The key of Expert pattern is to identify the *information expert* from the conceptual class model for a given responsibility. Consider ProcessSaleWithCashPay component for example, it has the responsibility to calculate the **total** of the **Sale**. This responsibility needs to be assigned to a class. When we assign responsibilities, we had better to state the responsibility clearly:

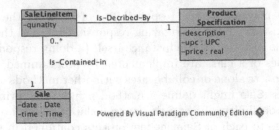

Fig. 53. Information expert for the total of Sale

Which object should be responsible for knowing the grand total of the Sale instance?

By pattern Expert, we should look for the class of objects which has the following information that is needed for calculating the grand total of the Sale:

- all the SaleLineItem instances of the Sale instance, and
- the sum of their subtotal of SaleLineItem instances.

Looking at the conceptual class diagram in Fig. 18 in Sect. 7 of Part II, we extract the partial class diagram in Fig. 53. This class diagram shows that only Sale knows the above two pieces of information for calculating the grand total of the Sale. Thus by Expert, Sale is the correct class for this responsibility.

We assign the responsibility of returning the total, represented by the method $total()$, to class Sale. This is shown in Fig. 54a as a message $1 : total()$ to object :Sale. Next the functionality is decomposed into responsibilities of *knowing the subtotal* of each SaleLineItem of Sale. And each SaleLineItem is the information expert of its subtotal. This is represented by the responsibility assignment of $1.2 : sub := subtotal()$ in Fig. 54a. Further, the subtotal functionality is decomposed into getting the price of the item and the quantity of item. The information expert of knowing the price is ProductionSpecification and the information expert of quantity is the SaleLineItem itself. This leads to a further responsibility assignment $1.2.1 : p := price()$ to ProductSpecification. The construction of the object sequence diagram shows that while looking for an information expert, further decomposition of responsibilities and looking for sub-information experts are often needed.

Notice the message $1 : t = total()$ to :Sale is not from the actor Cashier. This is because it is not an actor to trigger the operation $total()$. Instead the information of $total()$ is directly picked up by the GUI object for display. We do not discuss GUI design and how GUI objects are linked to the application objects.

Along the creation of object sequence diagrams, methods representing responsibilities are assigned to the classes. This is represented in the partial *design class diagram* in Fig. 54b. A **design class diagram** is a class diagram which contains classes and operations of classes, as well as attributes of classes

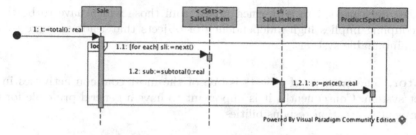

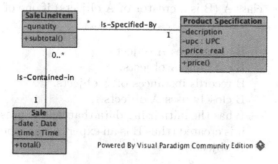

(a) Object sequence diagram for design of *total*()

(b) Design class diagram

Fig. 54. Design of *total*()

and associations among classes. The design of object sequence diagrams for operations thus also transforms the conceptual class diagram to a corresponding design class diagram.

To be precise, a class diagrams also contains information about directions of *navigability* (or *visibility*) of associations and *dependencies* among classes. Dependencies represent the directions of messages and flows of parameters of methods. It seems that Visual Paradigm does not support visual presentation of navigability, but the object sequence diagrams show the directions of messages anyway.

The pattern Expert is the most fundamental principle in object-oriented design. We will see it is used gain and again in the following subsection about the design of the operations of Process Sale with Cash Payment. Expert "expresses the common intuition that objects do things related to the information they have - fundamentally, objects do things related to information they know" [42]. A good analogy is that if a corporation is to produce the annual financial report of its business, it is obvious that this responsibility should be given to the chief financial officer, and then the chief financial officer would give the responsibilities for producing the different parts to different divisions of his or her departments which has the relevant information and data.

The use of Expert also maintains encapsulation, since objects use their own information to fulfil responsibilities. This also implies low coupling, which means no extra links needed to be formed apart from those which have to be there. Low coupling implies high independency of objects that leads to more robust and maintainable systems.

Creator. The creation of objects is one of the most common activities in an object system. Consequently, it is important to have a general principle for the assignment of creation responsibilities.

Pattern Name:	Creator.
Solution:	Assign class B the responsibility to create an instance of a class A (B is a creator of A objects) if one of the following is true:

- B aggregates A objects.
- B contains A objects.
- B records instances of A objects.
- B closely uses A objects.
- B has the initialising data that will be passed to A when it is created (thus B is an expert with respect to creating A objects).

Problem:	What should be responsible for creating a new instance of some class?

Consider the postconditions of *enterItem(upc:UPC, qty:Quantity)* of component ProcessSaleWithCashPay. We identify the responsibility "creating a SaleLineItem instance". Look into partial class diagrams in Fig. 53 as a part in the conceptual model in Fig. 18 in Sect. 7 of Part II. A Sale instance aggregates many SaleLineItem objects, Creator suggests Sale is a good candidate to be responsible for creating the SaleLineItem instance. The responsibility is then delegated to SaleLineItem to create itself. Notice that in all object-oriented programming languages a class always has "constructor" for creating objects of the class. However, the creator of an object o is the object which calls the constructor method of the class of o. This leads to a design of object sequence diagram in Fig. 55. The assignment of creating a SaleLineItem instance to Sale also identifies a method *makeLineItem(upc:UPC, qty: Quantity)* of class Sale, which should be added to the design class diagram in Fig. 54b.

Consider *makeCashPayment()*. Its postconditions indicates the responsibility of "creating a CashPayment instance". Which object should be the creator of the CashPayment? Creator suggests both Sale, which is closely related to CashPayment, and CashDesk, which represents the component of the sale handler handling payments too, can be candidates of the creator. Recall that contract of *makePayment()* also has a postcondition for the CashPayment created to be linked to the Sale. We have two alternative designs in Fig. 56a, b respectively.

Compare the two designs, the one in Fig. 56a is much simpler, and the link between :Sale and :CashPayment is naturally established through creation. Furthermore, look into the conceptual class diagram in Fig. 18 in Sect. 7 of Part II,

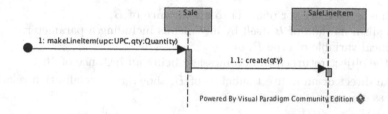

Fig. 55. Example of Creator pattern

we find that there is no direct association between **CashDesk** and **CashPayment**. The message 1.1 : $p=Create()$ from :**CashDesk** to :**CashPayment** cannot be sent unless we add an association. This also motivates the **Low Coupling** pattern.

Low Coupling. The design in Fig. 56a is preferable over the one in Fig. 56b because it does not need an extra link formed between **CashDesk** and **CashPayment**. Thus, the former keeps the "coupling" low. In object-oriented programming languages such as C++, Java, and Smalltalk, common forms of coupling from a class A to a class B to include:

- A has an attribute which refers to a instance of B, being represented by an association in a class diagram;
- A has a method which

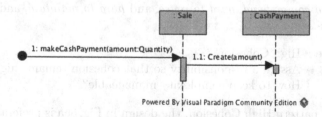

(a) Creator of *CashPayment*

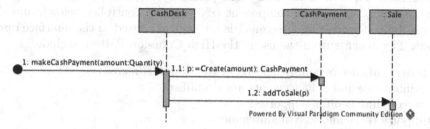

(b) An alternative Creator of *CashPayment*

Fig. 56. Two alternative Creators of *CashPayment*

- has a reference (or pointer) to an instance of B,
- calls a method of B itself by any means including a parameter,
- local variable of type B, or
- the object returned from a message being an instance of B;

- A is a direct or an indirect subclass of B, shown as specialisation relation in a class diagram.

Classes whose objects have too many links to other objects are not easy to be reused, as to reuse such a class the related class should be used. Components with classes of high coupling are difficult to maintain too, as changing to such a class would cause changes to the related classes. For better reusability and maintainability of components, the pattern of Low Coupling suggests that coupling should be kept low.

Pattern Name : Low Coupling.
Solution :   Assign a responsibility so that coupling remains low.
Problem :   How to support low dependency an increased reuse?

The design in Fig. 56a conforms to Lower Coupling.

High Cohesion. Cohesion is a measure of how strongly related and focused the responsibilities of a class are. A class with high cohesion has highly related functional responsibilities, and it is not overloaded with a large amount of responsibility. A class with low cohesion is undesirable as it suffers from the following problems: *hard to comprehend, hard to reuse*, and *hard to maintain*, and thus it is prone to errors.

Pattern Name : High Cohesion.
Solution :   Assign a responsibility so that cohesion remains high.
Problem :   How to keep complexity manageable?

According to pattern High Cohesion, the design in Fig. 56a is preferable over the one in Fig. 56b also. This is because **CashDesk** is the interface object of **ProcessSale**. Thus, it is naturally and primarily responsible for handling the provided operations of the component (see pattern Controller below), and the responsibility for creating a payment is not logical related to the interface operations. The benefits from the use of the High Cohesion Pattern include:

- clarity and ease of comprehension of the design is increased,
- maintenance and enhancements are simplified,
- low coupling is often supported,
- supports reuse and easy maintenance.

Controller. To create a design of a component, we need to assign the responsibility of handling the operations of component's provided interfaces. The question is which object should be responsible for receiving the provided interface operations from its actors, and then delegates the responsibilities specified by the contracts of the operations to further objects.

Pattern Name: Controller.

Solution: Assign the responsibility for handling a system (input) event to a class representing one of the following choices:

- Represents the "overall system" (facade controller)[18].
- Represents the overall business or organisation (facade controller).
- Represents something in the real-world that is active (for example, the role of a person) that might be involved in the task (role controller).
- Represents an artificial handler of all system (input) events of a use case (or 'operations of provided interfaces of a component'), usually named "⟨*UseCaseName*⟩*Handler*"' (use-case controller or 'component interface handler').

Problem: Who should be responsible for handling a system input event (or 'the operations of the provided interface of the component')?

Notice that we added some alternative interpretations in the single quotes, such as 'component interface handler' and 'operations of provided interfaces of a component', in relation to our component-based design. This pattern also suggests to use the same controller class for all system input events in the same use case. It also implies that a controller is a non-user interface object responsible for handling provided operations of the component.

With our component based model of architecture, it is become more obvious when deciding the controller classes as they are just the classes to implement the provided interfaces, and we have one controller class for each interface. Consider the use case Process Sale with Cash Payment (also component **Process-SaleByCash**), we have given the specification of the contracts of the operations *startSale()*, *enterItem()*, *finishSale()*, and *makeCashPayment()* of the use case. We need to assign these operations to a controller class. According to the pattern of Controller, we have the following candidates

1. **CashDesk**: represents a component interface handler[19].
2. **Store**: represents the overall business or organisation.
3. **Cashier**: represents something in the real-world (such as the role of a person) that is active and might be involved in the task.
4. **ProcessSaleHandler**: represents an artificial handler of all the operations of the use case[20].

---

[19] This does not explicitly indicated by Controller pattern, but it is an object that Cashier actor uses to handle the operations. It also represents the Cash Desk PC.

[20] The choice of **CashDesk** can also be seen as an artificial handler.

The decision on which of these four is the most appropriate controller is influenced by other factors, such as cohesion and coupling. In the next subsection, we will use CashDesk as the controller to show the design of the provided operations of the component ProcessSaleByCash. The reason is that it is already in the conceptual class diagram with associations naturally identified, and this object does not have much other functionality to carry out.

The relation between the controller class and the component provided interface is that former implements the latter. Thus, we have class CashDesk implements pIFProcessSaleCash and in Java this corresponding the class definition below

```
Interface pIFProcessSaleCash{
    startSale();
    enterItem();
    finishSale();
    makecashPayment()
}
```

```
Class CashDesk implements  pIFProcessSaleCash {
    startSale(){as designed in the next subsection};
    enterItem(){as designed in the next subsection};
    finishSale() {as designed in the next subsection};
    makeCashPayment(){as designed in the next subsection}
```

11.3   Design Component ProcessSaleWithCashPay

We first discuss the design of Start Up operation that creates the initial object structure of the system so that all business use processes reply on. Recall the post conditions of *StartUp* operation:

1. A Sore, CashDesk, Catalog and ProductSpecification were created (instance creation).
2. ProductSpecification was associated with Catalog.
3. Catalog was associated with Store.
4. CashDesk was associated with Store.
5. Catalog was associated with CashDesk.

This contract specifies the initialisation of the execution when an application is launched. The principle is to create an initial domain object first, and then through which the other objects that need to be created in the StartUp operation are created. The problem of how to create the initial domain object is dependent upon the object-oriented programming language and operating system. The following is, for example, how *StartUp()* is done using Java applet.

```
public class ProcessSaleApplet extends Applet {
    public void init() {
```

```
        cashDesk := store.getCashDesk();
        }
// Store is the initial domain object.
// The Store constructor creates other domain objects
        private Store store := new Store();
        private CashDesk cashDesk;
        private Sale sale;
    }
```

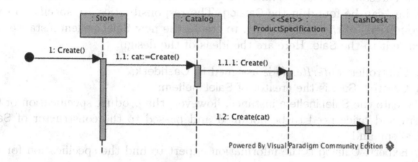

Fig. 57. Design of *StartUp()*

The object sequence diagram for the design of *StartUp()* operation does not show its controller so as to abstract the platform details away. Instead, the object sequence diagram will start from the creation of the initial domain object, and in this case it is **Store**. The design is shown in Fig. 57. After the *StartUp()* operation is executed. Some management use cases can be carried out to add product specifications to the **Catalog** instance **cat**. Notice that the creation of the **Catalog** instance **cat** also creates the (empty) set of **ProductSpecification** instances; and the creation of the **CashDesk** uses **cat** as a parameter so that the **CashDesk** is linked to the **Catalog**. Therefore the postconditions of *StartUp()* are all met by the design. Now we design the operations of Process Sale with Cash Payment.

Design of startSale(). The contract of *startSale()* assumes the preconditions of the existence of the objects **Store**, **CashDesk** and **Catalog** that were created by the *StartUp()* operation. The postcondition is simply to create a new **Sale** instance. By Controller, **CashDesk** it is also the Creator of the new **Sale** instance. The design is given in Fig. 58.

Design of enterItem(). This operation carries most of the complexity, compared to the other operations of the use case. Its contract assumes the existence of the **CashDesk** instance, the **Catalog** instance and its contained **ProductSpecifications**. The operation has input parameters **upc:UPC** and **qty:Quantity** of the item to

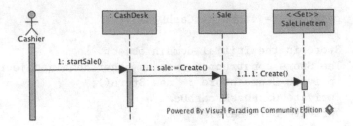

Fig. 58. Design of *startSale*()

create. The contract also assumes the precondition that product identity **upc** is valid, i.e., can be found in the **Catalog**. The responsibilities are specified in the postconditions of the contract, i.e., to create the new **SaleLineItem** instance and associate it to the **Sale**. Here are the ideas of the design

1. by Controller, *enterItem*() is assigned to **Cashdesk**;
2. by Creator, **Sale** is the creator of **SaleLineItem**;
3. to create the **SaleLineItem** instance, however, the product specification of the item and price need to be obtained and passed to the constructor of **Sale-LineItem**; and
4. by Expert, **Catalog** is the information expert to find the specification for the given **upc**.

This analysis leads to the design given in Fig. 59.

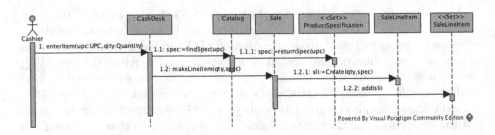

Fig. 59. Design of *enterItem*()

Creating the object sequence diagrams also improves the understanding of the preconditions of an operation. For example, the precondition that the **CashDesk** instance is linked with **Catalog** instance, establish by *StartUp*(); and that the existence of the **Sale** and the existence of the **ProductSpecification**, established by *startSale*() and some management use cases. On the other hand, an object sequence diagram can also be checked against the contract of the operation, that is all preconditions are checked and postconditions are established.

Design of finishSale(). This is a simple operation and its execution assumes the preconditions established by *startSale()* and *enterItem()*. The postcondition is simply to set the attribute **isComplete** attribute of **Sale**. By Controller **CashDesk** is the controller of *finishSale()*, and **Sale** is the expert for setting its attribute **isComplete** to true. The design is shown in Fig. 60.

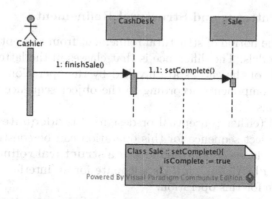

Fig. 60. Design of *finishSale()*

Design of makeCashPayment(). The precondition of this operation is that the **isComplete** attribute of the **Sale** is **true**. This has been established by *finishSale()*. The postconditions include creating of **CashPayment**, associating it to the **Sale** and associating the sale with the **Store** to log the complete sale. The Creator of **cashPayment** is designed to **Sale** in Fig. 56a. The expert for logging the complete **Sale** is **Store**, as it aggregates (complete) **Sale** instances. This analysis leads to the design in Fig. 61.

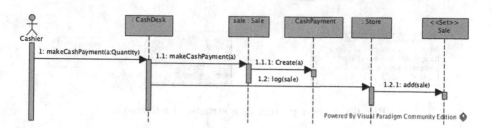

Fig. 61. Design of *makeCashPayment()*

The design of the object sequence diagrams of the operations also contributes significantly to the understanding and identification of the preconditions of the operations that are difficult to identify during the analysis of the use case sequence diagram and the contracts of their operations. The dependency of the preconditions of an operation on the postconditions established by other operations can be checked using the state machine diagram of the component. For example, the state machine diagram in Fig. 39 for component ProcessSaleWith-CashPay is used to guide the above discussion of the preconditions in the design of the operations.

11.4   Design Patterns and Structural Refinement

We now extend the notion of structural refinement from conceptual class models to design class models. The difference is that classes in the latter contain methods. The methods of the classes are invoked by the operations in the provided interfaces of the components according to the object sequence diagrams of the interface operations.

A class model (either conceptual or design) $\mathcal{C}$ is **adequate** for an interface operation if an object sequence for this operation can be constructed using the methods of in the classes. A class model $\mathcal{C}$ is a **structural refinement** of a class model $\mathcal{C}_1$, denoted by $\mathcal{C}_1 \sqsubseteq \mathcal{C}$, if $\mathcal{C}_1$ is adequate for an interface operation, then $\mathcal{C}$ is also adequate for this operation.

The expert pattern is then statement as a refinement rule shown in Fig. 62. We explain the diagram as follows

- a responsibility $S[c.(x)]$ is assigned to class C that contains a sub-responsibility $c(x)$,
- class B is the information expert of the responsibility of $c(x)$, here attributes x can contain role names to refer to associated objects of class B, and
- the responsibility is represented as a method $m()$ and assigned to class B.

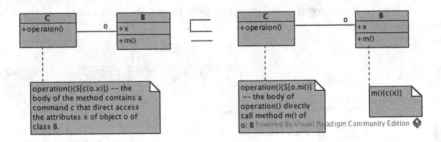

Fig. 62. Expert pattern as a structural refinement

A structural refinement rule for class decomposition is given in Fig. 63, that also reflects High Cohesion. We explained this refinement as follows

- assume class A contains two sets of attributes x and y (including role names of associations with class C);
- class C are given responsibilities represented by methods m and n, and m only refers to attributes x;

- we can decompose A into three classes A, B and D such that B maintains x only and it is assigned with the responsibility m;
- class A is responsible for coordinating the responsibilities of class B and D.

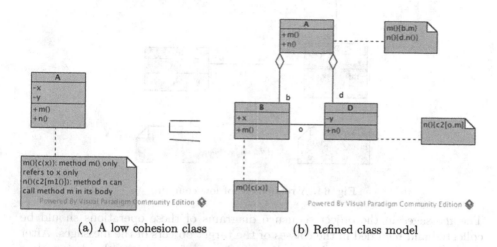

(a) A low cohesion class   (b) Refined class model

Fig. 63. Class decomposition

The class model in Fig. 64 also refines the low cohesion class in Fig. 63a, and clearly this model is of lower coupling than the class model in Fig. 63b.

The refinement in Figs. 62, 63 and 64 can be used in the context of any larger class models that contain them. The proposition about refinement in Subsect. 7.8 of Part II can now be extended as: a class model C is a structural refinement of a class model C_1, if C can be obtained by one of the following changes made to C_1:

- adding a class,
- adding an attribute to a class,
- adding an association between two classes,
- increasing the multiplicity of a role of an association (that is equivalent to adding attributes at the level of program code),
- promoting an attribute a subclasses to its superclass,
- promoting an association of a subclass to its superclass,
- adding a method to a class, and
- promoting a method of a subclass to its superclass.

Structural refinement supports incremental modelling and design.

11.5   Summary of Design

We have discussed all the operations of Process Sale with Cash Payment, or equivalently the operations of the interface of component ProcessSaleByCash.

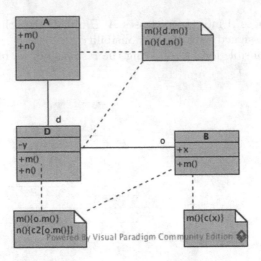

Fig. 64. A refinement of low coupling

The messages in the object sequence diagrams of these operations should be collected and recorded in the classes of the target objects of the messages. After doing these, the conceptual class diagram is transformed into the design class diagram, whose methods and directions of navigability (or visibilities) of the associations of the class are determined by the object sequence diagrams. With the design class diagram, the object sequence diagrams and the state machine diagrams of a component, an object-oriented program (skeleton) for the component can be generated. The skeleton contains the methods of the classes and object interactions as method calls (represented by the messages in the object sequence diagrams) in their bodies, only leaving significant algorithms for manipulation simple attributes of objects need to be coded. The detailed design model and the program skeleton are analysable and validatable against the requirements models.

The GRASP patterns and design are mainly from Larman's textbook [42]. However, we put the discussion in relation to the component-based architecture design given in Sect. 10.1. Furthermore, models of component-based architecture can be obtained at the requirements analysis level by decomposing the use cases. On the other hand, transformations of object sequence diagrams of a component can wrap some objects into a components and abstract away the details of some object interactions inside these wrapped components. These transformations can be supported by an interactive transformation tool [46]. This will further decompose the component-based model of architecture obtained in the component-based architecture design in Sect. 10.1.

Relation to the rCOS Formal Method. The informal object-oriented design presented in this section is the motivation of the development of the object-oriented extension [27] to Unifying Theories of Programs [32]. Based on this semantic theory, a sound and complete calculus of object-oriented structure refinement presented in [91], which also characterises the expert pattern (Creator is treated as a special case of Expert), low coupling and high cohesion as refinement rules, together with other refactoring rules. The application to the Trading System is shown in [15]. Formalisation of more design patterns can be found in [63]. Code generation from design is also presented in [62].

12   Summary and Future Work

We have presented, through informal but yet precise discussions, a model-driven design method for object-oriented component-based software systems. The theoretical underpinning of this method is formal model-driven method of component and object systems, knows as rCOS [15,27,37] and component interfaces [11,21,26,37,61], and formal semantics and relations of different UML models for requirements models and design [12,25,52,55].

The rCOS methods clearly reflect the model-driven development that *system design is carried out in a process through building system models* to gain confidence in requirements and designs. The process of model constructions emphases on

- the use of *abstraction* for information hiding so as to be well-focused and problem oriented;
- the use of the engineering principles of *decomposition* and *separation of concerns* for *divide and conquer* and *incremental development* and evolution; and
- the use of *formalisation* to allow the *process repeatable* and *artefacts (models) analysable*.

Alao, rCOS proposes a multiple diminutional approach to component-based architecture modelling, as shown in Fig. 65.

- First, it allows models of a component at different levels of abstract, from the top level models of *interface contracts* of components developed through use case analysis and conceptual class modelling, through models of interactions and dynamic behaviours of components, component-based architecture design and object-oriented design of individual components, to models of deployment and implementations.
- At each level of abstraction, a component has models of different viewpoints, including the *class model* (or *data model*), the specification of *static data functionality* (i.e., changes of data states), the *model of interaction protocol* with the environment (i.e., actors) of the components, and the *model of reactive behaviour*. These models of different viewpoints support the understanding of different aspects of the components and support different techniques of analysis, design and verification of different kinds of properties. Moreover, they support the separation of design and verification concerns - models of different viewpoints can be refined separately without affecting models of the other view viewpoints. For example, in the rCOS theory, we have proven that contact of the static functionality of an interface can be refined without

changing its contract of dynamic behaviour, and *vice versa*. Similarly, structure refinement of the class model preserves the specifications of contracts and interaction models.

– A model of a component is hierarchical and composed from models of 'smaller' components that interact and collaborate with each other through their interfaces. Some components can also control, monitor or coordinate other components. These compositions are realised by connector components.

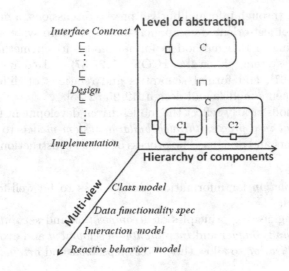

Fig. 65. rCOS modelling approach

We briefly summarise the iterative rCOS model of development process, driven by model constructions and model transformations/refinement, as followings

1. Through use case analyse and conceptual class modelling development a model of component-based architecture (Sects. 5–8).
2. Refine interface operations of components by using design patterns to generate a model object-oriented design, i.e., the collection of object-sequence diagrams and the design class diagram (Sect. 9).
3. Transform the model of object-oriented design to a model of component-based design for integration and maintenance/evolution [46] (this is not discussed in details in this chapter).
4. Realise the interfaces of components using appropriate middlewares, e.g., RMI, CORBA etc. (not covered in the these notes).
5. Code generation performed after Step 3 and Step 4.

An iteration of this process is shown in Fig. 66.

We can see that the rCOS method and development emphasis on the interface-based requirements analysis and design of components. We believe this

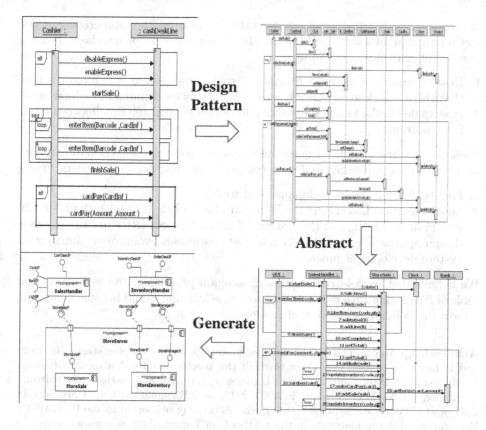

Fig. 66. rCOS development process

is becoming increasingly essential for the maintenance of and development of front end applications from modern complex evolving software-intensive systems [89]. These systems include Internet of Things (IoT) [48], Smart Cities [83] and Cyber-Physical Systems (CPS) [43]. They are becoming major networks of infrastructures for development of applications in all economic and social areas such as health and care health, environment management, transport, enterprises, manufacturing, agriculture, governance, culture, societies and home automation. These applications share a common model of architectures and involve different communication technologies and protocols among the architectural components. The research and applications thus require collaborations among experts with expertise in a variety of disciplines and various skills in software systems development.

The future development of the rCOS interface theory include its extension to models of *physical interfaces* in order to model *cyber-physical components* and their composition [54,72]. This will make the notion of interfaces very general. For example, a piece of wall or a window can be modelled interfaces between the temperatures outside and inside a room. Even the "air" between two sections of a room can modelled as an interface that transforms the temperature of one section to that of another. However, this general notion of interfaces poses a number of challenges, for example

1. How to develop a model of contract of such interfaces, as it is often the case that there is no known physical laws or functions for defining these interfaces?
2. How to define the formal semantics and the refinement relation between inter-face contracts?

These are the first significant questions to ask when developing a semantic theory for these CPS components and their compositions. Further challenges including

1. how to develop design techniques and tools,
2. how to combine David Parnas's Four-Variable Model, Michael Jackson's Prob-lem Frames Model, and the Rational Unified Process (RUP) of the use case driven approach systematically into the continuous evolutionary integration system development process?

We believe that model-driven approach is again promising, and techniques and tools of simulation with rich data and machine learning would become increasing important in building the correct models.

Acknowledgement. The development of materials of this chapter started in 1998, and it has been revised ever since through the teaching at the University of leices-ter during 1998–2001, United Nations University -International Institute for Software Technology (UNU-IIST, Macau) in 2001–2013, and Birmingham City University in 2015, and at many international training schools (mostly supported by the UNU-IIST). We acknowledge the materials in the textbook of Larman [42] as a major source of knowledge and ideas, that have developed in all the versions of the course notes. The extensive research at UNU-IIST on the rCOS method and the development of its tool support have significantly contributed to development of the understanding of theo-retical insight of object-oriented design, component-based design, and model-driven development, and their relations. We acknowledge the contribution from Xin Chen, Zhenbang Chen, Ruzheng Dong, He Jifeng, Wei Ke, Dan Li Xiaoshan Li, Jing Liu, Charles Morisset, Anders Ravn, Volker Stolz, Shuling Wang, Jing Yang, Liang Zhao, and Naijun Zhan.

Our special thanks go to Jonathan Bowen and Anders Ravn for their careful read-ing and constructive comments, without that we could not have made this chapter into its current form.

References

1. Hamilton, M.: The engineer who took the apollo to the moon. https://medium.com/@verne/margaret-hamilton-the-engineer-who-took-the-apollo-to-the-moon-7d550c73d3fa
2. Abrial, J.R.: The B-Book: Assigning Programs to Meanings. Cambridge University Press, Cambridge (1996)
3. Abrial, J.R.: Modeling in Event-B: System and Software Engineering. Cambridge University Press, New York (2010)

4. Limet, S., Robert, S., Turki, A.: Controlling an iteration-wise coherence in dataflow. In: Arbab, F., Ölveczky, P.C. (eds.) FACS 2011. LNCS, vol. 7253, pp. 241–258. Springer, Heidelberg (2012)
5. Bell, M.: Service-Oriented Modeling: Service Analysis, Design, and Architecture. Wiley & Sons, New Jersey (2008)
6. Booch, G.: Object-Oriented Analysis and Design with Applications. Addison-Wesley, Boston (1994)
7. Bowen, J.P., Hinchey, M.G.: Formal methods. In: Gonzalez, T.F., Diaz-Herrera, J., Tucker, A.B.(eds.) Computer Science Handbook, 3rd edn. Section XI, Software Engineering, vol. 1, Computer Science and Software Engineering, Part 8, Programming Languages, Chapter 71, pp. 1–25. CRC Press (2014)
8. Brooks, F.P.: No silver bullet: essence and accidents of software engineering. IEEE Comput. **20**(4), 10–19 (1987)
9. Brooks, F.P.: The mythical man-month: after 20 years. IEEE Softw. **12**(5), 57–60 (1995)
10. Chandy, K.M., Misra, J.: Parallel Program Design: a Foundation. Addison-Wesley, Reading. (1988)
11. Chen, X., He, J., Liu, Z., Zhan, N.: A model of component-based programming. In: Arbab, F., Sirjani, M. (eds.) FSEN 2007. LNCS, vol. 4767, pp. 191–206. Springer, Heidelberg (2007)
12. Chen, X., Liu, Z., Mencl, V.: Separation of concerns and consistent integration in requirements modelling. In: van Leeuwen, J., Italiano, G.F., van der Hoek, W., Meinel, C., Sack, H., Plášil, F. (eds.) SOFSEM 2007. LNCS, vol. 4362, pp. 819–831. Springer, Heidelberg (2007)
13. Chen, Z., et al.: Modelling with relational calculus of object and component systems - rCOS. In: Rausch, A., Reussner, R., Mirandola, R., Plášil, F. (eds.) The Common Component Modeling Example. LNCS, vol. 5153, pp. 116–145. Springer, Heidelberg (2008)
14. Chen, Z., Li, X., Liu, Z., Stolz, V., Yang, L.: Harnessing rCOS for tool support —the CoCoME experience. In: Jones, C.B., Liu, Z., Woodcock, J. (eds.) Formal Methods and Hybrid Real-Time Systems. LNCS, vol. 4700, pp. 83–114. Springer, Heidelberg (2007)
15. Chen, Z., Liu, Z., Ravn, A.P., Stolz, V., Zhan, N.: Refinement and verification in component-based model driven design. Sci. Comput. Program. **74**(4), 168–196 (2009)
16. Chen, Z., Liu, Z., Stolz, V.: The rCOS tool. In: Fitzgerald, J., Larsen, P.G., Sahara, S. (eds.) Modelling and Analysis in VDM: Proceedings of the Fourth VDM/Overture Workshop, pp. 15–24. No. CS-TR-1099 in Technical report Series, University of Newcastle upon Tyne (2008)
17. Chen, Z., Morisset, C., Stolz, V.: Specification and validation of behavioural protocols in the rCOS modeler. In: Arbab, F., Sirjani, M. (eds.) FSEN 2009. LNCS, vol. 5961, pp. 387–401. Springer, Heidelberg (2010)
18. Clarke, E.M., Emerson, E.A.: Design and synthesis of synchronization skeletons using branching-time temporal logic. In: Kozen, D. (ed.) Logics of Programs. LNCS, vol. 131, pp. 52–71. Springer, Heidelberg (1981)
19. Dijkstra, E.W., Scholten, C.S.: Predicate Calculus and Program Semantics. Springer, New York (1990)
20. Dijkstra, E.W.: The humble programmer. Commun. ACM **15**(10), 859–866 (1972). An ACM Turing Award lecture

21. Dong, R., Zhan, N., Zhao, L.: An interface model of software components. In: Liu, Z., Woodcock, J., Zhu, H. (eds.) ICTAC 2013. LNCS, vol. 8049, pp. 159–176. Springer, Heidelberg (2013)

22. Fischer, C.: Fault-tolerant programming by transformations. Ph.D. thesis, University of Warwick (1991)

23. Gamma, E., Helm, R., Johnson, R., Vlissides, J.: Design Patterns: Elements of Reusable Object-Oriented Software. Addison-Wesley, Boston (1994)

24. Harel, D.: Statecharts: a visual formalism for complex systems. Sci. Comput. Program. **8**(3), 231–274 (1987)

25. He, J., Li, X., Liu, Z.: Component-based software engineering. In: Van Hung, D., Wirsing, M. (eds.) ICTAC 2005. LNCS, vol. 3722, pp. 70–95. Springer, Heidelberg (2005)

26. He, J., Li, X., Liu, Z.: A theory of reactive components. Electr. Notes Theor. Comput. Sci. **160**, 173–195 (2006)

27. He, J., Liu, Z., Li, X.: rCOS: a refinement calculus of object systems. Theor. Comput. Sci. **365**(1–2), 109–142 (2006)

28. Heineman, G.T., Councill, W.T.: Component-Based Software Engineering: Putting the Pieces Together. Addison-Wesley Professional, Reading (2001)

29. Herold, S., et al.: CoCoME - the common component modeling example. In: Rausch, A., Reussner, R., Mirandola, R., Plášil, F. (eds.) The Common Component Modeling Example. LNCS, vol. 5153, pp. 16–53. Springer, Heidelberg (2008)

30. Hoare, C.A.R.: An axiomatic basis for computer programming. Commun. ACM **12**(10), 576–580 (1969)

31. Hoare, C.A.R.: Communicating Sequential Processes. Prentice-Hall, Upper Saddle River (1985)

32. Hoare, C.A.R., He, J.: Unifying Theories of Programming. Prentice-Hall, Upper Saddle River (1998)

33. Holzmann, G.J.: The SPIN Model Checker: Primer and Reference Manual. Addison-Wesley, Reading (2004)

34. Holzmann, G.J.: Conquering complexity. IEEE Comput. **40**(12), 111–113 (2007)

35. Johnson, J.: My Life is Failure: 100 Things You Should Know to Be a Better Project Leader. Standish Group International, West Yarmouth (2006)

36. Jones, C.B.: Systematic Software Development using VDM. Prentice Hall, Upper Saddle River (1990)

37. Ke, W., Li, X., Liu, Z., Stolz, V.: rCOS: a formal model-driven engineering method for component-based software. Front. Comput. Sci. China **6**(1), 17–39 (2012)

38. Ke, W., Liu, Z., Wang, S., Zhao, L.: A graph-based operational semantics of OO programs. In: Breitman, K., Cavalcanti, A. (eds.) ICFEM 2009. LNCS, vol. 5885, pp. 347–366. Springer, Heidelberg (2009)

39. Khaitan, S.: Design techniques and applications of cyber physical systems: a survey. IEEE Syst. J. **9**(2), 350–365 (2014)

40. Kroll, P., Kruchten, P.: The Rational Unified Process Made Easy: a Practitioner's Guide to the RUP. Addison-Wesley, Boston (2003)

41. Lamport, L.: Specifying Systems: the TLA+ Language and Tools for Hardware and Software Engineers. Addison-Wesley, Boston (2002)

42. Larman, C.: Applying UML and Patterns: An Introduction to Object-Oriented Analysis and Design and the Unified Process, 2nd edn. Prentice-Hall, Upper Saddle River (2001)

43. Lee, E.: Cyber physical systems: design challenges. Technical report No. UCB/EECS-2008-8, University of California, Berkeley (2008)

44. Leveson, N.G., Turner, C.S.: An investigation of the Therac-25 accidents. IEEE Comput. **26**(7), 18–41 (1993)
45. Li, D., Li, X., Liu, Z., Stolz, V.: Interactive transformations from object-oriented models to component-based models. Technical report 451, IIST, United Nations University, Macao (2011)
46. Li, D., Li, X., Liu, Z., Stolz, V.: Interactive transformations from object-oriented models to component-based models. In: Arbab, F., Ölveczky, P.C. (eds.) FACS 2011. LNCS, vol. 7253, pp. 97–114. Springer, Heidelberg (2012)
47. Li, D., Li, X., Liu, Z., Stolz, V.: Support formal component-based development with UML profile. In: 22nd Australian Conference on Software Engineering (ASWEC 2013), Melbourne, pp. 191–200. IEEE Computer Society, 4–7 June 2013
48. Li, X., Lu, R., Liang, X., Shen, X., Chen, J., Lin, X.: Smart community: an internet of things application. Commun. Mag. **49**(11), 68–75 (2011)
49. Li, X., Liu, Z., He, J.: Formal and use-case driven requirement analysis in UML. In: 25th International Computer Software and Applications Conference (COMPSAC 2001), Invigorating Software Development, Chicago, pp. 215–224. IEEE Computer Society, 8–12 October 2001
50. Li, X., Liu, Z., He, J.: A formal semantics of UML sequence diagram. In: 15th Australian Software Engineering Conference (ASWEC 2004), Melbourne, pp. 168–177. IEEE Computer Society, 13–16 April 2004
51. Li, X., Liu, Z., He, J.: Consistency checking of UML requirements. In: 10th International Conference on Engineering of Complex Computer Systems, pp. 411–420. IEEE Computer Society (2005)
52. Liu, J., Liu, Z., He, J., Li, X.: Linking UML models of design and requirement. In: Proceedings of the 2004 Australian Software Engineering Conference, pp. 329–338. IEEE Computer Society (2004)
53. Liu, Z.: Software development with UML. Technical Report 259, IIST, United Nations University, P.O. Box 3058, Macao (2002)
54. Liu, Z., Chen, X.: Interface-driven design in evolving component-based architectures, workshop of the 25 Anniversary of ProCoS, Proceedings to be Published in Springer Lecture Notes in Computer Science (2015)
55. Liu, Z., He, J., Li, X., Chen, Y.F.: A relational model for formal object-oriented requirement analysis in UML. In: Dong, J.S., Woodcock, J. (eds.) ICFEM 2003. LNCS, vol. 2885, pp. 641–664. Springer, Heidelberg (2003)
56. Liu, Z., Joseph, M.: Transformation of programs for fault-tolerance. Form. Asp. Comput. **4**(5), 442–469 (1992)
57. Liu, Z., Joseph, M.: Specification and verification of fault-tolerance, timing, and scheduling. ACM Trans. Program. Lang. Syst. **21**(1), 46–89 (1999)
58. Liu, Z., Kang, E.Y., Zhan, N.: Composition and refinement of components. In: Butterfield, A. (ed.) UTP 2008. LNCS, vol. 5713, pp. 238–257. Springer, Heidelberg (2010)
59. Liu, Z., Li, X., He, J.: Using transition systems to unify UML models. In: George, C.W., Miao, H. (eds.) ICFEM 2002. LNCS, vol. 2495, pp. 535–547. Springer, Heidelberg (2002)
60. Liu, Z., Mencl, V., Ravn, A.P., Yang, L.: Harnessing theories for tool support. In: Proceedings of the Second International Symposium on Leveraging Applications of Formal Methods, Verification and Validation (ISoLA 2006), pp. 371–382. IEEE Computer Society, full version as UNU-IIST Technical report 343 (2006)
61. Liu, Z., Morisset, C., Stolz, V.: rCOS: theory and tool for component-based model driven development. In: Arbab, F., Sirjani, M. (eds.) FSEN 2009. LNCS, vol. 5961, pp. 62–80. Springer, Heidelberg (2010)

62. Long, Q., Liu, Z., Li, X., He, J.: Consistent code generation from UML models. In: Australian Software Engineering Conference, pp. 23–30. IEEE Computer Society, UNU-IIST TR 319 (2005)
63. Long, Q., Qiu, Z., Liu, Z.: Formal use of design patterns and refactoring. In: Margaria, T., Steffen, B. (eds.) ISoLA 2008. Communications in Computer and Information Science, vol. 17, pp. 323–338. Springer, Berlin (2008)
64. Lynch, N.A., Tuttle, M.R.: An introduction to input/output automata. CWI Q. **2**(3), 219–246 (1989)
65. Manna, Z., Pnueli, A.: The Temporal Logic of Reactive and Concurrent Systems: Specification. Springer, New York (1992)
66. Milner, R.: Communication and Concurrency. Prentice-Hall Inc., Upper Saddle River (1989)
67. Naur, P., Randell, B. (eds.): Software engineering: report of a conference sponsored by the NATO science committee, Garmisch, 7–11 October 1968, Brussels, Scientific Affairs Division, NATO (1969)
68. Nielson, H., Nielson, F.: Semantics with Applications. A Formal Introduction. Wiley, Chichester (1993)
69. Nuseibeh, B., Easterbrook, S.: Requirements engineering: a roadmap. In: Proceedings of the Conference on the Future of Software Engineering, ICSE 2000, pp. 35–46. ACM, New York (2000)
70. Object Managment Group: Model driven architecture - a technical perspective, document number ORMSC, 01 July 2001
71. Oettinger, A.: The hardware-software complementarity. Commun. ACM **10**(10), 604–606 (1967)
72. Palomar, E., Liu, Z., Bowen, J.P., Zhang, Y., Maharjan, S.: Component-based modelling for sustainable and scalable smart meter networks. In: Proceeding of IEEE International Symposium on a World of Wireless, Mobile and Multimedia Networks, WoWMoM 2014, Sydney, pp. 1–6, 19 June 2014
73. Peter, L.: The Peter Pyramid. William Morrow, New York (1986)
74. Peterson, J.L.: Petri Nets. ACM Comput. Surv. **9**(3), 223–252 (1977)
75. Plotkin, G.D.: The origins of structural operational semantics. J. Log. Algebr. Program. **60**(61), 3–15 (2004)
76. Pressman, R.S.: Software Engineering: A Practitioner's Approach. The McGraw-Hill Companies, New York (2005)
77. Queille, J.P., Sifakis, J.: Specification and verification of concurrent systems in CESAR. In: Dezani-Ciancaglini, M., Montanari, U. (eds.) Symposium on Programming. LNCS, vol. 137, pp. 337–351. Springer, Heidelberg (1982)
78. Randell, B., Buxton, J. (eds.): Software engineering: report of a conference sponsored by the NATO science committee, Rome, Italy, 27–31 October 1969, Brussels, Scientific Affairs Division, NATO (1969)
79. Rausch, A., Reussner, R., Mirandola, R., Plášil, F.: Introduction. In: Rausch, A., Reussner, R., Mirandola, R., Plášil, F. (eds.) The Common Component Modeling Example. LNCS, vol. 5153, pp. 1–3. Springer, Heidelberg (2008)
80. Rayl, A.: NASA engineers and scientists-transforming dreams into reality (2008)
81. Robinson, K.: Ariane 5: flight 501 failure - a case study (2011)
82. Roscoe, A.W.: Theory and Practice of Concurrency. Prentice-Hall, Upper Saddle River (1997)
83. Shapiro, M.: Smart cities: quality of life, productivity, and the growth effects of human capital. Rev. Econ. Stat. **88**, 324–335 (2006)
84. Sommerville, I.: Software Engineering, 6th edn. Pearson Education Ltd., England (2001)

85. Spivey, J.M.: The Z Notation: a Reference Manual, 2nd edn. Prentice Hall, Upper Saddle River (1992)
86. Stellman, A., Greene, J.: Applied Software Project Management. O'Reilly Media (2005)
87. Stoy, J.E.: Denotational Semantics: the Scott-Strachey Approach to Programming Language Semantics. MIT Press, Cambridge (1977)
88. Szyperski, C.: Component Software: Beyond Object-Oriented Programming, 2nd edn. Addison-Wesley Longman Publishing Co. Inc., Boston (2002)
89. Wirsing, M., Banâtre, J.P., Hölzl, M.M., Rauschmayer, A. (eds.): Software-Intensive Systems and New Computing Paradigms - Challenges and Visions, vol. 5380. Springer, New York (2008)
90. Yang, L., Stolz, V.: Integrating refinement into software development tools. In: Pu, G., Stolz, V. (eds.) 1st International Workshop on Harnessing Theories for Tool Support in Software. Electronic Notes in Theoretical Computer Science, vol. 207, pp. 69–88. Elsevier, Amsterdam, UNU-IIST TR 385 (2008)
91. Zhao, L., Liu, X., Liu, Z., Qiu, Z.: Graph transformations for object-oriented refinement. Form. Asp. Comput. 21(1–2), 103–131 (2009)
92. Zhao, L., Wang, S., Liu, Z.: Graph-based object-oriented hoare logic. In: Liu, Z., Woodcock, J., Zhu, H. (eds.) Theories of Programming and Formal Methods. LNCS, vol. 8051, pp. 374–393. Springer, Heidelberg (2013)

Cyber-Physical Systems Engineering

Bernd-Holger Schlingloff$^{(\boxtimes)}$

Fraunhofer FOKUS and Humboldt-Universität zu Berlin, Berlin, Germany
hs@informatik.hu-berlin.de

Abstract. Building complex embedded- and cyber-physical systems requires a holistic view on both product and process. The constructed system must interact with its physical environment and its human users in a smooth way. The development processes must provide a seamless transition between stages and views. Different modeling techniques and methods have been proposed to achieve this goal. In this chapter we present the fundamentals of cyber-physical systems engineering: identification and quantification of system goals; requirements elicitation and management; modeling and simulation in different views; and validation to ensure that the system meets its original design goals. A special focus is on the model-based design process. All techniques are demonstrated with appropriate examples and engineering tools.

Keywords: Cyber-physical systems · Embedded systems · Model-based design · Systems analysis · Requirements analysis · Systems modeling · Block diagrams · State-transition systems · Code generation

1 Introduction

The systematic, model-based design of cyber-physical systems is a fascinating subject both for academic researchers and for practitioners from industry. Embedded systems, which control, activate and supervise technical systems, have become an integral part of our daily lives. Already at present (year 2015) there are more embedded systems than people on earth. Moreover, in the last decade the number of such systems has been exponentially increasing; it is estimated that by 2020 on average each human will possess around one hundred different embedded systems. Mostly we do not even notice that we are using such systems: a modern car contains between 50 and 100 electronic control units, from driver assistance systems to motor- and battery controllers. Also their functionality and usability is steadily being increased. More and more functions are realized by software, and the software running on each device becomes more and more complex. In some cases even human life depends on the correct functioning of the software. For example, think of an artificial pacemaker for the heart, or of a signalling device for a high-speed train.

Another order of magnitude in complexity is added by the fact that more and more embedded systems are being equipped with communication links, so that they can collaborate to deliver some combined service. Such *cyber-physical*

© Springer International Publishing Switzerland 2016
Z. Liu and Z. Zhang (Eds.): SETSS 2014, LNCS 9506, pp. 256–289, 2016.
DOI: 10.1007/978-3-319-29628-9_5

systems will be the next big revolution in information technology. Current keywords describing this fact are "the internet of things", "ambient intelligence", "smart environment", and others. However, this technological advance will only be possible if engineers can manage to master the ever increasing design complexity. The combined software in a "smart car" presently consists of more than 100,000,000 lines of code, written jointly by more than 1.000 software developers — imagine! For the development of these devices, conventional and ad-hoc engineering techniques are approaching their limits.

Thus, advanced design methods for these systems are absolutely necessary. In this chapter, we will describe the state of the art and some research directions for systematic engineering of embedded and cyber-physical systems. The material is based on a lecture series with the same title, where the overall curriculum is described in [Sch14]. We start in Sect. 2 by defining cyber-physical system and listing some of their characteristic attributes. In Sect. 3 we give a short introduction into systems analysis, and show how to define requirements with the example of a pacemaker. Section 4 comprises the main part of this chapter. It deals with modeling in various views: systems modeling in SysML, continuous modeling with block diagrams in Simulink/Scicos, and discrete-state modeling with UML state machines. In Sect. 5 we show how to transform these models into executable code. Finally, Sect. 6 concludes the chapter.

2   Embedded- and Cyber-Physical Systems

We begin with some definitions of relevant terms. The word *system* may be the most over-used word in computer science. From its Greek origins ($\sigma\upsilon\sigma\tau\eta\mu\alpha$) we can infer that a system is "something which is composed". Since probably everything in this world is composed from something else, the term does not define a class of objects; it does not separate those things which are systems from those which are not. However, it serves to describe an aspect of objects, namely being a combination of several other objects called *components*. Components are things "to be put together" to constitute a system. They can be elementary, meaning that we do not decompose them further, or subsystems, which are again composed. In a system, the components interact in some way, or else we would not consider them to be parts of the same system. The international standard ISO/IEC 15288:2008 [ISO08] defines a system to be "a combination of interacting elements organized to achieve one or more stated purposes". A similar definition is given in the "Systems Engineering Handbook" of the INCOSE (International Council of Systems Engineering) [INC00]:

> [A system is] an integrated set of elements, subsystems, or assemblies that accomplish a defined objective. These elements include products (hardware, software, firmware), processes, people, information, techniques, facilities, services, and other support elements.

Both of these definitions refer to an objective or purpose of the composition. That is, only those systems are included which are composed by humans. Natural systems such as ecosystems, biological systems, or social systems are not included in the considerations.

Human-made systems serve some purpose, the provide a *function*. In a *technical system* this function is to process matter or energy. By *processing* we refer to the *transformation* or *transport*, that is, the change of form or location of something.

Typical examples of technical systems are

- a thermal power plant (transforming one form of energy to another),
- an injection-moulding machine (transforming the shape of matter), and
- a forklift truck (transporting matter).

The function of a *computational system*, in contrast to the function of a technical system, is to process *information*. Similar to the notions of "matter" and "energy", the term "information" describes a basic concept which we will not try to define here. Typical computational systems are

- a pocket calculator,
- a word processor (transformation of information), and
- a mobile phone (transport of information).

The last of these examples exhibits a general problem of delimitation when dealing with information processing: Since the representation of information in a material world is always bound to physical objects, all information processing contains the processing of these physical objects. In order to decide whether a system is a technical or computational system, it is important which processing aspect is predominant. In case of a pocket calculator, the category is pretty clear: The function is best described as "a device performing arithmetic operations on the input and displaying the result". It would be strange to describe it as "a device transforming battery power into light signals and excess heat". In case of a phone the situation is not so clear: With the first "tele-phones" in the 1870s the (technical) aspect of transforming sound waves into electrical signals and back predominated. No information processing took place: the voltage level on the microphone or speaker directly reflected the amplitude of the corresponding sound waves. With modern smartphones, however, the information processing clearly is predominant: the wave forms are digitally recorded, split into packets, wrapped, encoded and decoded according to the chosen transmission protocol, etc.

With the above definitions of technical and computational system we can define a central term of this chapter.

Definition 1. *An* embedded system *is a computational system, which is a fixed component of a technical system.*

In other words, an embedded system is a computer which is an integral part of some machine. Without the embedded system, the machine would not work properly. In an embedded system, the information processing is designed, built and operated with a particular purpose in a technical process. A schematic diagram of this definition is given in Fig. 1: The embedded system is the computational system inside the technical system, which again is part of a physical environment. The embedded system communicates with the technical systems via sensors and actuators, whereas the technical system processes material and energy in the "real world".

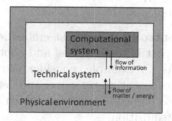

Fig. 1. Schematics of an embedded system

Typical examples of embedded systems are

- the attitude control of an Ariane space rocket,
- the TCAS (traffic collision avoidance system) of a commercial airplane,
- the ETCS OBU (on-board unit) of a high speed train,
- automotive electronic control units: ABS, ESC, cruise control, etc.,
- the temperature control of a nuclear power plant,
- the controller of an industrial punching machine,
- a bicycle computer, and
- an artificial pacemaker for the human heart.

The definition implies some characteristic properties of embedded systems. The following properties are fundamental:

- **Fixed part of a technical system:** An embedded system is usually physically attached to the technical system it belongs to. Its dimensions and capacities are fitted for the particular system, and it cannot be easily exchanged or replaced.
- **Dedication to a particular purpose:** Within the technical system, the embedded systems fulfills a predetermined function. In contrast to a universal Turing machine (or any general-purpose computer) often it can do certain special computations only, and cannot be arbitrarily programmed.
- **Interaction with a physical environment:** The technical system containing the embedded system performs a physical process, transforming matter or energy in the real world. To interact with this physical environment, the embedded system uses sensors and actuators.
- **Reactivity to external stimuli:** Pure computational systems usually terminate after finishing the calculation of their result. Since the function of an embedded system is determined by a physical process, it must be constantly

able to react to inputs from this process and cannot terminate. Often there are certain time limits for the computation of the output, thus the system must react in real time.

Besides these fundamental properties, there are some secondary attributes which embedded systems often, but not always, possess:

- **Supervising and controlling:** In most embedded systems, the function of the computational part is to supervise and control the technical system in which it resides. As an example, consider the controller of a washing machine which regulates motor, water valves and detergent flow, heating, etc. However, there are also embedded systems which are not control systems, e.g., devices for data acquisition.
- **Mass-produced:** Many embedded systems are integrated in end-consumer goods and thus have to be manufactured at extremely low cost. For example, for an automotive device which is to be incorporated in a million cars, saving 1ct in production saves 10,000 dollars in total. Nevertheless, there are also embedded devices which are unique, for example, a spacecraft on-board unit.
- **Difficult to maintain and extend:** Since the embedded system is distributed together with the technical system, software updates are often hard to realize or commercially unattractive. Since embedded systems are made for a particular purpose, it is mostly not possible to extend the functionality to a "version 2.0". For example, updating the software of an automotive device costs up to 100 dollars per car which can be very expensive if a large number of cars is concerned. However, a trend is to connect embedded devices to the internet in order to make upgrades possible.
- **Highly available, trustworthy and safety-critical:** Since embedded systems are becoming ubiquitous, we rely more and more on their availability and correct behaviour. For example, without electronic engine control it would be impossible to build a car or plane satisfying modern environmental standards. Embedded systems are increasingly also realizing safety-critical tasks, e.g., in an antilock braking system, where a failure might have fatal consequences.

An important trend in embedded systems is that they are being equipped with communication facilities (WLAN, Bluetooth, GSM/UMTS/LTE, Zigbee, etc.) so that they can exchange information with other computational systems. By the interconnection of a significant amount of embedded systems, new functionalities can be realized. This leads to the notion of *cyber-physical systems*.

Definition 2. *A cyber-physical system is a system of embedded systems which are interconnected and/or connected with other computational systems via communication networks.*

Of course, there is no strict separation between the notions of "embedded system" and "cyber-physical system": On the one hand, each embedded system is a cyper-physical system with just one component; on the other hand some embedded control devices consist of several interacting processors and thus can be viewed as a cyber-physical system. Thus, in this article, there will be no strict differentiation between these two notions.

By definition, the composition of embedded systems in a cyber-physical system is such that it accomplishes a defined objective. The objective is such that it cannot be achieved by any single one of the constituent technical systems. Typical examples of cyber-physical systems are

- the set of electronic control units in a car: In present-day cars there are typically between 50 and 80 electronic control units (ECUs) which are interconnected via different on-board networks (CAN, LIN, MOST, FlexRay, etc.). The interconnection serves to exploit or avoid certain interferences; e.g., if the electric tailgate is closed, ventilation is decreased to avoid a pressure increase in the car.
- the device controllers of an assembly line: In automated factories the different production machines are interconnected in order to enable a "just-in-time" production of individualized products.
- a sensor network for earthquake early warning: Whereas a single sensor node cannot make a solid statement about the epicenter and strength of an earthquake, a network of such nodes can predict the arrival of destructive waves in advance.
- a team of autonomous soccer robots: It is the declared target of the international RoboCup federation to have by 2050 a team of humanoid robots winning against a human team according to the usual FIFA rules. Already now there are annual competitions in this direction, with simplified rules.

3 Systems and Requirements Analysis

When constructing an embedded or cyber-physical system, the most important early phases are *systems analysis* and *requirements analysis*. Errors or omissions during these phases critically affect the complete project. Systems analysis is concerned with the design and construction processes of complex systems, and in requirements analysis processes are defined for the elicitation, management and linking of desired system properties.

Systems Analysis. The main problem in the development of "large" technical systems is the increasing complexity. Systems engineering tries to master this complexity by defining design and construction processes which take the whole development cycle into respect. All aspects of the system under construction are considered, both technical as well as non-technical ones such as user behaviour, commercial factors, operations, maintenance, and disposal. The subject of systems engineering is not limited to embedded or computational systems; e.g., also in building a new airport, systems engineering should be applied.

Systems analysis is the process of understanding, designing and developing a system as a whole (in contrast to the view of a system as a set of components). Essential to this is the holistic view of the system requirements, in particular with respect to the integration and operation of the system in its socio-technical context. The main methods of systems analysis are to focus on system goals, to continuously explore several design variants, and to maintain a holistic view on processes and activities during the design and implementation.

Systems engineering is an interdisciplinary approach and means to enable the realization of successful systems. It focuses on defining customer needs and required functionality early in the development cycle, documenting requirements, and then proceeding with design synthesis and system validation while considering the complete problem: operations, cost and schedule, performance, training and support, test, manufacturing, and disposal. Systems engineering considers both the business and the technical needs of all customers with the goal of providing a quality product that meets the user needs. [INC00]

A cyber-physical system admits several levels of abstraction or consideration. Sommerville [Som10] identifies five different levels (see Fig. 2): Hardware-, platform-, application-, process-, and organizational level. Each computational system is based on some *hardware* on which is running. This basic layer includes PCs, microcontrollers, processor boards, printed circuits, FPGAs, sensors, actuators etc. The next abstraction levels considers the *platform(s)* for the system, i.e., the basic software such as firmware, operating system, software libraries, middleware, protocol stacks, etc. Building on the platform level is the layer of *applications* or the *application software*, which realizes the user functionality and user interfaces. Above that, the *process* level is concerned with the technical and organizational conditions in which the system is operated. On top of that, all processes are performed by organizations, e.g., companies or public authorities; the *organizational* level considers activities within and interactions between organizations.

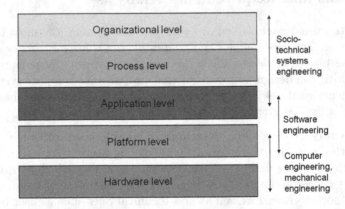

Fig. 2. Engineering levels for cyber-physical systems

Computer engineering integrates several fields of electrical engineering and computer science to develop artefacts on the hardware and platform levels. *Software engineering* is about developing artefacts on the platform and application level. *Systems engineering* is concerned with the process and organizational level; the artefacts usually are not directly executable, but consist of models and formalizations of goals and circumstances. An engineer working on a particular level must have knowledge of the adjacent levels, in order to know what to rely on from the level below, and what to guarantee to the level above. A holistic view, as it is advocated in systems engineering, must consider relevant aspects from all levels.

As an example for this layering, consider the development of an artificial cardiac pacemaker for the human heart [Bos07]. The hardware mainly consists of a pulse generator with electrodes. Here, aspects like casing materials, form factor, battery life time, mechanical faults etc. have to be considered. When designing the platform, operating system and software architecture must be decided. On the application layer the software for driving the pulse generation and communicating with the attending physician must be implemented. To this end, processes like implantation into the body, follow-up care, and long-term diagnosis are to be considered. These processes are executed in organisations like hospitals or doctors' offices. Without a certain understanding of the complete hierarchy, a project to develop a new pacemaker can not be successfully accomplished. As an example, it is necessary to understand the hospital's patient registration system in order to design a decent export function of the data-logging component in the pacemaker.

Requirements Analysis. Typical processes to be performed in systems engineering are the *stakeholder requirements definition* and the *requirements analysis* process: see [INC00]. In the stakeholder requirements definition, the needs and wishes of all people involved in the operation of the system under development are gathered. A stakeholder is "any entity (individual or organization) with a legitimate interest in the system" [INC00]. This is a more general term than the common term "user". In our pacemaker example, stakeholders are the patient, doctor, surgeon, nurse, hospital, developing and producing company, supplier, maintenance technician, ambulance, administrative authorities, and others.

The *stakeholder requirements document*, also called *user requirements specification* or similar, describes the services to be provided to the stakeholders, and the operational conditions necessary for delivering these services. This document is the main reference for all subsequent developments. It should be written in a language which is easily understandable by all stakeholders, and describes the desired functionality from the viewpoint of the user/stakeholder. That is, implementation aspects are unimportant for the specification. However, for embedded systems, also the physical operational environment must be specified. On the one hand, this means that environmental parameters like maximal admissible temperature or acceleration, sensor ranges etc. must be precisely described. On the other hand, the physical properties of the system under development must be part of the specification: maximal dimensions, plugs and connectors, etc. are also part of this document. In contrast to a software specification, the specification of an embedded system has to consider all aspects, including software, hardware, potential sensors, admissible tolerances and deviations, cost or power limitations, etc. However, no commitment to specific technical solutions is to be made; this is to be delayed to later development stages.

An example of an industrial stakeholder requirements document is the PACE-MAKER System Specification [Bos07]. This document has been made public to serve as a practical case study for scientific investigations. An in-depth modeling of certain aspects has been made in [KHCD13]. The excerpt in Fig. 3 describes part of the pulse generation functionality for rate-adaptive pacing. Subsequently, we will show how these requirements are reflected in the system's software design.

5.7 Rate-Adaptive Pacing: The device shall have the ability to adjust the cardiac cycle in response to metabolic need as measured from body motion using an accelerometer.

5.7.1 Maximum Sensor Rate: The Maximum Sensor Rate (MSR) is the maximum pacing rate allowed as a result of sensor control. The Maximum Sensor Rate shall be (1) required for rate adaptive modes, and (2) independently programmable from the URL (Upper Rate Limit)

5.7.2 Activity Threshold: The activity threshold is the value the accelerometer sensor output shall exceed before the pacemakers rate is affected by activity data.

5.7.3 Response Factor: The accelerometer shall determine the pacing rate that occurs at various levels of steady state patient activity. Based on equivalent patient activity: (1) The highest response factor setting (=16) shall allow the greatest incremental change in rate. (2) The lowest response factor setting (=1) shall allow a smaller change in rate.

5.7.4 Reaction Time: The accelerometer shall determine the rate of increase of the pacing rate. The reaction time is the time required for an activity to drive the rate from LRL (Lower Rate Limit) to MSR.

5.7.5 Recovery Time: The accelerometer shall determine the rate of decrease of the pacing rate. The recovery time shall be the time required for the rate to fall from MSR to LRL when activity falls below the activity threshold.

Fig. 3. Part of a pacemaker system specification

Many software projects fail due to an inadequate requirements analysis. There are some important properties a requirements specification must have. Such a document should be

- **understandable:** All stakeholders (not only the engineers involved) must be able to read and understand the document. Thus, e.g., it should contain a list of used terms and definitions, relevant standards, etc.
- **unambiguous:** When read by different stakeholders, the requirements must not leave any freedom of interpretation. With respect to the functionality, they must be precise, i.e., describing uniquely what the system shall or shall not do.
- **verifiable:** For each requirement, there must be a clear criterion whether it is correctly implemented in the final system or not. That is, it must be possible to design test cases which pass if and only if the requirement is satisfied. The test must be realistic, and the test result must be clearly defined.

- **complete:** The intended behaviour of the system under development must be fully determined by the specification. This includes the possibility of "leaving parts unspecified", if they are not necessary for the goals of the system.
- **consistent:** All requirements must be realizable, that is, must not be self-contradictory or impose insurmountable obstacles to an implementation. There must not be requirements which are in direct- or indirect conflict.
- **traceable:** For each requirement, it should be stated why it exists, who is the source of this requirement, where it is relevant, and how it contributes to the system's goals.
  Furthermore, it should be made clear what the significance of the requirement in the specification is, and which other requirements are connected to it.
- **abstract:** The requirements should focus on the stakeholder's perspective, not the developer's perspective onto the system. They should not unnecessarily constrain the implementation: If the same functionality can be realized in more than one way, this can be fixed at a later stage only.
- **adaptable:** The requirements document should be written in a way so that it can be modified and extended later on. All requirements should be largely independent, such that they can be deleted or replaced by alternatives, if this should turn out to be necessary.

There have been various methods proposed to achive a stakeholder requirements document which has the above properties. The first tasks during requirements engineering is the *requirements elicitation*, where the engineers communicate with all stakeholders to determine what their needs are. This can be supported by techniques such as guided interviews, brain-storming sessions, check lists, competitor analysis, etc.

The next step is the *requirements recording*, where the elicitation results are grouped and documented in a designated form, such as natural-language sentences, use cases, user stories, diagrams, or process specifications. Here, requirements management tools can be used which organize the items in a database of assets. Requirements are recorded as entries which can be searched for, selected, versioned, and linked to other entries. Many requirements management tools offer additional possibilities such as interaction to word processing and document generation software.

After the recording, the actual *requirements analysis* takes place. Here, the requirements are validated with respect to the above properties. Requirements which are unclear, ambiguous, not verifiable, incomplete or inconsistent must be re-written. Requirements where the origin or significance is unclear, which are written from a developer's perspective, or overlapping with other requirements should be modified. It is helpful to design some abstract models during this process, in order to apply academic tools such as model checkers, consistency checks, refinement and transformation.

The last part of the requirements engineering phase is the *requirements tracing*. This is an ongoing activity which spreads over the whole development cycle.

Here requirements are classified, prioritized, and linked with other artefacts. It is important to use software tools for tracing the requirements in order to keep track of their evolution. In particular, since most embedded systems are produced in several variants, the possibility of reusing certain requirements must be investigated. Variant management in software product lines is an active ongoing research field [PBvdL05].

Requirements can be classified into three groups: system goals, scenarios and strategies [Poh10]. A *system goal* is the intentional description of a characteristic feature of the system under development. For example, one goal of the pacemaker system is the following.

PSG 2.1.1 *The pacemaker system supports the needs of patients that require bradycardia pacing support. ... It supports the recovery process of a bradicardiac heart (i.e., a heart beating too slow) by providing dual chamber, rate adaptive pacing support.*

System goals are a refinement and elaboration of the overall conception of the system, and act as a guiding star to other artefacts. Each development step and each developed artefact should be justifiable by a system goal. In this way, system goals can be used to identify irrelevant activities and to evaluate and choose different design alternatives. Usually, system goals are organized as AND-OR-trees, where topmost goals have as children the direct subgoals (AND-node), and each goal may have different alternative realizations (OR-node).

A *scenario* is an operational description of the way that the system achieves its goals, by means of a concrete example run. It consists of a sequence of steps both of the system and its environment or user. This way, a scenario is a concretization of (some of) the system goals, giving a step-by-step description of the actions and reactions which ends in the satisfaction or dissatisfaction of the goal. A common way to write down a scenarios is in a so-called *user story* or *use case description* [Coc01]. Figure 4 gives as an example a use case description which isoperationalizing the requirements from Fig. 3.

1. The pacemaker is in operating mode "permanent" with an operational pacing rate of f, where $LRL \leq f \leq URL$.
2. The patient moves with an activity rate below the threshold.
3. The patient increases the activity above threshold.
4. The pacemaker increases the pacing rate by the appropriate reaction factor.
5. The patient further increases the activity.
6. The pacemaker increases the pacing rate only up to the maximum sensor rate MSR.
7. The patient stops the activity.
8. Within the set recovery time the pacemaker reduces the pacing rate from MSR to LRL.

Fig. 4. Pacemaker scenario: use case "rate-adaptive pacing"

A *strategy* is a high level plan to achieve some goals. In the context of cyber-physical systems engineering, a system strategy is the description of a plan to achieve a goal or to realize a scenario. Whereas a system goal determines *why* something should happen, and a scenario describes *what* should happen, a strategy answers the question *how* it should happen.

While formulating system strategies, it makes sense to distinguish between static (spatial) and dynamic (temporal) properties. Strategies can be seen under three different perspectives: the structural, functional, and behavioural perspective. The structural perspective forms a static viewpoint, whereas the functional and behavioural perspective focus on dynamic aspects of the system under development.

In the *structural perspective*, the composition of the system from parts, the relation between the individual parts, the data to be transmitted and processed, and the data attributes are described; as a catch-phrase: "this part sends data in such a format to that part". The *functional perspective* focusses on the transformation of data and information by the system; "this input signal is combined with that internal signal to yield those output signals". In the *behavioural perspective*, the reaction of the system to stimuli from the environment is described; "if the user does this, then the system does that".

For the formulation of strategies, various kinds of diagrams can be used. Typical diagrams for the structural perspective are block diagrams, as well as object and class diagrams. For the functional perspective, data and object flow diagrams are used. The behavioural perspective can be denoted with state-transition diagrams and activity diagrams. We will see examples for all three perspectives in the next section.

4 Modeling

Before actually building a technical system, it is good engineering practice to first construct a model. A model is a formal or semiformal representation of the system under development. It allows certain experiments to be performed even before the system is realized, thus providing early feedback and error-correction possibilities.

For the modeling of software, many different formalisms have been developed and are being used both in academia and industry. The software for cyber-physical systems differs from other software systems in that it has to interact with a physical environment. Whereas for a computational system it is usually adequate to model it with discrete states, modeling formalisms for physical objects often include continuous dimensions. For a technical system containing both computational and mechanical components, models thus include discrete and continuous parts.

Subsequently, we will describe how to transform requirements for cyber-physical systems into system models using SysML, the systems modeling language. Then, we will show how to refine system models into continuous and discrete models, representing, respectively, physical and computational aspects of the cyber-physical system under development.

4.1 Systems Modeling

Modeling has been performed ever since people began constructing complex systems. The word stems from the latin "modulus", which is the unit or gauge according to which scale the pillars of a temple are made. That is, the model of a temple describes the relative dimensions of the different parts it is made of, in small size. This is an essential feature of a model: it shows only some aspect of an object under consideration, reducing its size or complexity. In general, a *model* is a reduced representation of some object.

This object either already exists (e.g., a children's toy model of a race car). In this case, the model is an *image* of the original. Or, it can be an prototype of something which is to be built (e.g., a small-size design model of a new car). Here, the model is a *pre-image* of the real thing. In general, there exists a *reduction mapping* between an object and its model, which preserves only some aspects.

The reduction in size is made since it is much easier to produce a model car than an actual car. The main functionality of a car (to transport people) is obviously lost in the mapping. However, other important properties like aerodynamic efficiency can be demonstrated on a model as well as on an actual car. In general, each model is a *purposeful* reduction: it is made for specific reasons and serves some defined purposes. For example, the purpose of aerodynamic model is to optimise air resistance in a wind channel, whereas the purpose of a toy model might be to win an RC car race. Thus, an aerodynamic model of a car will be very different from a model used in RC races.

When designing a model, great care has to be taken that the aspects which are important for the intended purpose are preserved under the reduction mapping, i.e., that the model faithfully represents the actual system. "Modeling errors", i.e., deviations between the modeled and actual behaviour within the represented aspect, usually make the whole model useless.

In models of complex technical systems, often the reduction in comparison to the actual system is not with respect to the physical size, but with respect to the logical complexity. An *abstraction* is a special reduction mapping which reduces the information content of a concept or an observable phenomenon, selecting only those aspects which are relevant for a particular purpose. A technical model is an abstraction of a system, which is used to demonstrate some function or behaviour of the system, to help in the construction of the system, or to enable or simplify an analysis or investigation. Modeling a technical system is done by "leaving out unnecessary details", i.e., omitting structural or behavioural aspects which are not relevant.

Depending on the purpose, there might be several technical models of a system. E.g., for a building there might be statical models helping to calculate the stability, graphical 3D-models showing the architecture and facade, and floor plans giving detailed instructions where to build the walls. Consider, for example, an architectural floor plan. The abstraction function is then a simple mathematical scaling; and the property preserved under this scaling is whether objects overlap or not. Thats why the floor plan can be used for figuring out where your furniture can go in your new home, before you build it. Using computer models for the statics and appropriate architecture software, it is even possible to compare and modify different "virtual" buildings before actual construction work begins. Such analyses would be very hard or even impossible to do without models.

Subsequently, we use the following definitions:

Definition 3. *A* model *is a purposeful reduction of some existing or planned system. A* technical model *is an abstraction of a technical system, made for the purpose of demonstrating, constructing or analysing certain aspects of the system.*

Other definitions, which can be found in the literature, focus on special kinds or usages of models. For example, the aerospace standard DO-331 concentrates on the use of models in software construction and analysis: "A model is an abstract representation of a set of software aspects of a system that is used to support the software development process or the software verification process". The automotive standard ISO 26262 emphasizes the importance of models for requirements analysis and demonstration. It defines the process of building a model: "modeling is used for the conceptual capture of the functionality to be realised (open/closed loop control, monitoring) as well as for the simulation of real physical system behaviours (vehicle environment)".

For cyber-physical systems, which combine both physical and computational components, models fall into two classes:

- *Physical models* represent the operational environment and physical behaviour of the system under development. This includes models of mass and energy flow, the reaction of sensors to changes in pressure, heat, humidity, etc., the behaviour of actuators with respect to the supplied voltage, and so on. A model concentrates only on certain of these parameters (e.g., pressure and temperature), abstracting from all others physical actualities. Since "reality" is often considered to be continuous, physical models mostly use continuous elements and variables. An examples for a physical model is a system of differential equations over real numbers describing the temperature of a gas in a combustion chamber in relation to the applied pressure.
- *Logical models* are computer diagrams representing the computational parts of the system. They are used to model the *structure*, the *function* and the *behaviour* of the system under development. This includes the decomposition into modules, the data structures used, the message exchange protocols, etc. Logical models abstract from implementation details of the software, such as the used programming language, the internals of certain library functions, or the contents of certain variables. Since computation is mostly considered to take place in discrete steps, logical models normally use states variables over countable domains. An example for a logical model is a finite automaton translating input sequences of a's and b's into sequences of 0's and 1's.

Modeling of physical systems by differential equations has been practised by engineers for hundreds of years. Compared to that, software modeling is a relatively new discipline. Since the beginning of software engineering, the need has been recognized to deal with the ever increasing complexity of computer software. Thus, many different formalisms have been proposed to model software artefacts. Amongst these are classical formalisms for modeling the behaviour, such as flowchart diagrams and Nassi–Shneiderman diagrams; finite automata, labelled transition systems and state machines; Petri nets and activity diagrams; StateCharts, message sequence charts, etc. For modeling the structure of software, different sorts of architecture and component diagrams have been suggested.

Models denoted in one or several of such formalism have traditionally been used to document and visualize large software systems. A relatively new idea, however, is to use models also as "first-class citizens" in an embedded systems design process. For software systems, *model-based development and analysis* is a means to reduce the design complexity by using a model of the system. Traditional software design methods are usually ordered in stages such as stakeholder requirements definition and analysis, architectural design, module design, implementation, debugging and testing, system integration, installation and operation. Figure 5 gives a graphical representation of such a classical V-shaped cyberphysical engineering process. The horizontal arrows indicate that the artefacts on the left (constructive) half of the "V" correspond to those on the right (analytic) half.

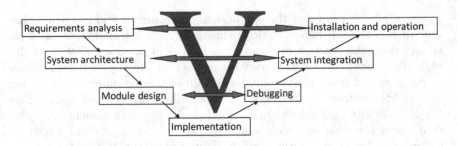

Fig. 5. A classical V-shaped engineering process

If different types of artefacts are being used as workflow results between the different design and analysis stages, gaps in the overall process appear. Stakeholder analysis produces a requirements document, which is used as the input for function and control system design. The resulting system specification document is used by programmers to implement software modules, which in turn are integrated into software systems. These systems are tested in various test environments and deployed onto the target hardware.

In a traditional development process, all these stages use different notations and formalisms for their work results. For example, a control system may be described via circuit diagrams, whereas its software may be implemented in the C programming language. These different notations lead to misunderstandings and to the introduction of errors between the phases. Moreover, different tools have to be used for each stage; thus, there are frequent incompatibilities between the artefacts, and no continuous work flow in the development is possible. Since the software system is available at a late development stage only, also testing can start only late, which leads to high costs for error correction.

Model-based development (also called *model-based design* or *model-based engineering*) is a paradigm which mitigates these deficits. In model-based development, there is one *system model* which is the central artefact of the whole design process. The development steps consist in transformation and enrichment of this system model. ISO 26262 defines *model evolution* to be the "evolution of the functional model from an early specification model via a design model to an implementation model and finally its automatic transformation into code".

Model-based development can be described by the following process steps. The system model is built at the earliest possible time, from the stakeholder requirements specification. Then, it is transformed and augmented with additional information, such that parts of the model can be executed. A *virtual prototype* can be derived from this initial system model, which is used to simulate and validate the behaviour of the target system, even before it physically exists. The main development process consists of a stepwise refinement of the system model to an *implementation model*. From the implementation model, executable code is generated automatically. If necessary, the target code is augmented with additional code (e.g., special library routines), and deployed onto host- and target platform.

Between the refinement steps, tests and simulations are applied frequently, to assure that each step preserves the desired behaviour. To this end, a *test model* can be developed from the requirements which is independent from the system model, and from which test suites are obtained by *model-based test generation*. The test cases are executed with respect to the system model (*model-in-the-loop testing*, MiL), with respect to the generated code (*software-in-the-loop*, SiL), and with respect to the target hardware (*hardware-in-the-loop*, HiL). Additionally, in highly safety-critical systems, the requirements can be formalized to a *logical specification* and the system model can be verified with respect to these formulas. (This process has been called *model checking*). Figure 6 displays the various artefacts and activities which can occur in model-based design.

Model-based development has shown to yield a significant increase in productivity and quality, reducing both the development time and the number of errors in the design [PHAB12]. The possibility for early demonstration and simulation of the systems' functions helps to detect specification errors. Virtual prototyping yields a better understanding of the functionality to be developed. Automatic code generation speeds up the time-consuming coding process, and continuous testing on all development stages avoids design errors. The system model serves as a basis for the technical documentation which is required for homologation of safety-critical systems. Therefore, it is expected that in the future this technique will be the major paradigm for cyber-physical systems engineering.

In order to effectively apply the model-based design technique, a modeling language is needed which supports as many phases of the process as possible.

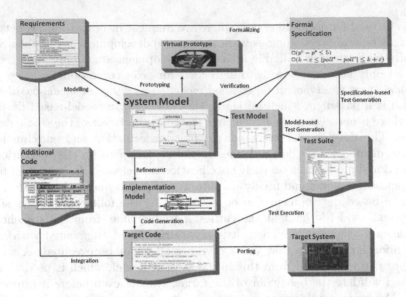

Fig. 6. Artefacts and activities in model-based development

UML, the unified modeling language [OMG15b], has been standardized by the Object Management Group (OMG) in order to harmonize and combine different modeling notations. For systems engineering, it has been augmented by SysML, the systems modelling language [OMG15a]. Furthermore, several variants and extensions of UML called *profiles* have been defined such as MARTE for the Modeling and Analysis of Real-Time and Embedded systems.

The goal of these standards is to provide a uniform, unique description language for (almost) all artefacts in the model-based design process. UML and SysML are targeting a common language basis for all stakeholders in cyber-physical systems engineering, in order to make continuous tool chains possible. Such an integrated tool chain would support all of the above mentioned model-based development activities, providing a seamless integration of artefacts and work result.

In particular, this involves engineers from mechanical and electrical design as well as software engineers. That is, an integrated development environment (IDE) for cyber-physical systems engineering would have to support concepts such as differential equations, flow diagrams, and state-transition systems. Furthermore, it would have to help maintaining the consistency of all artefacts throughout the whole process, as well as facilities to migrate and evolve models. Finally, it would enable quality assurance of both the model and the automatically generated code. Unfortunately, up to now this goal has only been reached partly. Although tool providers and researchers are working towards this ultimate goal, today there are still different languages and tools for different phases of the process.

SysML strives to integrate requirements engineering into the modeling activities. In principle, stakeholder and system requirements can be given in a variety of formats: as textual contract specification, as use-case descriptions, as algebraic or logical formulas, as component descriptions with pre- and postconditions, as state diagrams or automata, or even code and pseudo-code. This is a spectrum of possibilities, where in practice even combinations and profiles of the above mentioned formats are being used today. In order to deal with this situation, SysML provides the concept of a *requirement diagram*. These are particular model elements which provide a connection between informal and formal notation. Requirement diagrams allow to integrate textual requirements into a formal model. They are used to model the content and structure of a stakeholder or system requirements document.

Each UML/SysML model consists of *elements*, which are connected by *relations*, where relations themselves are model elements. Relations may be directed and contain multiplicities; typical directed relations are

- **generalisation**, characterizing the relation between a specialized element and its general classifier, and
- **composition**, characterizing the relation between a whole and its parts.

UML contains several other relations between elements such as associations, dependencies, inclusions, realizations, etc. In SysML, a requirements diagram contains one or more *requirement* elements. The <<requirement>> stereotype characterizes a named textbox which may include an identifier, the text of the requirement, and additional properties (such as the requirement category or its verification method). For requirements, the following relations can be used in addition to the ones above:

- **include:** This relation is drawn between requirements R_1 and R_2 to indicate that R_2 is a sub-requirement of R_1. For example, the requirement **5.7** on rate-adaptive pacing in Fig. 3 above includes requirement **5.7.1** about the maximum sensor rate.
- **derive:** This relation indicates that R_2 is a logical or physical consequence of R_1. For example, the requirement that the pacemaker device includes an acceleration sensor is derived from the requirement that it shall provide rate-adaptive pacing.
- **refine:** R_2 is a refinement of R_1, if it describes the same content, but with more detail than R_1, possibly eliminating some choices in the design space. For example, the requirement **5.7.1.2** that the MSR shall be independently programmable from the URL might be refined by a requirement **R** saying that there must be a variable msr in the non-volatile memory which can be set by the physician via the device-controller monitor.
- **verify:** A requirement may be verified by a test case. For example, the refined requirement **R** from before could be verified by a test case in which the variable msr is set to a certain value.
- **satisfy:** A requirement may be satisfied by a particular model element describing its implementation. For example, the requirement **R** could be

satisfied by an object diagram describing the non-volatile variables of the pacemaker.

In Fig. 7, a breakdown of the requirements from Fig. 3 in the open-source tool Papyrus [Ecl15] is presented. Papyrus builds on the Eclipse IDE, and is freely available.

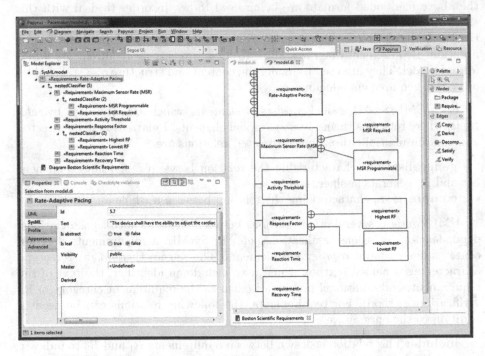

Fig. 7. Requirements diagram for the pacemaker in the Papyrus tool

4.2   Modeling of Continuous Components

Cyber-physical systems differ from pure computational systems in that they interact with a physical environment. For model-based development of the (software for the) embedded systems which constitute a cyber-physical system, we need a model of the physical environment and/or the technical system in which it is working. In some cases, this model can be rather trivial. For example, assume that the system has sensors to observe its environment. Then the simplest environment model is one where all sensors may give arbitrary values (within their respective ranges) at all times. As another example, assume we want to model a user operating the system with knobs and buttons. Then a very simple model is the one which expresses that the user may press any button or choose any knob setting at any time.

However, such a model might not be very useful. It ignores physical and logical dependencies within the environment. Firstly, the value of a physical observable in the environment usually can not change arbitrarily — often it is a *continuous* quantity. For example, the outside temperature just doesn't change instantaneously from minus 20° to plus 40° Celsius. Even with discrete parameters, physical side conditions may impose restrictions on the user behaviour. It is simply not possible to turn a knob from setting 1 to setting 5 without going through the intermediate settings 2, 3, and 4. Secondly, one physical parameter may rely on another one. For example, in a closed container, the temperature of a gas is proportional to the pressure applied to it. Or, a touch sensor may give a signal only if a certain height has been reached. Thirdly, and most importantly, the outputs of the embedded system affect the behaviour of the technical system in the environment, and thus also the inputs which the system gets from its environment. For example, turning on a motor might increase the pressure onto a gas and thus its temperature which is read by a thermo sensor. This type of feedback is called a *control loop* – the embedded system is controlling the technical environment, which in turn influences the behaviour of the embedded system.

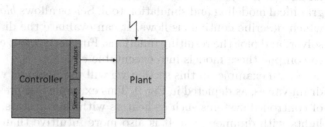

Fig. 8. Feedback loop between controller and plant

Control theory is a discipline traditionally concerned with such control loops between continuous input and output magnitudes. In control theory, the embedded system is called a *controller*, and the enclosing technical system is called the *plant*. The plant is a *dynamical system* which is described by some continuous parameters. These parameters are influenced by the outside world. Mathematically, a parameter in a dynamical system is just a continuous function from time points (real numbers) into values (real numbers). Some of the parameters can be observed by the controller via sensors, and some can be controlled via actuators. The environment imposes a disturbance on the controlled parameters, and the goal of the controller is to bring them back to some admissible values. Figure 8 above displays this basic control theory paradigm; note that it is just another visualization of the same actual situation as presented by Fig. 1.

The above discussion hopefully made clear that in order to design cyber-physical systems, there is a need for modeling formalisms with which the environment of an embedded system can be described. This "material world" to a large extent can be seen as a dynamical system, where measurable quantities such as length, volume, temperature, etc., evolve over time. To model such dynamical systems, concepts are needed such as the continuous change of some variable, the continuous sum of one or more flows, and the continuous dependency of one value upon others. In mathematics, real-valued functions, integrals, and differential equations provide such concepts. That is, mathematically the physical world can be described by a set of real-valued functions over time. In engineering, several other formalisms have been invented which build on mathematical modeling via differential equations, and which are generally accepted. Amongst these are several forms of diagrams such as electrical-circuit diagrams, fluid-mechanics diagrams, process-flow diagrams, and functional-block diagrams.

For computer science, no similar formalism is generally accepted. The main questions are how to come up with a convenient modeling notation for the relevant physical aspects of a cyber-physical system, and how to integrate it with computational modeling notations. Although SysML contains various mechanisms for dealing with continuous flows, there is not yet an adequate tool support to use them in an academic environment. In the industrial context, tools like Simulink (from MathWorks), Simplorer (from Ansys), LabVIEW from (National Instruments), Ascet (from ETAS), and Dymola (from Dassault) are being used for modeling dynamical systems. In these notes, we use Scicos, which is a free graphical modeling and simulation tool. Scicos allows *block diagrams* to be drawn which describe continuous flows. It can evaluate the diagrams with a numerical solver, and plot the resulting functions. Furthermore, it contains a code generator to compile these models into executable code.

As an example, in this section we will use a simple water tank with gain and drain valves, as depicted in Fig. 9. This example is representative for a large class of controlled systems such as heaters with thermostats, batteries with chargers, lights with dimmers, etc. It is also more intuitive than the pacemaker example since it requires only general knowledge of physical contexts and differential calculus. Subsequently we will model several variants of this system using block diagrams.

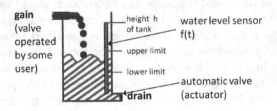

Fig. 9. Schematics of a water tank

A block diagram consists of a set of *blocks*, where each block has a dedicated number of *input* and *output ports*. Blocks without input are called *sources*, blocks without output are called *sinks*. In the diagram, each output of a block must be connected to at least one input of another port, and each input must be connected to some output. These connections are the signals or data values that flow between the blocks. Sources are, amongst others, a constant generator (a block with one output generating a constant value on this output), a ramp (generating a linear function), or a sinusoid generator (generating an output in the form of a sinus wave). Typical sinks are the various "Scope" blocks for displaying the input signal(s) on screen. Blocks which have both input and output ports are, for example, adder, multiplier, integrator and differentiator. In commercial tools, there is usually a huge library of blocks. Often, these are specialized for a particular domain, e.g., the modeling of temperature distribution in combustion engines, or the simulation of water flow in hydraulic machines.

As an example, consider the block diagram in Fig. 10. This diagram contains two sources (*gain* and *drain*) and one sink (the scope). The sources are arbitrary piecewise linear functions, which are multiplied by constant factors. The lower signal is subtracted from the upper, and the difference is integrated over time. The result $f(t)$, as displayed by the scope, is shown below the diagram. The diagram can be seen as a rough model of the water tank, with input pipe and output pipe. The different diameters of the pipes are modeled by the constant multiplication factors $c_1 = 3$ and $c_2 = 2$; opening and closing of the valves is modeled by the randomly chosen functions *gain* and *drain*. Function $f(t)$ then represents the resulting filling level of the tank; for the moment we abstract from the fact that each real tank has a limited capacity and can not contain a negative amount of water.

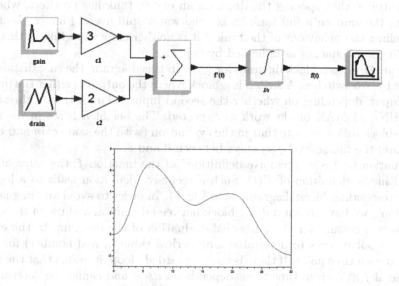

Fig. 10. A simple block diagram and its evaluation result

If we evaluate ("simulate") the diagram, the scope shows the function depicted in the lower part of Fig. 10. This evaluation is equivalent to the numerical solving of a system of ordinary differential equations (ODEs) Each block diagram using only standard mathematical blocks can be transformed into an

ODE as follows. We give each signal/connection a unique name. Then we equate
the output of a block to the function it represents, applied to the inputs of
the block. In the example of Fig. 10, this yields $v_0 = gain$, $v_1 = c_1 * v_0$, $v_2 = drain$, $v_3 = c_2 * v_2$, $v_4 = v_1 - v_3$, $v_5 = \int v_4$ Letting $v_5 = f(t)$ and elimination
all variables but v_4, we get

$$(*) \quad f'(t) = (c_1 * gain(t) - c_2 * drain(c)).$$

The translation works also in the other direction: each ODE can be represented by a block diagram. Instead of defining the general procedure, we just
give an example. In our water tank, let $g(t) = (c_1 * gain(t) - c_2 * drain(t))$ denote
the net flow in or out of the tank, and let h be the height of the tank. We refine
equation $(*)$ as follows.

$$(**) \quad f'(t) = \begin{cases} \max(0, g(t)), & \text{if } f(t) \leq 0, \\ \min(0, g(t), & \text{if } f(t) \geq h, \text{ and} \\ g(t), & \text{else, i.e., if } 0 < f(t) < h \end{cases}$$

The first case defines what happens if the water tank is empty ($f(t) \leq 0$): In this
case, water can only flow in; that is, if $g(t) > 0$ then $f'(t) = g(t)$, else $f'(t) = 0$.
Similarly, the second case defines the filling of a full tank: In this case, water
can only flow out; that is, $f'(t) = g(t)$ if $g(t)$ is negative, else $f'(t) = 0$. (You
could imagine that opening the drain on an empty tank has no effect, whereas
opening the gain on a full tank makes the water spill over.) Finally, the third
case defines the behaviour of the tank if it is neither empty nor full; in this case
the filling level changes as indicated by $(*)$.

Figure 11 gives a block diagram for $(**)$. In this diagram, the case distinction
is done by two switches. A switch is a block where the output is either the first or
third input, depending on whether the second input is larger than a threshold.
The MIN and MAX blocks work as expected. The height h is set in the right
switch-block to $h = 8$; note that in the evaluation (with the same $gain$ and $drain$
as before) the filling level $f(t)$ stays between 0 and 8.

Equation $(**)$ is a "recursive definition" of the function f: the value of $f(t)$
is used in the definition of $f'(t)$. Such a recursive definition leads to a loop in
the corresponding block diagram, as in Fig. 11. In order to avoid an "unguarded
recursion", we have to put a delay block between definition and use of the signal
f. This is necessary for the numerical evaluation of the diagram. In the evaluation, the solver tries to determine a numerical value (a real number) for each
signal at each time point. If there is an "unguarded" loop, it means that the value
of a signal f at a given time point depends $on\ itself$ and cannot be determined.
Putting a delay in the loop means that the value of f depends $on\ an\ earlier$
$value$ of f; thus it can be determined by calculating the values of all signals from
the beginning in fixed steps. Of course, one should be aware that this calculates
only an $approximation$ to the solution of the corresponding differential equation.
In general, differential equations need not have solutions; for example, consider

$$(***) \quad f'(t) = \begin{cases} -1, & \text{if } f(t) \geq 0, \\ 1, & \text{if } f(t) < 0 \end{cases}$$

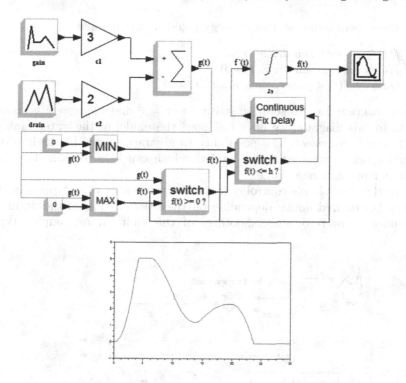

Fig. 11. Block diagram modeling a water tank

There is no function f defined on any subset of real numbers which is a solution to this equation. The numerical solution will oscillate depending on the chosen step size for the delay.

Block diagrams can also be used to model the behaviour of a controller. As shown in Fig. 8, a controller is a computational system influenced by and determining the behaviour of its technical environment, the plant. As an example, we consider our water tank as the plant which is regulated by a controller. That is, we extend our model of the water tank by a controller model. Since the drain valve is operated by the controller, it is no longer modeled by an arbitrary function; the *drain* signal is output from the controller to the plant. The gain-valve, which still is under control of some external user, and the rest of the tank model are left unchanged.

We assume that the controller can observe the actual water level by a sensor; thus, the signal $f(t)$ is fed from the tank model to the controller model. Consider the two marks *upper* and *lower*, mounted at the desired upper and lower filling level. The task of the controller is to keep the water level between the lower and upper mark, no matter how the gain-valve is opened or closed by the user. A simple strategy the controller could follow is

- if the water level exceeds the *upper* marking, open the drain, and
- if the water level falls below the *lower* marking, close the drain.

As mathematical formulas, this strategy could be written as

- if $f(t) \geq upper$, then $drain(t) = 1$
- if $f(t) \leq lower$, then $drain(t) = 0$
- if $lower < f(t) < upper$, then $drain'(t) = 0$

A block diagram for this solution (with $lower = 3$ and $upper = 5$ is shown in Fig. 12. In this diagram, we have collapsed the model of the water tank from Fig. 11 into a *superblock*. The possibility to abstract several blocks into one is a very important structuring mechanism which can help to make large block diagrams more understandable.

Note that this simple controller keeps the water level only "approximately" between the desired limits; depending on the reaction time of the drain valve there may be over- or undershootings of the limit. More complex type of

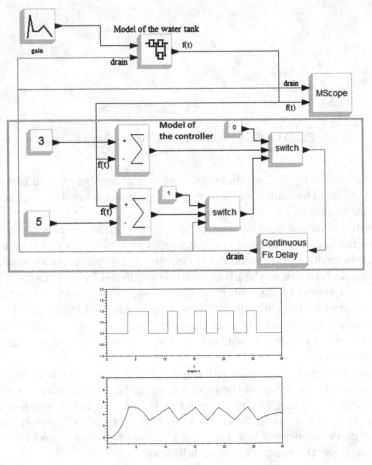

Fig. 12. Water tank with a simple controller

controllers can be modeled in this way, including so-called PID controllers, which can maintain the desired target value very accurately.

4.3   Discrete-State Modeling

Cyber-physical systems are networks of computational systems operating in a technical environment. Physical objects in this environment are mostly characterized by continuous parameters such as shape, size, position, movement, temperature, pressure, voltage, etc. Notable exceptions to this rule are switching elements such as mechanical switches, bistables, relays, and transistors. These can be seen as taking, at any given time, one of two or a finite set of possible values. In contrast, computations are usually discrete processes. The reason is that present computers are largely built from switching elements. Thus, they can only execute programs in discrete steps, and they can represent data only in a discrete, finite way. (There was a time when people experimented with continuous or hybrid computers, but those days are long gone...) Thus, each computer can assume only a finite (although very large) number of states, and each process executed by a computer can go only through a finite or countably infinite number of states.

Many different formalisms have been proposed for the description of discrete processes and machines. Most of them are based on the notions of state and event. A *state* of a system is a mapping of its parameters to values. An *event* is an instantaneous change in some state component(s), causing a *transition* between states. Mathematically, an event is a discontinuity in the trajectory of some variable(s).

Formally, a *state-transition system* (or simply *transition system*) consists of an alphabet $\mathcal{A}$, a set S of states, a set T of transitions, and an initial state s_0. Each transition between two states is labelled by a symbol from $\mathcal{A}$. A *run* or *execution* of a state-transition system is a finite or infinite sequence of states from S starting from the initial state s_0, where each pair of adjacent states is related by a transition from T.

For example, reconsider the pacemaker specification from Fig. 3. From Requirement 5.7.2, we learn that there exists an activity threshold which determines whether the pacing rate is affected by activity data or not. This can be modeled by a state-transition system as shown in Fig. 13.

In this transition system, there are two states, ACC_off and ACC_on, determining whether the accelerometer sensor data shall be taken into account or not. The alphabet $\mathcal{A}$ consists of only two symbols: $\mathcal{A} = \{$sd_gt_at, sd_le_at$\}$. The transition from ACC_off to ACC_on occurs when sd_gt_at happens, that is, when the sensor data becomes greater than the activity threshold. Likewise, when the sensor data becomes less or equal to the activity threshold, sd_le_at happens and a transition from ACC_on to ACC_off is performed. Initially, the transition system is in state ACC_off. Therefore, there is only one possible run of the system:

$$ACC\_off \xrightarrow{\text{sd\_gt\_at}} ACC\_on \xrightarrow{\text{sd\_le\_at}} ACC\_off \xrightarrow{\text{sd\_gt\_at}} ACC\_on \xrightarrow{\text{sd\_le\_at}} \ldots$$

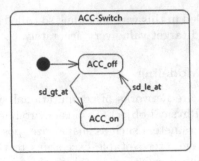

Fig. 13. A simple switch

Historically, state-transition systems have been investigated as Moore- and Mealy-machines, finite automata, Petri nets, neural networks, StateCharts, and others. Traditional research questions have been the relation of these formalisms to formal language theory, logic, and term rewriting. Mainly, the *expressiveness* and *complexity* was in the focus of research. Their potential as a modeling language in a model-based development process has been emphasized with the advent of UML [OMG15b]. The "Unified Modeling Language" has been defined in order to combine and unify several of the above formalisms. In its current version 2.5 (Mar. 2015), it contains 14 types of diagrams, for modeling both the structure and behaviour of computational systems.

State Machines are the UML diagram type which is closest to state-transition systems. In fact, our above Fig. 13 depicts a valid UML state machine, drawn with the Eclipse Papyrus Tool. However, in UML, the alphabet of state machines can be structured: each transition can have a number of triggers, a guard, and an effect. A trigger of a transition can be any event, e.g., the receipt of a message, or the execution of a message. The guard can be any boolean expression, formulated, e.g., in the Object Constraint Language OCL. The effect of a transition can be any behaviour, e.g. an assignment, an event, or even a state machine behaviour. A transition from s to s' which has event e as trigger, condition c as guard, and action a as effect is depicted as .75

$$s \xrightarrow{\ e\,[c]\,/\,a\ } s'.$$

Empty triggers, guards, and effects can be omitted. Thus, in Fig. 13, `sd_gt_at` and `sd_le_at` are events which occur due to an action of some outside component, and there are no transition guards and effects.

Besides the concept of "state" and "transition" UML state machines include concepts to include data and to structure states via hierarchies and parallelism. Let us explain these concepts via an example. Requirement 5.7.3 in Fig. 3 declares that there is a response factor for the accelerometer-induced increase of pacing rate. This factor has settings between 1 and 16. Assume that the setting can be increased by the event `inc` and decreased by `dec`. Then we can model this with 16 states, as shown in the upper half of Fig. 14 (drawn with the Eclipse Yakindu Statechart Tools).

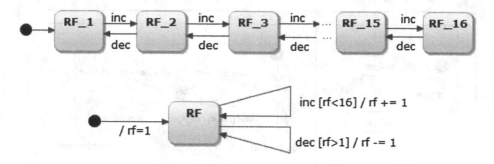

Fig. 14. Two different models of a counter

However, a more concise model can be obtained as shown in the lower half of this figure. Here, `rf` is an object of type `int`, which is set to 1 by entering the initial state, incremented upon event `inc` by the action `rf += 1` if its value is less than 16, and decremented upon `dec` by `rf -= 1` if its value is greater than 1.

For parallelism and hierarchies, we note that a UML a state machine consists of a set of regions, where each region contains states and transitions. All regions in a state machine are executed in parallel. A state itself can be simple or composite, where a composite state is one which again contains a number of regions. This way, a state can contain states, which contain states, etc.; this arbitrary nesting is similar to the nesting of blocks and superblocks which we have seen in Fig. 12.

As an example, consider the model in Fig. 13. Assume that there is a process `sdac` (sensor data acquisition) which is triggered in fixed intervals and reads the current activity level from the sensor into variable `sd`. Assume further that in order to smoothen this sensor reading, we are to switch into state `ACC_on` only if two consecutive sensor readings have been above the threshold, and likewise for state `ACC_off`. Then we can extend the model as shown in Fig. 15. Here, the events `ACC_off` and `ACC_on` are generated by the parallel region at the right if two successive readings are above or below threshold, respectively.

5   Model Transformation and Code Generation

A major advantage of a formal model, in cyber-physical systems engineering, is that it enables the engineer to automatically generate code from it. A prerequisite for this is, of course, that the model is treated as a "first-class citizen" in the development process. That is, the model is not just a means of documentation and illustration, but is on the same level of importance as, e.g., requirements, code segments, and test cases. Syntactic and semantic correctness of the model must be ensured similarly to the development of code. Furthermore, the model must be integrated, maintained, put under version control, and evolved, as the system is being further developed.

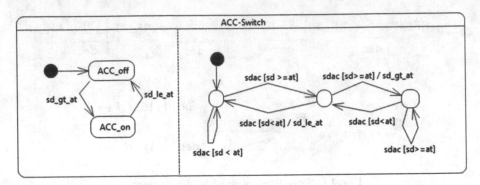

Fig. 15. Two parallel regions

Code generation from a model is a special type of *model transformation*. Here, executable code according to some programming language syntax is generated from a syntactically correct model. The transformation is described via the modeling concepts. The situation is similar to that of a classical compiler, which translates programs from a high-level programming language into machine code. The actions of the compiler are described via the syntax of the source language. Similarly, a code generator can be considered as a "model compiler".

5.1   Code Generation from Block Diagrams

According to the two kinds of models which we have met, block diagrams with continuous flows and state-machine diagrams with discrete transitions, there are two major ways to generate code. For continuous models, numerical solvers are employed which construct an approximation to the trajectories of all signals in the model.

Consider a block-diagram model of a controller, e.g., for our water-tank simulation. Figure 16 is the boxed (control) part of Fig. 12, where we replaced the

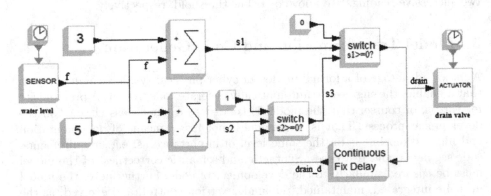

Fig. 16. Controller model for the water tank

feedback loop from and to the model of the water tank by a sensor and an actuator. The sensor represents an input function $f(t)$ to the controller, viz. the observed water level of the tank at a given moment. The actuator is an output function $drain(t)$ of the controller, viz. the controlled setting of the drainage valve at time t. Both of these models are time-triggered, i.e., they are read and written at designated times only (indicated by the clock input). This controller model has internal signals (s1, s2, s3, drain and drain_d) connecting the blocks, plus certain constant parameters. The code generator will generate code from this model which calculates, for a given time interval $[0, t_{max})$ the values of the output function from the values of the input function. It does so by starting with the initial values at time $t = 0$, and incrementing the time t in discrete steps. The values in between these steps are numerically approximated. In general, the translation follows the scheme

```
initialize all signals (default value is 0);
for (t:=0; t< tmax; t+=tstep)
    for all blocks
        out-signal := block-function(in-signals)
    end for all blocks
end for
```

For the evaluation of the **for all**-statement, the code generator has to construct an order of the blocks such that all in-signals are computed before the block-function itself is called. For a source block (e.g., a sensor), the block function has no input arguments. For a sink block (e.g., an actuator), the block function returns *void*. The calculation of the block function may involve previous values of this function, which must be stored in a buffer. As an example, the output of an integrator block can be approximated by

out-signal$(t+t_{step})$:= out-signal$(t)+t_{step}$*in-signal(t)

This method was first described by L. Euler in 1768; meanwhile, more exact mathematical methods have been developed. As another example, consider the **continuous fix delay** block which realizes a time shift of the input signal. It can be approximated by storing "sufficiently many" values of the input signal in a queue and outputting the earliest one. The following pseudo-code roughly describes the code generated from the controller model in Fig. 16; the actual code contains several optimizations.

```
s1 := 0; s2 := 0; s3 := 0; drain := 0; drain_d := 0;
for (t:=0; t< tmax; t+=tstep)
    if (trigger1) then f := sensor_read;
    s1 := 3 - f;
    s2 := f - 5;
    s3 := If (s2 ≥ 0) then 1 else drain_d;
    drain := if (s1 ≥ 0) then 0 else s3;
    drain_d := buffer1 . dequeue (); buffer1 . enqueue (drain);
    if (trigger2) then actuator_write(drain);
end for
```

The maximal simulation time t_{max} and step size t_{step} are parameters of the simulator. On a host computer, the maximal simulation time usually is finite, whereas for execution on an embedded target system, the upper limit usually is infinite. During a simulation, the step size may be adjusted in the main loop according to the dynamics of the system. For code which is to run on an embedded system, the step size should be chosen according to the speed of the target processor.

5.2   Code Generation from Transition Systems and State Machines

When programming an embedded system, an often used scheme is the so-called *simple control loop*:

```
while (true){
    sense: ⟨read sensor values⟩;
    think: ⟨calculate action⟩;
    act: ⟨write actuator values⟩;
}
```

Most code generators are constructed such that the code generated from a state machine follows this scheme. For example, for a transition system with alphabet $\mathcal{A}$, states S, transitions T and initial state s_0, the generated code could be as follows.

```
state s = s₀;
while (true){
    ⟨ get trigger a ∈ 𝒜⟩;
    if ∃s'((s, a, s') ∈ T) then s = s';
    ⟨ display state s ∈ S⟩;
}
```

Here, we assume that the transition system is *deterministic*, i.e., for any $s \in S$ and $a \in \mathcal{A}$ there is at most one s' such that $(s, a, s') \in T$. For nondeterministic transition systems, the **if**-statement must be replaced by a nondeterministic **choose**-statement. For execution on a (deterministic) machine, of course, the nondeterminism must be resolved according to some strategy.

For UML state machines, the trigger of a transition could be either an external event or a signal generated as the result of an action. Hence, at any given instant, there may be several events which can be processed by the state machine The semantics of UML determines that the processing of all internal events must be completed before the next external event is considered. Thus, occurrence and processing of an event are treated separately: If an event occurs either from an external source or as the consequence of an internal action, it is put into an *event pool*. From this pool, events which are the result of an internal action are prioritized whenever a new trigger is dispatched. This feature is called "run-to-completion" semantics: once an action is started, it will run until it is done, before any external signals are processed.

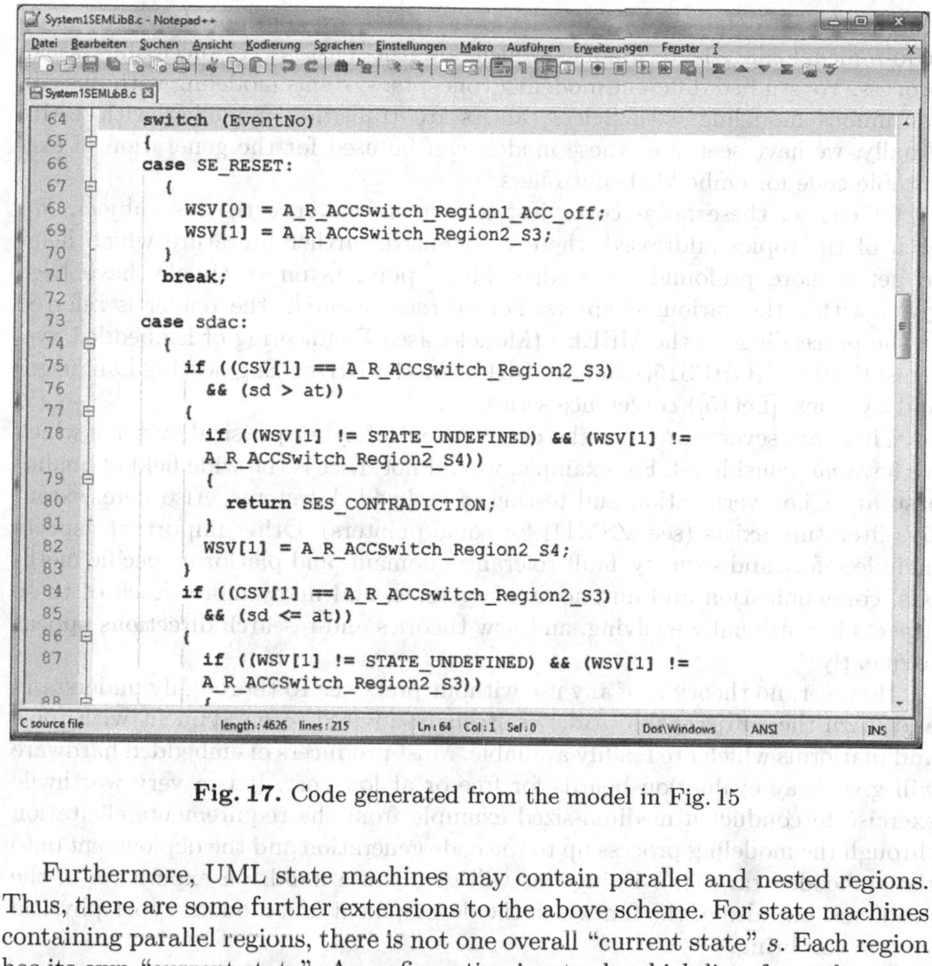

Fig. 17. Code generated from the model in Fig. 15

Furthermore, UML state machines may contain parallel and nested regions. Thus, there are some further extensions to the above scheme. For state machines containing parallel regions, there is not one overall "current state" s. Each region has its own "current state". A *configuration* is a tuple which lists for each region the current state of this region. Furthermore, if states and regions are nested, then each transition leaving a superstate exits all regions within that state. Thus, the current state of all sub-regions is affected by a transition from the enclosing state.

As an example for code generation from UML state machines, we use the industrial tool IAR visualSTATE. This tool is a "front end" for the IAR embedded workbench tool suite, which offers debugging and profiling support for embedded software. However, visualSTATE is able to generate C code for other tools as well. Figure 17 depicts part of the "readable" code generated from the model in Fig. 15 with this tool. This code can be compiled with standard C compilers, and executed on an embedded target.

6 Conclusion

In these notes, we have discussed the principles of model-based engineering of cyber-physical systems. We have seen the particular challenges which these systems pose to the software development. Then, we considered systems- and requirements-analysis techniques which are the basis of a successful design process. We studied different modeling concepts: systems modeling with SysML, continuous modeling with Scicos, and state transition modeling with UML. Finally, we have seen how these models can be used for the generation of executable code for embedded controllers.

Of course, these notes cover just a first encounter with this subject. For each of the topics addressed, there is extensive further literature which helps to get a more profound knowledge. Many pointers on textbooks have been given within the various chapters. For current research, the reader is referred to the proceedings of the MBEES (Model-Based Engineering of Embedded Systems, [GHPS14, GHPS15]) and MODELS (Model-Driven Engineering Languages and Systems, [Let15]) conference series.

There are several areas in the development of cyber-physical systems which we have *not* considered. For example, we did not discuss the wide field of quality assurance, i.e., verification and testing of embedded systems. Also here, extensive literature exists (see [ZSM11] for some pointers). Other important aspects include safety and security, fault tolerance, domain- and platform-specific methods, communication and autonomy of systems, and many more. Each of these aspects is continually evolving, and new theories and research directions appear frequently.

However, no theory is of any use without practice: To thoroughly understand and learn the subject, the reader is strongly advised to experiment with tools and platforms which are readily available. Most producers of embedded hardware will give away evaluation boards for free or at low cost. It is a very worthwile exercise to conduct a medium-sized example from the requirements elicitation through the modeling process up to the code generation and the deployment onto the embedded target(s). Doing this will give you a hands-on experience of the problems, but also of the fun which the development of a modern cyber-physical system can bring.

References

[Bos07] Boston Scientific Inc. PACEMAKER System Specification (2007). http://sqrl.mcmaster.ca/_SQRLDocuments/PACEMAKER. Accessed October 2015

[Coc01] Cockburn, A.: Writing Effective Use Cases. Addison-Wesley, Boston (2001)

[Ecl15] Eclipse Foundation. Papyrus 1.1.0, June 2015. https://eclipse.org/papyrus. Accessed October 2015

[GHPS14] Giese, H., Huhn, M., Phillips, J., Schätz, B. (eds.): Dagstuhl-Workshop MBEES: Model Based Engineering of Embeddedsystems X, Dagstuhl, Germany. fortiss GmbH, München (2014). https://www4.in.tum.de/~schaetz/papers/MBEES2014.pdf. Accessed October 2015

[GHPS15] Giese, H., Huhn, M., Phillips, J., Schätz, B. (eds.): Dagstuhl-Workshop MBEES: Model Based Engineering of Embeddedsystems XI, Dagstuhl, Germany. fortiss GmbH, München (2015). https://www4.in.tum.de/~schaetz/papers/MBEES2015.pdf. Accessed October 2015

[INC00] INCOSE (International Council on Systems Engineering). Systems Engineering Handbook, vol. 2.0. (2000)

[ISO08] ISO (International Organization for Standardization). ISO/IEC 15288:2008 – Systems engineering - System life cycle processes (2008)

[KHCD13] Kordon, F., Hugues, J., Canals, A., Dohet, A.: Embedded Systems: Analysis and Modeling with SysML, UML and AADL. ISTE, Wiley (2013)

[Let15] Lethbridge, T. (ed.): Proceedings of the 18th International Conference on Model Driven Engineering Languages and Systems, Ottawa. ACM/IEEE (2015)

[OMG15a] OMG (Object Management Group). SysML 1.4, June 2015. http://www.omgsysml.org. Accessed October 2015

[OMG15b] OMG (Object Management Group). UML 2.5, June 2015. http://www.omg.org/spec/UML. Accessed October 2015

[PBvdL05] Pohl, K., Böckle, G., van der Linden, F.: Software Product Line Engineering: Foundations, Principles, and Techniques. Birkhäuser, Heidelberg (2005)

[PHAB12] Pohl, K., Hönninger, H., Achatz, R., Broy, M.: Model-Based Engineering of Embedded Systems: The SPES 2020 Methodology. Springer, Heidelberg (2012)

[Poh10] Pohl, K.: Requirements Engineering: Fundamentals, Principles, and Techniques. Springer, Heidelberg (2010)

[Sch14] Schlingloff, B.-H.:Towards a curriculum for model-based engineering of embedded systems. In: Giese et al. [GHPS14]. https://www4.in.tum.de/~schaetz/papers/MBEES2014.pdf. Accessed October 2015

[Som10] Sommerville, I.: Software Engineering, 9th edn. Addison-Wesley, Boston (2010)

[ZSM11] Zander, J., Schieferdecker, I., Mosterman, P.J. (eds.): Model-Based Testing for Embedded Systems. Computational Analysis, Synthesis, and Design of Dynamic Systems. CRC Press, Boca Raton (2011)

Combining Formal and Informal Methods in the Design of Spacecrafts

Mengfei Yang[1] and Naijun Zhan[2]([✉])

[1] Chinese Academy of Space Technology, Beijing, China
[2] State Key Laboratory of Computer Science,
Institute of Software, CAS, Beijing, China
znj@ios.ac.cn

Abstract. In this chapter, we summarize our experience on combing formal and informal methods together in the design of spacecrafts. With our approach, the designer can either build an executable model of a spacecraft using the industrial standard environment *Simulink/Stateflow*, which facilitates analysis by simulation, or construct a formal model using Hybrid CSP (HCSP), which is an extension of CSP for formally modeling hybrid systems. HCSP processes can be specified and reasoned about by Hybrid Hoare Logic (HHL), which is an extension of Hoare logic to hybrid systems. The connection between informal and formal methods is realized via an automatic translator from *Simulink/Stateflow* diagrams to HCSP and an inverse translator from HCSP to *Simulink*. The advantages of combining formal and informal methods in the design of spacecrafts include

- It enables formal verification as a complementation of simulation. As the inherent incompleteness of simulation, it has become an agreement in industry and academia to complement simulation with formal verification, but this issue still remains challenging although lots of attempts have been done (see the related work section);
- It provides an option to start the design of a hybrid system with an HCSP formal model, and simulate and/or test it using *Matlab* platform economically, without expensive formal verification if not necessary;
- The semantic preservation in shifting between formal and informal models is justified by co-simulation. Therefore, it provides the designer the flexibility using formal and informal methods according to the trade-off between efficiency and cost, and correctness and reliability.

We will demonstrate the above approach by analysis and verification of the descent guidance control program of a lunar lander, which is a real-world industry example.

Keywords: Spacecraft · Lunar lander · *Simulink/Stateflow* · formal methods · hybrid systems

This work is supported partly by "973 Program" under grant No. 2014CB340701, by NSFC under grants 91118007 and 91418204, and by the CAS/SAFEA International Partnership Program for Creative Research Teams.

© Springer International Publishing Switzerland 2016
Z. Liu and Z. Zhang (Eds.): SETSS 2014, LNCS 9506, pp. 290–323, 2016.
DOI: 10.1007/978-3-319-29628-9_6

1   Introduction

Spacecraft control systems like most digital controllers are, by definition, hybrid systems as they interact with and/or try to control some aspects of the physical world, also typical safety-critical as any fault could result in the failure of the whole mission. Detailed behavior modeling with rigorous specification, extensive analysis and formal verification, required for reliability prediction, is a great challenge for hybrid system designers. Spacecraft control systems further intensify this challenge with extensive interaction between computing units and their physical environment and their mutual dependence on each other. On the other hand, designing a spacecraft control system is a complex engineering process, and therefore it is unlikely to demand engineers to apply formal methods in the whole process of design because of efficiency and cost. So, it is extremely necessary to have a way to combine formal and informal methods in the design so that the engineers can flexibly shift between formal and informal methods.

In order to efficiently develop reliable safety-critical systems, model-based design (MBD) has become a major approach in the design of computer controlled systems. Using this approach at the very beginning, an abstract model of the system to be developed is defined. Extensive analysis and verification on the abstract model are then conducted so that errors can be identified and corrected at the very early stage. Then the higher-level abstract model is refined to a lower-level abstract model step by step, until it can be composed with existing components. There have been huge number of MBD approaches proposed and used in industry and academia, e.g., *Simulink/Stateflow* [1,2], Modelica [41], SysML [3], MARTE [40], Metropolis [9], Ptolemy [20], hybrid automata [25], CHARON [6], HCSP [24,51], Differential Dynamic Logic [36], Hybrid Hoare Logic [29], etc. These approaches can be classified into two paradigms according to whether with a solid theoretical foundation, i.e., formal as [6,9,20,24,25,29, 36,51] and informal as [1–3,40,41].

It is commonly known that engineering informal methods for designing hybrid systems are very efficient and cheap, but cannot guarantee the correctness and reliability; in contrast, formal methods can guarantee the correctness and reliability of the system to be developed, but pay in low efficiency and high cost. Therefore it is desirable to provide the designer with the ability to choose between formal or informal analysis depending on the degree of confidence in the correctness of the design required by the application.

In this chapter, we report our experience on combing informal and formal methods together in the design of spacecrafts. The framework of our approach is as follows:

- We first build executable models of hybrid systems using the industrial standard environment *Simulink/Stateflow*, which facilitates analysis by simulation.
- Then, to complement simulation, formal verification of *Simulink/Stateflow* models is conducted via the following steps:
  1. first, we translate *Simulink/Stateflow* diagrams to Hybrid CSP (HCSP) processes by an automatic translator *Sim2HCSP*;

2. second, to justify the translation, another automatic translator H2S that translates from HCSP to *Simulink* is provided, so that the consistency between the original *Simulink/Stateflow* model and the translated HCSP formal model can be checked by co-simulation;

3. then, the obtained HCSP processes in the first step are verified by an interactive Hybrid Hoare Logic (HHL) prover;

4. during the verification, synthesizing invariants for differential equations and loops is needed.

– Of course, as an alternative, we can construct an HCSP formal model at the beginning of the design first, and then simulate and/or test the formal model economically if formal verification is not necessary.

Simulink [1] is an environment for the model-based analysis and design of embedded control systems, which offers an intuitive graphical modeling language reminiscent of circuit diagrams and thus appealing to the practising engineer. *Stateflow* [2] is a toolbox adding facilities for modeling and simulating reactive systems by means of hierarchical statecharts, extending *Simulink*'s scope to event-driven and hybrid forms of embedded control. Modeling, analysis, and design using *Simulink/Stateflow* (S/S) have become a de-facto standard in the embedded systems industry.

S/S relies on extensive simulation based on unverified numerical computation to validate system requirements, which is prone to incomplete coverage of open systems and possible unsoundness of analysis results due to numerical errors. As a result, existing errors in the model might not be discovered through simulation. If such incorrectly developed systems are deployed then any undetected errors can potentially cause a catastrophic failure. In safety-critical applications the risk of such failures is regarded as unacceptable. Reducing these risks by formal verification would be desirable, complementing simulation. Motivated by this, in our previous work [48,53,54], we presented a formal method for "closed-loop" verification of safety properties of S/S models. This is achieved by automatically translating S/S diagrams into HCSP [24,51], a formal modelling language for hybrid discrete-continuous systems. As formal analysis of HCSP models is supported by an interactive Hybrid Hoare Logic (HHL) prover based on Isabelle/HOL [29,47,52], this provides a gateway to mechanized verification of S/S models. To justify the translation from S/S to HCSP, in [14], we investigated how to translate HCSP formal models into *Simulink* graphical models, so that the consistency between the original *Simulink/Stateflow* model and the translated HCSP formal model can be checked by co-simulation.

In addition, in practice, people may start to build a formal model as a starting point of designing a system, based on which formal analysis and verification are conducted. However, a formal model is not easy to be understood by a domain expert or engineer, and therefore is not easy to be validated. In particular, the cost for formal verification of a formal model is quite expensive. In fact, many errors can be detected by testing and/or simulation in an economical way. Thus, it deserves to translate a formal model into a *Simulink* model, so that validation can be achieved by simulation; furthermore, detecting errors can be done with simulation in an economical way.

So, HCSP formal models can be simulated and/or tested using *Matlab* platform economically, without expensive formal verification when it is not necessary. Together with the work on translating S/S diagrams into HCSP, it provides the designer of embedded systems the flexibility using formal and informal methods according to the trade-off between efficiency and cost, and correctness and reliability.

We have implemented a toolchain called MARS [13] to support the above approach. MARS integrates a set of tools, including an automatic translator from S/S into HCSP, and an automatic translator from HCSP into *Simulink*, an HHL theorem prover, an invariant generator for hybrid systems which provides the options to synthesize an invariant with symbolic computation or numeric computation, and an abstractor to abstract an elementary hybrid system by a polynomial hybrid system.

The above approach and tool have been successfully applied in the design of spacecrafts, and we will demonstrate it by applying the approach to the design of a descent guidance control program of a lunar lander. A preliminary version of these results has been reported elsewhere [48].

1.1   Synopsis

This chapter first summarizes our experience on the design of spacecrafts before, most of which are joint work with other people. Then, we argue that combining formal and informal methods can provide the flexibility in the design of spacecrafts, but we do not provide any further technical contribution. The main results we used are listed as follows:

– HHL is a joint work with Chaochen Zhou, Shuling Wang, Dimitar Guelev, Jiang Liu, Jidong Lv, Zhao Quan, Hengjun Zhao and Liang Zou in [29,44,46], which extends classical Hoare logic to hybrid systems;
– Invariant generation of hybrid systems is a joint work with Jiang Liu and Hengjun Zhao in [30–32];
– The translation from S/S is based on the joint work with Martin Fränzle, Shengchao Qin, Shuling Wang and Liang Zou published in [53,54];
– The translation from HCSP to *Simulink* is based on the joint work in [14] with Anders P. Ravn, Mingshuai Chen, and Liang Zou;
– The tool implementation is based on the joint work [13,45,52] with Mingshuai Chen, Shuling Wang, Liang Zou, Tao Tang, Xiao Han and Hengjun Zhao;
– The case study part is based on the joint work in [48] with Hengjun Zhao, Bin Gu and Yao Chen.

Paper Organization. The rest of this paper is organized as follows. Section 2 briefly reviews *Simulink/Stateflow*, HCSP and HHL. Section 3 establishes a connection between S/S informal models and HCSP formal models. Section 4 focuses on the explanation of the toolchain MARS. In Sect. 5, we demonstrate our approach by analysis and verification of the GNC control program of a lunar lander. Section 6 introduces the related work. Section 7 draws a conclusion and discusses the future work.

2   *Simulink/Stateflow*, HCSP and HHL

In this section, we briefly introduce the industrial de-facto graphical modeling language *Simulink/Stateflow*, the formal modeling language Hybrid CSP (HCSP), the specification language Hybrid Hoare Logic and its prover. The reader is referred to [1, 2, 47] for more details.

2.1   Simulink

A *Simulink* model contains a set of blocks, subsystems, and wires, where blocks and subsystems cooperate by message transmission through the wires connecting them. An elementary block receives input signals and computes the output signals, and meanwhile, it contains some user-defined parameters to alter its functionality. One typical parameter is *sample time*, which defines how frequently the computation is performed. According to sample time, blocks are classified into two types: *continuous blocks* with sample time 0, and *discrete blocks* with sample time greater than 0. Blocks and subsystems in a *Simulink* model receive inputs and compute outputs in parallel, and wires specify the data flow between them.

Figure 1 gives a *Simulink* model of train movement, comprising four blocks, including continuous blocks v and p, that are *integrator* blocks of the *Simulink* library, and discrete blocks c and acc. The block v outputs the velocity of the train, which is the time integral of the input acceleration from acc; similarly, p outputs the distance of the train, which is the time integral of the input velocity from v, and acc outputs the acceleration computed according to the constant provided by c and the input distance from p.

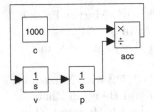

Fig. 1. A simple control system

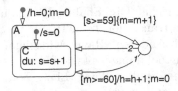

Fig. 2. A timer

2.2   Stateflow

As a toolbox integrated into *Simulink*, *Stateflow* offers the modeling capabilities of statecharts for reactive systems. It can be used to construct *Simulink* blocks, which can be fed with *Simulink* inputs to produce *Simulink* outputs. A *Stateflow* diagram has a hierarchical structure, which can be an *AND diagram*, for which states are arranged in parallel and all of them become active whenever the diagram is activated; or an *OR diagram*, for which states are connected with transitions and only one of them becomes active when the diagram is activated. A *Stateflow* diagram consists of an alphabet of events and variables, a finite set of states, and transition networks. In the following, we will explain the main ingredients of *Stateflow* and their intuitive meaning respectively.

Alphabet: The alphabet of a *Stateflow* diagram consists of a finite set of events and variables. An event can be an input or output of a diagram, which may be local to the diagram. A variable may also be set as input, output, or local, and moreover, it can be associated with an initial value if necessary.

States: A state describes an operating mode, possibly *active* or *inactive*. A state could be hierarchical, containing another *Stateflow* diagram inside. Because of hierarchy, transitions originating from a state are classified into two types depending on whether or not their target states are inside the same state: ingoing and outgoing transitions. All transitions are ordered by a strict priority so that there is no non-determinism in transition selection. A state may be associated with three types of actions (all are optional): *entry action*, that is executed when the state is activated; *during action*, that is executed when no valid transition is enabled; and *exit action*, that is executed when a valid transition leaves from the state, and as a consequence the state becomes inactive. The actions of *Stateflow* may be either assignments, or emissions of events, etc.

States in an AND diagram must be specified with different priorities, that determine the order of their executions. The parallel states are actually executed in sequential order according to their priority.

Transitions: A complete transition is a path from source state to target state. In *Stateflow*, a complete transition may consists of several transition segments by joining connective junctions, which form a transition network from source state to target state. A connective junction is a graphical object to connect different transition segments, but itself can not be seen as a source state nor a target state of a complete transition. Each transition segment is of the form $E[C]\{cAct\}/tAct$, where E is an event, C is the guard condition, $cAct$ the condition action, and $tAct$ the transition action. All these components are optional. $cAct$ will be executed immediately when event E is triggered and condition C holds, while $tAct$ will be put in a queue first and be executed after the corresponding transition is taken.

Default transitions with no source states or source junctions are allowed for OR diagrams, and they are used to choose an active state when an OR diagram is activated.

Next we explain intuitively how a *Stateflow* diagram is executed.

Initialization: Initially, the whole system is activated: for an AND diagram, all the parallel states are activated according to the priority order; and for an OR diagram, one of the states is activated by performing the default transition.

Broadcasting and Executing Transition: Each *Stateflow* diagram is activated either by sampling time periodically or by triggering events, depending on the user-settings. For the second case, as soon as one of the triggering event arrives, called *current event*, the event will be broadcasted through the whole diagram. For an AND diagram, the event will be broadcasted sequentially to the parallel states inside the diagram according to the priority order over states; while for an OR diagram, it will find out the active state of the diagram (i.e. the one with the default transition) and broadcast the event to it. It will then check the outgoing transitions of the current active state according to the priority order, and if there is one valid transition that is able to reach a state, the transition will be taken; otherwise, check the ingoing transitions in the same way. If there is neither an outgoing nor an ingoing valid transition enabled, the during action of the state will be executed, and then the event is broadcasted recursively to the sub-diagram inside the state. The transition might connect states at different levels in the hierarchical diagram. When a transition connecting two states is taken, it will first find the common ancestor of the source and target states, i.e. the nearest state that contains both of them inside, then perform the following steps: exit from the source state (including its sub-diagram) step by step and at each step execute the exit action of the corresponding state and set it to be *inactive*, and then enter step by step to the target state (including its sub-diagram), and at each step, set the corresponding state to be *active* and execute the corresponding entry action.

Example 1. Fig. 2 gives an example of *Stateflow*. The states A and C are activated initially, so variables h, m, and s are set to 0. A has a transition network to itself, which becomes enabled when s equals to 59. Once the transition network is enabled, the outgoing transition is executed, and thus m is increased by 1; then it will execute transition 1 as it is with a higher priority by increasing h by 1 and resetting m to 0 if m equals to 60, otherwise, execute transition 2.

Note that s is reset to 0 whenever the transition network becomes enabled, as the sub-diagram of A is initialized again.

Combination of Simulink and Stateflow. How *Simulink* and *Stateflow* work together is exemplified by using the two examples in Figs. 1 and 2. In order to implement the block acc in Fig. 1, we revise the *Stateflow* diagram in Fig. 2 as follows: We add a condition action $[True]\{acc = 1000/p + m/100\}$ to transition 2 of the *Stateflow* diagram, meaning that the acceleration of the train is updated every minute and the new acceleration is calculated as $1000/p + m/100$. We then replace blocks acc and c by the modified stateflow diagram, which inputs p from the simulink diagram and then calculates and outputs the acceleration acc back to the simulink diagram.

2.3 Hybrid CSP (HCSP)

HCSP is an extension of Hoare's Communicating Sequential Processes for modeling hybrid systems [24,51]. In HCSP, differential equations are introduced to model continuous evolution of the physical environment along with interrupts. The set of variables is denoted by $\mathcal{V} = \{x, y, z, ...\}$ and the set of channels is denoted by $\mathcal{C} = \{ch_1, ch_2, ch_3, ...\}$. The processes of HCSP are constructed as follows:

$$P ::= \text{skip} \mid x := e \mid\mid \text{wait } d \mid ch?x \mid ch!e \mid P;Q \mid B \to P \mid P \sqcup Q \mid X \mid$$
$$\mu X.P \mid \langle \mathcal{F}(\dot{s}, s) = 0\&B \rangle \mid \langle \mathcal{F}(\dot{s}, s) = 0\&B \rangle \trianglerighteq [\![_{i \in I}(io_i \to Q_i) \mid$$
$$\langle \mathcal{F}(\dot{s}, s) = 0\&B \rangle \mid \langle \mathcal{F}(\dot{s}, s) = 0\&B \rangle \trianglerighteq_d Q$$

$$S ::= P \mid S \| S$$

Here, P, Q, and Q_i represent sequential processes, whereas S stands for a (sub)system; $ch, ch_i \in \mathcal{C}$ are communication channels; while ch_i* is a communication event which can be either an input event $ch?x$ or an output event $ch!e$; B and e are the Boolean, and arithmetic expressions, respectively; and d is a non-negative real constant.

Process skip terminates immediately without updating variables, and process $x := e$ assigns the value of expression e to variable x and then terminates. Process $wait\ d$ keeps idle for d time units without changing the variables. Interaction between processes is based on two types of communication events: $ch!e$ sends the value of e along channel ch, and $ch?x$ assigns the value received along channel ch to variable x. Communication takes place when both the source and the destination processes are ready.

A sequentially composed process $P;Q$ behaves as P first, and if it terminates, as Q afterward. The alternative process $B \to P$ behaves as P only if B is true and terminates otherwise. Internal choice between processes P and Q denoted as $P \sqcup Q$ is resolved by the process itself. Communication controlled external choice $[\![_{i \in I}(ch_i* \to Q_i)$ specifies that as soon as one of the communications ch_i* takes place, the process starts behaving as process Q_i. The repetition P^* executes P for an arbitrary finite number of times, and the choice of the number of times is non-deterministic.

Continuous evolution is specified as $\langle \mathcal{F}(\dot{s}, s) = 0\&B \rangle$. The real variable s evolves continuously according to differential equations $\mathcal{F}$ as long as the Boolean expression B is true. B defines the domain of s. Interruption of the continuous evolution due to B (as soon as it becomes false) is known as *Boundary Interrupt*. The continuous evolution can also be preempted due to the following interrupts:

- *Timeout Interrupt:* $\langle \mathcal{F}(\dot{s}, s) = 0\&B \rangle \trianglerighteq_d Q$ behaves like $\langle \mathcal{F}(\dot{s}, s) = 0\&B \rangle$, if the continuous evolution terminates before d time units. Otherwise, after d time units of evolution according to $\mathcal{F}$, it behaves as Q.

- *Communication Interrupt:* $\langle \mathcal{F}(\dot{s}, s) = 0 \& B \rangle \trianglerighteq []_{i \in I}(ch_i* \rightarrow Q_i)$ behaves like $\langle \mathcal{F}(\dot{s}, s) = 0 \& B \rangle$, except that the continuous evolution is preempted whenever one of the communications ch_i* takes place, which is followed by respective Q_i.

Finally, S defines an HCSP system on the top level. A parallel composition $S_1 \| S_2$ behaves as if S_1 and S_2 run independently, except that they need to synchronize along the common communication channels. The concurrent processes can only interact through communication, and no shared variables are allowed. A detailed explanation can be found in [47].

2.4   Hybrid Hoare Logic

In [29], classical Hoare Logic was extended to hybrid systems, called *Hybrid Hoare Logic* (HHL). In HHL, a hybrid system is modeled by HCSP process. To capture both discrete and continuous behavior of HCSP, the assertion languages of HHL include two parts: one is first-order logic (FOL), used for specifying properties of discrete processes, and the other is a subset of Duration Calculus (DC) [49,50], called history formulas, for specifying the execution history for continuous processes. In HHL, a specification for a sequential process P is of the form $\{Pre\}\, P\, \{Post;\, HF\}$, where $Pre, Post$ represent precondition and postcondition, respectively, and are expressed by FOL to specify properties of variables held at starting and termination of the execution of P. HF is a history formula to record the execution history of P, including its real-time and continuous properties. The specification for a parallel process is then defined by assigning to each sequential component the respective precondition, postcondition, and history formula, that is

$$\{Pre_1, Pre_2\}\, P_1 \| P_2 \, \{Post_1, Post_2;\, HF_1, HF_2\}.$$

A proof system for HHL was provided in [29]. In particular, the notion of differential invariant [30,37] is used to characterize the behavior of differential equations.

HHL Prover. For tool support, we have implemented an interactive theorem prover for HHL based on Isabelle/HOL, please refer to [45,47,52] for more details.

3   Connection Between Informal and Formal Models

In this section, we show how to link informal and formal models via a translation from *Simulink/Stateflow* to HCSP and an inverse translation from HCSP to *Simulink*.

3.1 From *Simulink/Stateflow* to **HCSP**

3.1.1 Translating *Simulink*

The behavior of any block can be divided into a set of sub-behaviors, each of which is guarded by a condition. Moreover, these guards are mutually exclusive and complete, i.e., the conjunction of any two of them is unsatisfiable and the disjunction of them is valid. Hence, blocks can be interpreted by a transformation predicate over inputs and outputs as follows:

$$Seman_B(init, ps) \;\hat{=}\; out(0) = init \wedge \bigwedge_{k=1}^{m} (B_k(ps, in) \Rightarrow P_k(ps, in, out)), \quad (1)$$

where *init* stands for the initial output value set by user, *ps* are the user-set parameters that may change the function of the block, *in* and *out* are resp. the timed traces corresponding to input and output signals, $out(0)$ is the value of *out* at time 0. In the definition we assume that the block's behavior is split into m cases by B_k and in each case the behavior is specified by the corresponding predicate P_k. Additionaly, $\bigvee_{k=1}^{m} B_k(ps, in)$ is valid, and $B_i(ps, in) \wedge B_j(ps, in)$ is unsatisfiable for any $i \neq j$.

So, the semantics of a *Simulink* diagram is defined by

$$Seman_D \;\hat{=}\; \bigwedge_{j=1}^{n} Seman_B(init_j, ps_j), \quad (2)$$

where n is the number of blocks in the diagram, $init_j$ and ps_j are the initial output value and parameters of the j-th block.

Notice that different types of blocks, i.e. continuous and discrete blocks, have different definitions for B_k and P_k because the input signals for discrete blocks only refer to the value of the closest sample time point, i.e. the value of input signals at time t should refer to the time $(t - (t \bmod st))$ where st represents the sample time of the block.

Blocks

For a continuous block, its initialization is simply encoded as an assignment. A continuous block uses its B_ks as a partition of the whole state space, and continuously evolves following some differential equation $\mathcal{F}_k$ subject to the corresponding formula B_k. During the continuous evolution, the block is always ready for receiving new signals from in-ports, and sending the respective signals to out-ports (represented by io_i). Based on the continuous sample time, the blocks which receive signals from the continuous block via out-ports can always get the latest values. So, a continuous block can be encoded into the following process pattern:

$$PC(init, ps) \;\hat{=}\; out := init; P^*$$
$$P \;\hat{=}\; \langle \mathcal{F}_1(\dot{out}, out, in, ps) = 0 \& B_1(in, ps) \rangle \trianglerighteq [\!]_{i \in I}(io_i \to skip);$$
$$\dots;$$
$$\langle \mathcal{F}_m(\dot{out}, out, in, ps) = 0 \& B_m(in, ps) \rangle \trianglerighteq [\!]_{i \in I}(io_i \to skip)$$

For a discrete block, its initialization is also encoded as an assignment. However, a discrete block with sample time *st* only computes output signals at the time points whose values minus the initial time are divided by *st*, i.e. once every *st* time units. At the beginning of each period, it updates the input signal by receiving a new one from in-port, and after the computation, sends the new produced output signal to the out-port. Thus, the blocks which receive signals from the discrete block can always get the values of the last nearest period. Finally, a discrete block can be encoded as follows:

$$\mathcal{PD}(init, ps, n) \triangleq out := init; P^*$$
$$P \triangleq cin?in; P_{comp}; cout!out; \text{wait } st$$
$$P_{comp} \triangleq B_1(in, ps) \rightarrow P_{comp_1}(in, out, ps); ...;$$
$$B_m(in, ps) \rightarrow P_{comp_m}(in, out, ps)$$

Diagrams

A diagram is translated into an HCSP process via the following steps:

Step 1: *Computing inherited sample times.* A *Simulink* diagram may contain blocks with unspecified sample time, which is called *inherited* and is indicated with value −1. An inherited sample time of a block is determined when the sample times of all the input signals of the block are known, and then it is computed as the greatest common divisor (GCD) of the sample times of these input signals.

Step 2: *Translating wires.* In general, wires in *Simulink* diagrams can be considered as a special form of signals, and thus can be represented as variables. In addition, when a diagram is partitioned into a set of subdiagrams, we will model a wire between any two sub-diagrams as a pair of input and output channels for transmitting values.

Step 3: *Separating a diagram to a set of connected sub-diagrams.* We first classify wires to three categories: from continuous to continuous, from continuous to discrete (from discrete to continuous), and from discrete to discrete; and then partition a diagram to a set of largest connected blocks with the same type (that is either continuous or discrete) according to the following strategy:

(1) Wires between continuous blocks are modelled as shared variables, and hence, the two continuous blocks are put into one partition;

(2) Wires between a continuous block and a discrete block are modelled as channels, and thus, these two blocks are put into two disjoint partitions, and will transmit values via the channels;

(3) Wires between discrete blocks are hard to model because the control represented by the blocks may be centralized or distributed. In our approach, a control is assumed as centralized by default, and in this case, the wires between the discrete blocks are modelled as shared variables; and therefore, the two blocks are put in one partition. Please note that the general case in which the user options for control are allowed will be discussed later.

Step 4: *Translating each resulting continuous sub-diagram.* First, we collect all initialization parts of these continuous blocks in the continuous sub-diagram and put them in sequence as the initialization part; second, collect all communications happening in these continuous blocks and union them together as the communication part; third, cartesian the differential equations in these continuous blocks as the continuous evolution part, then construct a communication interruption by setting that the continuous evolution is interrupted by the communication part; finally, put the initialization part and the communication interruption in sequence.

Step 5: *Translating each resulting discrete sub-diagram.* As in the continuous case, we treat the sub-diagram as a discrete block. So, we first collect all initialization parts, inputs and outputs from the HCSP processes corresponding to these discrete blocks in the discrete sub-diagrams, and respectively put them in sequence according to the order of these blocks as the corresponding initialization, input and output in the final HCSP process for the sub-diagram; then we compute the greatest common divisor t of the sample times of these blocks as the sample time of the block; third, we update each computation part of these discrete block by letting it be computed every t time units, and then put all the updated computation parts in sequence together with the input and output to form the computation part of the block; finally, we introduce a timer to guarantee the computation part is executed periodically with period t.

Subsystems

A subsystem consists of a set of blocks, diagrams, and other subsystems. So, a system can be modeled hierarchically in *Simulink* with subsystems. In *Simulink*, there are three types of subsystems, i.e., *normal subsystems*, *triggered subsystems* and *enabled subsystems*. In the following, we show how to translate them into HCSP.

- A *normal subsystem* contains neither triggered nor enabled blocks inside. For this case, we flatten the subsystem directly by connecting the in-ports and out-ports attached to it to the corresponding in-ports and out-ports attached to the blocks inside it. The subsystem plus the outside blocks connected to it will then be reduced to a diagram, which can be translated as above.
- A *triggered subsystem* contains a triggered block inside it, and meanwhile, there is a corresponding input triggering signal targeting at the subsystem. The sample times of all the other input signals of the subsystem are equal to the one of the triggering signal. All the blocks except for the triggered block (called as normal blocks hereafter) inside the subsystem have unspecified sample time -1. They constitute a diagram, and will be activated by the trigger events. According to the change of the triggering signal, there are three types of *trigger events*: the rising, falling and changing of the sign of the triggering signal. Whenever a trigger event occurs, all the normal blocks inside the subsystem will be performed once. We flatten the rest of the triggered

subsystem except for the triggering signal and the triggered block, and then apply the above procedure to translate the resulting diagram. Taking the triggering signal into account, the computation part $procR$ is revised by

$$procR \leftarrow tri?; cin; procR; cout,$$

where tri represents the input triggering signal, indicating that the computation of the subsystem will be activated by signal $tri?$ from outside.

Meanwhile, we revise the translation of the outside block that outputs the triggering signal depending on its type as follows:

- *Discrete.* In this case, the computation part P_{comp} is replaced by the following process

$$osig := out_{tri}; P_{comp}; B_{tri}(osig, out_{tri}) \rightarrow tri!$$

In which, we introduce a variable $osig$ to record the output signal of last period at the beginning (here out_{tri} is used to represent the triggering signal); then after the computation part P_{comp} is performed, we compare the old signal $osig$ and the new output signal out_{tri}. If they satisfy the condition B_{tri} for triggering an event, then a triggering event $tri!$ occurs. The definition of B_{tri} depends on the triggering type, for instance, if the triggering signal is rising,

$$B_{tri}(osig, out_{tri}) \,\hat{=}\, osig < 0 \wedge out_{tri} \geq 0 \ \vee \ osig \leq 0 \wedge out_{tri} > 0$$

- *Continuous.* In this case, the differential equation part in P_{comp} is replaced by the following process

$$\langle \mathcal{F}_1(\dot{out}, out) = 0 \& B_1 \wedge \neg B_{tri} \rangle \trianglerighteq \cdots ;$$
$$\cdots$$
$$\langle \mathcal{F}_m(\dot{out}, out) = 0 \& B_m \wedge \neg B_{tri} \rangle \trianglerighteq \cdots ;$$
$$B_{tri} \rightarrow tri!;$$
$$\langle \mathcal{F}_1(\dot{out}, out) = 0 \& B_1 \wedge B_{tri} \rangle \trianglerighteq \cdots ;$$
$$\cdots$$
$$\langle \mathcal{F}_m(\dot{out}, out) = 0 \& B_m \wedge B_{tri} \rangle \trianglerighteq \cdots$$

where B_{tri} defines the condition for occurring a triggered event, in particular for the rising case, it can be defined as $out_{tri} = 0 \wedge \dot{out}_{tri} > 0$, i.e. the value of the output signal is 0 and its first derivative is greater than 0. As soon as B_{tri} holds, the event $tri!$ occurs, and then the process continuously evolves according to the differential equations of the block, till next time the trigger event occurs, when B_{tri} turns from false to true again.

- An *Enabled subsystem* P_{comp} contains an enabled block inside it, and meanwhile, there is a corresponding input enabling signal targeting at the subsystem. The blocks except for the enabled block (i.e. normal blocks) inside the enabled subsystem can be continuous or discrete, and whenever the input signal is greater than 0, they will be activated.

For both continuous and discrete cases, we model the wire connecting the block that outputs the enabling signal and the enabled subsystem as a shared variable en. When both the enabling signal and the enabled subsystem are continuous, first of all, for each normal block inside the subsystem, we add $en > 0$ as a conjunction with the domains of all its differential equations, and meanwhile, add an extra differential equation $\langle \dot{out} = 0 \& en \le 0 \rangle$ (meaning that the output is not changed when the signal is not enabled) to the block, thus the new domains for the block will be complete; then flatten the enabled subsystem, the resulting diagram plus the outside output block will constitute a new continuous diagram, which can be translated as above.

When both the enabling signal and the enabled subsystem are discrete and have the sample time, first of all, for each normal block inside the subsystem, we add the enabling condition $en > 0$ as a conjunction with the guards of the computation of the block; then flatten the enabled subsystem, the resulting diagram plus the outside output block will constitute a new discrete diagram, which can be translated as above.

The detail of the translation from *Simulink* to HCSP can be found in [54].

3.1.2   Translating *Stateflow*

A *Stateflow* diagram is translated as a process template $\mathcal{D}$, which is a parallel composition of the monitor process $\mathcal{M}$ and the parallel states $\mathcal{S}_1, \cdots, \mathcal{S}_n$ of the diagram, with the following form

$$\mathcal{D} \; \hat{=} \; \mathcal{M} \| \mathcal{S}_1 \| \cdots \| \mathcal{S}_n.$$

The monitor process $\mathcal{M}$ is an HCSP process, which monitors the broadcasting of the event among the states $\mathcal{S}_i$. Each $\mathcal{S}_i$ is also an HCSP process, which is the encoding of the corresponding state in the *Stateflow* diagram. When the diagram is an OR diagram, n will be 1, and the only state $\mathcal{S}_1$ corresponds to the virtual state that contains the diagram, which has neither (entry/during/exit) action nor transition associated to it.

$\mathcal{S}_i$ is an HCSP process corresponding to the i-th state. $\mathcal{S}_i$ first initializes the local variables of the state and activates the state by executing the entry action, defined by P_{init} and P_{entry} respectively; then it is triggered whenever an event E is emitted by the monitor $\mathcal{M}$ possibly with the shared data, and performs the following actions: first, initializes *done* to *False* indicating that no valid transition has been executed yet, and searches for a valid transition starting from $\mathcal{S}_i$ by calling a depth-first algorithm **TTN**; if *done* is still false, then executes the during action *dur* and all of its sub-diagrams. Note that for an OR diagram, the execution of the virtual state is essentially to execute the sub-diagram directly; finally, notifies the monitor the completion of the broadcasting and outputs the shared data.

Likewise, each sub-diagram (represented by P_{diag}) may be AND or OR sub-diagram. Different from the AND diagram at the outermost, for simplicity, we define the AND sub-diagram as a sequential composition of its parallel states.

This is reasonable because there is no true concurrency in *Stateflow* and the parallel states are actually executed in sequence according to their priorities. The OR diagram is encoded as a sequential composition of the connecting states, guarded by a condition $a_{S_i} == 1$ indicating that the i-th state is active. In a word, $\mathcal{S}_i$ can be represented by the following HCSP process:

$$\mathcal{S}_i \;\hat{=}\; P_{init}; P_{entry}; (BC_i?E; VOut_i?sv_i; \mathcal{S}_{du}; BO_i!; VIn_i!sv_i)^*,$$
$$\mathcal{S}_{du} \;\hat{=}\; done = False; \textbf{TTN}(\mathcal{S}_i, E, done); \neg done \to (dur, P_{diag}),$$
$$P_{diag} \;\hat{=}\; P_{and} \mid P_{or},$$
$$P_{and} \;\hat{=}\; \mathcal{S}_{1_{du}}; \cdots; \mathcal{S}_{m_{du}},$$
$$P_{or} \;\hat{=}\; (a_{S_1} == 1 \to \mathcal{S}_{1_{du}}); \cdots; (a_{S_k} == 1 \to \mathcal{S}_{k_{du}}).$$

Note that in the above, **TTN** returns an HCSP process corresponding to both outgoing and ingoing transitions from/to $\mathcal{S}_i$. In **TTN**, local events may be emitted, e.g. during executing actions of transitions or states. For such case, the current execution of the diagram needs to be interrupted by broadcasting the local event, and after the broadcasting is completed, the interrupted execution will be resumed.

The monitor process $\mathcal{M}$ in terms of HCSP coordinates the execution of broadcasted events. When an event is broadcasted, an OR diagram will broadcast the event to its active state, while an AND diagram will broadcast the event to each of its sub-diagrams according to the priority order. During the broadcasting, a new local event may be emitted inside some sub-diagram, and thus current execution will be interrupted by the local event. After the completion of the local event, the interrupted execution will be resumed. $\mathcal{M}$ can be defined by the following HCSP process:

$$\mathcal{M} \;\hat{=}\; num := 0; (\mathcal{M}_m)^*$$
$$\mathcal{M}_m \;\hat{=}\; (num == 0) \to (P_{tri}; CH_{in}?iVar; num := 1; EL := []; NL := [];$$
$$\textbf{push}(EL, E); \textbf{push}(NL, 1));$$
$$(num == 1) \to (BC_1!E; VOut_1!sv[](BR_1?E; \textbf{push}(EL, E); \textbf{push}(NL, 1); num := 1)$$
$$[](BO_1?; VIn_1?sv; num := num + 1; \textbf{pop}(NL); \textbf{push}(NL, num));$$
$$\cdots$$
$$(num == n) \to (BC_n!E; VOut_n!sv[](BR_n?E; \textbf{push}(EL, E); \textbf{push}(NL, 1); num := 1)$$
$$[](BO_n?; VIn_n?sv; num := num + 1; \textbf{pop}(NL); \textbf{push}(NL, num));$$
$$num == n + 1 \to (\textbf{pop}(EL); \textbf{pop}(NL); \textbf{isEmpty}(EL) \to (num := 0; CH_{out}!oVar);$$
$$\neg\textbf{isEmpty}(EL) \to (E := \textbf{top}(EL); num := \textbf{top}(NL)))),$$

where P_{tri} stands for the process corresponding to the triggered event, $CH_{in}?iVar$ for receiving the input of the triggered event, $CH_{out}!oVar$ for sending out the update during broadcasting the event, n for the number of parallel states of current diagram, E for current event, num for the sub-diagram to which current event is broadcasted. EL and NL are two stacks respectively to store the broadcasted events and the corresponding sub-diagrams to which these events are broadcasted.

Advanced features of *Stateflow* can also be handled well by HCSP, please see [53] for the detail.

3.1.3   Translating Combination of *Simulink* and *Stateflow*

Given a *Simulink*/*Stateflow* model, its *Simulink* and *Stateflow* parts are translated by using procedures in Sects. 3.1.1 and 3.1.2 respectively, and then put the resulting HCSP processes in parallel to form the whole model of the system. The *Simulink* and *Stateflow* diagrams in parallel transmit data or events via communications. The communications between them are categorized into the following cases:

- The input (and output) variables from (and to) *Simulink* will be transmitted through the monitor process to (and from) *Stateflow*;
- The input events from *Simulink* will be passed via the monitor to *Stateflow*;
- The output events (i.e. the ones occurring in $S_1, \cdots, S_n$ in the *Stateflow* diagram) will be sent directly to *Simulink*;
- The input/output variables and events inside *Simulink* part are handled as in Sect. 3.1.1

Please see [53] for the detail.

3.2   From HCSP to *Simulink*

In [14], we present a translation from HCSP to *Simulink* as an inverse procedure of the translation from *Simulink*/*Stateflow* to HCSP. The basic idea is to define an operational semantics for HCSP using *Simulink*. This means that everything in an HSCP model must be represented in *Simulink*. The latter is constituted from subsystems and therefore even arithmetic or Boolean expressions which are incorporated in HSCP must be translated to a *Simulink* subsystem in a consistent manner. For example, it is a natural way to define the meaning of any arithmetic (Bolean) expression as a normal subsystem, for instance, Fig. 3 is a *Simulink* subsystem corresponding to $x - 1 + y * ((-2)/3.4)$.

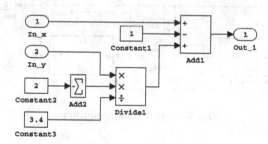

Fig. 3. $x - 1 + y * ((-2)/3.4)$

For modeling sequential composition, inspired by UTP [26], we therefore introduce a pair of Boolean signals ok and ok' into each subsystem, which is translated from an HCSP process, to indicate the relevant initiation and termination. If ok' is false, the process has not terminated and the final values of the process variables are unobservable. Similarly, if *ok* is false, the process has never started and even the initial values are unobservable. Additionally, *ok* and *ok'* are local to each subsystem corresponding to an HCSP process, which never occur in the process text. Furthermore, *ok* and *ok'* in a *Simulink* subsystem are constructed as an in-port signal named In_*ok* and an out-port signal named Out_*ok* respectively. For example, the semantics of skip is defined by a subsystem given in Fig. 4.

Fig. 4. Skip statement

The translation of a continuous evolution of HCSP is very involved, which is shown in Fig. 5, where the group of differential equations $\mathcal{F}$ and the Boolean condition B are encapsulated into a single subsystem respectively. The enabled subsystem F contains a set of integrator blocks corresponding to the vector s of continuous variables, and executes continuously whenever the value of the input signal, abbreviated as *en*, on enable-port is positive. Intuitively, subsystem B guards the evolution of subsystem F by taking the output signals of F as its inputs, i.e. $s_B = s'_F$, and partially controlling the enable signal of F via its output Boolean signal, denoted by B. As a consequence, an algebraic loop occurs between subsystem B and F which is not allowed in *Simulink*, and a plain solution is to insert an unit delay block with an initial value 1 insert after subsystem B.

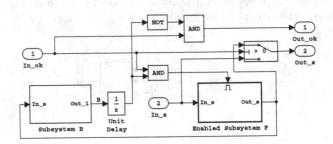

Fig. 5. Continuous Evolution

The full description and justification of the translation can be found in [14].

4   Tool Implementation

We have implemented all the above theories and integrated them as a tool-chain named *MARS* for Modelling, Analyzing and veRifing spacecraft control

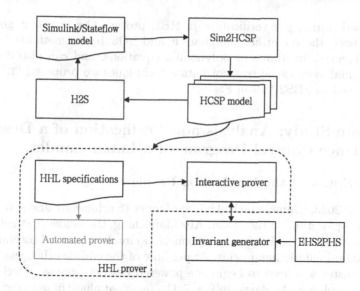

Fig. 6. Verification architecture

systems [13]. As shown in Fig. 6, the architecture of MARS is composed of three parts: a linking between informal and formal models, consisting of a translator Sim2HCSP from *Simulink/Stateflow* to HCSP and a translator from HCSP to *Simulink*, an HHL prover, and an invariant generator.

The translator Sim2HCSP is designed to translate *Simulink/Stateflow* models to HCSP. By applying Sim2HCSP, the translation from *Simulink/Stateflow* to HCSP is fully automatic, and to justify its correctness, another automatic inverse translator H2S is implemented. We use H2S to translate the HCSP model resulting from Sim2HCSP back to *Simulink*, and check the consistency between the output *Simulink/Stateflow* model and the original *Simulink/Stateflow* model by co-simulation.

The HHL prover is then applied to verify the above HCSP models obtained from Sim2HCSP. HHL prover is a theorem prover for Hybrid Hoare Logic (HHL) [29]. As the input of HHL prover, the HCSP models are written in the form of HHL specifications. Each HHL specification consists of an HCSP process, a pre-/post-condition to specify the initial and terminating states of the process, and a history formula to record the whole execution history of the process, respectively. HHL defines a set of axioms and inference rules to deduce such specifications. Finally, by applying HHL prover, the specification to be proved will be transformed into an equivalent set of logical formulas, which will be proved by applying axioms of corresponding logics in an interactive or automatic way.

To verify differential equations, we use the concept *differential invariants* to characterize their properties without solving them [30]. For computing differential invariants, we have implemented an independent invariant generator, which will be called during the verification in HHL prover. The invariant generator integrates both the quantifier elimination and SOS based methods for computing differential invariants of polynomial equations, and can also deal with non-polynomial systems by transformation techniques we proposed [32], which is implemented as EHS2PHS in Fig. 6.

5   A Case Study: Analysis and Verification of a Descent Guidance Control Program of a Lunar Lander

5.1   Description of the Verification Problem

At the end of 2013, China launched a lunar lander to achieve its first soft-landing and roving exploration on the moon. After launching, the lander first entered an Earth-Moon transfer orbit, then a 100 km-high circular lunar orbit, and then a 15 km × 100 km elliptic lunar orbit. At perilune of the elliptic orbit, the lander's variable thruster was fired to begin the powered descent process, which can be divided into 6 phases. As shown in Fig. 7, the terminal phase of powered descent is the slow descent phase, which should normally end several meters above the landing site, followed by a free fall to the lunar surface. One of the reasons to shut down the thruster before touchdown is to reduce the amount of stirred up dust that can damage onboard instruments.

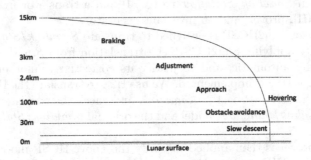

Fig. 7. The powered descent process of the lunar lander.

Powered descent is the most challenging task of the lunar lander mission because it is fully autonomous. Due to communication delay, it is impossible for stations on earth to track the rapidly moving lander, and remote control commands from earth cannot take effect immediately. The lander must rely on its own guidance, navigation and control (GNC) system to, in real time, acquire its current state, calculate control commands, and use the commands to adjust its attitude and engine thrust. Therefore the reliable functionality of the GNC system is the key to the success of soft-landing.

Clearly, the powered descent process of the lander gives a specific hybrid system (HS), i.e. a sampled-data control system composed of the physical plant and the embedded control program, which forms a closed-loop with the following prominent features: (1) the physical dynamics is modelled by ordinary differential equations (ODEs) with general elementary functions (rational, trigonometric, exponential functions etc.); (2) the program has complex branching conditions and numerical computations; (3) the physical process is frequently interrupted by control inputs from the program; (4) the system suffers from various uncertainties. Due to the high complexity, analysis and verification of such a system is very hard and beyond the capacity of many existing verification tools.

As a case study, we show how to apply the above approach to analysis and verification by focusing on one of the 6 phases, i.e. the slow descent phase, of the powered descent process. Through such verification, trustworthiness of the lunar lander's control program is enhanced. According to the framework of our approach, analysis and verification procedure can be outlined as follows:

(1) we first build a *Simulink/Stateflow* model of the closed-loop system and analyze its behaviour by simulation;
(2) then, with the tool Sim2HCSP [53,54], the *Simulink/Stateflow* graphical model is automatically translated to a formal model given by HCSP;
(3) subsequently, to justify the above translation, using the translator H2S [14], the resulted HCSP process is translated to a *Simulink* diagram inversely, so that the consistency between the original *Simulink/Stateflow* model and the translated HCSP model can be checked by co-simulation;
(4) finally, a formal verification of the system is conducted using HHL Prover [52]. During the verification, we need to call the tool EHS2PHS [32] first to abstract the considered elementary hybrid system to a polynomial hybrid system, and then exploit the tool invariant generator [30] to synthesize an invariant of the obtained polynomial HS.

All the above procedure is fully supported by the toolchain MARS [13].

5.1.1 Overview of the Slow Descent Phase

The slow descent phase begins at an altitude (relative to lunar surface) of approximately 30 m and terminates when the engine shutdown signal is received. The task of this phase is to ensure that the lander descends slowly and smoothly to the lunar surface, by nulling the horizontal velocity, maintaining a prescribed uniform vertical velocity, and keeping the lander at an upright position. The descent trajectory is nearly vertical w.r.t. the lunar surface (see Fig. 8).

The operational principle of the GNC system for the slow descent phase (and any other phases) can be illustrated by Fig. 9. The closed loop system is composed of the lander's dynamics and the guidance program for the present phase. The guidance program is executed periodically with a fixed sampling period. At each sampling point, the current state of the lander is measured by IMU (inertial measurement unit) or various sensors. Processed measurements are then input into the guidance program, which outputs control commands, e.g. the magnitude and direction of thrust, to be imposed on the lander's dynamics in the following sampling cycle.

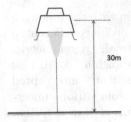

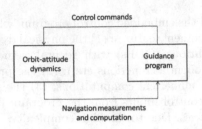

Fig. 8. The slow descent phase.

Fig. 9. A simplified configuration of GNC.

We next give a mathematical description of the lander's dynamics as well as the guidance program of the slow descent phase. For the purpose of showing the technical feasibility and effectiveness of formal methods in the verification of aerospace guidance programs, we neglect the attitude control as well as the orbit control in the horizontal plane, resulting in a one-dimensional (the vertical direction) orbit dynamics.

Dynamics. Let the upward direction be the positive direction of the one-dimensional axis. Then the lander's dynamics is given by

$$
\begin{cases}
\dot{r} = v \\
\dot{v} = \frac{F_c}{m} - gM \\
\dot{m} = -\frac{F_c}{Isp_1} \\
\dot{F}_c = 0 \\
F_c \in [1500, 3000]
\end{cases}
\quad \text{and} \quad
\begin{cases}
\dot{r} = v \\
\dot{v} = \frac{F_c}{m} - gM \\
\dot{m} = -\frac{F_c}{Isp_2} \\
\dot{F}_c = 0 \\
F_c \in (3000, 5000]
\end{cases}
, \text{ where} \qquad (3)
$$

- r, v and m denote the altitude (relative to lunar surface), vertical velocity and mass of the lunar lander, respectively;
- F_c is the thrust imposed on the lander, which is a constant in each sampling period;
- gM is the magnitude of the gravitational acceleration on the moon, which varies with height r but is taken to be the constant $1.622\,\mathrm{m/s^2}$ in this paper, since the change of height ($0 \le r \le 30$m) can be neglected compared to the radius of the moon;
- $Isp_1 = 2500$N· s/kg and $Isp_2 = 2800$N· s/kg are the two possible values that the *specific impulse*[1] of the lander's thrust engine can take, depending on whether the current F_c lies in $[1500, 3000]$ or $(3000, 5000]$, and thus the lander's dynamics comprises two different forms as shown in (3);
- note that the terms $\frac{F_c}{m}$ in (3) make the dynamics non-polynomial.

Guidance Program. The guidance program for the slow descent phase is executed once for every 0.128 s. The control flow of the program, containing 4 main blocks, is demonstrated by the left part of Fig. 10.

---

[1] Specific impulse is a physical quantity describing the efficiency of rocket engines. It equals the thrust produced per unit mass of propellant burned per second.

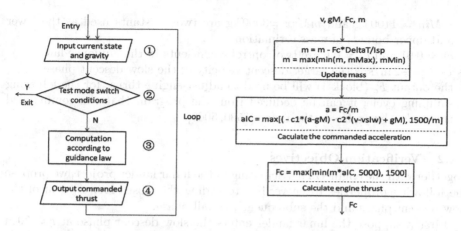

Fig. 10. The guidance program for the slow descent phase.

The program first reads data given by navigation computation (block 1), and then decides whether to stay in the slow descent phase or switch to other phases by testing the following conditions (block 2):

(SW1) shutdown signal 1, which should normally be sent out by sensors at the height of 6m, is received, and the lander has stayed in slow descent phase for more than 10s;

(SW2) shutdown signal 2, which should normally be sent out by sensors at the height of 3m, is received, and the lander has stayed in slow descent phase for more than 10s;

(SW3) no shutdown signal is received and the lander has stayed in the slow descent phase for more than 20s.

If any of the above conditions is satisfied, then the GNC system switches from slow descent phase to no-control phase and a shutdown command is sent out to the thrust engine; otherwise the program will stay in the slow descent phase and do the guidance computation (block 3) as shown in the right part of Fig. 10, where

- v and gM are the vertical velocity and gravitational acceleration from navigation measurements or computation; note that we have assumed gM to be a constant;
- F_c and m are the computed thrust and mass estimation at last sampling point; they can be read from memory;
- $DeltaT = 0.128\,$s is the sampling period;
- Isp is the specific impulse which can take two different values, i.e. 2500 or 2800, depending on the current value of F_c;

312   M. Yang and N. Zhan

- $mMin = 1100\,\text{kg}$ and $mMax = 3000\,\text{kg}$ are two constants used as the lower and upper bounds of mass estimation;
- $c_1 = 0.01$ and $c_2 = 0.6$ are two control coefficients in the guidance law;
- $vslw = -2\,\text{m/s}$ is the target descent velocity of the slow descent phase;
- the output F_c (block 4) will be used to adjust engine thrust for the following sampling cycle; it can be deduced from the program that the commanded thrust F_c always lies in the range $[1500, 5000]$.

5.1.2 Verification Objectives

Together with the engineers participating in the lunar lander project, we propose the following properties to be verified regarding the closed-loop system of the slow descent phase and the subsequent free fall phase.

Firstly, suppose the lunar lander enters the slow descent phase at $r = 30\,\text{m}$ with $v = -2\,\text{m/s}$, $m = 1250\,\text{kg}$ and $F_c = 2027.5\text{N}$. Then

(P1) **Safety 1:** $|v - vslw| \leq \varepsilon$ during the slow descent phase and before touchdown[2], where $\varepsilon = 0.05\,\text{m/s}$ is the tolerance of fluctuation of v around the target $vslw = -2\,\text{m/s}$;
(P2) **Safety 2:** $|v| < vMax$ at the time of touchdown, where $vMax = 5\,\text{m/s}$ is the upper bound of $|v|$ to avoid the lander's crash when contacting the lunar surface;
(P3) **Reachability:** one of the switching conditions (SW1)-(SW3) will finally be satisfied so that the system will exit the slow descent phase.

Furthermore, by taking into account such factors as uncertainty of initial state, disturbance of dynamics, sensor errors, floating-point calculation errors etc., we give

(P4) **Stability and Robustness:** (P2) and (P3) still holds, and an analogous of (P1) is that v will be steered towards $vslw = -2\,\text{m/s}$ after some time.

5.2 Analysis by Simulation

We first build a *Simulink/Stateflow* model of the closed-loop system for the slow descent phase. Then based on the model we analyze the system's behaviour by simulation.

The physical dynamics specified by (3) is modelled by the *Simulink* diagram shown in Fig. 11.

In Fig. 11, several blocks contain parameters that are not displayed:

---

[2] Note that if no shutdown signal is received, there exists possibility that the lander stays in the slow descent phase after landing.

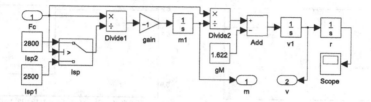

Fig. 11. The *Simulink* diagram of the dynamics for the slow descent phase.

- the threshold of Isp is 3000, which means Isp outputs 2800 when F_c is greater than 3000, and 2500 otherwise;
- the initial values of m, v and r ($m = 1250\,\text{kg}$, $r = 30\,\text{m}$, $v = -2\,\text{m/s}$) are specified as initial values of blocks m1, v1 and r respectively.

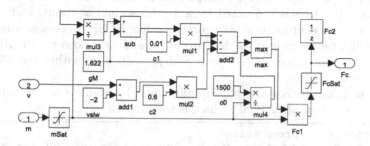

Fig. 12. The *Simulink* diagram of the guidance program for the slow descent phase.

As specified in Fig. 10, The guidance program includes three parts: updating mass m, calculating acceleration aIC, and calculating thrust F_c. The *Simulink* diagram for the guidance program is shown in Fig. 12, in which the sample time of all blocks are fixed as 0.128 s, i.e. the period of the guidance program. In Fig. 12, blocks m and mSat are used to update mass m, blocks Fc1 and FcSat are used to calculate thrust F_c, and the rest are used to calculate acceleration aIC. Blocks mSat and FcSat are saturation blocks from *Simulink* library which limit input signals to the upper and lower bounds of m and F_c respectively.

The simulation result is shown in Fig. 13. The left part shows that the velocity of the lander is between -2 and -1.9999, which corresponds to (P1); the right part shows that if shutdown signal 1 is sent out at 6 m and is successfully received by the lander, then (SW1) will be satisfied at time 12.032s, which corresponds to (P3).

5.3 From *Simulink/Stateflow* Model to HCSP Model

Given a *Simulink/Stateflow* model, Sim2HCSP translates its *Simulink* and *Stateflow* parts separately. With the approach in [54], the *Simulink* part is translated into HCSP processes, while using the approach in [53], the *Stateflow* part

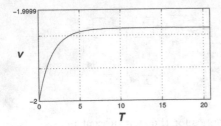
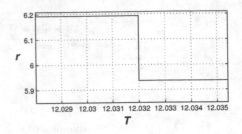

Fig. 13. The simulation result.

is translated into another HCSP processes. Then, these HCSP processes are put together in parallel to form the whole model of the system. The *Simulink* and *Stateflow* diagrams in parallel transmit data or events via communications. Please refer to [53,54] for details. Sim2HCSP takes *Simulink/Stateflow* models (in xml format, which is generated by a *Matlab* script) as input, and outputs several files as the definitions for the corresponding HCSP processes, which contain three files for defining variables, processes, and assertions for the *Simulink* part, and the same three files for each *Stateflow* diagram within the *Stateflow* part.

Then the manually constructed *Simulink* model is translated into annotated HCSP using the tool Sim2HCSP, which is basically as

```
definition P :: proc where
''P == PC_Init; PD_Init; t:=0; (PC_Diff; t:=0; PD_Rep)*''
```

In process P, PC_Init and PD_Init are initialization procedures for the continuous dynamics and the guidance program respectively; PC_Diff models the continuous dynamics given by (3) within a period of 0.128 s; PD_Rep calculates thrust F_c according to

$$F_c' := -0.01 \cdot (F_c - m \cdot gM) - 0.6 \cdot (v - vslw) \cdot m + m \cdot gM \qquad (4)$$

for the next sampling cycle; variable t denotes the elapsed time in each sampling cycle. Hence, process P is initialized at the beginning by PC_Init and PD_Init, and behaves as a repetition of dynamics PC_Diff and computation PD_Rep afterwards.

5.4   Consistency Checking by Co-Simulation

To validate the above translated HCSP model, we translate it into a *Simulink* model using the tool H2S inversely, which consists of 63 nested subsystems. The top-level overview of the translated *Simulink* model is shown in Fig. 14, where a parallel pattern interprets the physical plant *PC* and the control program *PD*.

To validate the formal model, the translated *Simulink* model is simulated with a fixed simulation step of 0.0001 s, and the evolution of the lander is shown

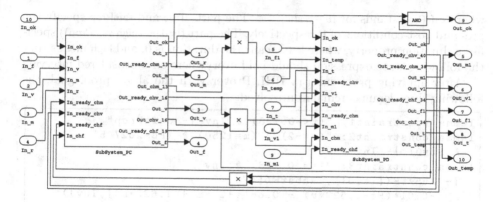

Fig. 14. The top-level overview of the translated *Simulink* model

as the solid curve in Fig. 15. For velocity, we also illustrate the corresponding results of the original *Simulink* model in the dash curve, showing that the translation loop well keeps the system behaviours consistently. Moreover, the left part shows that the velocity of the lander is between −2 and −1.9999 m/s, which corresponds to (R1); the right part shows that if shut-down signal is sent out at 6 m and is successfully received by the lander, then (R3) is satisfied at time 12.0569 s; and then with a subsequent free fall, (R2) is guaranteed.

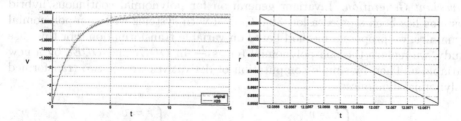

Fig. 15. The evolution in physical plant *PC*

By combining formal and informal approaches in validation and verification of the lunar lander, the reliability was indeed improved, and the domain experts and engineers were also convinced.

5.5   Verification

In this section, we formally verify the property (P1), and the proof for the other properties (P2)-(P4) can be found in [48].

In order to verify property (P1), we give the following proof goal in HHL Prover:

```
lemma goal : ''{True} P {safeProp; (l=0 | (high safeProp))}''
```

where safeProp stands for $|v - vslw| \leq \varepsilon$. The parts True and safeProp specify the pre- and post-conditions of P respectively. The part (l=0 — (high safeProp)) specifies a duration property, where l=0 means the duration is 0, and high means that the following state expression should hold everywhere on a considered interval.

After applying proof rules in HHL Prover with the above proof goal, the following three lemmas remain unresolved:

```
lemma constraint1: "(t<=0.128) & Inv |- safeProp"
lemma constraint2: "(v=-2) & (m=1250) & (Fc=2027.5)
  & (t=0) |- Inv"
lemma constraint3: "(t= 0.128) & Inv
  |- substF([(t,0)], substF([(Fc,
    -0.01*(Fc-1.622*m) - 0.6*(v+2)*m + 1.622*m)],Inv))"
```

In a more readable way, the three lemmas impose the following constraints:

(C1) $0 \leq t \leq 0.218 \wedge Inv \longrightarrow |v - vslw| \leq \varepsilon$;
(C2) $v = -2 \wedge m = 1250 \wedge F_c = 2027.5 \wedge t = 0 \longrightarrow Inv$;
(C3) $t = 0.128 \wedge Inv \longrightarrow Inv(0 \leftarrow t; F'_c \leftarrow F_c)$, with F'_c defined in (4);
(C4) Inv is the invariant of both constrained dynamical systems

$$\langle ODE_1; 0 \leq t \leq 0.128 \wedge F_c \leq 3000 \rangle \text{ and } \langle ODE_2; 0 \leq t \leq 0.128 \wedge F_c > 3000 \rangle,$$

where ODE_1 and ODE_2 are the two dynamics defined in (3).

Invariant Generation. Invariant generation for polynomial continuous/hybrid systems has been studied a lot [30]. To deal with systems with non-polynomial dynamics, we propose a method based on variable transformation. For this case study, we replace the non-polynomial terms $\frac{F_c}{m}$ in ODE_1 and ODE_2 by a new variable a. Then by simple computation of derivatives we get two transformed polynomial dynamics:

$$ODE'_1 \triangleq \begin{cases} \dot{r} = v \\ \dot{v} = a - 1.622 \\ \dot{a} = \frac{a^2}{2500} \end{cases} \text{ and } ODE'_2 \triangleq \begin{cases} \dot{r} = v \\ \dot{v} = a - 1.622 \\ \dot{a} = \frac{a^2}{2800} \end{cases}. \tag{5}$$

Furthermore, it is not difficult to see that the update of F_c as in (4) can be accordingly transformed to the update of a given by

$$a' \triangleq -c_1 \cdot (a - gM) - c_2 \cdot (v - vslw) + gM. \tag{6}$$

As a result, if we assume Inv to be a formula over variables v, a, t, then (C2)-(C4) can be transformed to:

(C2') $v = -2 \wedge a = 1.622 \wedge t = 0 \longrightarrow Inv$;
(C3') $t = 0.128 \wedge Inv \longrightarrow Inv(0 \leftarrow t; a' \leftarrow a)$, with a' defined in (6);
(C4') Inv is the invariant of both constrained dynamical systems $\langle ODE'_1; 0 \leq t \leq 0.128 \rangle$ and $\langle ODE'_2; 0 \leq t \leq 0.128 \rangle^3$ with ODE'_1 and ODE'_2 defined in (5).

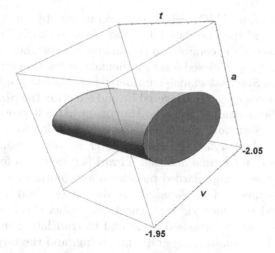

Fig. 16. The invariant for HHL Prover.

Note that the constraints (C1) and (C2')-(C4') are all polynomial. Then the invariant *Inv* can be synthesized using the SOS (sum-of-squares) relaxation approach in the study of polynomial hybrid systems [28]. With the *Matlab*-based tool YALMIP and SDPT-3, an invariant $p(v, a, t) \leq 0$ as depicted by Fig. 16 is generated. Furthermore, to avoid the errors of numerical computation in *Matlab*, we perform post-verification using the computer algebra tool RAGLib[4] to show that the synthesized $p(v, a, t) \leq 0$ is indeed an invariant. Thus we have successfully completed the proof of property (P1) by theorem proving. On the platform with Intel Q9400 2.66 GHz CPU and 4 GB RAM running Windows XP, the synthesis costs 2 s and 5 MB memory, while post-verification costs 10 min and 70 MB memory.

6 Related Work

6.1 Related Formalization of Sumulink/Stateflow

There has been a range of work on translating *Simulink* into modelling formalisms supported by analysis and verification tools. Tripakis *et al.* [43] presented an algorithm for translating discrete-time *Simulink* models to Lustre, a synchronous language featuring a formal semantics and a number of tools for validation and analysis. Cavalcanti *et al.* [11] put forth a semantics for discrete-time *Simulink* diagrams using Circus, a combination of Z and CSP. Meenakshi *et al.* [34] proposed an algorithm that translates a subset of *Simulink* into the input language of the finite-state model checker NuSMV. Chen *et al.* [12] presented an algorithm that translates *Simulink* models to the real-time specification language

---

[3] We have abstracted away the domain constraints on F_c.

[4] http://www-polsys.lip6.fr/safey/RAGLib/.

Timed Interval Calculus (TIC), which can accommodate continuous *Simulink* diagrams directly, and they validated TIC models using an interactive theorem prover. Their translation is confined to continuous blocks whose outputs can be represented explicitly by a closed-form mathematical relation on their inputs.

Beyond the pure *Simulink* models considered in the above approaches, models comprising reactive components triggered by and affecting the *Simulink* dataflow model have also been studied recently. Hamon *et al.* [23] proposed an operational semantics of *Stateflow*, which serves as a foundation for developing tools for formal analysis of *Stateflow* designs. Scaife *et al.* [39] translated a subset of *Stateflow* into Lustre for formal analysis. Tiwari [42] defines a formal semantics of *Simulink/Stateflow* using guarded pushdown automata, in which continuous dynamical systems modeled by *Simulink* are discretized, and he discussed how to verify a guarded sequence via type checking, model checking and theorem proving. Agrawal *et al.* [5] proposed a method to translate *Simulink/Stateflow* models into hybrid automata using graph flattening, and the target models represented by hybrid automata can then be formally analyzed and verified by model checkers for hybrid systems. Their approach induces certain limitations, both for the discrete-continuous interfaces in *Simulink/Stateflow* models, where the output signals of *Stateflow* blocks are required to be Boolean and to immediately connect to the selector input of an analog switch block, and for the forms of continuous dynamics, as most of current model checkers for hybrid systems support only very restricted differential equations. Miller *et al.* [35] proposed a method to translate discrete *Simulink/Stateflow* models into Lustre for formal analysis.

In contrast, the formal semantics for *Simulink/Stateflow* given here is based on the work of [53,54], in which the meanings of most of syntactic entities and features of *Simulink/Stateflow* are well handled by using HCSP. E.g., the meaning of all continuous blocks can be well defined by using the notions of differential equations and invariants in the HCSP encodings, advanced features like *early return logic, history junction, nontermination* of *Stateflow* can be easily handled by using the notion of *recursion* of HCSP, which are not addressed in most of the existing work. The payment is that we have to resort to interactive theorem proving instead of automatic model checking for discharging the proof obligations.

6.2   Related Verification of Embedded Systems

Verification of full feedback system combining the physical plant with the control program has been advocated by Cousot [16] and Goubault et al. [22]. There are some recent work in this trend which resembles our approach in this paper. In [10], Bouissou et al. presented a static analyzer named HybridFluctuat to analyze hybrid systems encompassing embedded software and continuous environment; subdivision is needed for HybridFluctuat to deal with large initial sets. In [33], Majumdar *et al.* also presented a static analyzer CLSE for closed-loop control systems, using symbolic execution and SMT solving techniques;

CLSE only handles linear continuous dynamics. In [7], Saha *et al.* verified stability of control software implementations; their approach requires expertise on analysis of mathematical models in control theory using such tools as Lyapunov functions.

6.3   Related Verification Tools

Some tools are available for formal verification of *Simulink/Stateflow* based on numerical simulation or approximation. STRONG [17] performs bounded time reachability and safety verification for linear hybrid systems based on robust test generation and coverage. Breach [18] uses sensitivity analysis to compute approximate reachable sets and analyzes properties in the form of MITL based on numerical simulation. C2E2 [19] analyzes the discrete-continuous *Stateflow* models annotated with discrepancy functions by transforming them to hybrid automata, and then checks bounded time invariant properties of the models based on simulation.

There are many tools developed for formal modelling and verification of hybrid systems. The tool d/dt [8] provides reachability analysis and safety verification of hybrid systems with linear continuous dynamics and uncertain bounded input. iSAT-ODE [4] is a numerical SMT solver based on interval arithmetic that can conduct bounded model checking for hybrid systems. Flow* [15] computes over-approximations of the reachable sets of continuous dynamical and hybrid systems in a bounded time. However, due to the undecidable reachability problem of hybrid systems, the above tools based on model checking are incomplete. Based on the alternative deductive approach, the theorem prover KeYmaera [38] is proposed to verify hybrid systems specified using differential dynamic logic. Compared to our work, it supports a simple set of hybrid constructs that do not cover communications and parallel composition.

6.4   Related Industrial Case Studies

There are some recent work on application of formal methods in the aerospace industry. For example, in [27] Johnson *et al.* proved satellite rendezvous and conjunction avoidance by computing the reachable sets of nonlinear hybrid systems; in [21] Katoen *et al.* reported on their usage of formal modelling and analysis techniques in the software development for a European satellite.

7   Conclusions

In this paper, we summarize our experience on combining formal and informal methods in the design of spacecrafts. The ingredients of our approach include

- A translation from S/S to HCSP, implemented as Sim2HCSP;
- A translation from HCSP to *Simulink*, implemented as H2S;
- A deductive way to verify a translated S/S model via HHL prover;

- An abstraction of elementary hybrid systems by polynomial hybrid systems, implemented as EHS2PHS;
- Invariant generation of polynomial hybrid systems, implemented as invariant generator.

The advantages of our approach include

- It enables formal verification as a complementation of simulation. As the inherent incompleteness of simulation, it has become an agreement in industry and academia to complement simulation with formal verification, but this issue still remains challenging although lots of attempts have been done (see the related work section);
- It provides an option to start the design of a hybrid system with an HCSP formal model, and simulate and/or test it using *Matlab* platform economically, without expensive formal verification if not necessary.
- The semantic preservation in shifting between formal and informal models is justified by co-simulation. Therefore, it provides the designer the flexibility using formal and informal methods according to the trade-off between efficiency and cost, and correctness and reliability.

The effectiveness of our approach has been demonstrated in the successful analysis and verification of the descent guidance control program of a lunar lander.

Acknowledgements. We thank all of our collaborators with whom the joint work are reported in this chapter, including Prof. Chaochen Zhou, Prof. Martin Fränzle, Prof. Shengchao Qin, Prof. Anders P. Ravn, Prof. Tao Tang, Prof. Bin Gu, Dr. Jiang Liu, Dr. Jidong Lv, Dr. Shuling Wang, Dr. Hengjun Zhao, Dr. Liang Zou, Dr. Yao Chen, Mr. Mingshuai Chen and Mr. Zhao Quan.

References

1. Simulink User's Guide (2013). http://www.mathworks.com/help/pdf_doc/simulink/sl_using.pdf
2. Stateflow User's Guide (2013). http://www.mathworks.com/help/pdf_doc/stateflow/sf_using.pdf
3. SysML V 1.4 Beta Specification (2013). http://www.omg.org/spec/SysML
4. Eggers, A., Fränzle, M., Herde, C.: SAT modulo ODE: a direct SAT approach to hybrid systems. In: Cha, S.S., Choi, J.-Y., Kim, M., Lee, I., Viswanathan, M. (eds.) ATVA 2008. LNCS, vol. 5311, pp. 171–185. Springer, Heidelberg (2008)
5. Agrawal, A., Simon, G., Karsai, G.: Semantic translation of simulink/stateflow models to hybrid automata using graph transformations. Int. Workshop Graph Transform. Visual Model. Tech. **109**, 43–56 (2004)
6. Alur, R., Henzinger, T.A.: Modularity for timed and hybrid systems. In: Mazurkiewicz, A., Winkowski, J. (eds.) CONCUR 1997. LNCS, vol. 1243. Springer, Heidelberg (1997)
7. Anta, A., Majumdar, R., Saha, I., Tabuada, P.: Automatic verification of control system implementations. In: EMSOFT 2010, pp. 9–18 (2010)

8. Asarin, E., Dang, T., Maler, O.: The d/dt tool for verification of hybrid systems. In: Brinksma, E., Larsen, K.G. (eds.) CAV 2002. LNCS, vol. 2404, pp. 365–370. Springer, Heidelberg (2002)

9. Balarin, F., Watanabe, Y., Hsieh, H., Lavagno, L., Passerone, C., Sangiovanni-Vincentelli, A.L.: Metropolis: an integrated electronic system design environment. IEEE Comput. **36**(4), 45–52 (2003)

10. Bouissou, O., Goubault, E., Putot, S., Tekkal, K., Vedrine, F.: HybridFluctuat: a static analyzer of numerical programs within a continuous environment. In: Bouajjani, A., Maler, O. (eds.) CAV 2009. LNCS, vol. 5643, pp. 620–626. Springer, Heidelberg (2009)

11. Cavalcanti, A., Clayton, P., O'Halloran, C.: Control law diagrams in circus. In: Fitzgerald, J.S., Hayes, I.J., Tarlecki, A. (eds.) FM 2005. LNCS, vol. 3582, pp. 253–268. Springer, Heidelberg (2005)

12. Chen, C., Dong, J.S., Sun, J.: A formal framework for modeling and validating simulink diagrams. Formal Asp. Comput. **21**(5), 451–483 (2009)

13. Chen, M., Han, X., Tang, T., Wang, S., Yang, M., Zhan, N., Zhao, H., Zou, L.: MARS: A toolchain for modeling, analysis and verification of spacecraft control systems. Technical Report ISCAS-SKLCS-15-04, State Key Laboratories of Computer Science, Institute of Software, CAS (2015)

14. Chen, M., Ravn, A., Yang, M., Zhan, N., Zou, L.: A two-way path between formal and informal design of embedded systems. Technical Report ISCAS-SKLCS-15-06, State Key Laboratories of Computer Science, Institute of Software, Chinese Academy of Sciences (2015)

15. Chen, X., Ábrahám, E., Sankaranarayanan, S.: Flow*: an analyzer for non-linear hybrid systems. In: Sharygina, N., Veith, H. (eds.) CAV 2013. LNCS, vol. 8044, pp. 258–263. Springer, Heidelberg (2013)

16. Cousot, P.: Integrating physical systems in the static analysis of embedded control software. In: Yi, K. (ed.) APLAS 2005. LNCS, vol. 3780, pp. 135–138. Springer, Heidelberg (2005)

17. Deng, Y., Rajhans, A., Julius, A.A.: STRONG: a trajectory-based verification toolbox for hybrid systems. In: Joshi, K., Siegle, M., Stoelinga, M., D'Argenio, P.R. (eds.) QEST 2013. LNCS, vol. 8054, pp. 165–168. Springer, Heidelberg (2013)

18. Donzé, A.: Breach, a toolbox for verification and parameter synthesis of hybrid systems. In: Touili, T., Cook, B., Jackson, P. (eds.) CAV 2010. LNCS, vol. 6174, pp. 167–170. Springer, Heidelberg (2010)

19. Duggirala, P.S., Mitra, S., Viswanathan, M., Potok, M.: C2E2: a verification tool for stateflow models. In: Baier, C., Tinelli, C. (eds.) TACAS 2015. LNCS, vol. 9035, pp. 68–82. Springer, Heidelberg (2015)

20. Eker, J., Janneck, J., Lee, E.A., Liu, J., Liu, X., Ludvig, J., Neuendorffer, S., Sachs, S., Xiong, Y.: Taming heterogeneity - the ptolemy approach. Proc. IEEE **91**(1), 127–144 (2003)

21. Esteve, M.-A., Katoen, J.-P., Nguyen, V., Postma, B., Yushtein, Y.: Formal correctness, safety, dependability, and performance analysis of a satellite. In: ICSE 2012, pp. 1022–1031 (2012)

22. Goubault, E., Martel, M., Putot, S.: Some future challenges in the validation of control systems. In: ERTS 2006 (2006)

23. Hamon, G., Rushby, J.: An operational semantics for stateflow. Int. J. Softw. Tools Technol. Transf. **9**(5), 447–456 (2007)

24. He, J.: From CSP to hybrid systems. In: Roscoe, A.W. (ed.) A Classical Mind, Essays in Honour of C.A.R. Hoare, pp. 171–189. Prentice Hall International (UK) Ltd, Hertfordshire (1994)

25. Henzinger, T.A.: The theory of hybrid automata. In: LICS 1996, pp. 278–292, July 1996

26. Hoare, C.A.R., He, J.: Unifying Theories of Programming, vol. 14. Prentice Hall, Englewood Cliffs (1998)

27. Johnson, T.T., Green, J., Mitra, S., Dudley, R., Erwin, R.S.: Satellite rendezvous and conjunction avoidance: case studies in verification of nonlinear hybrid systems. In: Giannakopoulou, D., Méry, D. (eds.) FM 2012. LNCS, vol. 7436, pp. 252–266. Springer, Heidelberg (2012)

28. Kong, H., He, F., Song, X., Hung, W.N.N., Gu, M.: Exponential-condition-based barrier certificate generation for safety verification of hybrid systems. In: Sharygina, N., Veith, H. (eds.) CAV 2013. LNCS, vol. 8044, pp. 242–257. Springer, Heidelberg (2013)

29. Liu, J., Lv, J., Quan, Z., Zhan, N., Zhao, H., Zhou, C., Zou, L.: A calculus for hybrid CSP. In: Ueda, K. (ed.) APLAS 2010. LNCS, vol. 6461, pp. 1–15. Springer, Heidelberg (2010)

30. Liu, J., Zhan, N., Zhao, H.: Computing semi-algebraic invariants for polynomial dynamical systems. In: EMSOFT 2011, pp. 97–106 (2011)

31. Liu, J., Zhan, N., Zhao, H.: Automatically discovering relaxed lyapunov functions for polynomial dynamical systems. Math. Comput. Sci. **6**(4), 395–408 (2012)

32. Liu, J., Zhan, N., Zhao, H., Zou, L.: Abstraction of elementary hybrid systems by variable transformation. In: Bjørner, N., de Boer, F. (eds.) FM 2015. LNCS, vol. 9109, pp. 360–377. Springer, Heidelberg (2015)

33. Majumdar, R., Saha, I., Shashidhar, K.C., Wang, Z.: CLSE: closed-loop symbolic execution. In: Goodloe, A.E., Person, S. (eds.) NFM 2012. LNCS, vol. 7226, pp. 356–370. Springer, Heidelberg (2012)

34. Meenakshi, B., Bhatnagar, A., Roy, S.: Tool for translating simulink models into input language of a model checker. In: Liu, Z., Kleinberg, R.D. (eds.) ICFEM 2006. LNCS, vol. 4260, pp. 606–620. Springer, Heidelberg (2006)

35. Miller, S.P., Whalen, M.W., Cofer, D.D.: Software model checking takes off. Commun. ACM **53**(2), 58–64 (2010)

36. Platzer, A.: Differential dynamic logic for hybrid systems. J. Autom. Reasoning **41**(2), 143–189 (2008)

37. Platzer, A., Clarke, E.M.: Computing differential invariants of hybrid systems as fixedpoints. In: Gupta, A., Malik, S. (eds.) CAV 2008. LNCS, vol. 5123, pp. 176–189. Springer, Heidelberg (2008)

38. Platzer, A., Quesel, J.-D.: KeYmaera: a hybrid theorem prover for hybrid systems (system description). In: Armando, A., Baumgartner, P., Dowek, G. (eds.) IJCAR 2008. LNCS (LNAI), vol. 5195, pp. 171–178. Springer, Heidelberg (2008)

39. Scaife, N., Sofronis, C., Caspi, P., Tripakis, S., Maraninchi, F.: Defining and translating a safe subset of simulink/stateflow into lustre. In: EMSOFT 2004, pp. 259–268. ACM (2004)

40. Selic, B., Gerard, S.: Modeling and Analysis or Real-Time and Embedded Systems with UML and MARTE: Developing Cyber-Physical Systems. The MK/OMG Press, Burlington (2013)

41. Tiller, M.: Introduction to Physical Modeling with Modelica, vol. 615. Springer, New York (2001)

42. Tiwari, A.: Formal semantics and analysis methods for Simulink Stateflow models. Technical report, SRI International, (2002)

43. Tripakis, S., Sofronis, C., Caspi, P., Curic, A.: Translating discrete-time Simulink to Lustre. ACM Trans. Embed. Comput. Syst. **4**(4), 779–818 (2005)

44. Wang, S., Zhan, N., Guelev, D.: An assume/guarantee based compositional calculus for hybrid CSP. In: Agrawal, M., Cooper, S.B., Li, A. (eds.) TAMC 2012. LNCS, vol. 7287, pp. 72–83. Springer, Heidelberg (2012)
45. Wang, S., Zhan, N., Zou, L.: An improved hhl prover: an interactive theorem prover for hybrid systems. In: Butler, M., et al. (eds.) ICFEM 2015. LNCS, vol. 9407, pp. 382–399. Springer, Heidelberg (2015). doi:10.1007/978-3-319-25423-4_25
46. Zhan, N., Wang, S., Guelev, D.: Extending Hoare logic to hybrid systems. Technical report ISCAS-SKLCS-13-02, State Key Laboratory of Computer Science, Institute of Software, Chinese Academy of Sciences (2013)
47. Zhan, N., Wang, S., Zhao, H.: Formal modelling, analysis and verification of hybrid systems. In: Liu, Z., Woodcock, J., Zhu, H. (eds.) Unifying Theories of Programming and Formal Engineering Methods. LNCS, vol. 8050, pp. 207–281. Springer, Heidelberg (2013)
48. Zhao, H., Yang, M., Zhan, N., Gu, B., Zou, L., Chen, Y.: Formal verification of a descent guidance control program of a lunar lander. In: Jones, C., Pihlajasaari, P., Sun, J. (eds.) FM 2014. LNCS, vol. 8442, pp. 733–748. Springer, Heidelberg (2014)
49. Zhou, C., Hansen, M.R.: Duration Calculus – A Formal Approach to Real-Time Systems. Monographs in Theoretical Computer Science. An EATCS Series. Springer, Heidelberg (2004)
50. Zhou, C., Hoare, C.A.R., Ravn, A.: A calculus of durations. Inf. Process. Lett. **40**(5), 269–276 (1991)
51. Chaochen, Z., Ji, W., Ravn, A.P.: A formal description of hybrid systems. In: Alur, R., Sontag, E.D., Henzinger, T.A. (eds.) HS 1995. LNCS, vol. 1066. Springer, Heidelberg (1996)
52. Zou, L., Lv, J., Wang, S., Zhan, N., Tang, T., Yuan, L., Liu, Y.: Verifying chinese train control system under a combined scenario by theorem proving. In: Cohen, E., Rybalchenko, A. (eds.) VSTTE 2013. LNCS, vol. 8164, pp. 262–280. Springer, Heidelberg (2014)
53. Zou, L., Zhan, N., Wang, S., Fränzle, M.: Formal verification of simulink/stateflow diagrams. In: Finkbeiner, B., Pu, G., Zhang, L. (eds.) ATVA 2015. LNCS, vol. 9364, pp. 464–481. Springer, Heidelberg (2015). doi:10.1007/978-3-319-24953-7_33
54. Zou, L., Zhan, N., Wang, S., Fränzle, M., Qin, S.: Verifying Simulink diagrams via a hybrid hoare logic prover. In: EMSOFT 2013, pp. 1–10 (2013)

Author Index

Printed in the United States
By Bookmasters